RSVP: The College Reading, Study, and Vocabulary Program

RSVP:

The College
Reading,
Study, and
Vocabulary
Program

FOURTH EDITION

James F. Shepherd
Queensborough Community College, Emeritus
The City University of New York

HOUGHTON MIFFLIN COMPANY Boston Toronto

Dallas Geneva, Illinois
Palo Alto Princeton, New Jersey

Sponsoring Editor: Mary Jo Southern
Senior Project Editor: Barbara Roth
Design Coordinator: Martha Drury
Senior Production Coordinator: Renée Le Verrier
Manufacturing Coordinator: Sharon Pearson
Marketing Manager: Diane Gifford

Printed in the U.S.A.

ISBN: 0-395-47204-0

ABCDEFGHIJ-WC-954321

Book design: George McLean
Unit opener photographs: One: Frank Ward/© Amherst College;
Two: © Beryl Goldberg; Three: © Susan Lapides; Four: Frank Ward/
© Amherst College; Five: © Larry Kolvoord/TEXAS STOCK
Mechanical art: Commonwealth Printing, Hadley, MA
Hand-drawn art: Marsha Goldberg

We would like to acknowledge and thank the following sources for permission to reprint material from their work:

Pages 3–44: Chapters 1 through 4 are based on material in *College Study Skills*, 4th ed., Copyright © 1990, by James F. Shepherd. Used by permission of Houghton Mifflin Company.

Pages 47–92: Chapters 5 through 8 are based on material in *College Vocabulary Skills*, 4th ed., Copyright © 1991, by James F. Shepherd. Used by permission of Houghton Mifflin Company.

Pages 61–72: Dictionary definitions Copyright © 1980 by Houghton Mifflin Company. Reprinted by permission from THE AMERICAN HERITAGE DICTIONARY, paperback edition. Dictionary definitions Copyright © 1981 by Houghton Mifflin Company. Adapted and reprinted by permission from THE AMERICAN HERITAGE DICTIONARY OF THE ENGLISH LANGUAGE.

Page 80: Excerpts from Douglas A. Bernstein, and others, *Psychology*, 1988. Used by permission of Houghton Mifflin Company.

Page 84: Dictionary definitions Copyright © 1981 by Houghton Mifflin Company. Adapted and reprinted by permission from THE AMERICAN HERITAGE DICTIONARY OF THE ENGLISH LANGUAGE.

Pages 95–96: "Inferences" from PSYCHOLOGY, 3/e by Andrew B. Crider, et al., p. 268. Copyright © 1989 by Andrew B. Crider, George R. Goethals, Robert D. Kavanaugh, and Paul R. Solomon. Reprinted by permission of HarperCollins Publishers.

Page 100: "Alcoholic Beverages" from Marvin R. Levy, et al., ESSENTIALS OF LIFE AND HEALTH, 5th ed., Copyright © 1988, pages 109–110. Used by permission of McGraw-Hill Publishing Company.

(Credits continued on page 432)

Contents

Preface

RSVP: The College Reading, Study, and Vocabulary Program orients students to college life and shows them how to improve the reading, study, test-taking, and vocabulary skills essential for academic success. A complete text and workbook, *RSVP* has been used in its first three editions by thousands of students, both in classes under the supervision of instructors and in other settings, including learning centers and skills laboratories.

The text features clear, concise, but complete explanations, and more than 200 practical exercises for skills development. Students respond favorably to the exercises because they are of obvious utility, they have varied formats, and they are challenging without being frustratingly difficult.

Instructors' comments suggest that *RSVP*'s popularity is due largely to two factors. First, it develops reading and study skills using dozens of actual textbook selections from a wide range of topics that are interesting to students. Second, it offers more comprehensive vocabulary and test-taking instruction than other reading and study skills texts.

Organization of the Text

The twenty-eight chapters are arranged in the sequence most instructors have indicated they prefer; however, chapters are written so they may be taught in any sequence appropriate for specific students or groups of students. The text is composed of five parts:

Part One, "Prepare to Succeed," orients students to college life, offers suggestions for managing time and increasing concentration, and explains course and degree requirements.

Part Two, "The Vocabulary Program," teaches how to determine word meanings by studying context, analyzing word structure, or using a dictionary, and explains methods for learning new words.

Part Three, "The Reading Program," develops literal, inferential, and critical reading comprehension and lays the foundation for improving underlining and note-taking skills.

Part Four, "The Study Program: Preparing for Tests," explains how to take good class notes, survey textbooks and chapters, mark books, make notes for books, and recite and review information in preparation for tests.

Part Five, "The Study Program: Taking Tests," presents instruction for improving skill in answering true-false, multiple-choice, matching, fill-in, and essay questions.

The text concludes with an appendix that consists of an entire textbook chapter, a Master Vocabulary List that contains definitions of words in textbook selections that may be unfamiliar to students, a glossary, an index, forms for keeping records of assignments, and forms for study schedules.

Improvements in the Fourth Edition

This new Fourth Edition of *RSVP* includes updated exposition, improved exercises, and many other changes, including the following:

- The textbook chapter in the appendix is the basis for exercises in surveying (Chapter 19), marking books (Chapter 20), making notes for books (Chapter 21), reciting and reviewing for tests (Chapter 22), and taking tests (Chapter 23). Both the Instructor's Resource Manual and Chapter 23 contain tests based on information in this chapter.

- Throughout the book, words in textbook excerpts that may be unfamiliar to students are underscored in blue; these words are defined in the Master Vocabulary List on pages 413–425.

- Exercises in Chapter 5, "Learning New Words," provide students with the opportunity to learn the meanings of from 50 to 275 of the words defined in the Master Vocabulary List. Tests based on these words are provided in the Instructor's Resource Manual.

- New boxed inserts with titles such as "How to Take a Test," "Bar Graphs," and "Time Lines" highlight important information or summarize text instruction.

- More than half of the 120 excerpts from college textbooks are new to this edition.

- Part One, "Prepare to Succeed," is reorganized to emphasize basic techniques for college success rather than the grading system.

- "The Vocabulary Program" is now located in Part Two, to precede reading instruction, and the chapters are rearranged to emphasize instruction in how to learn new words and make effective use of a dictionary.

- Part Three, "The Reading Program," has been improved by reorganizing chapters, increasing the number and types of exercises in most chapters, and introducing instruction in expository patterns (Chapter 13).

- Part Four, "The Study Program: Preparing for Tests," contains two new chapters: Chapter 16, which provides an overview of the steps in the study process, and Chapter 19, "Survey Chapters," which includes an exercise for surveying the textbook chapter in the appendix.

- Chapter 1, "Do Your Best," now includes suggestions about how to select curriculums and courses, build good relations with instructors, and purchase study equipment.

- Chapter 2, "Manage Your Time," suggests ways to make better use of time and keep well-organized assignment records. Assignment record forms are provided at the back of the book.

- Chapter 5, "Learning New Words," includes exercises for learning words underscored in blue in textbook excerpts throughout the book.

- Chapter 6, "Dictionaries," includes a discussion of and exercise for idioms.

- Chapter 7, "Study Context," and Chapter 8, "Analyze Word Structure," include exercises based on excerpts from college textbooks.

- Chapter 14, "Visual Materials," now offers instruction in interpreting cartoons, photographs, classification charts, and process charts.

- Chapter 17, "Take Good Class Notes," has more detailed explanations about improving listening skills, keeping well-organized notes, and increasing speed in taking notes.
- Chapter 20, "Mark Your Books," explains how to keep underlining to a minimum by using numbers and marginal notes.
- Chapter 21, "Make Notes for Books," includes explanations, examples, and exercises on how to make notes in six formats: major and minor details; paragraph summaries; definitions of terminology; classification charts; time lines; and maps.

Teaching Suggestions

As explained above, the chapters are arranged in a logical sequence, but they are written so that students can study any one of them without first having studied any others. Thus, skills may be taught in any order. However, I recommend that the chapters about topics, main ideas, and major and minor details be taught in the sequence in which they are presented (Chapters 10–12). Also, students should read the overview of the study process in Chapter 16 before they study the following chapters, which explicate the steps of the procedure.

Instructor's Resource Manual

RSVP is accompanied by an Instructor's Resource Manual that contains teaching suggestions, quizzes, tests, and a complete answer key to exercises. The manual is printed on 8½- by 11-inch paper to facilitate duplicating the materials for classroom use.

Acknowledgments

I am deeply indebted to the talented editorial, art, and production staffs of Houghton Mifflin Company for the expert assistance they provided me in preparing this revision. I am also grateful to the following reviewers for comments and suggestions that helped me in revising this book:

Elaine Coffey, *Black Hawk College, Moline, Illinois*
Susan M. Martin, *University of South Florida, Tampa*
Carol Paskuly, *Erie Community College, Buffalo, New York*
Larry Silverman, *Seattle Central Community College*
David A. Strong, Jr., *Dyersburg State Community College, Dyersburg, Tennessee*

In writing this revision, I was inspired by the students I taught at Queensborough Community College for more than twenty years.

    I want *RSVP* to be as useful to you as I can make it. Therefore, please let me know what I should and should not change when I prepare the fifth edition. If you write to me, I will answer you. Address your letter to James F. Shepherd, c/o Marketing Services, College Division, Houghton Mifflin Company, One Beacon Street, Boston, Massachusetts 02108.

J.F.S.

To the Student

The information about reading, studying, test-taking, and learning vocabulary in *RSVP* is the information thousands of students told me was most helpful to them in improving their skills.

It is not possible to learn everything in *RSVP* all at once. When you have a study problem, consult the index at the back of the book for help. For example, if you know that you must answer essay questions for a test, consult the index to find where essay questions are discussed. Then study those pages.

I sincerely hope that you use what you learn in this book to do your best in school. I—and many others you have never met—want you to enjoy the benefits of a college education.

I am very interested in your opinion of *RSVP*. If you write to me about this book, I will write to thank you. Address your letter to James F. Shepherd, c/o Marketing Services, College Division, Houghton Mifflin Company, One Beacon Street, Boston, Massachusetts 02108.

J.F.S.

One

Prepare to Succeed

If you are wondering what your life will be like when you graduate from college, I am glad to tell you that it may be better than you can imagine.

When I graduated from college, I did not know that I would become a teacher and author. But, of course, if I had not graduated from college, I would never have had the opportunity to do the work that I enjoy—teaching and writing books for students.

My experiences are similar to those of thousands of other college graduates; our lives are better because we went to college. We are pleased that you have joined us. We believe that you are wise to want a college education and that your successful experiences in college will make it possible for you to live a life that is better in ways that you cannot imagine today.

RSVP was written to help you learn how to do well in your courses, stay in school, and thus acquire a college education. Chapters 1 through 4 explain some strategies that successful college students use, ways to increase concentration while studying, basic information about college life and degree requirements, and sources of help in case of academic difficulty.

Do Your Best

Many people who are famous entertainers today had to work at everyday jobs in restaurants, offices, and factories before they became successful in show business. But we don't think of these celebrities as waiters, office workers, or laborers. We think of them as the actors, musicians, comedians, and dancers they have become by doing the things that are necessary to succeed in the entertainment industry.

The same is true of your college ambitions. Today others may think of you as a high school student, working person, or homemaker, but you can become known as a successful college student by doing the things that successful college students do:

- Enjoy learning
- Be serious about each course you take
- Know what teachers expect of you
- Do the things teachers expect of you

This chapter explains methods you may want to use to help ensure that you will have a successful experience in college.

Know Why You Are Attending College

It may seem obvious that the reason people go to college is to acquire an education, but the reasons for attending a college or university are actually extremely varied. Young people who have completed high school recently may go to college because they cannot find work; older people may go to college because the opportunity has been made available to them by their employers.

The "Checklist of Reasons for Attending College" on page 4 lists the reasons students most often give for being in college. Read the list and check the boxes in front of the three reasons that best describe why you are in school.

Checklist of Reasons for Attending College

Check the boxes in front of the three reasons that best describe why you are in school.

- ☐ I want to earn a college degree.
- ☐ I need a better education to get a good job.
- ☐ I want to prepare myself for a specific occupation.
- ☐ I want to be a well-educated person.
- ☐ I want to increase my appreciation for the arts.
- ☐ I want to learn to think more clearly.
- ☐ I want to be more responsible for my own life.
- ☐ I want a better job than the one I have now.
- ☐ I want to be promoted at the place where I work.
- ☐ I want to decide what I will do with my life.
- ☐ I want to use the money that is available for my tuition.
- ☐ I cannot find a job right now.
- ☐ I do not want to go to work right now.
- ☐ My parents want me to go to college.
- ☐ I like the social life at college.
- ☐ I like the feeling it gives me to be on campus.
- ☐ I want to find a boyfriend or girlfriend.
- ☐ I want to find a husband or wife.

Most students check three boxes in front of the first ten reasons, which are all ways of saying "I want to improve myself."

Did you check boxes in front of the reasons that are all ways of saying "I want to improve myself"? If so, you believe in the possibility of a better life for yourself and that college will help you attain it. If, however, you are attending school *only* to please your parents, *only* because you cannot find work, *only* for some reason other than self-improvement, you may not have sufficient motivation to do well in school.

Enroll in the Right Curriculum

You will be awarded a degree when you satisfactorily complete all the course work and other requirements in your **curriculum***, or program of study. On page 5 is the first-semester program for accounting students at a college in New York City.

* **Boldface** terms are defined in the glossary.

		Credits
BU-101	Principles of Accounting I	4
BU-210	Business Organization	3
BU-205	Business Management	3
EN-101	English Composition I	3
HE-202	Health Education	1
PE-	Physical Education	1
		15

If you do not have a copy of your curriculum, ask your counselor or adviser where you can get one. It is extremely important for you to know exactly what courses you must take to earn a degree.

When you obtain a copy of your curriculum, read the descriptions of the courses you are required to take and decide if they are the types of things that you want to study. You will benefit from college more if most of your requirements are courses that you really want to take.

If you are not pleased with your curriculum, examine the courses that are required for *other* curriculums at your school; you may find a program of study that is more appealing to you and change to that curriculum. For most people, college is a time to explore possibilities and to learn about themselves; more than half of all college students change their curriculum at least once during their college careers.

Take the Right Courses

In addition to enrolling in the right curriculum, it is important that you take the right courses. Use the following suggestions to guide you during **registration:**

- Enroll in courses as early in the registration period as you can; if you wait until the last minute, the courses you want may be filled.

- Enroll in prerequisite courses. A **prerequisite** is a course for which you must receive a satisfactory grade before you can enroll in some other course. For instance, the prerequisite for Accounting II may be a grade of C or better in Accounting I. It is essential for you to enroll in prerequisites so that you will take courses in the correct sequence and not be delayed in graduating from college.

- Enroll in learning skills courses. Colleges usually test students' reading, writing, and mathematics skills when they apply for admission. After testing, many students are required or advised to improve learning skills. Take full advantage of any learning skills instruction that you are offered. The faculty of your school believes that this instruction will help you do your best and earn a degree. Many of the students who do poorly in college did not improve their skills before they took regular course work.

- Schedule difficult classes at the times you are most alert and concentrate best. If you like to get up early, schedule difficult classes as early in the day as you can. If you're not fully awake until noon, schedule challenging courses after lunch or late in the day.

- Enroll in courses taught by teachers who have been recommended to you by students whose judgment you trust. At some schools the student government compiles students' evaluations of instructors and makes them available at the student government office or student affairs office.

- If you believe you might eventually change your curriculum, study your catalogue to find courses that apply to any curriculum to which you may someday transfer and take those courses as electives.

Find Enjoyment in Learning

If you have ever had the opportunity to teach young children, you know that they find great enjoyment in learning. Children are eager to learn, and they are proud to show their artwork, printing, and solutions to arithmetic problems. Perhaps this is partly because as they learn, they are very much aware that they are learning. One day they cannot write their names, but the next day they can; one moment they cannot add 3 + 4, but the next moment they can. Learning is a vivid and exciting experience for children.

But sometime between the first day of kindergarten and the last day of high school, many students lose the great joy they used to derive from learning. People who had fun learning how to dance and drive a car may find little pleasure in learning about the mysteries of life in a biology class or learning how to speak, read, and write Spanish. Perhaps this is because there are immediate and obvious benefits to knowing how to dance and drive, but it is less obvious how life will be enriched when one can look at nature with increased understanding or hold conversations with Spanish-speaking people.

Every subject taught in college is fascinating to many very intelligent people. If you find yourself thinking that a subject is uninteresting or boring, ask yourself this question: "Why is this subject interesting to some people but not to me?" If you find the answer to this question, then you will know why the subject is interesting. In fact, you may become more interested in the subject yourself.

Often, if you analyze your feelings about a subject that you think is boring or uninteresting, you may discover that there is something about it that makes you uncomfortable or anxious. Following are some methods you may use to help yourself feel better about subjects that make you uncomfortable:

1. Don't underestimate your abilities. Some people feel that there are certain subjects they are incapable of learning. If you feel this way about a subject, ask yourself this question: "Why do I feel that I cannot learn this subject when I know that people *just like me* learn it and do well in it?" If you answer this question, you may discover that the only thing preventing you from learning a subject is your erroneous belief that you cannot learn it.

2. Devote sufficient time to difficult subjects. A subject that you find difficult to learn may require more time than you are devoting to it. Ask yourself this question: "Could I learn this subject if I spent more time studying it?" If so, give the subject the additional time it requires. You will then have the satisfaction of learning something that you thought you could not learn; you will discover that you can do things that you thought you could not do. This will improve your opinion of yourself.

3. Don't insist that you be perfect. You may find it helpful to keep in mind that you do not need to be outstanding in every subject you study in college. If you are majoring in business and receive low grades in your business courses, then you have a serious problem. But if you are majoring in business, you do not need to be outstanding in every course outside your specialization.

4. Enjoy difficult courses. Keep in mind that you do not need to be outstandingly good at something in order to enjoy it. For instance, you may have a singing voice that nobody would pay to hear and yet derive great pleasure from singing. The same is true of subjects you study in college. Give yourself permission to enjoy all the subjects you study, even the ones in which you do not excel.

If you use these suggestions, you are likely to find that some subjects are much more interesting than you once thought, and you will also probably be less anxious when you study. If these suggestions don't help, you may find that the subject you dislike is one for which you lack necessary skills in reading, writing, or mathematics. If that is the case, seek help to improve your skills.

Know Your Teachers' Requirements

Students who don't know what their instructors require usually don't do all the things their instructors expect of them. As a result, they usually do not earn very good course grades.

During the first class meeting instructors usually give an overview of the course, explain course requirements, and distribute a syllabus or other handout. **A syllabus** is a printed outline of the main topics of a course. When course requirements are listed in a syllabus or on other printed pages, keep them in a safe place; when they are presented orally, maintain accurate and complete notes about them. In either case, understand them completely and follow them exactly.

A "Checklist for Course Requirements" appears on page 8. Use it to make certain that you know exactly what your instructors expect of you. Some teachers require only that students take midterm and final examinations, but others require most of the things that are mentioned in the checklist.

Attend Classes Faithfully

At some colleges there are teachers who do not take attendance, so students may mistakenly believe that it is not important for them to attend classes. However, if classes were not important, colleges would not maintain classrooms or pay a faculty.

Checklist for Course Requirements

Use this checklist for each course you are taking.

☐ I have purchased the books and other required materials.
☐ I must take books or other materials to class.
☐ I must take notes during class.
☐ I must participate in class discussions.
☐ I must do homework assignments.
☐ I must attend a laboratory (and I know where it is located and when I must attend it).
☐ I must have conferences with the teacher (and I know when and where I must go for them).
☐ I must write a paper (and I know the format for the paper and when it is due).
☐ I must attend concerts, visit museums, or go on field trips.
☐ I know how many tests I must take and when they will be given.
☐ I know how my final grade will be determined.

If you are uncertain about requirements for a course, ask the instructor to explain them.

To succeed in college you must accept complete responsibility for everything that happens in each of your classes, even if you are absent. If you accept this responsibility, you will avoid many unnecessary difficulties. Do the following if you are absent from a class.

- Contact a classmate to learn about assignments or tests announced in your absence.
- Hand copy or photocopy notes taken by a classmate while you were absent.
- Deliver assignments to the instructor as soon as possible.

When you return to a class, check with your teacher to make certain that your classmate gave you correct information about assignments and tests and ask the instructor for suggestions about how you can catch up with work you missed.

Do not ask an instructor, "Did I miss anything?" The answer is yes. Also, do not tell a teacher that an absence is "excused" because of illness or some similar reason. Excused absences are noted in high school but not in most colleges and universities. When a student is absent from a college class, the teacher assumes that the absence is unavoidable.

If an injury or illness makes it impossible for you to attend class for an extended period, contact the health services office of your school. Someone in that office may notify your instructors as to why you are not attending classes. If so, your teachers may make special arrangements for you to catch up with course work; if they do not make special arrangements, you may need to withdraw from your courses (see page 37).

In addition to attending all classes, arrive on time. Students who are frequently late to class communicate the message to their teachers and classmates that they are disorganized, inconsiderate, or immature. If you arrive on time not only can you avoid creating an unfavorable impression of yourself, you will know everything that happens during class.

Use the Right Study Equipment

Professional chefs don't try to cook gourmet meals without the right cooking utensils and qualified carpenters don't try to build houses without the tools of their trade, but many students try to pursue a college career with not much more than a ballpoint pen and a spiral notebook.

You will find that it is easier to be a student if you have the equipment that you need to do the work of a student efficiently. The "Study Equipment Checklist" on page 10 may include some items that you need to purchase.

Give highest priority to purchasing your textbooks. Some students encounter unnecessary difficulty in their courses because they wait too long to purchase their books or because they try to get by without buying the books they need. Experienced students who are determined to do well in school purchase their required books immediately and get a head start in their classes by beginning to read them even before teachers give reading assignments.

When you buy your required books, also take great care in purchasing a notebook; the notebook you select can help or hinder you in maintaining the well-organized records of class notes you need in order to do well in your college courses. Though most students use spiral notebooks, there are several advantages to using a ring binder.

Reasons for Using a Ring Binder

- A ring binder can hold all the notes for all of your classes.
- Since you will have only one ring binder, you will always take the right notebook to class.
- You can add paper to a ring binder. As a result, you can always have enough paper in your notebook for courses in which teachers give long lectures.
- If you are absent, you can insert notes you copy from a classmate exactly where they belong.
- You can have an assignment section in a ring binder, so you don't have to have a separate assignment book.

When a desk is too small to accommodate a ring binder comfortably, remove some paper from the binder for note-taking. Or leave your ring

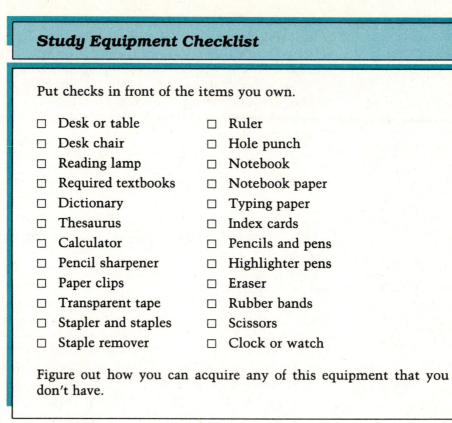

Study Equipment Checklist

Put checks in front of the items you own.

☐	Desk or table	☐	Ruler
☐	Desk chair	☐	Hole punch
☐	Reading lamp	☐	Notebook
☐	Required textbooks	☐	Notebook paper
☐	Dictionary	☐	Typing paper
☐	Thesaurus	☐	Index cards
☐	Calculator	☐	Pencils and pens
☐	Pencil sharpener	☐	Highlighter pens
☐	Paper clips	☐	Eraser
☐	Transparent tape	☐	Rubber bands
☐	Stapler and staples	☐	Scissors
☐	Staple remover	☐	Clock or watch

Figure out how you can acquire any of this equipment that you don't have.

binder at home, take notes on loose-leaf paper that you carry in a folder with double pockets, and insert the notes where they belong in your ring binder when you return home.

If you decide to use spiral notebooks, it is a good idea to purchase a separate notebook for each class. Buy notebooks with pockets on the inside covers so you will have a place to keep papers your teachers distribute. Write the names of your courses in large print on the outside front covers of your notebooks to ensure that you take the right notebooks to your classes.

Organize Your Notebook

No matter what kind of notebook you choose for class notes, be sure you set aside a place to keep records about assignments, tests, instructors, and classmates.

- Information about assignments should explain exactly what they are, how they are to be done, and when they are due.
- Information about tests should include exactly what materials and topics will be covered on each test and the dates the tests will be given.
- Information about instructors should include their names, office locations, office telephone numbers, and office hours.

- Information about classmates should include the names, addresses, and telephone numbers of at least two people in each class whom you can contact for assignments and notes you miss when you are absent.

On page 21 there is an explanation of a method you may want to use to keep accurate records of your assignments.

Keep Up-to-Date with Course Work

College terms start out slowly. They gradually get busier and busier, reaching a peak of activity at final examination time. If you fall behind in the work for a course, you may find yourself trying to catch up just when you are very busy with all of your other courses. Don't fall behind—keep up-to-date with course work.

This is doubly important when you must master information or skills taught early in a course in order to learn information or skills that are taught later in the course. Mathematics, science, technology, and foreign language courses are some of the courses that fit this description. When you study, ask yourself this question: "Do I need to learn this information or skill in order to learn other information or skills later in the course?" If the answer to this question is yes, learn the information or skill immediately and review it often.

Do Assignments on Time

Instructors give assignments to provide practice for skills and for other purposes. They expect students to have assignments ready on time; many teachers do not accept late work, and others give lower grades for late assignments. Some teachers give assignments that they review in class but do not collect and grade. Do these assignments faithfully; their purpose is to help you acquire a skill or to learn other things that you need to know.

Teachers sometimes require students to write papers that are five, ten, or more pages long. The grades for papers such as these usually account for substantial proportions of course grades. Before you start work on them, make certain that you know the answers to the following questions:

- How many pages long must the paper be?
- What topics are acceptable for the paper?
- In what format must the paper be presented?
- When is the paper due?

When you are uncertain about the requirements for a paper, schedule a conference with the teacher to receive the clarification you need.

It is wise to begin work on long papers as soon as they are announced. Visit your library to learn about the research facilities available there. Start reading about your topic right away and make notes about information you want to include in your paper. If you put off writing a paper, you may find you have to devote many hours to it just when you need to prepare for midterm tests or final examinations. Therefore, arrange your schedule so that the time you spend writing long papers is spread over as many weeks as possible.

Also, before you submit any written work, keep in mind that college instructors usually give higher grades to papers that are neat and free of errors than to ones that are sloppy looking and full of mistakes. Ask a friend or relative to proofread your written work before you give it to an instructor, and submit only papers that are as neat as you can make them.

If you do not know how to use a word processor, it would be a good idea for you to learn. Computers are probably available for you to use in an instructional resource center or some other facility on your campus. Studies have found that teachers tend to give higher grades to papers that are prepared on word processors than to those that are typed or handwritten. It is very time consuming to retype or rewrite an entire page to make a minor change; however, slight changes can be made very easily and quickly on a word processor, and a corrected page can be retyped by simply pushing a button. Papers written using a word processor tend to receive higher grades because they usually have fewer errors than typed or handwritten papers.

Keep a photocopy of each paper you write so you will not need to rewrite it if a teacher misplaces or loses it, and so you will have a record of references and other information in the paper to which you may want to refer in the future.

Be Prepared for Tests

Many first-year students make the mistake of not preparing properly for the first test their teachers give. Being poorly prepared, they do not go to class on test day, or they take the test and receive a low grade. Either way they start the term at a great disadvantage.

If you are absent the day a test is given, you may be required to take a make-up test that is more difficult than the test the other students took. Or if a teacher does not offer make-up tests, you may be given a failing grade for the test you missed.

If you receive a low grade for the first test in a course, you might become discouraged because you realize that it will be extremely difficult for you to earn a good grade in the course. Do not create an unnecessary source of discouragement for yourself. Be prepared to do your best on all tests.

Chapters 16 through 22 explain how to prepare for examinations, and Chapters 23 through 28 describe effective methods for answering various kinds of test questions.

Build Good Relations with Instructors

It is to your benefit to have good relations with your instructors. If you have a problem, teachers will be more interested in helping you find a solution if you have made a favorable impression on them. Also, when they can't decide which of two grades to give you, they are more likely to give you the higher grade if they have positive feelings about you.

One way to make favorable impressions on your teachers is to address them by the titles they prefer. Notice the titles they place before their names on materials they distribute to you. If your instructors write their names as "Prof. Joseph Hosey," "Dr. Elaine Morton," "Mr. John Snyder," and "Ms. Kitty Bateman" they probably would like you to use these titles.

Students also create a good impression on an instructor when they do what he or she requires, attend class faithfully, arrive on time, sit in an attentive position facing the instructor, smile, and show that they are willing and ready to learn. In addition, since we tend to like best the people we know best, get to know your teachers. One way to do this is to ask them questions after class or during office hours.

Following are examples of behaviors that do *not* help a student build good relations with instructors.

- Be absent
- Arrive late to class
- Slouch in a chair
- Appear to be annoyed
- Talk excessively about your experiences and beliefs
- Hold conversations while the teacher is teaching

Students who engage in annoying behaviors such as these create an unfavorable impression of themselves.

Make New Friends

You will enjoy your college experience more if you have friends to talk with before and after your classes. In addition, you need to have friends in your classes whom you can call to learn about assignments you miss when you are absent and from whom you can copy notes taken on days you are not in class. You may also find it helpful to discuss assignments or study for tests with students who are taking the same courses you are taking. Make a special effort to introduce yourself to people you meet in your classes and to make friends in every class you take.

Enjoy Campus Life

You can make your college experience even more enjoyable if you take part in the social life on your campus. Make a special effort to attend social functions and to join a club.

Your student government sponsors social events such as movies, concerts, athletic events, and dances. These and other activities are available to you at little or no cost. Read student newspapers and notices on bulletin boards for announcements of these events.

In addition, the students at your school have organized clubs for interests that may range from bowling to creative writing and from photography to karate. There are probably organizations for students who want to learn more about various religions, countries, or hobbies, and opportunities for students to play basketball, baseball, volleyball, or other team sports. Information about clubs may be printed in a brochure or pamphlet that was distributed during orientation. Clubs not only provide you with opportunities to participate in activities you enjoy; they are also a way for you to meet people and make new friends.

If you have difficulty learning about social events and clubs, visit the student government office, student activities office, or student affairs office. Somebody there can give you the information that you need to involve yourself in campus life.

Find Help If You Need It

Most students have difficulty with a course at some time during their college careers. If you have an academic problem, your first source for help is books you may own, purchase, or borrow from a library.

RSVP provides help for taking class notes, studying for tests, answering test questions, and many other study problems. You may also own other books that contain solutions to problems you encounter in college courses. For example, your English book may explain the format to use for a research paper you must write for a psychology course, or your math book may provide the review of mathematics you need for an accounting or a chemistry course.

Advisers, counselors, teachers, and other students are also sources of help when academic difficulties arise. **Advisers** are teachers who are assigned to help students select courses; the services counselors provide are explained on page 32.

Teachers can sometimes offer solutions that do not occur to students. A young man told his chemistry teacher that he was having trouble because his laboratory sessions were taught by an inexperienced laboratory assistant. His instructor arranged for him to sit in on laboratory sessions taught by another assistant. Instead of attending one laboratory each week, he attended two, but he did well in his chemistry course.

Teachers, counselors, and advisers usually know if there are study groups, laboratories, **tutors,** or other sources of help available. If they do not know, they may direct you to the office of the department that offers the course that is causing problems. Or they may suggest visiting an office of academic skills, a learning center, a tutorial service, or some other department or service on campus.

Students who have already taken a course that gives you trouble may be your best source of help—they have already solved problems you are having. Make friends with second-, third-, and fourth-year students who are enrolled in your curriculum and who will give you suggestions on how to study for courses they have already taken.

EXERCISE 1.1   ## Checklist for Course Requirements

Use the "Checklist for Course Requirements" on page 8 to analyze what your teachers require. Use your analyses to write a summary of the requirements for each of your courses.

EXERCISE 1.2   **Attendance Requirements**

Find the answer to the first question in your college catalogue.

1. What are the official attendance requirements at your college?

_____

_____

_____

2. If any of your teachers have attendance requirements that are stricter than those stated in your college catalogue, write their requirements on the following lines.

_____

_____

_____

_____

EXERCISE 1.3   **Social Activities**

List the names of three clubs sponsored by your student government that you may want to join.

1. _____

2. _____

3. _____

EXERCISE 1.4   **Your Teachers' Names**

List the names of all your instructors and the titles by which they prefer to be addressed.

1. _____

2. _____

3. _____

4. _____

5. _____

6. _____

EXERCISE 1.5   **Help in This Book**

Consult the table of contents in the front of this book to answer the following questions.

1. What chapter teaches how to take good lecture notes?

   _____

2. What chapter teaches how to recite and review for tests?

   _____

3. What chapter teaches how to select correct answers to multiple-choice questions?

   _____

EXERCISE 1.6   **Helpful People**

Seek the help of faculty or other students if you have academic problems.

1. List the names of all your current teachers. Then place a check in front of those with whom you would feel comfortable discussing any difficulty you might have in fulfilling requirements for their courses.

   _____   _____

   _____   _____

   _____   _____

2. List the names of two counselors or advisers with whom you would talk if you were having difficulty with a course.

   _____   _____

3. List the names and phone numbers of at least three second-, third-, or fourth-year students enrolled in your curriculum from whom you would seek help if you were having difficulty with a course.

   _____   _____

   _____   _____

EXERCISE 1.7   **Course Information Chart**

List information about your courses, instructors, classmates, and tests on the "Course Information Chart" on the inside front cover of this book.

Manage Your Time

One of the most noticeable differences between high school and college is the way in which classes are scheduled. High school students usually attend classes five days each week, and all their time in school is scheduled for them. In college, on the other hand, students don't necessarily attend classes every day, and they sometimes have long breaks between classes. In addition, they have to plan when to study for their courses.

As you have probably discovered, studying in college requires more time than studying in high school. In a typical term, full-time college students may read five, six, or more textbooks, complete a major project in each course, and take many tests. With a great deal to accomplish in the few weeks of a term, successful college students find it is essential to schedule how they will use their time. This chapter explains four steps for scheduling study time:

- Decide how much to study
- Determine how much time you have available for studying
- Decide what you will study
- Decide when you will study

The box on page 19 summarizes these four steps. Refer to it when you need a quick review of the information in this chapter.

Figure 2.1, on page 18, is an example of a weekly study schedule. The hours that are crossed out in the schedule are hours the student cannot study because she is attending class, working, traveling, or engaging in other activities. Important things to do and social obligations are written in the schedule, and the times the student will study various subjects are shaded in light blue. "Free" indicates the hours that she may use for additional studying or for leisure activities.

Decide How Much to Study

Teachers often tell students that they should spend two hours studying outside of class for each hour they spend in the classroom. For instance, when students take a course that meets for three class hours each week,

FIGURE 2.1

A Weekly Study Schedule

	SAT	SUN	MON	TUE	WED	THU	FRI
	Oct. 7	Oct. 8	Oct. 9	Oct. 10	Oct. 11	Oct. 12	Oct. 13
8-9	Eng – Revise +	Free	Chem –	Psych – Read Ch.9	Math – Odd	Psych – Read Ch 10	Chem – Ex 12.1,
9-10	type paper	Free	Ex 11.1-11.5	Prep to discuss ques 1, 4, & 6	problems 1-19, PP 187-188	Prep to discuss ques 1-17	12.3, 12.7-12.9
10-11	Hist – Read	Chem –	X	X	X	X	X
11-12	Ch. 8, pp 231-252	Read Ch. 11	X	X	X	X	X
12-1	X	↑	X	X	X	X	X
1-2	Hist – Work on	Lunch and movie with George	Hist – Read	Math – Prep for	Hist – Answer	Eng – Research	X
2-3	paper (Library)	↕	Ch. 8, pp 243-279	quiz on Ch. 4-6	ques 1-12, pp 180-181	for paper (Library)	Hist – Work on
3-4	X	↓	X	Eng – Outline	X	X	paper (Library)
4-5	X	– Do Laundry	Math – Odd	for paper (Library)	X	X	↓
5-6	X	– Wash Car	problems 21-39, pp 172-174	Free	X	Free	X
6-7	Free	– Plan dinner	X	Free	X	Free	X
7-8	Free	for Oct. 14	X	X	X	X	Free
8-9	Free	Math – Odd problems	Free	Chem –	↑ Photography Club	Chem – Read	Free
9-10	Free	1-19, PP 171-172	Free	Ex 11.6 - 11.11	Photography Club	Ch. 12	Free
10-11	Free	X	X	X	↓	X	Free

instructors customarily recommend that they study for six hours each week outside of class. This is good advice, but it doesn't take into account that some students need to devote more time to studying than others.

One way to find out how much *you* must study is to keep records of how long it actually takes you to study for your courses. For example, when you read a textbook, write the time in pencil on the page where you begin. After you have finished reading, write the time again. Then count the number of pages you read and figure out how many minutes it took you to read them. If you do this a few times with each book you are studying, you will soon be able to estimate very accurately how long it takes you to read ten, twenty-five, or fifty pages in any book you are studying. Use this information to help in deciding how much time you need to study.

Another way to decide how much time to spend working on an assignment or preparing for a test is to answer the following questions:

How to Schedule Study Time

Use the following procedure to schedule the time you will spend studying for your college courses.

- Decide how much you want to study (by figuring out how much time you need to study to get the grades you want).
- Determine how much time you have available for studying (by referring to your list of "things to do," your calendar, and your analysis of times you can't study because you're engaged in other activities).
- Decide what you will study (by keeping records of assignments on a form that lists them in the sequence in which they must be completed).
- Decide when you will study (by scheduling short study sessions rather than long ones at times you are not engaged in other activities).

- Will the assignment help me master a skill that is important to my long-term goals? (For example, a business student should give priority to English composition assignments because the ability to write well is important to success in business.)
- How will my grade for the assignment or test affect my final course grade? (For example, a student of electrical technology should give priority to written assignments in his electrical technology courses because his instructors use assignment grades to compute final course grades.)
- How important is my grade in the course to helping me achieve my long-term goals? (For example, a student at a school in Florida may want high grades in all of her courses so she can transfer credits for the courses she takes in Florida to a school in Illinois.)

You probably want to do your best in each course you take. However, when you have insufficient time to study as much as you want, establish your priorities by spending your study time in the ways that will benefit you most in the future.

Determine Time Available for Study

Use three steps to determine how many hours are available to you each week that you can spend studying. *First,* keep a list of chores and other things that you have to do each week. The study schedule in Figure 2.1, on page 18, includes the items in this list:

> *Things to do*
> Wash the car
> Do the laundry
> Plan dinner for Sat. (10/14)
> Buy birthday present for Mom
> Lose five pounds

Second, prepare a calendar of social activities and important dates such as exams or assignment due dates. Some of the activities shown in the calendar below are included in the study schedule in Figure 2.1.

Third, determine the times you cannot study because you are engaged in activities such as attending class, working, traveling, eating meals, dressing and grooming, sleeping, exercising, socializing, and watching television.

When you analyze how much time you have for studying, you may find that you don't have enough time to study because you devote a great deal

OCTOBER

Sunday	Monday	Tuesday	Wednesday	Thursday	Friday	Saturday
1	2	3 Psych Quiz	4	5	6	7 Jane's party 9 PM
8 Lunch/movie with George	9	10	11 Photography Club 8 PM	12	13	14 Friends for dinner 7 PM
15	16	17	18 History paper due	19 Football game 2 PM	20	21
22	23 Mom's birthday	24	25	26 Chemistry test	27	28 Rita visits campus
29	30	31 Halloween party 9 PM				

of time to work, sports, family responsibilities, or some other activity. If you are so busy with another activity that it interferes with your ability to do well in college, you may need to reduce the number of courses you take each semester, or you may need to spend less time engaging in the conflicting activity.

For example, many students have difficulty in college because they are working. If you have a job, check the boxes in front of any of the following statements that describe you:

☐ I sometimes miss classes because of my job.

☐ I am sometimes late to classes because of my job.

☐ I am sometimes tired in classes because of my job.

☐ I am sometimes unable to complete assignments on time because of my job.

☐ I have missed a test or been underprepared for a test because of my job.

If you checked any box, your job is interfering with your ability to do your best in college. Following are some alternatives for full-time students:

■ Work a great deal during the summer and very little, or not at all, during the school year.

■ If you spend much time traveling to and from work, find a job on campus, near campus, or near where you live (even if it pays less money).

■ If the hours that you must work are the problem, find a job with more suitable hours (even if it pays less money).

■ If you are working only because you want to enjoy a luxury, such as an expensive automobile, consider doing without the luxury.

■ If you are working mainly because you receive more approval from your parents for working than you do for being a student, consider explaining the demands of college study to your parents.

If none of these alternatives is a solution for you, or if you are a part-time student working full-time to support yourself or your family, you may need to enroll in fewer courses next term.

Decide What You Will Study

Students sometimes make the mistake of studying first for the courses they *prefer* to study rather than for the courses for which they *need* to study. Avoid this mistake by keeping your assignments in the format that is illustrated in Figure 2.2, on page 22.

The record of assignments in Figure 2.2 was used to prepare the study schedule in Figure 2.1, on page 18. For example, compare Figure 2.2 with Figure 2.1 to notice that the student plans to complete Thursday's assignments on Wednesday and Thursday.

At the back of this book are forms that you may use to keep records of your assignments. Make photocopies of one of the forms, punch holes in the copies, and put them in the assignment section of your ring binder.

FIGURE 2.2

A Method for
Keeping
Assignments

COURSE	MON Oct 9	TUE Oct 10	WED Oct 11	THU Oct 12	FRI Oct 13
English	Revise the two-page paper Type neatly		Bring outline for research paper		Bring list of references for research paper (at least 10)
Math	Odd problems 1-19, pp. 171-172	Odd problems 20-39, pp. 172-174	Quiz on chapters 4-6	Odd problems 1-19, pp. 181-188	
Chemistry	Read Ch. 11 Do Ex. 11.1-11.5 (Test Oct 26)		Do Ex. 11.6 - 11.11		Read Ch. 12 Do Ex. 12.1, 12.3, +12.7-12.9
History	Read Ch. 8, pp. 231-252 (Paper due Oct 18)	Read Ch. 8, pp. 253-279		Write answers to questions 1-12, pp.180-181	
Psychology		Read Ch. 9 Prepare for discussion questions 1,4,+6		Read Ch. 10 Prepare for discussion questions 1-7	

Decide When to Study

Observe yourself when you study to determine whether you are most alert early in the morning, in the afternoon, in the evening, or late at night. Use what you learn to schedule study periods at the time of day you concentrate best.

In addition, when you prepare study schedules, plan many short study sessions rather than a few long ones. For example, when you schedule six hours to study for a test, plan six one-hour study sessions rather than one six-hour or two three-hour study sessions. Short study sessions are more effective than long ones because it is tiring to study for long periods, and we do not learn well when we are tired. When you must study a subject for several consecutive hours, take a five- or ten-minute break every hour.

Also use the following suggestions to help you decide when you will study for the courses you are taking.

■ *Before class* is the best time for studying about the lecture topic for the class because the topic will be fresh in your mind when you listen to the lecture.

■ *After class* is the best time for reviewing and correcting notes taken during the class; if you don't understand your notes right after class, you won't understand them later when you study them to prepare for a test.

■ *Just before sleep* is the best time for learning information for tests; there is evidence that we remember more information when it is learned just before sleep than when it is learned at other times.

It is necessary to revise study schedules often to accommodate changing school, social, and other obligations. Also, some weeks have holidays, which offer uninterrupted stretches of time for working on major projects and preparing for examinations. There are study schedule forms at the back of this book, which you may photocopy. You may want to make one copy for each week of the term because no two weeks are exactly alike.

Make Better Use of Time

You may find that you can make better use of your time by combining activities and by using short periods more effectively. Following are some practical ways to do two things at once:

■ Record material you want to learn and listen to it while you are driving or doing household chores.

■ Write material on 3-by-5-inch cards and study the information while you walk from place to place or ride on a bus.

■ Think about what you will do during your next study session while you are walking, driving, or doing routine chores.

■ Study while you wash clothes, while you wait for a favorite television program to start, or while you wait for a friend to arrive.

You may also find that you have more time by making better use of short periods. Following are some suggestions:

Time	Activities You Could Do
Five minutes	Review words you are learning
	Revise your list of things to do
	Plan your next study session
	Do some sit-ups or pushups
	Take out the garbage
	Clean the bathroom sink
Fifteen minutes	Pay a bill
	Review notes
	Survey a chapter
	Wash dishes
	Solve a math problem
	Pick the topic for a paper
	Work out on an exercise bike

Thirty minutes   Run an errand
Write a letter
Locate material in the library
Review notes
Read five pages in a textbook
Buy birthday cards
Jog three miles

If you analyze how you spend your time, you may find that you waste time each day that you could use doing things you need to do.

EXERCISE 2.1 **Decide How Much to Study**

List the courses you are taking, the grade you want for each course, and the number of hours you will need to study for each course during each week in order to earn the grade you want.

Courses	Grades I want	Hours I need to study
_____	_____	_____
_____	_____	_____
_____	_____	_____
_____	_____	_____
_____	_____	_____
_____	_____	_____

What is the total number of hours you will study each week? _____

EXERCISE 2.2 **Make a Calendar for the Term**

Make a calendar for the entire term.

1. Obtain a calendar of the type illustrated on page 20. (They are sometimes available free in bookstores and card shops.)
2. Consult your school's catalogue for holidays, vacations, final examinations, and other important dates in your school's academic calendar.
3. Use syllabuses, outlines, and other materials your instructors give you to find the dates of tests and the dates papers and other course projects are due.
4. Use the school newspaper or other student government publications to find the dates of important athletic and social events you want to attend.
5. Use your personal records to find the dates of weddings, birthdays, anniversaries, and other important events you will observe with your relatives and friends.

Include these and other important dates in your calendar.

EXERCISE 2.3   ## Prepare a List of Things to Do

Prepare a list of the things you need to do next week. Include chores, social obligations, and other things you want to accomplish.

Things to Do Next Week

_____

_____

_____

_____

_____

_____

_____

_____

_____

_____

_____

_____

EXERCISE 2.4   ## Determine Time Available for Study

Referring to your list of things to do, your calendar, and your class schedule, use one of the forms at the back of this book to analyze how many hours you have available *next* week that you can use for studying. Cross out the times when you cannot study because you are attending class, working, traveling, eating meals, or engaging in other activities of the type listed on page 21. Be certain to cross out enough time for each activity. If it takes you an hour each morning to get dressed and eat breakfast, cross out an hour, not half an hour. Also, be certain to allow enough time for meals and relaxation; they are essential to your enjoyment of life and your physical and mental well-being.

How many hours do you have available for studying *next* week?

_____

If you have fewer hours than you need for studying, figure out how you can make more time available or consider whether you overestimated the number of hours you will need for studying when you did Exercise 2.1.

EXERCISE 2.5   ## Decide What to Study First

Use one of the assignment forms in the back of this book to list the assignments you must do next week. Also, on the following lines list days tests will be given and the days reports are due.

Tests and Reports

_____

_____

_____

_____

_____

EXERCISE 2.6   ## Decide When to Study

Referring to the materials you prepared when you did Exercise 2.5, enter in your study schedule the exact times you will study for each of your courses next week.

3

Increase Concentration

In order to make the best use of your study time, you must be able to focus your thought and attention on studying during the time you set aside for this purpose. Yet you may find that you are unable to concentrate for long stretches of time. Some students report that their minds begin to wander after as few as five minutes of reading. Others complain that they can't concentrate on studying for more than ten or fifteen minutes.

This chapter explains a number of strategies for increasing concentration, which are summarized in the box entitled "How to Increase Concentration for Studying" on page 28. In addition, when you study Chapters 9 through 22, you will learn methods that will keep your mind active and less likely to wander when you read and study.

Select a Specific Place to Study

Select a place where you prefer to study and always study there. If you do not have a place to study at home, you may find a quiet place to study in a friend's home, a library, an empty classroom, or even a quiet booth in the corner of a cafeteria. Avoid using this place for reading magazines, watching television, chatting on the telephone, eating, and other similar activities. When you go to this place, you will sense your purpose for being there, and your mind will prepare itself to concentrate on studying.

Provide your study area with the necessary equipment, including a brightly lit desk or table and a firm but comfortable chair (see page 10). Good light will help you read without tiring quickly and it will focus your attention on the material you are studying; a firm chair will keep you alert.

Explain to friends and relatives that you do not want to be disturbed while you are studying because it will interrupt your concentration. You may devise a method to signal that you are studying. One of my students uses a silk rose to indicate that she doesn't want to be disturbed; when her husband and children see her seated at the kitchen table wearing the pink rose they know that she is studying, and they don't bother her.

If you have friends who insist on interrupting you while you are studying, try to replace them with more considerate companions. You deserve friends who respect your study time and who want you to do well in college.

How to Increase Concentration for Studying

Use these strategies to improve your ability to concentrate on studying for longer periods.

■ Always study in the same place and explain to your friends and relatives that you do not want to be interrupted while you are studying.

■ Keep records of how long you concentrate when you study and try to concentrate longer the next time you study.

■ Keep your list of things to do handy and add items to it as they come into your mind while you are studying.

■ Decide that you really want to study rather than do something else.

■ Begin study sessions by doing routine or easy tasks.

■ Do large tasks a bit at a time.

■ Accept that you must do difficult tasks to achieve your goal of getting a college education.

■ Reward yourself for studying.

■ Use the methods for reading and studying that are explained in Chapters 9 through 22 of *RSVP*.

Keep Records of Concentration

When you begin to study, make a note of the time. Then, when you first become aware that your attention is not focused on studying any longer, record the time again. Compare the two times and make a note of how many minutes passed before you lost your concentration. Next, spend a few minutes doing something other than studying; you might stand up and stretch or look out the window. When you begin to study again, make another note of how long you concentrate.

Continue in this way until you are satisfied with the length of time you are able to concentrate. Many students report that keeping these kinds of records helps them to double or triple their attention span very quickly.

Use Your List of Things to Do

Your list of things to do, explained on page 20, provides a handy method for dealing with distracting thoughts such as "do the laundry," "call Dad," and "photocopy the report for history." When you study, keep your list of things to do handy and add items to it as they come into your mind. By writing the things you want to do in the place they belong, you free your mind to concentrate on studying rather than on trying to keep track of other obligations.

Decide That You Want to Study

Once your mind drifts off, you are no longer studying. You might be thinking about something that happened earlier in the day, something that is worrying you, or something that you would rather be doing—but you are not studying!

If you want to make the best use of your study time, decide that you *want* to study rather than daydream, listen to music, watch television, or do other things you enjoy. If you don't decide that you really want to spend your study time studying, you may become resentful and grow to feel that studying is a punishment. If you feel that you are being punished when you study, your thoughts will be about your suffering. These thoughts will keep you from concentrating on reading or studying.

Do Routine Tasks First

Keep a list of your assignments that is arranged in the sequence they must be completed and start each study session by examining the list to choose first what is either most routine or easy (see Exercise 2.5 on page 26). If it is equally important to proofread a draft of a paper for an English course and to study for a chemistry test, do first whichever of the assignments is easier for you.

Another way to begin a study session is to review things you have studied previously. For instance, before trying to solve a new type of problem for a mathematics course, spend a few minutes solving a kind of problem you already know how to do. You will provide yourself with the review practice you need, and you will put yourself in the right frame of mind for learning how to solve the new type of problem.

Do Large Tasks a Bit at a Time

It is sometimes difficult to concentrate on a task that seems impossible to accomplish. For instance, the thought of reading and learning everything in a 600-page textbook can be overwhelming. However, reading and learning the information in a textbook is accomplished one step at a time, using methods that are explained in following chapters of *RSVP*. Similarly, English handbooks explain how to do the small tasks that make it possible to write long term papers.

Mathematics, science, technology, and foreign language courses are among the ones for which information must be learned a bit at a time. If you do not keep up-to-date with the work in courses such as these, you may find it extremely difficult to catch up.

Accept Difficult Tasks

When your mind is focused on the thought that a task is difficult or unpleasant, it cannot concentrate on accomplishing the task. Replace the thought "I don't want to do this difficult task" with the thought "To achieve a worthwhile goal, I accept that I must do this and other difficult tasks."

Those who achieve important goals do difficult or unpleasant things they would not do *except* for the fact that they are intent on attaining their objectives. For example, if you are determined to own an expensive automobile, you may work long hours at a difficult or unpleasant job that you would not work at *except* that you are determined to have the car you want. In the same way, if your goal is to earn a college degree, you may have to do difficult or unpleasant tasks that you would rather not do *except* that you are determined to have the benefits of a college education.

Reward Yourself for Studying

You can motivate yourself to concentrate by arranging your schedule so that you can follow studying with something pleasant to do. Before you begin to study, plan that after an hour or two you will telephone a friend, read a magazine, go jogging, or engage in some other activity that you enjoy. When you study on a Saturday afternoon, plan that in the evening you will visit a friend, go to a movie, or do something else that entertains you.

Study followed by a reward is usually productive. If you know that you have only three hours to study because you've scheduled some fun for yourself, you may be inspired to make the best use of the three hours that you set aside for studying.

EXERCISE 3.1   ## Keeping Records of Concentration

When you begin to read for a college course, make a note of the time in pencil at the place where you begin reading. Then, when you detect that your attention is not focused on reading, record the time again. Compare the two times and make a note of how many minutes you read before you lost your concentration. Continue in this way, striving each time to concentrate longer than you did the time before.

EXERCISE 3.2   ## Do Routine Tasks First

1. Refer to Exercise 2.5 on page 26 to identify the first two assignments you will do next week. Decide which of these two assignments is easier, more routine, or more interesting, and do it first.

2. Decide for which of your courses it is appropriate to begin a study session by reviewing things you have studied previously.

EXERCISE 3.3   ## Unpleasant or Difficult Tasks

List the most unpleasant or difficult tasks you must do this term, and ponder whether your college education is important enough to you to do them.

Understand College Ways

If this is your first week in college, you may feel somewhat uncomfortable because you're not sure of the difference between a *bursar* and a *registrar*, a *credit* and an *hour*, or a *GPA* and an *INC*. If so, this chapter contains information that will be of interest to you.

The Catalogue or Bulletin

Your college publishes a book called a **catalogue** or **bulletin** that contains important information, such as descriptions of courses, graduation requirements, names of instructors, and locations of buildings and offices. If you do not have a copy of your school's catalogue, obtain one immediately. It is probably available at the admissions office of your school.

The School Calendar

Colleges prepare calendars that list holidays and other important days such as the ones for orientation, registration, and final examinations. If you do not find a calendar printed in your catalogue, ask a counselor or adviser for a copy. It is important for you to familiarize yourself with your school's calendar. For one thing, holidays at your school are not necessarily the same as the holidays at local public schools or at other colleges in your community.

Academic calendars are divided into **terms,** which are periods of study that usually end with final examinations. A term may be a semester, a quarter, or a trimester. When a school uses the **semester system,** the school year is divided into two parts, usually a fall and a spring term of about fifteen weeks each. When either the **quarter system** or the **trimester system** is used, the school year is usually divided into fall, winter, and spring terms of about ten weeks each.

Some colleges offer students opportunities to study during summer sessions or intersessions, which are not regarded as terms for the purposes of school business. A **summer session** is a period in the summer during which students may take courses; an **intersession** is a short session of study offered between two terms, such as a four-week session offered in January between a fall and a spring term.

Counseling Services

Most colleges have **counselors** who provide students with guidance in achieving their educational and occupational goals and in resolving their personal problems. In addition, counselors are usually experts in helping students with such problems as changing curriculums and dropping courses.

Read the "Checklist for Counseling Services" on page 33. If any statements on the checklist describe you, a counselor at your school can either help you or tell you where you can find help. You may be advised to visit another office on campus. Or, if you have a problem for which your school provides no services, you may be advised to visit an agency in the community that can give you the assistance you need.

Health Services

Most colleges have an office that provides health services for students who become ill or injured while they are on campus. Call this office if you have an illness or injury that prevents you from attending classes for an extended period. Someone in the office may notify your teachers that you called so they can make special arrangements for you during the time you are unable to attend classes.

Departments, Divisions, and Schools

You are probably taking courses from several different departments. A **department** is an organizational unit that offers courses in a specific subject or a specific group of subjects. For example, a history department may offer courses only in history, but a social science department may offer courses in psychology, sociology, anthropology, and other subjects.

At some colleges, departments are organized into groups called **divisions.** For example, the social science division of a college may include a psychology department, a sociology department, an anthropology department, and other departments. Some universities refer to divisions as **schools.** For instance, schools of business, schools of law, and schools of medicine are usually divisions of universities.

The President and Deans

The senior administrative officer at most colleges and universities is the **president;** he or she has ultimate responsibility for all aspects of the functioning of the school. **Deans** are members of the administration who are in

---

Checklist for Counseling Services

Check any statement in this list that describes you.

☐ I need a part-time job.
☐ I need a place to live.
☐ I need financial assistance.
☐ I need somebody to care for my children.
☐ I want to improve my grades.
☐ I am very anxious when I take tests.
☐ I want an explanation of my placement test scores.
☐ I want help in deciding what occupation to pursue.
☐ I want help in deciding what I should study in college.
☐ I want to know about job opportunities after I graduate.
☐ I want to transfer to another college.
☐ I am extremely displeased with one of my teachers.
☐ I have a serious physical disability or chronic illness.
☐ I have been out of school for years, and I feel lost.
☐ I feel very lonely.
☐ I have a serious problem with my parents (or spouse).
☐ I have poor relations with members of the opposite sex.
☐ I want help to overcome my drug (or alcohol) problem.

A counselor at your school can help you with your problems or tell you where you can find help.

---

charge of specified areas of the school's activities, such as a dean of students or a dean of instruction. Sometimes there are also deans of divisions or schools within a college or university.

At some schools the senior administrative officer is called a **chancellor,** and deans are sometimes called **vice chancellors** or **vice presidents.** At a few schools a chancellor or **ombudsman** is a special assistant to the president.

The Registrar and Admissions Office

The administration includes a **registrar,** who oversees registering students for courses and keeps records of the courses they take and the grades they receive. Shortly after you complete each term, the registrar will send you a **transcript,** which is a report of your grades for the courses you took.

The registrar may be located in the registrar's office, the student records office, or the admissions office. Visit this office when you have questions about your transcript or your registration in courses, and when you want a transcript mailed to an employer or another school.

The Bursar and Business Office

The **bursar,** or **cashier,** is the person responsible for money transactions; he or she may be located in the bursar's office, cashier's office, business office, or office of the treasurer. Visit this office when you have questions about tuition or fees or when you need to pay a bill.

Degrees

When students graduate from colleges and universities, they are awarded **degrees,** which are ranks for those who successfully complete specified courses and other requirements.

If this is your first year in college, you are probably studying for an associate degree or a bachelor's degree. **Associate degrees** are usually offered by two-year and community colleges. They are most commonly the A.A. (Associate of Arts), the A.S. (Associate of Science), and the A.A.S. (Associate of Applied Science). **Bachelor's degrees** are offered by four-year colleges and universities. They are usually the B.A. (Bachelor of Arts) and the B.S. (Bachelor of Science). Some colleges and universities offer **master's degrees** and **doctoral degrees.**

Credits and Hours

Credits and hours are assigned to most college courses. **Credits** are units given for the satisfactory completion of study that applies toward a degree. **Hours** are units that designate time spent in classrooms, laboratories, or conferences—they may be shorter or longer than sixty minutes. For example, at many colleges students earn three credits when they satisfactorily complete a three-credit English composition course. However, the students devote *four* hours each week to the course—*three* hours in class and *one* hour in conference with their composition teachers.

Letter and Number Grades

Instructors evaluate papers, tests, and other student work using letter or number grades. Figure 4.1, on page 35, shows the correspondences among letter grades and number grades used at most schools. Notice, for example, that the **letter grade** of B+ corresponds to the **number grades** 87, 88, and 89. Study your catalogue to learn the correspondences between letter grades and number grades used at your school. Sometimes there are important differences among colleges. For instance, some schools offer the letter grade of A+ and do not offer the grade of D−.

FIGURE 4.1

The Usual Correspondences Among Letter Grades, Number Grades, and GPA Values

Letter grades	Meaning	Number grades	GPA values	
			System 1	*System 2*
A	Excellent	96–100	4.00	4.00
A−		90–95	4.00	3.70
B+		87–89	3.00	3.30
B	Good	84–86	3.00	3.00
B−		80–83	3.00	2.70
C+		77–79	2.00	2.30
C	Satisfactory	74–76	2.00	2.00
C−		70–73	2.00	1.70
D+		67–69	1.00	1.30
D	Passing	64–66	1.00	1.00
D−		60–63	1.00	0.70
F	Failing	0–59	0.00	0.00

Final Course Grades

It may surprise you to learn that most instructors find grading to be their most painful responsibility. A few teachers avoid the discomfort of grading by giving all students high grades. But most accept the obligation to make comparisons among students and to award the highest grades to students who do the best work and the lowest to students who do the poorest work.

Instructors use a variety of methods for computing final grades; it is impossible to list them all. Following are descriptions of three commonly used methods:

1. An instructor may determine final course grades by finding the averages for students' number grades. For example, if a student has test grades of 77, 82, 86, and 75, an instructor will add the scores (320) and divide by the total number of scores (4) to find the average, which is 80. Figure 4.1 shows that a number grade of 80 is equivalent to a letter grade of B−; this is the final course grade the instructor will submit for the student.

2. An instructor may determine final course grades by finding the average for letter grades students have received. For example, if a student has the three letter grades of C+, B, and B+, the instructor may convert these letter grades to the GPA values shown in Figure 4.1 (2.70, 3.00, and 3.30), add the values (9.00) and divide by the total number of grades (3) to find the average, which is 3.00. Figure 4.1 shows that 3.00 is equivalent to a letter grade of B. The instructor will enter a final course grade of B.

3. An instructor may give extra value to one score in a set of scores. For example, one psychology professor computes final grades from scores on a term paper, a midterm examination, and a final examination, giving

double value to the final examination score. Following is an example of how the teacher computed a student's final grade:

Term paper	B+	= 3.30 × 1 =	3.30
Midterm exam	B	= 3.00 × 1 =	3.00
Final exam	A	= 4.00 × 2 =	8.00
		4	14.30

The professor divided 14.30 by 4 to find the average, which is 3.57. Figure 4.1 shows that 3.57 is equivalent to B+ (3.70 is needed for an A−). The student's final course grade is B+.

These are only three examples of the many different methods instructors may use to determine final course grades. If an instructor does not tell you how he or she will determine your final grade, ask, so that you will know what you must do to earn the grade you want for the course.

The Grade Point Average (GPA)

Most colleges compute students' average grades using the **grade point average,** or **GPA,** which is a number that ranges from 0.00 to 4.00. Following final examinations, instructors submit letter grades to the registrar, who enters the grades on students' transcripts and assigns numerical values to them for the purpose of computing GPAs.

Figure 4.1, on page 35, shows two widely used methods for assigning **GPA values** to letter grades. Notice in Figure 4.1 that in System 1, letter grades have the same value whether they are accompanied by a plus or minus (for example, B+, B, and B− all have a value of 3.00). But in System 2, letter grades have larger values when they are accompanied by a plus and smaller values when they are accompanied by a minus (for example, B has a value of 3.00, but B+ has a value of 3.30 and B− has a value of 2.70).

"How to Compute the GPA" on page 37 explains methods you may use to compute your grade point average.

Importance of Your GPA

Some first-year college students believe that they do well when they pass all of their courses; however, this is not necessarily true, because most colleges require students to maintain a minimum GPA of 2.00. Students who have passing grades of D often have GPAs lower than 2.00.

You must have a satisfactory GPA to stay in school, and the credits you accumulate have no value toward earning a degree unless your grade point average meets minimum requirements. If you transfer to another college, the new school will not give you credit for courses in which you received low grades, and a transcript showing a low GPA will not help you find a good job. These are just a few reasons it is important for you to maintain a good grade point average.

When students' GPAs drop below 2.00, it is usually difficult or impossible for them to raise them up to a satisfactory level. For example, a student who completes fifteen credits in the first term with a GPA of 1.65 must

How to Compute the GPA

Letter grades	Credits		GPA values		Grade points
A	3	×	4.00	=	12.00
B−	6	×	2.70	=	16.20
C−	6	×	1.70	=	10.20
	15				38.40

$$\frac{38.40}{15} = 2.56 \text{ GPA}$$

The grade point average is computed using the following procedures.

- Assign GPA values to letter grades.
- Multiply GPA values by credits.
- Add credits and add grade points to find totals.
- Divide total grade points by total credits.

In the example above, the GPA of 2.56 was found by dividing total grade points (38.40) by total credits (15).

have a GPA of at least 2.35 for fifteen credits in the second term to bring the GPA up to 2.00. Unfortunately, students who have D+ averages in their first term seldom have C+ averages in their second term. On the other hand, the GPA works to the advantage of students who earn good grades. If you have a GPA in the 2.50 to 3.50 range for many courses, you can receive a D, D+, or C− in one or two courses and still have a good average.

The W Grade

The **withdrawal grade,** or **W,** is for students who must either leave school or drop a course that is giving them serious difficulty. The W grade is not usually used to compute grade point averages, so it usually does not lower (or raise) GPAs. However, there are strict limitations on the time period during which this grade may be requested.

It is advisable to request a W grade when your final course grade is likely to be an F. Also, it is usually wiser to request a W than to accept a low grade, such as a D. A grade of D is acceptable only for an extremely difficult course that is not in your area of specialization. For example, if you were majoring in computer technology, you might be satisfied with a grade of D in a very difficult history course but not in a computer course.

Also, before you request a W grade, keep in mind that when you drop a course, you may end up with fewer credits than you need for full-time student status. If you lose full-time status, you may lose important benefits such as financial aid or the privilege of playing varsity athletics. Therefore, before you withdraw from a course, you may want to discuss your intentions with a financial aid counselor or other adviser.

The INC Grade

The **incomplete grade,** or **INC,** is given to students who did satisfactory work in a course but who did not complete a term paper or other important project. For instance, if a student performs satisfactorily on all tests for a course but does not submit a required written report, the instructor may give her an INC rather than a grade such as B or C. When she completes the report, the instructor will change the INC grade to A, B, C, or some other letter grade.

However, most schools have deadlines after which past-due work is not accepted. At these schools INC grades are automatically changed to Fs if work is not turned in by these deadlines. It is much better to keep up-to-date with course work than to request an INC grade and run the risk of having it changed to an F.

Some schools also have a special grade for students who miss a final exam in a course for which all their other work is satisfactory. This grade is similar to the INC grade; if the student does not take a make-up test by a specified deadline, the grade is usually changed to an F. Investigate whether your school has a special grade for students who miss final exams.

EXERCISE 4.1   ## Your School's Calendar

The following questions are about your school's calendar, which may be printed in the front of your catalogue.

1. What is the next day when there will be no classes because your school is observing a holiday?

_____

2. What is the next week when there will be no classes because your school is observing a recess of one week or longer?

_____

3. What is the last day of classes for the current term at your school?

_____

4. On what days will final examinations be given for the current term at your school?

_____

EXERCISE 4.2   **Office Locations**

The answers to these questions are probably in your catalogue and in materials that you got during orientation.

1. Where are the counselors' offices located?

   _____

2. Where is the registrar's office located? (It may be called the admissions office or the student records office.)

   _____

3. Where is the bursar's office located? (It may be called the cashier's office, the business office, or the office of the treasurer.)

   _____

4. Where is the financial aid office located?

   _____

5. Where is the office of testing located?

   _____

6. Where is the student activities office located?

   _____

7. Where is the health services office located?

   _____

   What is the telephone number of this office (in case you must report that you are unable to attend classes for an extended period because of illness)?

   _____

8. List the names and locations of the offices of the departments that offer the courses you are taking now.

   a. _____

   b. _____

   c. _____

   d. _____

   e. _____

EXERCISE 4.3   ## Your Curriculum

Obtain a copy of the requirements for your curriculum or program of study. A list of the requirements is probably printed in your catalogue.

1. How many credits are required in your curriculum?   _____

2. What is the minimum number of credits for which you must register in order to be classified as a full-time student?

_____

3. What is the maximum number of credits for which you can register without receiving special permission?

_____

EXERCISE 4.4   ## Letter Grades and Number Grades

Study your catalogue to learn the correspondences between letter grades and number grades at your school. Then write the letter grades that correspond to the following number grades.

1.	85 _____	8.	84 _____	15.	89 _____
2.	70 _____	9.	90 _____	16.	76 _____
3.	77 _____	10.	79 _____	17.	73 _____
4.	63 _____	11.	83 _____	18.	69 _____
5.	74 _____	12.	64 _____	19.	60 _____
6.	59 _____	13.	67 _____	20.	87 _____
7.	66 _____	14.	80 _____	21.	86 _____

EXERCISE 4.5   ## Letter Grades and GPA Values

Study your catalogue to learn the correspondences between letter grades and GPA values at your school. Then write the GPA values that correspond to the following letter grades.

1.	C _____	5.	D _____	9.	C− _____
2.	B+ _____	6.	B _____	10.	F _____
3.	A− _____	7.	D+ _____	11.	A _____
4.	C+ _____	8.	D− _____	12.	B− _____

EXERCISE 4.6   **Your Teachers' Grading Practices**

Find the answers to the following questions:

1. What grading policies do your teachers have for assignments that are turned in late?
2. What grading policies do your teachers have for students who are frequently late to class?
3. What arrangements do your teachers make for students who are absent on the days when tests are given?
4. How will your final grades be determined for the courses you are taking this term?

EXERCISE 4.7   **Minimum Grade Requirements**

1. What is the minimum GPA required for graduation?

   _____

2. Most schools have lower minimum GPA requirements for the first term or two of study and higher requirements for subsequent terms. If your school has such a policy, describe it below.

   _____

   _____

3. A college may require students to have minimum grades in specified courses (such as grades of at least C for courses in major subjects). If your school has minimum grade requirements for specified courses, state them below.

   _____

   _____

4. List the grades that have a value of 0.00 for computing the GPA at your school.

   _____

5. When students are put on probation because of low grades, how much time are they given to raise their grades?

   _____

6. What action is taken against students who fail to raise their grades sufficiently during the time they are on probation?

   _____

EXERCISE 4.8   **W and INC Grades**

The answers to the following questions are probably printed in your catalogue.

1. What is the last day this term to request a W grade?

   _____

2. What is the deadline for completing past-due work for INC grades students receive at the end of this term?

   _____

3. What happens to INC grades when past-due work is not completed by the deadline?

   _____

   _____

4. If your school has a grade for students doing satisfactory work who are absent from the final exam, write the grade on the line.

   _____

   What happens to this grade when a final exam is not made up by the deadline?

   _____

   _____

EXERCISE 4.9   **Computation of the GPA**

Compute GPAs for the following problems, using the method that is used at your school. If you own a calculator, use it to help you make the computations.

1.

Letter grades	Credits		GPA values		Grade points
A	4	×		=	
B	4	×		=	
C	4	×		=	_____

   GPA = _____

2. **Letter grades**   **Credits**   **GPA values**   **Grade points**

    B   3   ×   =
    C   6   ×   =
    D   <u>3</u>   ×   =   _____

    GPA = _____

3. **Letter grades**   **Credits**   **GPA values**   **Grade points**

    A   12   ×   =
    B   8   ×   =
    C   <u>15</u>   ×   =   _____

    GPA = _____

4. **Letter grades**   **Credits**   **GPA values**   **Grade points**

    B   10   ×   =
    C   6   ×   =
    D   <u>2</u>   ×   =   _____

    GPA = _____

5. **Letter grades**   **Credits**   **GPA values**   **Grade points**

    B   6   ×   =
    C   6   ×   =
    D   6   ×   =
    F   <u>3</u>   ×   =   _____

    GPA = _____

6. **Letter grades**   **Credits**   **GPA values**   **Grade points**

    B   6   ×   =
    C   7   ×   =
    D   <u>4</u>   ×   =   _____

    GPA = _____

7. **Letter grades**   **Credits**   **GPA values**   **Grade points**

B+	5	×	=	
C	4	×	=	
C−	<u>6</u>	×	=	_____

GPA = _____

Two

The Vocabulary Program

There are more than 500,000 English words, but experts estimate that average well-educated Americans make practical use of fewer than 30,000 of them. As you pursue college study, you may expect that any one of more than 470,000 words that are unfamiliar to you may suddenly appear in books, articles, and other materials you read. You must be able to identify quickly and accurately the meanings of most of these words so that you can understand fully what you read. In addition, you will need to learn many new words to understand the subjects you study in college.

Chapter 5 explains efficient methods for learning the meanings of new words, and the other chapters in this part of *RSVP* explain three methods for determining the meanings of unfamiliar words you encounter in your reading.

Chapter 6 explains how to locate definitions and other information about words in standard desk dictionaries. When you study Chapter 7 you will learn how to find, or figure out, the meanings of unfamiliar words by studying context. Finally, Chapter 8 teaches how to determine meaning by analyzing words to locate base words, prefixes, and other elements.

Learning New Words

If you are like most students, you will learn the meanings of about 1,500 words each year you are in college. College will stimulate your desire to enlarge your vocabulary, and you will need to learn new words to understand the subjects you study in college. This chapter explains how to select words to learn and how to learn their meanings.

Learn Words of General Interest

One practical way to find words you want to learn is to keep a list of words you recognize when you read or hear them but that you do not use when you write or speak. Words of this type will be easy for you to learn because you already know something about them, and you will be motivated to learn them because you know you are likely to encounter them again.

Search for these words whenever you listen to lectures, conversations, radio, or television and whenever you read. For example, read the following paragraph from an American history textbook and underline any words you recognize but do not use when you speak or write.

The Jazz Age

The Jazz Age, as the decade of the 1920s is sometimes called, owed its name to music that grew out of black urban culture. Evolving from African and black American folk music, early jazz communicated unrestrained freedom that black people seldom knew in their public, working, or political lives. With its emotional rhythms and emphasis on improvisation, jazz blurred the distinction between composer and performer and created new intimacy between performer and audience.

As he read this paragraph, one student underlined the following words he recognizes but does not use: *evolving* (meaning "developing gradually"), *unrestrained* (meaning "not controlled or restricted"), *improvisation*, (meaning "something done on the spur of the moment and without preparation"), and *intimacy* (meaning "closeness"). He added these four words to a list of words that he wants to learn.

Learn Terminology

Also, learn the new words you need to know in order to understand the subject matter of your courses. Over half of the questions on some college tests directly or indirectly test students' knowledge of **terminology**—words or phrases that are used with specific meanings when a subject is discussed. "Examples of Terminology" on page 49 lists examples of terminology in four college subjects.

While you are a college student you will learn the terminology of the subjects you study, adding to your vocabulary words found in the vocabularies of most well-educated people, who studied the same subjects that you will study during your college career.

Textbook authors and publishers use three methods to emphasize important terminology: they print terms in boldface or italics, they list terminology at the ends of chapters, and they define important words in glossaries.

1. Important terminology in textbooks may be printed in boldface or *italics*. *Anarchism* and *libertarian* are printed in boldface in the following excerpt from an American government textbook.

How Much Government?

Some people believe that government is unnecessary and that all the problems now solved by government can be left to other social institutions, such as the family or private organizations. This set of beliefs, called **anarchism,** has very few followers in the United States. Another group of people wants government to do no more than what is minimally necessary to maintain law and order, protect basic individual rights, and provide for national defense. This extremely individualistic view has been associated with the **libertarian** movement in recent years.

The meanings of *anarchism* and *libertarian* are stated in this excerpt.

2. Important terminology is sometimes listed at the end of textbook chapters under a heading such as "Important Words," "Key Concepts," or "Terms Used in This Chapter." The following list appears at the end of the first chapter of an American government textbook.

Key Terms

government	conservatism	anarchism
politics	liberalism	libertarian
democracy	democratic socialism	ideology
republic	communism	myths

Examples of Terminology

The following words are terminology of psychology, history, business, and English.

Psychology	History	Business	English
aggression	abolitionism	acquisition	ambiguity
altruism	agrarian	arbitration	analogy
aphasia	anarchist	boycott	anecdote
biofeedback	antitrust	bylaws	cliché
closure	capitalism	collateral	concise
delusion	carpetbagger	commodities	ellipsis
empathy	civil rights	defendant	euphemism
extravert	coalition	entrepreneur	fallacy
hallucination	embargo	flextime	hyphen
homeostasis	equal rights	franchise	imply
insight	fascism	grievance	jargon
introspection	feminism	hierarchy	non sequitur
libido	Holocaust	injunction	parallelism
mania	imperialism	jurisdiction	plagiarism
obsession	materialism	liability	pretentiousness
prejudice	megalopolis	monopoly	red herring
schema	pluralism	option	redundancy
stereotype	renaissance	reciprocity	syntax
superego	vaudeville	royalty	thesis
synapse	zero option	syndicate	usage

Notice that this list of key terms includes the terms *anarchism* and *libertarian*, which are defined in the paragraph entitled "How Much Government?" on page 48.

3. Important terminology is also often defined in a glossary. A glossary is a list of important words and their definitions; it is usually located at the back of a book, but sometimes a book contains a short glossary in each chapter. The glossary entries at the top of page 50 include definitions for *anarchism* and *libertarianism*.

Glossary

Anarchism The belief that government is unnecessary and that all problems now solved by government can be left to other social institutions.

Bicameral Refers to a legislature that is divided into two separate houses, such as the U.S. Congress.

Executive privilege The traditional right, claimed by presidents since Washington, to withhold information from Congress.

Libertarianism The belief that government should do no more than what is minimally necessary to maintain law and order, protect basic individual rights, and provide for national defense in order to allow the greatest possible freedom for the individual.

Lobbying Named after the public rooms in which it first took place, lobbying is the act of trying to influence government decision makers.

Patronage The providing of services, jobs, or contracts in return for political support that party committee members supervise and use to court voters.

The meanings of *anarchism* and *libertarian* are also stated in the paragraph entitled "How Much Government?" on page 48, and they are included among the "Key Terms" on the same page.

FIGURE 5.1

Notes on Notebook Paper

bicameral	Composed of two houses, such as the U.S. Congress which is composed of the Senate and the House of Representatives
détente	The relaxation of tension between the U.S. and Soviet bloc countries
gerrymander	To draw congressional district lines to gain an unfair advantage in elections
libel	The use of print or pictures to harm someone's reputation
slander	The use of speech to harm a person's reputation or well-being

Make Notes for Words

After you have decided that you want to learn a word, make a note of the word and information that you want to learn about it. Make your notes on notebook paper or on 3-by-5-inch cards.

Figure 5.1 illustrates notes made on notebook paper using the following procedure:

How to Make Notes on Notebook Paper

- Draw or crease a vertical line about 2½ inches from the left edge of the page.
- Write words to the left of the vertical line.
- Write definitions to the right of the vertical line.
- Skip a line between each definition.

Figure 5.2 illustrates notes made on a 3-by-5-inch card using the following procedure:

How to Make Notes on Cards

- Write a word, its part of speech, and its pronunciation on the unlined side of the card.
- Write additional information on the lined side of the card, upside down in relation to the material written on the front.

FIGURE 5.2

**Notes on a
3-by-5-Inch Card**

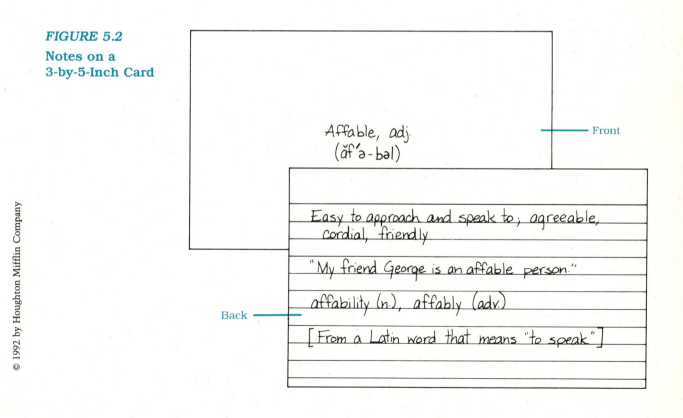

If you use this procedure, information on the backs of cards will be in the proper position for reading when you turn the cards over.

When you make notes for a word, include only the information that you want to learn about it. Figure 5.1 illustrates notes for learning only the definitions of words. In contrast, Figure 5.2 illustrates very complete notes that include a word's part of speech, pronunciation, definition, **synonyms, etymology,** and a sentence showing how the word is used.

When you write sentences to show how words are used, it is helpful to make the sentences about yourself, someone you know, or something you can visualize.

- **Write sentences about yourself.** If you want to learn that *euphoric* means "high-spirited," you might write a sentence about an experience that caused you to experience extremely high spirits: "I was *euphoric* when I received an A on a chemistry test."
- **Write sentences about someone you know.** The student who made the notes in Figure 5.2 associated *affable* with someone she knows—George, who is affable.
- **Write sentences about something you can visualize.** If you want to learn that *retail* means "the selling of goods directly to consumers," write a sentence about something you can visualize: "The Gap is a *retail* clothing store."

One way to better understand and learn the meanings of words is to relate them to your own experiences in sentences such as these.

Recite from Your Notes

Reciting is the act of repeating information silently or aloud so you will remember it. By reciting from your notes, you will read and hear words as many times as you need to learn their meanings. Use the following procedure:

How to Recite

- Read the word or term that is written to the left of the vertical line on notebook paper or on the unlined side of a card.
- Without looking at the information written to the right of the vertical line on notebook paper or on the lined side of a card, try to say the information silently or aloud.
- Read the information about the word to make certain that you recited it correctly. If you did not, reread the information and then immediately try to recite it again.
- Repeat this procedure later until you recall the information that you want to learn about the word.

The purpose of reciting is to learn information, not to memorize words. Since information may usually be stated in several different ways, you may often recite information correctly without repeating words exactly as they are written in your notes.

You may find that you learn words more quickly when you organize them into logical groups, such as words that are synonyms and words that share a common element.

- Synonyms. *Fantastic, bizarre, grotesque,* and *exotic* are a logical group because they are synonyms used to describe something that is "very strange or strikingly unusual."
- Words that share a common element. *Maternal, maternity, matriarch,* and *matricide* are a logical group because they share the element *mater-,* which means "mother."

Experiment with grouping words. One student grouped *affable, compassionate,* and *gullible* because they all describe people's personalities, and she put *choreographer, actuary, meteorologist,* and *thespian* in a group because they all name occupations.

Since we remember best what we review most, it is also necessary for you to review your notes in the way explained on pages 318–320.

EXERCISE 5.1 **Notes on Notebook Paper**

Make notes for learning the meanings of five words you need to know for a psychology, chemistry, business, or other college course you are taking. See Figure 5.1 on page 50 for an example of the kind of notes you are to make.

EXERCISE 5.2   **Notes on a 3-by-5-Inch Card**

Select a word of general interest that you want to learn and make notes for learning it on the form for a 3-by-5-inch card below. See Figure 5.2 on page 52 for an example of the kind of notes you are to make.

EXERCISE 5.3 **Vocabulary List 1**

The following words are underscored in blue in textbook excerpts that appear on pages 102–122 of Chapter 9, and the meanings of the words are provided in the Master Vocabulary List on pages 413–425. Use the methods explained in this chapter to learn the meanings of any of the words that you do not know.

1. acute		31. integral
2. alternative		32. intricate
3. ambiguous		33. levy
4. analogy		34. lewd
5. anticipatory		35. literal
6. asset		36. maim
7. connotation		37. mandate
8. constraint		38. menial
9. denotation		39. motivate
10. depict		40. niche
11. derive		41. obese
12. devotee		42. overplay
13. discrepancy		43. patronage
14. discrimination		44. perception
15. diversify		45. pit
16. embroil		46. prevail
17. entity		47. profound
18. envision		48. spontaneous
19. ethical		49. stereotype
20. euphemism		50. stipulate
21. exclusive		51. succinct
22. expenditure		52. taboo
23. explicit		53. terminal
24. imprecision		54. terminate
25. induce		55. unseemly
26. incentive		56. validity
27. inevitable		57. wangle
28. inference		58. willful
29. initial		59. zealous
30. injunction		

EXERCISE 5.4 **Vocabulary List 2**

The following words are underscored in blue in textbook excerpts that appear on pages 124–146 of Chapter 9, and the meanings of the words are provided in the Master Vocabulary List on pages 413–425. Use the methods explained in this chapter to learn the meanings of any of the words that you do not know.

1. aberrant	32. low-ball
2. affluence	33. martyrdom
3. ambivalent	34. norm
4. attribute	35. nurture
5. autonomy	36. oblige
6. bias	37. obscure
7. coin	38. oppress
8. compliance	39. optimize
9. concise	40. orientation
10. deteriorate	41. ostensible
11. deterioration	42. perspective
12. dilemma	43. pious
13. directive	44. prospective
14. ecclesiastical	45. ratify
15. ego	46. rationale
16. eject	47. résumé
17. embodiment	48. revere
18. empathy	49. self-esteem
19. euphoric	50. simultaneous
20. exploitation	51. sophisticated
21. extol	52. spectrum
22. frustration	53. superimpose
23. heresy	54. theoretical
24. heretic	55. trauma
25. imperialist	56. ultimate
26. impulsive	57. undercut
27. incur	58. vacillate
28. indicative	59. valid
29. indifference	60. victimize
30. internalize	61. virtually
31. liken	

EXERCISE 5.5   Vocabulary List 3

The following words are underscored in blue in textbook excerpts that appear on pages 151–168 of Chapters 10 and 11, and the meanings of the words are provided in the Master Vocabulary List on pages 413–425. Use the methods explained in this chapter to learn the meanings of any of the words that you do not know.

1. adhere	31. implicit
2. adherent	32. incapacitation
3. appalling	33. incompetent
4. ascetic	34. indistinguishable
5. barter	35. indoctrination
6. burgeon	36. inept
7. cardinal	37. innovation
8. confidant	38. interrogation
9. constructive	39. invest
10. convention	40. legacy
11. decapitate	41. medium
12. delusional	42. monetary
13. delve	43. nuance
14. deter	44. nutrient
15. determinant	45. placidity
16. deviate	46. provinces
17. devise	47. punctual
18. distinctive	48. regiment
19. dogmatism	49. regression
20. drudgery	50. rehabilitation
21. dullard	51. retribution
22. elliptical	52. revelation
23. enhance	53. sanction
24. erotic	54. sibling
25. ethics	55. staggering
26. ethnic	56. static
27. ethnicity	57. subject
28. facilitate	58. subtle
29. flamboyant	59. traumatic
30. frenzy	60. tortuous

EXERCISE 5.6   ## Vocabulary List 4

The following words are underscored in blue ink in textbook excerpts that appear on pages 171–194 of Chapters 12, 13, and 15, and the meanings of the words are provided in the Master Vocabulary List on pages 413–425. Use the methods explained in this chapter to learn the meanings of any of the words that you do not know.

This list includes a review of the following sixteen words you learned when you studied the first three lists: asset, enhance, ethical, ethnic, facilitate, frustration, impulsive, incentive, initial, literal, norm, orientation, perception, prospective, self-esteem, and virtually.

1. absorption
2. antipathy
3. asset
4. channel
5. compassionate
6. compatible
7. competence
8. compulsive
9. context
10. criterion
11. crucial
12. disreputable
13. elastic
14. emanate
15. emulation
16. enhance
17. entail
18. ethical
19. ethnic
20. evolve
21. extract
22. facet
23. facilitate
24. factor
25. frustration
26. habitual
27. idiosyncratic
28. impoverished
29. impulsive
30. incentive
31. initial
32. liability
33. literal
34. mainstream
35. martyr
36. norm
37. offset
38. orientation
39. parallel
40. perception
41. phenomenon
42. predominant
43. procreation
44. pronounced
45. prospective
46. reciprocal
47. retailer
48. scourge
49. self-esteem
50. thrive
51. virtually
52. wane
53. wary

EXERCISE 5.7   Vocabulary List 5

The following words are underscored in blue in textbook excerpts that appear on pages 278–296 of Chapter 20, and the meanings of the words are provided in the Master Vocabulary List on pages 413–425. Use the methods that are explained in this chapter to learn the meanings of any of the words that you do not know.

1. abrasion	30. inactivate
2. abstract	31. indifferent
3. affective	32. inhibit
4. affiliate	33. intact
5. allocate	34. intervention
6. altruism	35. irreversible
7. arbitrary	36. jeopardy
8. assertive	37. nip in the bud
9. bizarre	38. normative
10. brash	39. optimal
11. breach	40. orifice
12. caption	41. passive
13. chaos	42. perceive
14. coercive	43. pertinence
15. compassion	44. plum
16. competent	45. prestigious
17. concrete	46. provocative
18. conjure	47. recipient
19. connotative	48. reciprocity
20. consolidation	49. salient
21. denotative	50. segmentation
22. dialect	51. shoestring
23. disclosure	52. spatial
24. documentary	53. subsequent
25. dogmatic	54. susceptible
26. equity	55. technology
27. grist for the mill	56. tirade
28. harbor	57. vehicle
29. imposing	58. virulent

Dictionaries

Dictionaries are alphabetically arranged lists of words that include a great deal of information about words, including spellings, pronunciations, definitions, and synonyms. You should own a paperback dictionary to carry with you to classes and a desk dictionary to use where you study. Paperback dictionaries are handy reference sources, but they do not include sufficient information for a college student's needs. Compare the following excerpts beginning with *Virgil* and ending with *Virginia* from the desk and paperback editions of *The American Heritage Dictionary*.

Desk Edition

Vir·gil (vûr′jəl). Also **Ver·gil.** Full name, Publius Vergilius Maro. 70–19 B.C. Roman poet; author of the epic poem *Aeneid.* —**Vir·gil′i·an** *adj.*

vir·gin (vûr′jĭn) *n.* **1.** A person who has not experienced sexual intercourse. **2.** A chaste or unmarried woman; a maiden. **3.** An unmarried woman who has taken religious vows of chastity. **4.** *Capital* **V.** Mary, the mother of Jesus. Preceded by *the.* Also called "the Blessed Virgin." **5.** Any female animal that has not mated. **6.** *Capital* **V.** The constellation and the sign of the zodiac, **Virgo** (*see*). —*adj.* **1.** Characteristic of or appropriate to a virgin; chaste; maidenly. **2.** In a pure or natural state; untouched; unsullied: *virgin snow.* **3.** Unused, uncultivated, or unexplored: *"The North American drive had been towards the virgin west"* (Gordon K. Lewis). **4.** Existing in native or raw form; not processed or refined. **5.** Happening for the first time; initial: *"guiding my virgin steps on the hard road of letters"* (Maugham). **6.** Obtained directly from the first pressing. Said of vegetable oils. [Middle English, from Old French *virgine,* from Latin *virgō†* (stem *virgin-*).]

vir·gin·al¹ (vûr′jə-nəl) *adj.* **1.** Pertaining to, characteristic of, or befitting a virgin; chaste; pure. **2.** Remaining in a state of virginity. **3.** Untouched or unsullied; fresh.

vir·gin·al² (vûr′jə-nəl) *n.* A small, legless rectangular harpsichord popular in the 16th and 17th centuries. Often used in the plural: *a pair of virginals.* [From VIRGIN (because it was played by young girls).]

virgin birth. *Theology.* The doctrine that Jesus was miraculously begotten by God and born of Mary, who was a virgin.

Vir·gin·ia¹ (vər-jĭn′yə). A feminine given name. [French, from Latin, feminine of *Virginius,* name of a Roman gens.]

Vir·gin·ia² (vər-jĭn′yə). *Abbr.* **Va.** A Southern state of the United States, occupying 40,815 square miles in the east on the Atlantic; one of the original 13 states. Population, 4,648,000. Capital, Richmond. See map at **United States of America.** [From Latin *virgō* (stem *virgin-*), VIRGIN (after Queen Elizabeth I of England, the "virgin queen").] —**Vir·gin′ian** *adj.* & *n.*

Paperback Edition

Vir·gil (vûr′jəl). 70–19 B.C. Latin poet.

vir·gin (vûr′jĭn) *n.* **1.** One who has not experienced sexual intercourse. **2.** A chaste or unmarried woman. **3. the Virgin.** Mary, the mother of Jesus. —*adj.* **1.** Chaste. **2.** In a pure or natural state: *virgin snow.* [< L *virgō.*] —**vir·gin′i·ty** *n.*

vir·gin·al (vûr′jə-nəl) *adj.* **1.** Chaste; pure. **2.** Remaining in a state of virginity. **3.** Untouched or unsullied.

Vir·gin·ia (vər-jĭn′yə). A state of the SE U.S.

Notice that the desk edition gives many more definitions than the paperback edition and that the definitions in the desk edition are more complete. When desk dictionaries are condensed to fit on the pages of paperback books, a great deal is lost. Desk dictionaries list about 150,000 words, but paperback dictionaries list only about 50,000 words.

Of the several excellent dictionaries, I especially recommend the following four, which are available in most well-stocked bookstores.

The American Heritage Dictionary of the English Language
Webster's New World Dictionary of the American Language
Webster's Ninth New Collegiate Dictionary
Random House Webster's College Dictionary

If you do not own a good desk dictionary, compare these four dictionaries and buy the one with definitions that are easy for you to understand. It is essential that you own a dictionary that explains word meanings clearly; if you do not understand the definitions in your dictionary, you probably will not use it often.

Definitions, Synonyms, and Examples

Dictionaries explain the meanings of words using definitions, synonyms, and examples. **Definitions** are statements of the meaning of words; the definition of *happy* is "having a feeling of great pleasure." **Synonyms** are words that have the same or nearly the same meaning; synonyms of *happy* include *glad, pleased, delighted,* and *joyous.* **Examples,** in dictionary entries, are phrases or sentences that illustrate the ways words are used. The following sentence is an example of the way *happy* is used: "We are *happy* that it didn't rain the day of the picnic."

The following entry for *emanate* includes a definition, synonyms, and an example.

> **em·a·nate** (ĕm′ə-nāt′) *v.* -nated, -nating, -nates. —*intr.* To come forth or proceed, as from a source or origin; issue; originate: *"there was no light of any kind emanating from lamp or candle"* (Poe). —*tr.* To send forth; emit. [Latin *ēmānāre,* flow out : *ex-,* out + *mānāre,* to flow (see **mā-³** in Appendix*).] —**em′a·na′tive** *adj.*

Notice that semicolons separate the definition and synonyms and that a colon introduces the example, which is printed in italics.

- The definition is "To come forth or proceed, as from a source or origin."
- The synonyms are *issue* and *originate.*
- The example is "there was no light of any kind emanating from lamp or candle."

(Poe) following the italicized sentence indicates that it was written by Edgar Allan Poe, an American writer best known for short stories such as "The Fall of the House of Usher" and poems such as "The Raven."

Multiple Meanings

Since most words have more than one meaning, it is usually necessary to read two or more definitions of a word to locate the one that pertains to a specific context. The italicized word in the following sentence has several meanings.

Albert Einstein is the *personification* of brains.

Which of the following four definitions of *personification* pertains to the word as it is used in this sentence?

> **per·son·i·fi·ca·tion** (pər-sŏn′ə-fĭ-kā′shən) *n.* **1.** The act of personifying or something that personifies. **2.** A rhetorical figure of speech in which inanimate objects or abstractions are endowed with human qualities or are represented as possessing human form, as in *Hunger sat shivering on the road* or *Flowers danced about the lawn.* **3.** The artistic representation of an abstract quality or idea as a person. **4.** A person or thing typifying a certain quality or idea that is outstanding; an embodiment; exemplification: *"He's invisible, a walking personification of the Negative."* (Ralph Ellison).

Only the fourth definition explains the meaning that applies to *personification* as it is used in the sentence about Einstein.

Etymologies

An **etymology** is information about the origin and development of a word. The etymology for *tuxedo* is enclosed in brackets at the end of the following entry.

> **tux·e·do** (tŭk-sē′dō) *n., pl.* **-dos.** Also **Tux·e·do. 1.** A man's jacket, usually black, with satin or grosgrain lapels worn for formal or semiformal occasions. Also called "dinner jacket." **2.** A complete outfit including this jacket, black trousers with a stripe down the side, and a black bowtie. [From the name of a country club in *Tuxedo* Park, New York, where it became popular.] — An etymology

This etymology states that *tuxedo* comes from the name Tuxedo Park, New York. Etymologies often state interesting information about words that can aid you in learning or remembering their meanings.

Subject Labels

Desk dictionaries provide subject labels to help you locate definitions that pertain to subjects you study in college. **Subject labels** are terms printed in italic type that indicate the fields of knowledge to which the definitions apply. The following entry for *regression* includes three subject labels: the italicized words *Psychoanalysis, Statistics,* and *Astronomy.*

> **re·gres·sion** (rĭ-grĕsh′ən) *n.* **1.** Reversion; retrogression. **2.** Relapse to a less perfect or developed state. **3.** *Psychoanalysis.* Reversion to a more primitive or less mature behavior pattern. **4.** *Statistics.* The tendency for the expected value of one of two jointly correlated random variables to approach more closely the mean value of its set than the other. **5.** *Astronomy.* Retrogradation.

If you study psychology, the third definition will be of special interest to you. If you study statistics, the fourth definition is the one you want, and if you study astronomy, the fifth definition may be helpful to you.

Synonyms

Desk dictionaries are excellent sources of information about **synonyms**—words that have the same or nearly the same meaning. The following entry for *amiable* is accompanied by explanations of the synonyms *affable, good-natured, obliging, agreeable,* and *pleasant.*

> **a·mi·a·ble** (ā′mē-ə-bəl) *adj.* **1.** Pleasantly disposed; good-natured: agreeable. **2.** Cordial; friendly; sociable; congenial: *an amiable gathering.* [Middle English, from Old French, from Late Latin *amicābilis,* AMICABLE.] —**a′mi·a·bil′i·ty, a′mi·a·ble·ness** *n.* —**a′mi·a·bly** *adv.*
>   Synonyms: amiable, affable, good-natured, obliging, agreeable, pleasant. These refer to a tendency to please in social relations. *Amiable* implies friendliness and sweetness of disposition. *Affable* especially fits a person who is easy to approach and difficult to anger. *Good-natured* suggests an easygoing disposition. *Obliging* specifies disposition to comply with the will of others; *agreeable* adds to this a sense of eagerness to please. *Pleasant* applies to favorable manner or appearance.

— Synonyms

The synonyms discussed in this entry all refer to a tendency to please in social relations. You will find discussions of synonyms in desk dictionaries but not in paperback dictionaries.

Idioms

An **idiom** is a phrase that has a meaning that is not clear from the common meanings of the words in the phrase; it is an accepted phrase that cannot be interpreted literally. For example, the common meanings of the words in the phrase *green thumb* suggest that it refers to a thumb the color of grass. However, idiomatically, *green thumb* refers to a talent for growing plants.

> **green thumb.** The ability to foster the growth and health of plants.

Desk dictionaries provide the meanings of idioms such as *black sheep, cold turkey, elbow grease,* and *tit for tat.*

Affixes

In addition to defining words, dictionaries give the meanings of **affixes**—prefixes and suffixes of the kinds explained in Chapter 8. Entries for prefixes are followed by a hyphen (-), as in the following entry for *inter-.*

> **inter-.** Indicates: **1.** Between or among; for example, **inter-collegiate, international. 2.** Mutually or together; for example, **interact, intermingle.**

Similarly, entries for suffixes are preceded by a hyphen, as in the following entry for *-ful*.

> **–ful.** Indicates: **1.** Fullness or abundance; for example, **playful**. **2.** Having the characteristics; for example, **masterful**. **3.** Tendency or ability; for example, **useful**. **4.** The amount or number that will fill; for example, **armful**. [Middle English *-ful*, Old English *-ful*, *-full*, from *full*, FULL.]

Entries for combining forms are also followed or preceded by hyphens. On page 84 there are dictionary entries for the combining forms *biblio-* and *-phile*.

People, Places, and Other Topics

Desk dictionaries include entries for people, places, and many other topics. Entries for people range from famous historical figures to prominent individuals in politics, art, music, film, and sports.

> **King** (kĭng), **Martin Luther, Jr.** 1929–1968. American Baptist minister and civil-rights leader; awarded Nobel Peace Prize (1964); assassinated.

Entries for places include bodies of water, mountains, and deserts as well as cities, states, and countries.

> **Ti·ti·ca·ca** (tē′tē-kä′kä). A lake of South America, occupying 3,200 square miles in the Andes between Peru and Bolivia, at an altitude of 12,507 feet.

Desk dictionaries also list entries for a wide variety of other topics.

> **punk rock**. A form of rock music characterized by a stabbing, insistent rhythm and simple three-chord harmony, amplified sound, and lyrics that deal with subjects full of trouble and strife such as anarchy, alienation, violence, drugs, sex, and teen-age rebellion. Punk performers and followers adopt outlandishly vulgar behavioral patterns and clothing, often leading to acts of violence by performers and audience alike.
> **Purple Heart.** *Abbr.* **PH, P.H.** The U.S. Armed Forces medal of the Order of the Purple Heart, awarded to servicemen wounded in action.
> **World War II.** *Abbr.* **W.W.II** A war fought from 1939 to 1945, in which Great Britain, France, the Soviet Union, the United States, and other allies defeated Germany, Italy, and Japan. Also called "Second World War."

When you want basic facts about a topic, you are likely to find them in a modern desk dictionary.

EXERCISE 6.1 **Dictionary Checklist**

Use the following checklist to determine whether a dictionary that you own or are considering purchasing contains all the features you need in a dictionary. Write the title of the dictionary that you evaluate.

Title: _____

Yes   **No**

_____ _____   1. The dictionary was published no more than four years ago.

_____ _____   2. The definitions of words are easy to understand.

_____ _____   3. Biographical information is given (look up *Noah Webster*).

_____ _____   4. Geographical information is given (look up *New Mexico*).

_____ _____   5. Idioms are defined (look up *rule of thumb*).

_____ _____   6. Foreign phrases are defined (look up *bête noire*).

_____ _____   7. Prefixes, suffixes, and combining forms are defined (look up *retro-*, *-ish*, and *patho-*).

_____ _____   8. Abbreviations are defined (look up *P.S.*).

_____ _____   9. The dictionary has good illustrations and maps.

_____ _____   10. Some definitions have subject labels (look up *depression* to see whether some definitions are labeled *Economics*, *Astronomy*, or *Psychology*).

_____ _____   11. Some definitions have usage labels (look up *bug* to see whether a definition is labeled *Slang*, *Colloquial*, or *Informal*).

_____ _____   12. Meanings of synonyms are discussed (look up *old* to see whether its definitions are followed by a discussion of the meanings of words such as *ancient*, *antique*, and *archaic*).

EXERCISE 6.2   **Studying Dictionary Entries**

Answer the following questions by referring to the entries listed at the bottom of this page.

1. On what continent is the *Amazon* River located and approximately how many miles long is it?

   _____

2. Which is correct: "the *data* is" or "the *data* are"?

   _____

3. What is the meaning of the combining form *helio-*?

   _____

4. In what years was *John F. Kennedy* born and assassinated?

   _____

5. During what years was the *Korean War* fought?

   _____

6. What gives the main flavor to sauce *Mornay*?

   _____

7. Spell *love* in *pig Latin*.

   _____

8. Exactly where is your *uvula* located?

   _____

Am·a·zon² (ăm′ə-zŏn′, -zən). A river of South America rising in the Peruvian Andes and flowing about 4,000 miles north and then east through northern Brazil to the Atlantic Ocean; navigable by ocean vessels to Iquitos, Peru, 2,400 miles inland.

da·ta (dā′tə, dăt′ə, dä′tə) *pl.n. Singular* **datum** (dā′təm, dăt′əm, dä′təm). See Usage note below. **1.** Information, especially information organized for analysis or used as the basis for a decision. **2.** Numerical information in a form suitable for processing by computer. [Latin, plural of DATUM.]

helio-. Indicates the sun or of or by the sun; for example, **helio-graph, heliotrope.** [From Greek *hēlios,* the sun. See **săwel-** in Appendix.*]

Ken·ne·dy (kĕn′ə-dē), **John Fitzgerald.** 1917–1963. Thirty-fifth President of the United States (1961–63); assassinated.

Korean War. A military action between North Korea and United Nations forces (1950–53).

Mor·nay (môr-nā′) *n.* A white sauce flavored with grated Swiss or Parmesan cheese. [Probably after Philippe de *Mornay* (1549–1623), French Huguenot leader.]

pig Latin. A coded jargon in which the initial consonant of each word is transposed to the end of that word with *-ay* (ā) added to form a new syllable, as *igpay atinlay* for *pig Latin.*

u·vu·la (yōō′vyə-lə) *n.* The small, conical, fleshy mass of tissue suspended from the center of the soft palate above the back of the tongue. [Middle English, from Late Latin, "small grape" (from the shape of the uvula), diminutive of Latin *ūva,* a grape. See **óg-** in Appendix.*]

EXERCISE 6.3 Multiple Meanings

Referring to the entries at the bottom of this page, write the number of the definition that pertains to each word printed in **boldface.**

_____ 1. The 2,000-page manuscript of a novel was **abridged** to a reasonable length before publication.

_____ 2. *Indian* is an **ambiguous** word because it can refer to natives of India or to natives of North and South America.

_____ 3. I would like him more if he would refrain from making **caustic** comments about my friends.

_____ 4. His wife suggested that he **compose** himself before responding to an insulting letter.

_____ 5. It used to be a **convention** for men to remove their hats in the presence of women.

_____ 6. The painting **depicts** Abraham Lincoln addressing a crowd at Gettysburg, Pennsylvania.

_____ 7. They hired a **dynamic** young lawyer to represent them in court.

_____ 8. Missionaries persuaded many natives of Hawaii to **embrace** Christianity.

_____ 9. She studied dancing with a teacher who is an **exponent** of the Russian style of ballet.

---

a·bridge (ə-brĭj′) *tr.v.* **abridged, abridging, abridges.** **1.** To reduce the length of (a written text); condense. **2.** To curtail; cut short. [Middle English *abregen,* from Old French *abregier,* from Late Latin *abbreviāre,* ABBREVIATE.] —**a·bridg′er** *n.*

am·big·u·ous (ăm-bĭg′yŏŏ-əs) *adj.* **1.** Susceptible of multiple interpretation. **2.** Doubtful or uncertain. [Latin *ambiguus,* uncertain, "going about," from *ambigere,* to wander about : *ambi-,* around + *agere,* to drive, lead (see **ag-** in Appendix*).] —**am·big′u·ous·ly** *adv.* —**am·big′u·ous·ness** *n.*

caus·tic (kôs′tĭk) *adj.* **1.** Able to burn, corrode, dissolve, or otherwise eat away by chemical action. **2.** Marked by sharp and bitter wit; cutting: *"Her new clothes were the subject of caustic comment."* (Willa Cather). **3.** *Optics.* Of or pertaining to light emitted from a point source and reflected or refracted from a curved surface. —See Synonyms at **sarcastic.** —*n.* A caustic material or substance. [Latin *causticus,* from Greek *kaustikos,* from *kaiein,* to burn. See **kēu-** in Appendix.*] —**caus′ti·cal·ly** *adv.* —**caus·tic′i·ty** (kôs-tĭs′ə-tē) *n.*

com·pose (kəm-pōz′) *v.* **-posed, -posing, -poses.** —*tr.* **1.** To make up the constituent parts of; constitute or form. See Usage note at **comprise.** **2.** To make or create by putting together parts or elements. **3.** To create or produce (a literary or musical piece). **4.** To make (one's mind or body) calm or tranquil; to quiet. **5.** To settle (arguments); reconcile. **6.** To arrange aesthetically or artistically.

con·ven·tion (kən-vĕn′shən) *n. Abbr.* **conv. 1.** A formal assembly or meeting of members, representatives, or delegates of a group, such as a political party or fraternal society. **2.** The body of persons attending such an assembly. **3.** An agreement or compact; especially, an international agreement dealing with a specific subject, as the treatment of war prisoners. **4.** General agreement on or acceptance of certain practices or attitudes. **5.** A practice or procedure widely observed in a group, especially to facilitate social intercourse; custom. **6.** A widely used and accepted device or technique, as in drama, literature, or painting: *the theatrical convention of the "aside."* [Middle English *convencioun,* from Old French *convention,* from Latin *conventiō,* assembly, agreement, from *convenīre,* to come together, CONVENE.]

de·pict (dĭ-pĭkt′) *tr.v.* **-picted, -picting, -picts.** **1.** To represent in a picture or sculpture. **2.** To represent in words; describe. [Latin *dēpingere* (past participle *dēpictus*) : *dē-,* completely + *pingere,* to picture (see **peig-¹** in Appendix*).] —**de·pic′tion** *n.*

dy·nam·ic (dī-năm′ĭk) *adj.* Also **dy·nam·i·cal** (-ĭ-kəl). **1.** Of or pertaining to energy, force, or motion in relation to force. **2.** Characterized by or tending to produce continuous change or advance. **3.** Energetic; vigorous; forceful. **4.** Of or pertaining to variation of intensity, as in musical sound. —See Synonyms at **active.** [French *dynamique,* from Greek *dunamikos,* powerful, from *dunamis,* power, from *dunasthai,* to be able. See **deu-²** in Appendix.*] —**dy·nam′i·cal·ly** *adv.*

em·brace¹ (ĕm-brās′, ĭm-) *v.* **-braced, -bracing, -braces.** —*tr.* **1.** To clasp or hold to one with the arms, usually as a display of affection. **2. a.** To encircle or surround. **b.** To twine around. **3.** To include within its bounds; encompass: *"Nor can conventional narrative history really embrace the complexities of cultural change."* (Crane Brinton). **4.** To take up; adopt (a cause or doctrine, for example). **5.** To avail oneself of; accept eagerly: *embrace an opportunity.* **6.** To take in with the eyes or mind. **7.** To submit to with dignity or fortitude: *embrace misfortune.*

ex·po·nent (ĕk-spō′nənt, ĭk-) *n.* **1.** One that defines, expounds, or interprets. **2.** One that speaks for, represents, or advocates: *an exponent of international cooperation.* **3.** *Mathematics.* Any number or symbol, as 3 in $(x+y)^3$, placed to the right of and above another number, symbol, or expression, denoting the power to which the latter is to be raised. In this sense, also called "power." —*adj.* Expository; explanatory. [Latin *expōnēns,* present participle of *expōnere,* to EXPOUND.]

EXERCISE 6.4 **Subject Labels**

Referring to the entries at the bottom of this page, write the number of the definition that pertains to each subject listed in the second column. For instance, refer to the entry for *degradation* to find the number in front of the definition that pertains to the study of geology.

Word	Subject	Definition that pertains
1. degradation	geology	_____
2. node	mathematics	_____
3. phrase	music	_____
4. rectify	chemistry	_____
5. regression	psychology	_____
6. sleep	botany	_____
7. truss	engineering	_____
8. valid	logic	_____

deg·ra·da·tion (dĕg'rə-dā'shən) *n.* **1.** The act or process of degrading, specifically: **a.** A deposition, removal, or dismissal from rank or office. **b.** A reduction in worth or standing. **2.** A process of transition from a higher to a lower quality or level. **3.** The state or condition of being degraded; deterioration; degeneration. **4.** *Geology.* A general lowering of the earth's surface by erosion or transportation in running water. **5.** *Chemistry.* Decomposition of a compound by stages, exhibiting well-defined intermediate products. —See Synonyms at **disgrace.**
node (nōd) *n.* **1.** A knob, knot, protuberance, or swelling: *a lymph node.* **2.** *Botany.* The often enlarged point on a stem where a leaf, bud, or other organ diverges from the stem to which it is attached; a joint. **3.** *Physics.* A point or region of minimum or zero amplitude in a periodic system. **4.** *Mathematics.* The point at which a continuous curve crosses itself; the **crunode** (*see*). **5.** *Astronomy.* **a.** Either of two diametrically opposite points at which the orbit of a planet intersects the ecliptic. **b.** Either of two points at which the orbit of a satellite intersects the orbital plane of a planet. [Latin *nōdus,* a knob, knot. See **ned-** in Appendix.*] —**nod'al** *adj.*
phrase (frāz) *n. Abbr.* **phr.** **1.** Any sequence of words intended to have meaning. **2.** A brief, apt, and cogent expression, such as *behind the iron curtain.* **3.** A word or group of words read or spoken as a unit and separated by pauses or other junctures. **4.** *Grammar.* Two or more words in sequence that form a syntactic unit or group of syntactic units, less completely predicated than a sentence. **5.** *Dance.* A series of movements forming a unit in a choreographic pattern. **6.** *Music.* A segment of a composition, usually consisting of four or eight measures.
rec·ti·fy (rĕk'tə-fī') *tr.v.* **-fied, -fying, -fies.** **1.** To set right; correct. **2.** To correct by calculation or adjustment. **3.** *Chemistry.* To refine or purify, especially by distillation. **4.** *Electricity.* To convert (alternating current) into direct current. **5.** To adjust (the proof of alcoholic beverages) by adding water or other liquids. —See Synonyms at **correct.** [Middle English *rectifien,*

from Old French *rectifier,* from Medieval Latin *rēctificāre* : Latin *rēctus,* straight (see **reg-**[1] in Appendix*) + *facere,* to make (see **dhē-**[1] in Appendix*).] —**rec'ti·fi'a·ble** *adj.* —**rec'ti·fi·ca'·tion** (-fə-kā'shən) *n.*
re·gres·sion (rĭ-grĕsh'ən) *n.* **1.** Reversion; retrogression. **2.** Relapse to a less perfect or developed state. **3.** *Psychoanalysis.* Reversion to a more primitive or less mature behavior pattern. **4.** *Statistics.* The tendency for the expected value of one of two jointly correlated random variables to approach more closely the mean value of its set than the other. **5.** *Astronomy.* Retrogradation.
sleep (slēp) *n.* **1.** A natural, periodically recurring physiological state of rest, characterized by relative physical and nervous inactivity, unconsciousness, and lessened responsiveness to external stimuli. **2.** A period of this form of rest. **3.** Any similar condition of inactivity, such as unconsciousness, dormancy, or hibernation. **4.** *Botany.* The folding together of leaves or petals at night or in the absence of light.
truss (trŭs) *n.* **1.** *Medicine.* A supportive device worn to prevent enlargement of a hernia or the return of a reduced hernia. **2.** *Engineering.* A framework of wooden beams or metal bars, often arranged in triangles, to support a roof, bridge, or similar structure. **3.** *Architecture.* A bracket. **4.** Something gathered into a bundle; a pack. **5.** *British.* A bundle of a set weight of straw or hay, generally 60 pounds of new hay, 56 pounds of old hay, or 36 pounds of straw. **6.** *Nautical.* An iron fitting by which a lower yard is secured to a mast. **7.** A compact cluster of flowers at the end of a stalk.
val·id (văl'ĭd) *adj.* **1.** Well-grounded; sound; supportable: *a valid objection.* **2.** Producing the desired results; efficacious: *valid methods.* **3.** Legally sound and effective; incontestable; binding: *a valid title.* **4.** *Logic.* **a.** Containing premises from which the conclusion may logically be derived: *a valid argument.* **b.** Correctly inferred or deduced from a premise: *a valid conclusion.* **5.** *Archaic.* Of sound health; robust.

EXERCISE 6.5 Synonyms

Use the discussions of synonyms to match sentences *1* through *4* with words *a* through *d* and sentences *5* through *8* with words *e* through *h*.

fan·tas·tic (făn-tăs′tĭk) *adj.* Also **fan·tas·ti·cal** (-tĭ-kəl). **1.** Bizarre in form, conception, or appearance; strange; wondrous; fanciful. **2.** Existing in the fancy; unreal; illusory. **3.** Unrestrainedly fanciful; extravagant: *fantastic hopes.* **4.** Capricious or fitful, as a person or mood. **5.** *Informal.* Wonderful or superb; remarkable; uncanny. —*n. Archaic.* A person who is unrestrainedly fanciful or eccentric in behavior or appearance. [Middle English *fantastik*, from Old French *fantastique*, from Medieval Latin *fantasticus*, from Late Latin *phantasticus*, imaginary, from Greek *phantastikos*, able to produce the appearance of, from *phantazein*, to make visible. See **fantasy.**] —**fan·tas′ti·cal′i·ty, fan·tas′ti·cal·ness** *n.* —**fan·tas′ti·cal·ly** *adv.*
  Synonyms: *fantastic, bizarre, grotesque, fanciful, exotic.* These adjectives apply to what is very strange or strikingly unusual. *Fantastic* can mean literally apart from reality, but in this comparison it more often describes what seems to have slight relation to the real world because of its strangeness or extravagance. *Bizarre* stresses oddness of character or appearance that is heightened by striking contrasts and incongruities and that shocks or fascinates. *Grotesque* refers principally to appearance or aspect in which deformity and distortion approach the point of caricature or even absurdity. *Fanciful* suggests a character, nature, or design strongly influenced by imagination, caprice, or whimsy rather than by fact, reality, reason, or experience. *Exotic* means foreign in origin or character and alluring in effect.
small (smôl) *adj.* **smaller, smallest.** *Abbr.* **s., sm. 1.** Measurably less in size, number, quantity, magnitude, or extent; little. **2.** Limited in importance or significance; trivial. **3.** Limited in degree, scope, or intensity. **4.** Lacking position, influence, or status; minor: *"A crowd of small writers had vainly attempted to rival Addison."* (Macaulay). **5.** Engaged in business or other activity on a limited scale. **6.** Unpretentious; modest. **7.** Not fully grown; very young. **8.** Characterized by littleness of mind or character; petty. **9.** Belittled; humiliated. **10.** Diluted; weak. Said of alcoholic beverages. **11.** Soft; low: *a small voice.* —*adv.* **1.** In small pieces: *Cut it up small.* **2.** Softly. **3.** In a small manner. —*n.* **1.** Something smaller than the rest: *the small of the back.* **2.** *Plural.* **a.** Small things collectively. **b.** *British.* **Smallclothes** (*see*). [Middle English *smal(l)*, Old English *smæl.* See **mēlo-** in Appendix.*] —**small′ness** *n.*
  Synonyms: *small, little, diminutive, minute, miniature, minuscule, tiny, wee, petite.* These adjectives describe persons or things whose physical size is markedly below that of the average. *Small* and *little* can often be used interchangeably. In general, *small* has the wider application; with reference to physical size, *little* is usually more emphatic in implying sharp reduction from the average. *Little* is sometimes used also to add a sense of charm, endearment, or pathos to the term modified. *Diminutive* means very, often abnormally, small. *Minute* describes what is small to the point of being difficult to see. *Miniature* applies to a representation of something on a greatly reduced scale. *Minuscule* refers to what is very small, and is occasionally used in the sense of miniature. *Tiny* and *wee* both mean exceptionally small and are often interchangeable, though *wee* generally implies endearment or humor. *Petite* is applied principally to the feminine figure in the sense of small and trim.

_____ 1. A windowless fifty-story building that is painted black would be

_____ 2. A restaurant decorated with a waterfall, a stream, and trees to recreate a forest setting would be

_____ 3. Those who have never traveled down the Amazon River in a banana boat may find the experience to be

_____ 4. If you were given one million dollars, that would be

   a. fantastic.   b. grotesque.   c. fanciful.   d. exotic.

_____ 5. Adult women who weigh about one hundred pounds are

_____ 6. An almost invisible cavity in a tooth is

_____ 7. A two-ounce serving of roast beef is

_____ 8. Full-grown men who are less than four feet tall are

   e. diminutive.   f. minute.   g. minuscule.   h. petite.

EXERCISE 6.6 Idioms

Answer the following questions by placing checks in the boxes in front of the correct answers. If necessary, refer to the dictionary entries at the bottom of this page.

1. The **alpha and omega** are the
   - ☐ a. beginning and end.
   - ☐ b. top and bottom.
   - ☐ c. best and worst.
   - ☐ d. blessed and damned.

2. **Crocodile tears** are
   - ☐ a. big.
   - ☐ b. watery.
   - ☐ c. frightening.
   - ☐ d. false.

3. The **eleventh hour** is
   - ☐ a. with time to spare.
   - ☐ b. at the last minute.
   - ☐ c. an hour before midnight.
   - ☐ d. an hour before noon.

4. A **gravy train**
   - ☐ a. slips and slides.
   - ☐ b. pays well.
   - ☐ c. tastes good.
   - ☐ d. spills and leaks.

5. An **Indian summer** is
   - ☐ a. a summer crops grow well.
   - ☐ b. a summer of yesteryear.
   - ☐ c. warm fall weather.
   - ☐ d. much hotter than usual.

6. An **ivory tower** is a
   - ☐ a. retreat from reality.
   - ☐ b. center for research.
   - ☐ c. church or cathedral.
   - ☐ d. hospital or school.

7. **Lip service** is
   - ☐ a. rudeness.
   - ☐ b. kisses.
   - ☐ c. insincere agreement.
   - ☐ d. talk with no action.

8. A **red herring** is
   - ☐ a. distracting.
   - ☐ b. smelly.
   - ☐ c. colorful.
   - ☐ d. tasty.

9. A **sacred cow** is
   - ☐ a. large and religious.
   - ☐ b. immune from criticism.
   - ☐ c. worshiped devoutly.
   - ☐ d. a boring issue.

10. **Tongue-in-cheek** means
   - ☐ a. humorous.
   - ☐ b. serious.
   - ☐ c. quizzical.
   - ☐ d. commanding.

alpha and omega. **1.** The first and the last: "*I am Alpha and Omega, the beginning and the ending, saith the Lord*" (Revelation 1:8). **2.** The most important part of something.
crocodile tears. False tears; an insincere display of grief. [From the belief that crocodiles weep after eating their victims.]
eleventh hour. The latest possible time. [By allusion to the parable (Matthew 20:1–16) in which the workers hired at the eleventh hour received the same wages as those hired earlier.]
gravy train. *Slang.* An occupation or job that requires little effort while yielding considerable profit.
Indian summer. **1.** A period of mild weather, occurring in late autumn or early winter. **2.** A pleasant, tranquil, or flourishing period occurring during the end of a condition or period.

ivory tower. A place or attitude of retreat, especially, preoccupation with lofty, remote, or intellectual considerations rather than with practical everyday life.
lip service. Insincere agreement or payment of respect.
red herring. **1.** A smoked herring having a reddish color. **2.** Something that draws attention from the matter or issue at
sacred cow. A person, idea, or object sarcastically regarded as immune from reasonable criticism.
tongue-in-cheek (tŭng′ən-chĕk′) *adj.* Meant or expressed ironically or facetiously.

EXERCISE 6.7   Etymologies

Referring to the etymologies in the entries at the bottom of this page, fill in the information that is missing from the following sentences.

1. **Foible,** which means "a minor weakness," comes from a _____ _____ word that means _____.

2. **Lilliputian,** which means "very small," was first used by Jonathan Swift in his book _____.

3. **Maverick,** which means "an independent person," comes from Samuel Maverick, a Texas cattleman who did not _____ his _____.

4. **Narcissism,** which means "excessive self-love," comes from Narcissus, a mythical youth who rejected the love of _____ and fell in love with his own image.

5. **Ostracize,** which means "to banish or exclude from a group," comes from a _____ word that means _____.

6. **Utopia,** which means "a place of perfection," was first used by _____ in the year _____.

---

foi·ble (foi′bəl) *n.* **1.** A minor weakness or failing of character; a small but persistent personal fault. **2.** The weaker section of a sword blade, from the middle to the tip. In this sense, compare **forte.** —See Synonyms at **fault.** [Obsolete French, from adjective, "feeble," from Old French *feble,* FEEBLE.]

Lil·li·pu·tian (lil′ə-pyōō′shən) *n.* **1.** One of the tiny inhabitants of an island in Jonathan Swift's *Gulliver's Travels.* **2.** *Often small* l. A very small person or being. **3.** *Often small* l. A person of little intelligence, worth, or significance. —*adj. Often small* l. **1.** Very small; diminutive. **2.** Trivial: petty.

mav·er·ick (măv′ər-ĭk, măv′rĭk) *n.* **1.** An unbranded or orphaned range calf or colt, traditionally considered the property of the first person who brands it. **2.** A horse or steer that has escaped from a herd. **3. a.** One who refuses to abide by the dictates of his group; a dissenter: *"Pitt was a maverick among Whig politicians in that he adhered to Tory diplomacy and strategy."* (W.L. Morton). **b.** One who resists adherence to or affiliation with any single organized group or faction; an independent. Often used attributively: *maverick politicians.* [After Samuel A. *Maverick* (1803–1870), Texas cattleman who did not brand his calves.]

nar·cis·sism (när′sə-sĭz′əm) *n.* Also **nar·cism** (när′sĭz′əm). **1.** Excessive admiration of oneself. **2.** *Psychoanalysis.* An arresting of development at, or a regression to, the infantile stage of development in which one's own body is the object of erotic interest. [After NARCISSUS.] —**nar′cis·sist** (när′sə-sĭst) *n.* —**nar′cis·sis′tic** (när′sə-sĭs′tĭk) *adj.*

Nar·cis·sus (när-sĭs′əs). *Greek Mythology.* A youth who, having spurned the love of Echo, pined away in love for his own image in a pool of water and was transformed into the flower that bears his name.

os·tra·cize (ŏs′trə-sīz′) *tr.v.* **-cized, -cizing, -cizes. 1.** To banish or exclude from a group; shut out; shun. **2.** To banish by ostracism, as in ancient Greece. [Greek *ostrakizein,* from *ostrakon,* shell, shard (from the shard with which the Athenian citizen voted for ostracism). See **osth-** in Appendix.*]

U·to·pi·a (yōō-tō′pē-ə). An imaginary island that served as the subject and title of a book by Sir Thomas More in 1516 and that was described as a seat of perfection in moral, social, and political life. [New Latin, "no-place" : Greek *ou†,* not, no + *topos,* place (see **topic**).]

Study Context

A **context** is a sentence, paragraph, or longer unit of writing that surrounds a word and determines its meaning. For example, *depression* sometimes refers to sadness and dejection, but the context of the following sentence determines another meaning for the word.

> Millions of people were homeless and unemployed during the *depression* of the 1930s.

In the context of this sentence *depression* refers to a period of economic decline.

This chapter explains how to use context to locate or figure out word meanings. If you become more skillful at finding word meanings in context, you will have less need to look for definitions in a dictionary.

Stated Word Meanings

Writers often give straightforward definitions of words. Underline the definition of the italicized term in the following sentence:

> Your *receptive vocabulary* is the words you know when you read and listen.

You should have underlined the last nine words in the sentence.

Word meanings are also often set off in sentences by punctuation such as parentheses, commas, and dashes. Underline the meanings of *progeny*, *orthography*, and *plagiarize* that are set off in the following sentences.

Parentheses

The *progeny* (offspring) of one insect can number in the thousands, but most of them do not live for long.

Commas

Learn the rules of *orthography*, or spelling, that are explained in many English handbooks.

A Dash

When you write papers for your college courses, take care that you do not *plagiarize*—present the words or ideas of others as your own.

For *progeny* you should have underlined "offspring," for *orthography* "spelling," and for *plagiarize* "present the words or ideas of others as your own."

When writers use punctuation to set off the meanings of words in sentences, their purpose is clearly to state those meanings. However, word meanings are also frequently stated in less obvious ways. Underline the meaning of *panacea*, which is stated in the following sentence.

> After her divorce, Terry moved to Chicago, hoping that the move would be a remedy for her problems; however, Chicago was not a *panacea* for her difficulties.

Notice that in stating information about Terry, the sentence also gives the meaning of *panacea*: a remedy, solution, or cure-all. You should have underlined *remedy*.

Exercises 7.1 and 7.2, on pages 76 and 77, provide practice in locating word meanings that are stated in context.

Implied Word Meanings

When the meaning of a word is not stated in a context, it may be suggested, hinted, or **implied.** You may infer the meaning of a word that is implied by a context. To **infer** is to use reasoning to arrive at a conclusion or decision. Infer the meaning of *incarcerated* that is implied by the general sense of the following sentence.

General Sense

> Murderers are usually *incarcerated* for longer periods of time than robbers.

Since you know that those found guilty of murder and robbery are usually sentenced to serve time in prison, this context implies that *incarcerated* means "locked up in a jail, prison, or penitentiary."

When the meaning of a word is not implied by the general sense of a context, it may be implied by examples. Infer the meaning of *discipline* that is implied by examples in the following sentence.

Examples

> My history professor is an expert in three *disciplines*—history, architecture, and philosophy.

Since history, architecture, and philosophy are three branches of knowledge, this context implies that a *discipline* is a "branch of knowledge, learning, or study."

When the meaning of a word is not implied by the general sense of a context or by examples, it may be implied by a contrasting thought. Infer the meaning of *credence* that is implied by a contrast in the following sentence.

Contrast

Dad gave *credence* to my story, but Mom's reaction was one of total disbelief.

Since this sentence contrasts Dad's reaction of *credence* with Mom's reaction of "total disbelief," it implies that *credence* is very different from "total disbelief." *Credence* means "belief."

Exercises 7.3 and 7.4, on pages 78 and 79, provide practice in inferring word meanings that are implied by context. As you do these exercises, do not be discouraged if, at first, you have difficulty inferring the exact meanings of words. It is also an accomplishment to infer the general meanings of sentences that contain unfamiliar words.

EXERCISE 7.1 Stated Meanings

Underline the synonyms or definitions of the **boldface** words in the following sentences.

1. He understood his mother's frown to be **adverse,** or unfavorable, criticism.

2. Some people do not **condone** smoking in their homes, but others forgive, or overlook, their guests' smoking.

3. She **contends** that the death penalty should be abolished, but he argues that there are times when death is the only appropriate penalty.

4. Our thoughts are **covert;** they are concealed, or hidden, from others until we share them.

5. **Criteria** are standards by which something is judged, such as the standards teachers use when they evaluate students' writing.

6. When you go from bright daylight into a darkened room, the pupils of your eyes **dilate** (enlarge) to compensate for the loss of light.

7. The library is the most prominent **edifice** on campus; it towers above all the other buildings.

8. If I say, "Please call me Jim," it is **explicit** (or clearly stated) that I want you to call me Jim.

9. Some people are **gullible**—easily cheated or tricked because they believe everything that others say.

10. If I introduce myself to you as "Jim," it is **implicit**—suggested, though not directly stated—that I want you to call me "Jim."

11. The death sentence is sometimes carried out by **lethal** injection—a shot in the arm with a deadly chemical.

12. If you needed to make a choice between being rich and being loved, which would you **opt** for?

13. As supervisor, it is his task to familiarize new workers with company rules and to **orient** them to the responsibilities of their jobs.

14. When we laugh, our thoughts become **overt;** laughter makes it apparent, or clear, that we are amused.

15. The notion that it is sophisticated to smoke is **passé**—it's as old-fashioned and out-of-date as greasy hair.

EXERCISE 7.2   **Stated Meanings**

Underline the synonyms or definitions of the **boldface** words in the following sentences.

1. Your **peers** are your equals—your classmates, for instance.

2. When the going gets tough, the tough get going; they continue in spite of difficulty—they **persevere.**

3. The speaker's jokes were amusing and **pertinent;** they were directly related to the points she made in her speech.

4. The doctor's **prognosis** (prediction about recovery) is that Luis will be strong enough to go back to work in three days.

5. A **protégé** is a person who is guided and helped by a more influential person.

6. Establish good **rapport** (a warm relationship) with your college teachers.

7. Attorneys for defendants attempt to **refute** (disprove) claims of guilt.

8. Anthony owns a **replica** of the Venus de Milo—a copy of the famous armless statue housed in a museum in Paris.

9. Most office jobs are **sedentary**—they require workers to sit much of the time.

10. I have a brother and sister, but my best friend has no **sibling.**

11. My English teacher claims that the argument in my paper is **specious**—it seems true but it is false.

12. The contract specifies the number of hours we will work each week, and it **stipulates** the pay we will receive for each hour's work.

13. I can give evidence to prove that I paid the bill; my canceled check will **substantiate** my claim.

14. A circle is **symmetrical;** when a circle is divided in half, it has an identical form on either side of the dividing line.

15. Those who want careers as motion picture actors must be **tenacious**—persistent and stubbornly determined to succeed.

EXERCISE 7.3 **Implied Meanings**

Infer the meanings of the **boldface** words and write them on the lines provided.

1. Aspirin, fresh air, or something to eat will often **alleviate** a minor headache.

   _____

2. The insurance adjuster had to **ascertain** the exact value of the missing jewelry.

   _____

3. He was an **astute** lawyer—always to be found on the winning side.

   _____

4. She took a job during the summer to **augment** the salary she earns as a teacher.

   _____

5. We were assigned to write a **concise,** one-page summary of a five-hundred-page book.

   _____

6. The students reached a **consensus** that they would rather write a research paper than take a final examination.

   _____

7. Eating in restaurants became so expensive that we had to **curtail** dining out from once a week to once a month.

   _____

8. He is having his teeth straightened in the hope that his smile will be **enhanced.**

   _____

9. My English teacher read us an **excerpt** from a play written by Shakespeare.

   _____

10. Microwave ovens **facilitate** the quick preparation of meals.

   _____

EXERCISE 7.4 **Implied Meanings**

Infer the meanings of the **boldface** words and write them on the lines provided.

1. It is not **feasible** to drive from New York to Los Angeles in two days.

   _____

2. Only a few new businesses are successes—most are **fiascoes.**

   _____

3. We left the waitress a $5.00 **gratuity** because she was pleasant and gave us excellent service.

   _____

4. I assure you that the error was **inadvertent;** we never intend to overcharge our customers.

   _____

5. When he totaled his debts, he realized that he must get a more **lucrative** job in order to pay them.

   _____

6. The jury found him guilty because they decided that his alibi was not **plausible.**

   _____

7. It is **prudent** to purchase paper towels, light bulbs, laundry soap, and other household essentials when they are on sale.

   _____

8. My psychology professor sometimes shows us films that are **relevant** to topics we study in her class.

   _____

9. As she spoke in French, the interpreter gave us a **simultaneous** translation in English.

   _____

10. She had a C average her first semester, but a B average in all **subsequent** semesters.

   _____

EXERCISE 7.5   **Stated and Implied Meanings**

The excerpts in this exercise are from *Psychology* by Douglas A. Bernstein and others (Houghton Mifflin, 1988). The meanings of the **boldface** words are stated in or implied by the passages. If the meaning of a word is stated, underline the meaning: if the meaning of a word is implied, write the meaning in the left margin.

1. **Puberty**—the condition of being able for the first time to reproduce—is also characterized by fuller breasts and rounder curves in females, broad shoulders and narrow hips in males. Facial, underarm, and pubic hair grows. Voices deepen, and acne appears. (p. 64)

2. In western cultures, early adolescence, from twelve to sixteen or so, is **fraught** with ups and downs. Moods swing wildly from one extreme to another: from **elation** at a girlfriend's kiss to **dejection** at a failed exam. (p. 64)

3. **Mnemonics** are strategies for placing information in an organized context in order to remember it. For example, to remember the names of the Great Lakes, you simply remember the mnemonic HOMES, and the lake names follow easily: Huron, Ontario, Michigan, Erie, and Superior. (p. 311)

4. Experiments like Epstein's have demonstrated that **syntax,** the pattern of word order, plays a very important role in the comprehension of sentences. (p. 355)

5. Two assumptions guided Binet when he created his set, or **battery,** of questions. First, he assumed that intelligence is involved in many reasoning, thinking, and problem-solving activities. (p. 370)

6. **Trauma,** a shocking physical or emotional experience, can create what is perhaps the ultimate stress situation. Such catastrophes as rape, assault, military combat, fire, tornadoes, plane crashes, torture, or bomb blasts are only a few examples. (p. 476)

7. For reasons that are not always clear, the regulation of food intake sometimes goes **awry,** resulting in eating disorders. (p. 418)

8. Sometimes communicators try to change attitudes by **instilling** fear in the audience. A health organization, for example, may suggest that, if you do not eat a healthy diet, you are likely to die prematurely. (p. 635)

9. Boredom, or understimulation, is the opposite of pressure, but it, too, can be a stressor, especially if it continues for a long time. The agony of solitary confinement in prison or the **tedium** of a remote military post are probably the most extreme examples. (p. 476)

10. A **morpheme** is the smallest unit of language that has meaning. Word stems like *dog* and *run* are morphemes, but so are prefixes like *un-* and suffixes like *-ed,* because they have meaning even though they cannot stand alone. (p. 352)

Analyze Word Structure

When a context does not state or imply a word meaning, you can sometimes figure out the meaning by studying the base and prefix or suffix in the word. This chapter explains how to determine word meanings by analyzing their parts.

Suffixes

A **suffix** is a letter or group of letters that is added to the end of a base word. For example, in *truthful*, the base is *truth* and the suffix is *-ful*. Words you have never seen in print before may sometimes consist of a base word you know and an added suffix.

> How many years was her *mayoralty*?

Mayoralty is a word that does not appear very often in print; it may be unfamiliar to you. However, by locating the base word in *mayoralty* you can easily understand that the question is "For how many years was she mayor?"

Words you know may be the base words for five, ten, fifteen, or more other words that you do not read or hear often. For example:

*adapt*able	*adapt*ation	*adapt*er
*adapt*ableness	*adapt*ational	*adapt*ive
*adapt*ability	*adapt*ationally	*adapt*iveness

If you know that *adapt* means "to make suitable," you know the essential meaning of these nine words, even if you have never seen some of them in print before. Notice that some of the words contain two suffixes. For instance, *adaptableness* contains the suffixes *-able* and *-ness*.

A suffix usually identifies the part of speech of a word without giving important information about the word's meaning. For instance, *adapt* is a verb, *adaptable* is an adjective, and *adaptation* is a noun. *Adapt, adaptable,* and *adaptation* represent different parts of speech but they have similar meanings. Since they are different parts of speech, they cannot be used correctly in identical grammatical constructions.

> She can *adapt* to difficult situations.

> She is *adaptable* to difficult situations.

> She can make *adaptations* to difficult situations.

Though *adapt* is a verb, *adaptable* is an adjective, and *adaptation* is a noun, all three of these sentences have very similar meanings.

The most common adjective, noun, verb, and adverb suffixes are italicized in the following words.

Common Suffixes

- **Adjective suffixes:** approach*able*, critic*al*, depend*ent*, fear*ful*, angel*ic*, child*ish*, life*less*, danger*ous*, sleep*y*
- **Noun suffixes:** annoy*ance*, differ*ence*, preven*tion*, novel*ist*, real*ity*, punish*ment*, great*ness*
- **Verb suffixes:** fals*ify*, social*ize*
- **Adverb suffixes:** quick*ly*, after*ward*

It is sometimes difficult to locate base words because their spellings frequently change when suffixes are added to them.

How to Locate Base Words

- If a base word ends in *e*, the *e* may be dropped when a suffix is added to it: *mature + -ity = maturity*.
- If a base word ends in *y*, the *y* may be changed to *i* when a suffix is added to it: *harmony + -ous = harmonious*.
- Base words may undergo other spelling changes when suffixes are added to them: *reclaim + -ation = reclamation* (the *i* in *reclaim* is dropped).

Keep this information in mind as you do Exercises 8.1, 8.2, and 8.3, on pages 85, 86, and 87.

Prefixes

A **prefix** is a letter or group of letters that is added to the beginning of a base word. For example, in *untrue* the prefix is *un-* and the base word is *true*. Words that are unfamiliar to you may sometimes consist of a base word you know and an added prefix. For instance:

> We were shocked to learn of the *illimitability* of the dictator's power.

Illimitability is a word that does not appear very often in print; it may be unfamiliar to you. However, you can probably locate its base word, *limit*, which means "to restrict." If you also know that the prefix *il-* means "not," you should be able to determine that *illimitability* refers to that which has

© 1992 by Houghton Mifflin Company

no limits or restrictions. The sentence means, "We were shocked to learn that there is no limit to the dictator's power."

The preceding discussion of suffixes includes a list of nine words in which *adapt* is the base word. Following are fifteen of the more than thirty words in which *adapt* is preceded by a prefix.

mal*adapt*ation	non*adapt*ive	re*adapt*ation
mal*adapt*ed	pre*adapt*	un*adapt*able
mis*adapt*ation	pre*adapt*ation	un*adapt*ableness
non*adapt*able	re*adapt*ability	un*adapt*ively
non*adapt*ation	re*adapt*able	un*adapt*iveness

If you know that *adapt* means "to make suitable" and you also know the meanings of the prefixes *mal-*, *mis-*, *non-*, *pre-*, *re-*, and *un-*, you know the essential meanings of these fifteen words, even if you have not read or heard them before.

Unabridged dictionaries (the very large ones) list thousands of words that begin with the common prefixes. For example, most unabridged dictionaries list more than 10,000 words that begin with *non-* and more than 400 words that begin with *pseudo-*. If you know the meanings of *non-* and *pseudo-*, you know something important about the meanings of more than 10,400 words.

By mastering the meanings of twenty-one prefixes, you can increase the words you know by hundreds, or even thousands, in a very short time.

Following are the most useful meanings of the common English prefixes.

Prefix	Meaning	Example
1. un-	not; no	*un*happy means *not* happy
2. non-	not; no	*non*living means *not* living
3. dis-	not; no	to *dis*trust is *not* to trust
4. in-	not; no	*in*direct means *not* direct
5. im-	not; no	*im*perfect means *not* perfect
6. ir-	not; no	*ir*rational means *not* rational
7. il-	not; no	*il*legal means *not* legal
8. a-	not; without	*a*typical means *not* typical
9. de-	remove	to *de*frost is to *remove* frost
10. pre-	before	*pre*war means *before* a war
11. post-	after	*post*war means *after* a war
12. anti-	oppos(ing)	*anti*war means *opposing* war
13. pro-	favor(ing)	*pro*war means *favoring* war
14. inter-	between	*inter*state means *between* states
15. intra-	within	*intra*state means *within* a state
16. hyper-	excessive(ly)	*hyper*active means *excessively* active

17.	mal-	bad(ly)	*mal*nutrition is *bad* nutrition
18.	mis-	incorrect(ly)	to *mis*spell is to spell *incorrectly*
19.	pseudo-	false(ly)	a *pseudo*science is a *false* science
20.	semi-	partly	*semi*public means *partly* public
21.	re-	again	to *re*write is to write *again*

Exercises 8.4 and 8.5, on pages 88 and 89, provide practice for learning these prefixes. Other prefixes that are worth knowing include the following: *ante-* (before or prior to), *auto-* (self), *circum-* (around), *contra-* (opposed to), *counter-* (opposite, contrary to), *extra-* (outside, beyond), *hemi-* (half), *hypo-* (under, beneath), *intro-* (into, within), *retro-* (backward, back), *sub-* (under, beneath), *super-* (over), and *trans-* (across, on the other side).

Combining Forms

Combining forms are Greek and Latin word parts that are joined with other combining forms or base words. For example, the combining forms *graph-* and *-ology* may be combined to form *graphology*, and the base word *Egypt* may be combined with *-ology* to form *Egyptology*. *Graphology* is the study of handwriting to discover clues about personality, and *Egyptology* is the study of the civilization of ancient Egypt.

The principal way in which prefixes and suffixes differ from combining forms is that prefixes and suffixes are not joined, or combined, to create words, but combining forms are. For instance, the prefix *un-* cannot be joined with the suffix *-ness* to make a word (*unness* is not a word), but the combining forms *biblio-* and *-phile* can be joined to create the word *bibliophile*. Read the following dictionary entries for *biblio-*, *-phile*, and *bibliophile*.

> **biblio–.** Indicates books; for example, **bibliomania.** [From Greek *biblion*, book. See **Bible.**]
> **–phile, –phil.** Indicates one having love or strong affinity or preference for; for example, **Anglophile.** [French *-phile* or New Latin *-philus*, from Greek *-philos*, from *philos*, beloved, dear, loving. See **bhilo-** in Appendix.*]
> **bib·li·o·phile** (bĭb′lē-ə-fīl′) *n.* Also **bib·li·o·phil** (-fĭl′), **bib·li·oph·i·list** (bĭb′lē-ŏf′ə-list). **1.** One who loves books. **2.** A book collector. [French : BIBLIO- + -PHILE.] —**bib′li·oph′i·lism′** *n.* —**bib′li·oph′i·lis′tic** *adj.*

Notice that the meanings of *biblio-* and *-phile* are very closely related to the meaning of *bibliophile*.

Knowledge of the meanings of combining forms is usually essential for the study of natural science. For example, it is important for students of biology to know the meanings of *amph-* (both), *derma-* (skin), *gastro-* (stomach), *necro-* (death), *nephr-* (kidney), *para-* (alongside), *soma-* (body), and many other combining forms. If you study biology, chemistry, or other natural sciences, you may find a list of combining forms or Greek and Latin roots in your textbook. If so, learn their meanings.

Exercises 8.6, 8.7, and 8.8, on pages 90, 91, and 92, provide practice for learning the meanings of combining forms.

EXERCISE 8.1   **Suffixes**

Locate the base words in the **boldface** words and write them on the lines provided.

1. He overcame the **adversity** of poverty to succeed.

   He overcame _____ conditions to succeed.

2. We established the **authenticity** of our antique chair.

   We have an _____ antique chair.

3. The flood was a **calamitous** event.

   The flood was a _____.

4. The automobile accident left her **comatose.**

   The accident left her in a _____.

5. He had **comparative** good luck.

   If you _____ his luck to her luck, his luck was good.

6. Please prepare a **compilation** of the facts.

   Please _____ the facts.

7. The stages of life are **cyclical.**

   The stages of life occur in a _____.

8. Traffic laws are a **deterrent** to reckless driving.

   Traffic laws _____ reckless driving.

9. Who were the **disputants?**

   Who engaged in the _____?

10. She has a **distinctive** way of speaking.

    Her speech is _____ from others' speech.

EXERCISE 8.2   **Suffixes**

Locate the base words in the **boldface** words and write them on the lines provided.

1. We selected children's furniture for its **durability.**

   We selected _____ children's furniture.

2. We find his good humor **enviable.**

   We _____ his good humor.

3. Its **expiration** date is December 31, 1999.

   It will _____ on December 31, 1999.

4. We experienced many **familial** difficulties.

   We experienced many difficulties in our _____.

5. We thank you for your **leniency.**

   We thank you for being _____.

6. He has a **maniacal** laugh.

   He laughs like a _____.

7. Your work is **meritorious.**

   Your work has _____.

8. This machine has a **multiplicity** of parts.

   This machine has _____ parts.

9. The rain forest was not **penetrable.**

   They could not _____ the rain forest.

10. They give the elderly **preferential** treatment.

    They show a _____ for the elderly.

EXERCISE 8.3 **Base Words**

Locate the base words in the following forty words and write them on the lines provided.

1. angularity	_____	21. grievous	_____
2. civility	_____	22. habituate	_____
3. climatic	_____	23. hardiness	_____
4. collegiate	_____	24. hindrance	_____
5. combative	_____	25. icily	_____
6. commutation	_____	26. inclusive	_____
7. compliance	_____	27. lyricist	_____
8. continual	_____	28. mobilize	_____
9. contractual	_____	29. muscly	_____
10. conveyance	_____	30. notably	_____
11. corruption	_____	31. phraseology	_____
12. curative	_____	32. porosity	_____
13. demonstrable	_____	33. reclamation	_____
14. devastation	_____	34. satanic	_____
15. dictatorial	_____	35. sensual	_____
16. embodiment	_____	36. slavish	_____
17. equatorial	_____	37. sobriety	_____
18. erroneous	_____	38. torturous	_____
19. expertise	_____	39. victimize	_____
20. fluidity	_____	40. witticism	_____

EXERCISE 8.4 Prefixes

Write the meanings of the prefixes and the base words in the **boldface** words.

1. A lawyer **maladministered** the money she inherited.

   Prefix meaning: _____   Base word: _____

2. It is **atypical** for short men to be professional basketball players.

   Prefix meaning: _____   Base word: _____

3. The castle was **impenetrable** to ancient armies.

   Prefix meaning: _____   Base word: _____

4. He **invariably** eats lunch at noon.

   Prefix meaning: _____   Base word: _____

5. I was offended by his **hypercritical** remarks.

   Prefix meaning: _____   Base word: _____

6. Her decision was final and **irrevocable.**

   Prefix meaning: _____   Base word: _____

7. We sent the memo through **interdepartmental** mail.

   Prefix meaning: _____   Base word: _____

8. His testimony was a **misrepresentation** of the facts.

   Prefix meaning: _____   Base word: _____

9. Negotiators must often be **noncommittal.**

   Prefix meaning: _____   Base word: _____

10. The story is **pseudobiographical.**

    Prefix meaning: _____   Base word: _____

EXERCISE 8.5   **Prefixes**

Write the meanings of the prefixes and the base words in the **boldface** words as you did for Exercise 8.4.

1. Many well-groomed people use an **antiperspirant** when the weather is hot and humid.

   Prefix meaning: _____   Base word: _____

2. The paper was written in **illegible** handwriting.

   Prefix meaning: _____   Base word: _____

3. After a long sea voyage, we had to **reorient** ourselves to walking on land.

   Prefix meaning: _____   Base word: _____

4. The patient was **semiconscious** a few hours after the operation.

   Prefix meaning: _____   Base word: _____

5. Our team is **prequalified** to run in the marathon.

   Prefix meaning: _____   Base word: _____

6. His mother's death left him **disconsolate.**

   Prefix meaning: _____   Base word: _____

7. My algebra teacher sometimes tells jokes that are **irrelevant** to the study of mathematics.

   Prefix meaning: _____   Base word: _____

8. Her doctor advised her to drink **decaffeinated** coffee.

   Prefix meaning: _____   Base word: _____

9. The jurors were **proacquittal** after only an hour of deliberation.

   Prefix meaning: _____   Base word: _____

10. Some baseball players fear **intramuscular** pain in their pitching arms.

    Prefix meaning: _____   Base word: _____

EXERCISE 8.6   Numbers

Write the correct word on each blank line in this exercise by referring to the meanings of the combining forms listed below.

Combining form	Meaning	Combining form	Meaning
mono-, uni-	one	sept-	seven
bi-	two	octo-	eight
tri-	three	deca-, deci-	ten
quadri-	four	multi-	more than two

1. A **monolingual** person knows only _____ language.

2. A _____ person uses two languages.

3. A _____ person uses more than two languages.

4. A **unilateral** decision is made by _____ person or country.

5. A _____ decision affects two people or countries.

6. If a thing is **unique**, it is the only _____ like it.

7. A **bicentennial** is a _____ hundredth anniversary celebration.

8. A _____ is a four hundredth anniversary celebration.

9. A **biennial** event occurs every _____ years.

10. A _____ event occurs every three years.

11. A **quadruped** is an animal with _____ feet.

12. A _____ is an animal with two feet.

13. To **decimate** an army is to kill every _____ man.

14. There are _____ events in the **decathlon**.

15. **Septuagenarians** are people 70 to _____ years old.

16. **Octogenarians** are people _____ to

_____ years old.

EXERCISE 8.7   **Branches of Learning**

Use the meanings of the following combining forms to write the correct word on each blank line in this exercise. The answers to problems 1 through 12 end in "*-logy,*" which indicates "science" or "study of," and the answers to problems 13 and 14 end in "*-ist,*" which indicates "one who practices."

Combining form	Meaning	Combining form	Meaning
anthropo-	human	gyneco-	woman
archaeo-	ancient times	neuro-	nerves
audio-	hearing	patho-	disease
bio-	life	psycho-	mind
chrono-	time	seismo-	earthquake
geo-	earth	theo-	God or gods

1. _____ is the study of the origin and development of humankind.

2. _____ is the study of dates and the sequences of events in time.

3. _____ is the scientific study of disease.

4. _____ is the study of objects left from life and culture in ancient times.

5. _____ is the medical science of women's health.

6. _____ is the study of hearing.

7. _____ is the study of the origin and structure of the earth.

8. _____ is the scientific study of behavior and the processes of the mind.

9. _____ is the scientific study of earthquakes.

10. _____ is the study of living things.

11. _____ is the study of religious truth and the nature of God.

12. _____ is the scientific study of the nerves and the nervous system.

13. An _____ is a student of anthropology.

14. A _____ is a student of gynecology.

EXERCISE 8.8   **Using What You Have Learned**

Use what you learned when you did Exercises 8.7 and 8.8 to write the correct word on each blank line in this exercise.

1. That which is **archaic** belongs to _____ times.

2. A **chronic** headache lasts for a long _____.

3. A **psychic** has extraordinary _____ abilities.

4. **Seismic** activity is caused by an _____.

5. The **biotic** elements of nature are the _____ elements.

6. The **abiotic** elements of nature are _____ living.

7. A **theist** is a person who believes in _____.

8. An **atheist** is a person who does _____ believe in

_____.

9. **Polytheism** is a belief in more than one _____.

10. **Monotheism** is the belief in _____

_____.

11. A **chronometer** measures _____ precisely.

12. An **audiometer** measures _____.

13. A **seismometer** records _____.

14. **Geophysics** is the science of the physics of the _____.

15. **Biochemistry** is the chemistry of _____ things.

16. A **gynecocracy** is the rule of a state by _____.

17. A **theocracy** is the _____ of a state by

_____.

18. A **pathogen** is an agent that can cause _____.

19. **Chronological** sequence is _____ sequence.

20. A **monologue** is a long speech by _____ speaker.

Three

The Reading Program

In a typical term of study, full-time college students read five, six, or more textbooks. The chapters in this part of *RSVP* explain how to read textbooks efficiently and with good comprehension. You will learn:

1. How to find information that is hinted at or suggested in books as well as information that is directly stated.

2. How to locate topics, main ideas, and details.

3. How to identify when textbook passages define words, explain methods, describe sequences, or present lists of various kinds.

4. How to interpret visual materials such as cartoons, photographs, graphs, tables, diagrams, and charts.

5. How to read critically.

Excerpts from books of the kinds you are studying, or will soon be studying, are used to illustrate these reading skills. And you will practice the skills by applying them to similar passages from these kinds of books. This will help you meet the challenge of reading books that are more difficult than the ones you read in high school.

Stated and Implied Information

Written material contains both stated and implied information. You can answer questions about stated information in a passage by pointing to words in the selection or by copying them. **Implied** information, on the other hand, is not directly stated; it is only suggested or hinted. You can **infer** the answers to questions about the implied information in a passage; that is, by using the material stated in a selection you can make inferences to arrive at logical conclusions about additional information that is implied by the passage.

Making Inferences

In doing research for this fourth edition of *RSVP*, I found the following excellent explanation of inferences in *Psychology*, Third Edition, by Andrew W. Crider and others (Scott, Foresman and Company, 1989). The word *subjects* in the passage refers to people who took part in psychological experiments.

> Inference* is the process by which we fill in information missing from a story using general knowledge already stored in memory. There is now substantial evidence to indicate that when subjects read a series of sentences they store not only the meaning of the sentences, but also inferences drawn from the sentences. In one study subjects were asked to read the following statements:
>
> A burning cigarette was carelessly discarded. The fire destroyed many acres of virgin forest.
>
> Later, the subjects were asked to indicate if the following statement was true or false:
>
> The discarded cigarette started the fire.

* Words underscored in blue are defined in the Master Vocabulary List on pages 413–425, and the exercises on pages 56–57 are based on these words.

Interestingly, 96 percent of the subjects regarded the statement as true, even though the original statements did not <u>explicitly</u> state that the cigarette started the fire (Kintsch, 1974). To reach this conclusion the subjects had to make the inference that the burning cigarette started the forest fire. The fact that carelessly discarded cigarettes often start forest fires is part of the information stored in the long-term memories of most people.

Inferences are often quite useful in helping us fill in missing pieces of information. But sometimes inference can be used to convey a false piece of information. One of the best examples of this is in television commercials. Several years ago an aspirin manufacturer presented a commercial promoting Aspirin A. The announcer stated that studies from a university and a leading hospital showed Aspirin A was more effective for pain *other than headache*. The commercial went on to present some other information about the product, and then the announcer reappeared saying, "So, the next time you have a headache, take Aspirin A." Even though we were not told that Aspirin A was more effective for headache, most of us probably combined the information in the announcer's two statements to draw the inference that it was. In fact there is experimental evidence to indicate that subjects who listen to commercials often draw false inferences about the advertised products (Harris & Monaco, 1978).

References

Harris, R.J., and Monaco, G.E. (1978). Psychology of Pragmatic Implication: Information Processing Between the Lines. *Journal of Experimental Psychology*, 7, 269–279.

Kintsch, W. (1974). *The Representation of Meaning in Memory*. Hillsdale, NJ: Erlbaum.

This passage makes three important points about inference: (1) inference helps us fill in missing pieces of information, (2) people sometimes make incorrect inferences, and (3) inference is sometimes used to convey false information.

Stated Information

When you do the exercises in this chapter, you will be asked to decide whether answers to questions are stated in or implied by passages. Following are the statements used in the experiment described in the psychology textbook passage on pages 95–96.

A burning cigarette was carelessly discarded. The fire destroyed many acres of virgin forest.

Check the boxes in front of the questions whose answers are stated in these two sentences.

☐ 1. What was carelessly discarded?
☐ 2. What was destroyed?
☐ 3. Did flames leap high in the air?
☐ 4. Did the air fill with smoke?
☐ 5. By what means was forest destroyed?

The answers to questions 1, 2, and 5 are stated in the sentences. The answers to questions 3 and 4 are implied; we know that large fires produce flames and smoke.

Inferring Answers

Questions on college tests will often require you to infer answers; they will require you to use information you have learned to arrive at conclusions about correct answers. The exercises in this chapter are designed to help you improve your ability to make accurate inferences. Read the following short passage and then answer the multiple-choice questions, which are similar to the kinds of questions you will answer when you do the exercises in this chapter.

Sex-Typing

Parents engage in *sex-typing* when they encourage their children to behave in ways that have been traditionally considered appropriate for males and females. For instance, when parents encourage a son to wrestle but discourage a daughter from wrestling, they are sex-typing.

Check the boxes in front of correct answers and then circle the numbers in front of questions whose answers are implied by the passage but not directly stated in it.

1. Parents engage in sex-typing when they
   ☐ a. encourage traditional behaviors.
   ☐ b. write pornographic literature.
   ☐ c. teach female children to type.
   ☐ d. discourage sons from wrestling.

2. Parents are sex-typing when they encourage a
   ☐ a. girl to ride a bike.
   ☐ b. boy to care for a cat.
   ☐ c. girl to clean a house.
   ☐ d. boy to cook meals.

3. Sex-typing can be done by
   ☐ a. parents.
   ☐ b. teachers.
   ☐ c. clergy.
   ☐ d. all of the above.

4. Which of the following is *not* an example of sex-typing?
   ☐ a. telling a boy not to cry
   ☐ b. teaching a girl to fight back
   ☐ c. teaching a girl to be sweet
   ☐ d. teaching a boy to fight back

You should have circled the numbers in front of the second, third, and fourth questions; the answers to these three questions are not stated in the passage—they are implied. Following are explanations of the correct answers to the questions:

1. The answer, *a,* is stated in the first sentence; the other answers are not stated in the passage.

2. The answer, *c,* is implied; you should have circled "2." Cleaning house and cooking have traditionally been considered more appropriate for females than for males. Riding bikes and caring for pets are not usually considered more appropriate for one sex than for the other.

3. The answer, *d,* is implied; you should have circled "3." Sex-typing can be done by any adult who influences a child's behavior, including parents, grandparents, aunts, uncles, teachers, and clergy.

4. The answer, *b,* is implied; you should have circled "4." Fighting back has traditionally been considered more appropriate for males than for females. Boys have traditionally been encouraged not to cry, and girls have traditionally been encouraged to be sweet.

Don't become discouraged if you have difficulty answering questions correctly when you do the first few exercises in this chapter. Rather, try to understand your instructor's explanations of the correct answers. There are many exercises, so you have an opportunity to improve, and you are almost certain to become better at answering questions about stated and implied information if you understand *why* you sometimes select incorrect answers.

EXERCISE 9.1   **Types of Advertising**

There are three basic types of advertising. *Selective advertising* promotes the sale of specific brand name products, such as Bayer aspirin, Ford automobiles, and Maxwell House coffee. *Primary-demand advertising* encourages the total demand for a product without promoting any specific brand. The advertisements for Florida oranges are examples of this; those ads seek to increase the sale of Florida oranges whether consumers purchase fresh oranges or any specific brand of frozen or bottled orange juice. The third type, *institutional advertising*, has as its purpose to create good will toward the advertiser. For example, when an electric company runs an ad that explains what the company is doing to keep utility costs down, this is an example of institutional advertising. Any ad designed to make you think well of a company or organization and that does not request you to make a specific purchase is an example of institutional advertising.

Check the boxes in front of correct answers and then circle the numbers in front of questions whose answers are implied by the passage but not directly stated in it.

1. Selective advertising is used to promote the
   □ a. sale of a specific brand product.
   □ b. demand for a general type of product.
   □ c. good will of consumers toward an advertiser.
   □ d. purchase of any product or service.

2. Primary-demand advertising could be used to sell
   □ a. Green Giant peas.
   □ b. Wisconsin cheeses.
   □ c. Wrigley chewing gum.
   □ d. Lipton tea bags.

3. Selective advertising is *not* used to advertise
   □ a. Bayer aspirin.
   □ b. Ford automobiles.
   □ c. Maxwell House coffee.
   □ d. Japanese computers.

4. A telephone company does *not* use institutional advertising when it publishes an advertisement about
   □ a. women who do "men's" work.
   □ b. an employee who saved a baby's life.
   □ c. the times long-distance calls are cheapest.
   □ d. a movie it will sponsor on public television.

EXERCISE 9.2   Alcoholic Beverages

The different forms of alcoholic beverages vary greatly in strength, as measured by the concentration of alcohol they contain. The most common alcoholic beverages—beers, wines, and distilled spirits—are made by different processes.

- *Beer* and *ale* are derived from various grains by a brewing process; they generally contain from 3 to 6 percent alcohol.

- *Wines* are made by fermenting the juice of grapes or other fruits. Table wines, which are often served with meals, have a natural alcohol content ranging from 9 to 12 percent. Other varieties, such as sherry, port, and muscatel, are reinforced by the addition of distilled spirits to bring their alcohol content up to as much as 18 to 22 percent.

- *Distilled spirits*—the strongest alcoholic beverages, such as gin, whiskey, brandy, and rum—are manufactured by distilling brewed or fermented products so that liquids containing from 35 to 50 percent alcohol are recovered. Ounce for ounce, the amount of pure alcohol in most distilled liquors is ten to twelve times as great as that in beer. *But* when a person has a beer, he or she drinks 12 ounces of beer (in contrast to the typical shot glass of whiskey, which contains about 1 ounce).

The term **proof** indicates the concentration of ethyl alcohol in a beverage. Proof can be converted to percent by dividing the proof number in half. Thus, 80-proof whiskey is 40 percent alcohol, and 100-proof whiskey is 50 percent alcohol. Every ounce of 100-proof whiskey, then, contains one-half ounce of pure ethyl alcohol.

Check the correct answers and then circle the numbers in front of questions whose answers are implied by the passage but not directly stated in it.

1. Common alcoholic beverages are made by
   - ☐ a. distilling, fermenting, or brewing.
   - ☐ b. brewing, reinforcing, or distilling.
   - ☐ c. processing various grains.
   - ☐ d. isolating alcohol in vegetation.

2. Distilled spirits are made from products that have been
   - ☐ a. reduced to 35 to 50 percent alcohol.
   - ☐ b. previously brewed or fermented.
   - ☐ c. rejected for use as wine or beer.
   - ☐ d. processed in sterile laboratories.

3. How much ethyl alcohol is in a 40-proof liqueur?
   - ☐ a. 40 percent
   - ☐ b. 30 percent
   - ☐ c. 20 percent
   - ☐ d. 10 percent

EXERCISE 9.3　Palindromes

Palindromes are words, phrases, or sentences that spell the same backward and forward; for instance, *radar, deed, civic,* and *nun.* The first palindromic sentence is believed to have been created in the early 1600s. Here is a modern version of it.

Evil I did dwell; lewd did I live.

The most famous palindromic sentence is probably the one that Napoleon is supposed to have uttered when he went into exile: "Able was I ere I saw Elba." No palindrome tells a good story more succinctly than the well-known "A man, a plan, a canal—Panama."

Check the boxes in front of correct answers and then circle the numbers in front of questions whose answers are implied by the passage but not directly stated in it.

1. Palindromes are *not*
   - ☐ a. words.
   - ☐ b. phrases.
   - ☐ c. sentences.
   - ☐ d. books.

2. Which of the following is *not* a palindrome?
   - ☐ a. noon
   - ☐ b. repaper
   - ☐ c. pump
   - ☐ d. level

3. Which of the following is *not* a palindrome?
   - ☐ a. Did Mom read what Dad did?
   - ☐ b. A man, a plan, a canal—Panama.
   - ☐ c. Able was I ere I saw Elba.
   - ☐ d. Evil I did dwell; lewd did I live.

4. Which of the following is *not* a palindrome?
   - ☐ a. a Toyota
   - ☐ b. Don't give in.
   - ☐ c. Dennis sinned.
   - ☐ d. Madam, I'm Adam.

5. Which of the following is *not* a palindrome?
   - ☐ a. Pull up if I pull up.
   - ☐ b. Was it a car or a cat I saw?
   - ☐ c. Was it Otto's auto I saw?
   - ☐ d. In a regal age ran I.

EXERCISE 9.4 **Euphemisms**

A euphemism is an acceptable or inoffensive word or phrase used to describe something that is distasteful, unpleasant, or intimate. For instance, some retailers specialize in selling clothing for "big" men; "big" is a euphemism for distasteful words such as *fat, overweight,* and *obese.* Similarly, in our society, we are likely to use the euphemisms "passed away," "departed this life," or "was put to eternal rest" rather than say "died." Euphemisms are also substituted for taboo words. For instance, visitors to your home may ask, "Where is the bathroom?" rather than use four-letter words to explain why they want to know where your toilet is located.

Check the boxes in front of correct answers and then circle the numbers in front of questions whose answers are implied by the passage but not directly stated in it.

1. Euphemisms are words or phrases that
   □ a. do not offend others.
   □ b. are distasteful or unpleasant.
   □ c. take the place of "big" words.
   □ d. are intended to deceive or trick.

2. Which of the following is *not* a euphemism for describing elderly people?
   □ a. They are senior citizens.
   □ b. They are in their golden years.
   □ c. They are older than God.
   □ d. They have the benefit of experience.

3. Which of the following is *not* a euphemism for "died"?
   □ a. He passed away.
   □ b. He dropped dead.
   □ c. He departed this life.
   □ d. He was put to eternal rest.

4. We do *not* use a euphemism when we say
   □ a. an ugly picture is "not too good-looking."
   □ b. a poor country is "not too rich."
   □ c. a dumb animal is "not too bright."
   □ d. a kind person is "not too cruel."

5. Which of the following is *not* a euphemism?
   □ a. "Gave their lives" (for "were killed")
   □ b. Workers were "let go" (for "fired")
   □ c. "Full-figured" woman (for "overweight")
   □ d. Take a "shine" to (for take a "liking" to)

EXERCISE 9.5   **Urbanization**

Cities grew in number, size, and population as a result of industrialization. No longer just seats of government and commerce, they became places of manufacture and industry as well. Before 1800, about 10 percent of the European population lived in cities (20 percent did in Great Britain and the Netherlands, the leading areas of urban living). A mere forty-five cities in the world had more than 100,000 people. Halfway through the nineteenth century, 52 percent of the British lived in cities, although only 25 percent of the French, 36 percent of the Germans, 7 percent of the Russians, and 10 percent of U.S. inhabitants did. Most of the shift from rural to urban living in Europe and the United States has taken place in the twentieth century, but the increase in Europe's urban population during the 1800s was acute in its influence. In some regions, industrial areas grew up almost overnight—the Midlands in England, the Lowlands in Scotland, the northern plains in France, the German Rhineland, the U.S. northeast, and parts of northern Italy.

Industrial cities in the nineteenth century, particularly in England, grew rapidly, without planning or much regulation by local or national governments. Government and business were often reluctant to use taxation to finance remedies for poor working and living conditions. Civic pride and private patronage were too weak to combat the effects of unregulated private enterprise. On the European continent, where industrialization came later, states were more willing to regulate industrial and urban development.

Check the boxes in front of correct answers and then circle the numbers in front of questions whose answers are implied by the passage but not directly stated in it.

1. In which of these places did industrial areas grow rapidly in the 1800s?
   - ☐ a. The Lowlands in England
   - ☐ b. The Highlands in Scotland
   - ☐ c. The northeast United States
   - ☐ d. The southern plains in France

2. Before 1800, which of the following countries had the greatest percentage of its population living in cities?
   - ☐ a. Germany
   - ☐ b. Great Britain
   - ☐ c. France
   - ☐ d. Italy

3. Which of the following countries probably did the most to regulate industrial and urban development in the 1800s?
   - ☐ a. England
   - ☐ b. Scotland
   - ☐ c. Ireland
   - ☐ d. Germany

EXERCISE 9.6   **The Pygmalion Effect**

The *Pygmalion Effect* is a theory about the power of other people's expectations for you and your resulting behavior. The term was first used by Dr. Robert Rosenthal, a professor at Harvard University, and is based on a Greek legend about Pygmalion, the king of Cyprus. In the legend, the king longs for an ideal wife. Since no mortal woman meets his expectations, he fashions a statue of his ideal woman out of ivory and eventually falls in love with his creation. His desire to make the statue his wife is so intense that his belief brings it to life. Modern behavioral science is beginning to support the validity of the Pygmalion Effect; that is, people can be greatly influenced by the expectations of others. For example, athletes can be convinced by their coaches to give superlative performances. If teachers expect students to be high achievers, they will tend to live up to those expectations. And if people are labeled "low achievers," they will fulfill those expectations as well. Employees, as a rule, will succeed to the degree their supervisors believe they can. The coaches, teachers, and supervisors act as Pygmalions to those whose lives they influence.

Check the boxes in front of correct answers and then circle the numbers in front of questions whose answers are implied by the passage but not directly stated in it.

1. According to the Pygmalion legend, a king
   ☐ a. made a statue of his ideal woman.
   ☐ b. fell in love with the statue.
   ☐ c. caused the statue to come to life.
   ☐ d. all of the above

2. The Pygmalion Effect is a theory that states that
   ☐ a. the expectations of others influence our behavior.
   ☐ b. our behavior influences the expectations of others.
   ☐ c. athletes, students, and workers need encouragement.
   ☐ d. coaches, teachers, and employers have expectations.

3. It seems that Dr. Rosenthal is a student of
   ☐ a. history (especially of ancient Greece).
   ☐ b. human behavior (especially of achievement).
   ☐ c. mythology (especially of Greek legends).
   ☐ d. sculpture (especially of carving in ivory).

4. Which of the following is *not* an example of the Pygmalion Effect?
   ☐ a. A team wins because its coach expects it to.
   ☐ b. A team loses because its coach expects it to.
   ☐ c. A student succeeds because she knows she can.
   ☐ d. A student succeeds because her dad knows she can.

EXERCISE 9.7 **The Old Testament**

The Old Testament represents Hebrew literary and oral tradition dating from about 1250 to 150 B.C. Compiled by religious <u>devotees</u>, not research historians, it understandably contains factual errors, <u>im-precisions</u>, and <u>discrepancies</u>. However, there are also passages that contain reliable history, and historians find the Old Testament an indispensable source for studying the ancient Near East. Students of literature study it for its poetry, legends, and themes, all of which are an <u>integral</u> part of the Western literary tradition. But it is as a work of religious inspiration that the Old Testament attains its <u>profoundest</u> importance.

The Old Testament is the record of more than 1,000 years of ancient Jewish history; containing Jewish laws, wisdom, hopes, legends, and literary expressions, it describes an ancient people's efforts to compre-hend the ways of God. The Old Testament emphasizes and values the human experience; its heroes are not <u>demigods</u>, but human beings. It <u>depicts</u> human strength as well as weakness. Some passages exhibit cruelty and <u>unseemly</u> revenge, while others express the highest <u>ethical</u> values. As set forth in the Old Testament, the Hebrew idea of God and his relationship to human beings is one of the foundations of the Western tradition.

Check the boxes in front of correct answers and then circle the numbers in front of questions whose answers are implied by the passage but not directly stated in it.

1. The Old Testament contains
   □ a. factual errors.
   □ b. imprecisions.
   □ c. reliable history.
   □ d. all of the above

2. The greatest importance of the Old Testament is in its
   □ a. poetry.
   □ b. legends.
   □ c. religious inspiration.
   □ d. all of the above

3. The Old Testament emphasizes
   □ a. the Hebrew God.
   □ b. the human experience.
   □ c. poetry, legends, and themes.
   □ d. laws, wisdom, and hopes.

4. The Old Testament is studied by students of
   □ a. theology.
   □ b. history.
   □ c. literature.
   □ d. theology, history, and literature.

EXERCISE 9.8   The Double Bind

The "double bind" is a particular type of communication between parents and children in disturbed families. A classic double-bind message is the injunction "Be spontaneous!" If you obey this command, you have disobeyed it—you cannot deliberately be spontaneous. With a double bind, you are "damned if you do and damned if you don't"; the meaning of the message is ambiguous and confusing. Other double-bind messages are "Don't be so obedient!" "You should love me!" and "Have you stopped lying to me?" There is no reasonable response to these messages; if you obey the first message, you must disobey it. The second message suggests that loving and not loving are willful actions rather than feelings. The third message cannot be answered affirmatively or negatively unless the child confesses to lying. What is the meaning communicated with messages such as these? The child cannot decide.

Check the boxes in front of correct answers and then circle the numbers in front of questions whose answers are implied by the passage but not directly stated in it.

1. Which of the following is a double-bind question?
   - ☐ a. "Are you married or single?"
   - ☐ b. "Have you stopped beating your wife?"
   - ☐ c. "Do you enjoy swimming and hiking?"
   - ☐ d. "Would you rather work or play?"

2. The basic problem with double-bind messages from parents to children is that children
   - ☐ a. are wrong however they respond.
   - ☐ b. learn to make confusing statements.
   - ☐ c. are punished if they laugh or snicker.
   - ☐ d. are exposed to illogical thinking.

3. Double-bind communications are
   - ☐ a. made only by parents to children.
   - ☐ b. heard only in disturbed families.
   - ☐ c. meant to be taken as jokes.
   - ☐ d. confusing, ambiguous messages.

4. The message "You should love me more!"
   - ☐ a. suggests that loving is an act of the will.
   - ☐ b. must be disobeyed to obey it.
   - ☐ c. forces children to confess that they are lying.
   - ☐ d. assumes children instinctively love their parents.

EXERCISE 9.9   **Persuasion**

If you want to convince people of something, you should first convince them that you know what you are talking about. Then, as a speaker, you need to decide whether to use a one-sided message or a two-sided argument. In general, a two-sided argument is more effective in changing people's minds; a one-sided argument reinforces the opinions people already hold. Don't ask people to change their ideas just a little. If you shoot for a major change, you will be more effective. Also, most studies have shown that fear used as a persuasive device is not effective (this is the way your lungs will look if you smoke). If you want to scare people into changing, you must also give them some suggestions about ways to reduce their fear. Of course the higher the amount of fear you can arouse, the greater will be the change in their attitudes, unless you overplay your hand to the point where people ask, "What's the use?"

Check the boxes in front of correct answers and then circle the numbers in front of questions whose answers are implied by the passage but not directly stated in it.

1. If you want to convince people of something, first convince them that
   - ☐ a. you know what you're talking about.
   - ☐ b. they should make a major change.
   - ☐ c. their lives need to be improved.
   - ☐ d. you know what is best for them.

2. If you want to scare people into stopping smoking
   - ☐ a. show them photographs of smokers' lungs.
   - ☐ b. give them statistics about smokers' death rates.
   - ☐ c. show how stopping will reverse lung damage.
   - ☐ d. introduce them to people who have lung cancer.

3. If you want to motivate people who have been smoking cigarettes for many years to become nonsmokers, ask them to
   - ☐ a. gradually smoke fewer cigarettes.
   - ☐ b. change to a brand with less tar and nicotine.
   - ☐ c. smoke cigarettes without inhaling.
   - ☐ d. stop now and never smoke again.

4. Which of the following is *not* a method to use when trying to convince others to change their minds?
   - ☐ a. Convince them that you know what you're talking about.
   - ☐ b. Use a two-sided rather than a one-sided argument.
   - ☐ c. Ask for a major rather than a minor change.
   - ☐ d. Use fear as a motivation to make a change.

EXERCISE 9.10   Displaying Feelings

Most of us have developed patterns for displaying our feelings. As we witness other people's displays of feelings, we are likely to see at least four different patterns. (1) *Some people <u>deintensify</u> clues to their feelings.* For instance, when some people are afraid, happy, or hurt, they attempt to look less afraid, happy, or hurt than they really are. When people who are deintensifying bang their heads getting into their cars so hard that a bump appears, they may act as if the bang were only a minor injury. (2) *Some people <u>overintensify</u> or amplify clues to their feelings.* When these people are only slightly happy, or injured, they are likely to display a much greater amount of emotion than they really feel. Children who suffer a little pain but who are trying to get attention may scream as if they have been <u>maimed</u>. (3) *Some people give neutral clues to their feelings.* Whether these people are happy, afraid, sad, or angry, we see no real difference. We call the neutral position a "poker face." (4) *Some people mask clues to their feelings.* People who mask purposely look different from what we would expect. If these people are hurt, they may smile.

Check the boxes in front of correct answers and then circle the numbers in front of questions whose answers are implied by the passage but not directly stated in it.

1. Those who deintensify their feelings appear to be
   □ a. happy when they are hurt.
   □ b. happy when they are happy.
   □ c. more happy or hurt than they are.
   □ d. less happy or hurt than they are.

2. We do *not* expect "macho" men to
   □ a. deintensify their feelings.
   □ b. overintensify their feelings.
   □ c. give neutral clues to their feelings.
   □ d. mask clues to their feelings.

3. Those who mask their feelings are likely to
   □ a. smile if they are hurt.
   □ b. not show if they are hurt.
   □ c. look pained if they are hurt.
   □ d. hide behind a false face.

4. These four patterns for displaying feelings all
   □ a. help us understand others better.
   □ b. help us understand ourselves better.
   □ c. disguise what people are feeling.
   □ d. make clear what people are feeling.

EXERCISE 9.11   **Roman Baths**

The conquest of the Mediterranean world brought the Romans leisure, and Hellenism influenced how they spent their free time. During the second century B.C., the Greek custom of bathing became a Roman passion and an important part of the day. In the early Republic Romans had bathed infrequently, especially in the winter. Now large buildings containing pools and exercise rooms went up in great numbers, and the baths became an essential part of the Roman city. Architects built intricate systems of aqueducts to supply the bathing establishments with water. The baths included gymnasia, where men exercised and played ball. Women had places of their own to bathe, generally sections of the same baths used by men; for some reason, women's facilities lacked gymnasia. The baths contained hot-air rooms to induce a good sweat and pools of hot and cold water to finish the actual bathing. They also contained snack bars and halls where people chatted and read. The baths were socially important places where men and women went to see and be seen. Social climbers tried to talk to "the right people" and wangle invitations to dinner; politicians took advantage of the occasion to discuss the affairs of the day.

Check the boxes in front of correct answers and then circle the numbers in front of questions whose answers are implied by the passage but not directly stated in it.

1. The Romans adopted the custom of bathing sometime between
   - ☐ a. 1 and 100 B.C.
   - ☐ b. 101 and 200 B.C.
   - ☐ c. 201 and 300 B.C.
   - ☐ d. 201 and 300 A.D.

2. Water for Roman baths was supplied by
   - ☐ a. slaves carrying buckets.
   - ☐ b. wells beneath the baths.
   - ☐ c. aqueducts made of stone.
   - ☐ d. water pipes made of wood.

3. While in the baths, Romans would
   - ☐ a. eat.
   - ☐ b. exercise.
   - ☐ c. read.
   - ☐ d. all of the above

4. Ancient Romans would feel at home in our
   - ☐ a. health clubs.
   - ☐ b. schools.
   - ☐ c. churches.
   - ☐ d. gymnasiums.

EXERCISE 9.12   Consumer Income

Purchasing power is created by income. However, as every taxpayer knows, not all income is available for spending. For this reason, marketers consider income in three different ways: **Personal income** is the income an individual receives from all sources *less* the Social Security taxes that the individual must pay. **Disposable income** is personal income *less* all additional personal taxes. These taxes include income, estate, gift, and property taxes levied by local, state, and federal governments. About 6 percent of all disposable income is saved. On the average, about 60 percent is spent on such necessities as food, clothing, and shelter. **Discretionary income** is disposable income *less* savings and expenditures on food, clothing, and housing. Discretionary income is of particular interest to marketers, because consumers have the most choice in spending it.

Check the boxes in front of correct answers and then circle the numbers in front of questions whose answers are implied by the passage but not directly stated in it.

1. Discretionary income is *not* used to purchase
   □ a. automobiles.
   □ b. movie tickets.
   □ c. candy bars.
   □ d. work clothes.

2. Personal income is the money one receives *less*
   □ a. federal income tax.
   □ b. state income tax.
   □ c. Social Security tax.
   □ d. state sales tax.

3. About 60 percent of disposable income is spent on
   □ a. necessities.
   □ b. clothing.
   □ c. shelter.
   □ d. food.

4. Approximately how many dollars out of every $10,000 of disposable income are saved?
   □ a. $6
   □ b. $60
   □ c. $600
   □ d. $6,000

EXERCISE 9.13 **Flextime**

The changing work force has changing lifestyles and needs. In congested urban areas, rush-hour traffic makes the commute to work an unbearable ordeal for some. Two-career couples with children must perform miracles of scheduling and routing to make sure that the kids get to school or babysitter and that they get to work on time; single parents have half the resources and twice the problem. And more workers are going back to school or taking a second job in order to afford housing and cars. No wonder many workers have found **flextime** a desirable option. Instead of working the standard nine-to-five day, five days a week, they choose their own hours within certain limits. For instance, a company may stipulate that everyone has to be at work between 10:00 A.M. and 2:00 P.M., but workers may arrive or depart whenever they want as long as they work a total of eight hours. Such flexibility helps people arrange their complicated lives. When they don't have outside problems to worry about, they are more likely to work productively and happily on the job. The sense of control they get from arranging their own schedules is in itself motivating for many people.

Check the boxes in front of correct answers and then circle the numbers in front of questions whose answers are implied by the passage but not directly stated in it.

1. Workers with flextime schedules work
   - ☐ a. at times of their choice.
   - ☐ b. on days of their choice.
   - ☐ c. different hours each day.
   - ☐ d. different days each week.

2. Flextime did *not* gain popularity because some
   - ☐ a. people work two jobs.
   - ☐ b. couples with children both work.
   - ☐ c. parents raise children alone.
   - ☐ d. companies have limited work space.

3. Benefits of flextime do *not* include that it helps workers
   - ☐ a. arrange their complicated lives.
   - ☐ b. earn more money while working fewer hours.
   - ☐ c. work more productively and happily.
   - ☐ d. feel control in arranging their schedule.

4. Flextime is probably most likely to be used by
   - ☐ a. blue-collar workers in cities.
   - ☐ b. blue-collar workers in small towns.
   - ☐ c. white-collar workers in cities.
   - ☐ d. white-collar workers in small towns.

EXERCISE 9.14 Denotation and Connotation

The <u>denotations</u> of words are the actual things, behaviors, or characteristics to which they refer. For example, the denotation of *mother* is a female parent, the denotation of *Philadelphia* is a city by that name, and the denotation of *slender* is "having little fat." Denotations are contrasted with <u>connotations</u>, which are the associations suggested by words. For example, the denotation of *slender* and *skinny* are the same; however, *slender* has pleasant associations, but *skinny* does not. *Slender* connotes being slim, trim, and fit, but *skinny* connotes being abnormally thin and, perhaps, possessing an unhealthy lack of fat or flesh.

Check the boxes in front of correct answers and then circle the numbers in front of questions whose answers are implied by the passage but not directly stated in it.

1. When she called her boyfriend a "tiger," she used the word
   ☐ a. denotatively.
   ☐ b. connotatively.
   ☐ c. accurately.
   ☐ d. inaccurately.

2. In which of the following sentences is the word *fire not* used denotatively?
   ☐ a. The building was completely burned by fire.
   ☐ b. Fire provides light as well as heat.
   ☐ c. The mayor is under fire from the citizens.
   ☐ d. Take care when you fire the machine gun.

3. Connotations are
   ☐ a. associations suggested by words.
   ☐ b. actual things to which words refer.
   ☐ c. pleasant thoughts conveyed by words.
   ☐ d. unpleasant associations of words.

4. *Slender* does *not* connote being
   ☐ a. slim.
   ☐ b. trim.
   ☐ c. fit.
   ☐ d. smart.

5. Which of the following is a connotative meaning of the word *home*.
   ☐ a. a house where people live
   ☐ b. an apartment where people live
   ☐ c. a restful, congenial place
   ☐ d. the home plate in baseball

EXERCISE 9.15   **Minority Groups**

In a sociological sense, a minority is a category of people that society at large singles out for <u>discrimination</u> or selective, unfavorable treatment. Historically, blacks have perhaps suffered the most severe discrimination: it was not until World War I that blacks in large numbers worked next to whites in factory assembly lines. Because they were the last to be hired, they were often the first to be fired under the <u>seniority</u>-protection rules that <u>prevailed</u> in most businesses. But many Spanish-<u>surnamed</u> Americans have also been assigned to low-paying, <u>menial</u> jobs, as have many women. (Women are actually a majority numerically speaking, but they are a minority in the sense that they have suffered discrimination.) Job discrimination against minorities has been a "<u>vicious cycle</u>." Because they could not hope for better jobs, many minority-group members have had little <u>incentive</u> to seek education. And because they have not had an adequate education, many have not been able to qualify for those jobs that have been available to them.

Check the boxes in front of correct answers and then circle the numbers in front of questions whose answers are implied by the passage but not directly stated in it.

1. Women are considered a minority because they
   ☐ a. are a small proportion of the population.
   ☐ b. are mostly black or Spanish-surnamed.
   ☐ c. have been a target of discrimination.
   ☐ d. select others for unfavorable treatment.

2. Which of the following is *not* a minority group?
   ☐ a. Jews
   ☐ b. Chinese
   ☐ c. migrant farm workers
   ☐ d. men

3. Since minorities cannot hope for better jobs, they do not seek education; and since they have inadequate education, they are unqualified for available jobs. This is an example of
   ☐ a. a vicious cycle.
   ☐ b. frozen mobility.
   ☐ c. job discrimination.
   ☐ d. minority-group stagnation.

4. Blacks did not often work next to whites in assembly lines until about
   ☐ a. one hundred years ago.
   ☐ b. seventy-five years ago.
   ☐ c. fifty years ago.
   ☐ d. twenty-five years ago.

EXERCISE 9.16   Stereotypes

Perhaps the greatest barrier to our accurate judgment of others is our tendency to stereotype. Stereotyping is a standardized mental picture of a person or group that represents an oversimplified opinion, an emotional attitude, or an uncritical judgment. It involves labeling or categorizing things and people; it also involves placing things and people into the categories we have created. In practice, then, stereotyping assumes (1) that a person has the same characteristics as all other people in that group or (2) that a group has the same characteristics as one person who happens to be a part of that group. Stereotyping is a judgment about an entire group with little or no regard for individual differences within the group. You are likely to develop generalized opinions about any group you come in contact with. Your opinions may be true in a very broad sense, partially true, or totally false, depending on the accuracy and breadth of your perceptions. When you learn that a person is a member of a given group (recognition may come as a result of perception of skin color, a religious medal, gray hair, or any of a number of other signs), you may automatically project your general opinions on the individual person.

Check the boxes in front of correct answers and then circle the numbers in front of questions whose answers are implied by the passage but not directly stated in it.

1. A stereotype is an
   □ a. oversimplified opinion.
   □ b. emotional attitude.
   □ c. uncritical judgment.
   □ d. all of the above

2. In summary, the problem with stereotypes is that they
   □ a. involve placing people into various categories.
   □ b. pay too little attention to individual differences.
   □ c. assume a person has the characteristics of a group.
   □ d. assume a group has the characteristics of one person.

3. Which of the following is *not* a clue to group membership?
   □ a. skin color
   □ b. gray hair
   □ c. leather shoes
   □ d. a religious medal

4. Which of the following is *not* a stereotype?
   □ a. All teachers like to give tests.
   □ b. All students try to avoid studying.
   □ c. All infants need adult care.
   □ d. All fat people are jolly.

EXERCISE 9.17   **Retail Stores**

Department stores and chain stores helped to create and serve consumerism. The great boom in department-store growth occurred between 1865 and 1900, when companies like Macy's, Wanamaker's, Jordan Marsh, and Marshall Field became fixtures of metropolitan America. With their open displays of clothing, housewares, and furniture—all available in large quantities to anyone who had the purchase price—department stores effected a merchandising revolution. Not only did they offer wide variety; they added home deliveries, liberal exchange policies, and charge accounts. The Great Atlantic Tea Company, founded in 1859, became the first chain-store system. Renamed the Great Atlantic and Pacific Tea Company in 1869 and known more familiarly as A&P, the firm's stores sold groceries on a cash-and-carry basis. By buying in volume, the chain could sell to the public at low prices. By 1912 there were almost five hundred A&P stores, and more were being built in communities of all sizes across the nation. Other chains, such as Woolworth's, grew rapidly during the same period.

Check the boxes in front of correct answers and then circle the numbers in front of questions whose answers are implied by the passage but not directly stated in it.

1. Early department stores did *not*
   ☐ a. insist on cash payment for goods.
   ☐ b. deliver merchandise to customers' homes.
   ☐ c. have liberal exchange policies.
   ☐ d. offer a wide variety of merchandise.

2. Early department stores sold to
   ☐ a. very rich people.
   ☐ b. middle-class people.
   ☐ c. working-class people.
   ☐ d. everyone who could pay for goods.

3. The great growth in department stores took place in the
   ☐ a. late eighteenth century.
   ☐ b. early nineteenth century.
   ☐ c. late nineteenth century.
   ☐ d. early twentieth century.

4. Which of the following types of stores did *not* grow rapidly during the years 1865–1912?
   ☐ a. chain grocery stores
   ☐ b. chain drugstores
   ☐ c. variety stores
   ☐ d. department stores

EXERCISE 9.18   Memory Systems

Although we typically think of memory as a single entity, it can actually be broken down into three systems: sensory memory, short-term memory, and long-term memory. In this chapter we will be discussing each of these systems. Before we begin, however, let us consider briefly how each of these three systems contributes to human memory. Consider the following example. It is 11:30 on a Friday night and you are famished. You decide to order a pizza, so you look up the number of the local pizza parlor, 458-8604, in the phone book. You close the phone book, dial the number, and place the order. Let's trace this phone number through the three memory systems.

Sensory memory registers information that enters through one or more of the five senses. It holds a nearly literal image of the sensory stimulus for a very brief period of time. In our example, the phone number is presented visually, so it enters through the eyes. Sensory memory holds an enormous amount of information. When you look up the phone number in the book, the number 458-8604 gets stored along with many other names and numbers on the page. Although this memory system can store an enormous amount of information, it is not very useful in remembering the phone number, since the memory lasts less than 1 second. To remember the phone number long enough to dial, we have to transfer it from sensory memory into a somewhat longer-lasting memory system called **short-term memory.**

Short-term memory is a temporary storage system that lasts less than 20 seconds and has the capacity to hold only about seven separate pieces of information. In our example this is ideal, since the phone number only contains seven digits and we only need to remember it long enough to dial the phone, about 15 to 20 seconds. Once we have finished using the information in short-term memory it can either be transferred to a permanent memory system called long-term memory or it can be lost (forgotten). Information that we do not feel we will need again is forgotten. This is perhaps best illustrated when 5 minutes after ordering a pizza, we decide to add mushrooms and onions and once again have to look up the phone number. If, however, when we initially looked up the phone number we decided we would use it many times in the future, we might have rehearsed or practiced it in such a way as to place it in long-term memory. In contrast to short-term memory, which is a temporary memory system, **long-term memory** is a relatively permanent storehouse of knowledge. It has the capacity to store enormous amounts of information over long periods of time, perhaps a lifetime.

When discussing sensory, short-, and long-term memory, psychologists treat them as separate systems. They even diagram them as separate boxes. When first learning about memory, you may find it easier to think of memory systems as actual physical objects and to envision short-term memory as a little "box" residing somewhere in the brain.

Although the three memory storage systems we will discuss are very useful in helping to organize and understand what psychologists know about human memory, it is important to recognize that this is only a *model* of how psychologists think memory *might* work. A model is an analogy for or a representation of reality.

Check the boxes in front of correct answers and then circle the numbers in front of questions whose answers are implied by the passage but not directly stated in it.

1. When you search for a telephone number in a telephone book, numbers that you are not searching for are briefly held in your
   □ a. sensory memory.
   □ b. short-term memory.
   □ c. long-term memory.
   □ d. both *a* and *b*

2. The fact that we forget most information in less than 20 seconds is
   □ a. somewhat of a disadvantage.
   □ b. somewhat of an advantage.
   □ c. a great advantage.
   □ d. a great disadvantage.

3. We forget information in less than 20 seconds unless
   □ a. it is easy to understand.
   □ b. we rehearse or practice it.
   □ c. it is in sensory memory for more than 20 seconds.
   □ d. it is verbal rather than numerical information.

4. Information remains in long-term memory as long as
   □ a. one year.
   □ b. ten years.
   □ c. twenty-five years.
   □ d. a lifetime.

5. Sensory memory lasts
   □ a. ten seconds.
   □ b. five seconds.
   □ c. one second.
   □ d. less than one second.

6. □ T □ F   When you remember the telephone number of a movie theater only long enough to dial it, you store the number in your short-term memory.

7. □ T □ F   Psychologists know exactly how much and for how long information can be stored in long-term memory.

8. □ T □ F   The smell and taste of food registers in sensory memory.

9. □ T □ F   If information is not transferred from short-term to long-term memory, it is forgotten.

10. □ T □ F   The three types of memory reside in three compartments of the brain.

EXERCISE 9.19   Brands and Trademarks

Regardless of what type of product a company sells, it may want to create a **brand** identity by using a unique name or design that sets the product apart from those offered by competitors. Tide, Oldsmobile, and Bic are *brand names.* McDonald's golden arches, the Jolly Green Giant, the Pillsbury doughboy, and the Prudential rock are *brand symbols.*

Brand names may be owned by wholesalers and retailers as well as by producers of a product. Macy's, for example, buys merchandise from many manufacturers, which it then sells under some 50 in-house private labels.[1] A & P, the supermarket chain, purchases canned fruits, jellies, rice, household cleaning products, and frozen foods from hundreds of suppliers and offers them under the Jane Parker, A&P, and Ann Page brand names. Brands owned by national manufacturers are called **national brands.** Brands owned by wholesalers and retailers, such as Macy's and A & P, are **private brands.**

As an alternative to branded products, some retailers also offer **generic products,** which are packaged in plain containers that bear only the name of the product. These products are most often standard rather than first quality. They cost up to 40 percent less than brand-name products because of uneven quality, plain packaging, and lack of promotion. Generic goods have found a definite market niche, as a look at your local supermarket shelves will demonstrate. However, sales of generics have declined in the 1980s, partly because inflation has moderated, partly because consumers are disappointed with the uneven quality, and partly because brand-name producers have fought back with cents-off coupons that reduce the generics' cost advantage.[2]

Brand names and brand symbols may be registered with the Patent and Trademark Office as trademarks. A **trademark** is a brand that has been given legal protection so that its owner has exclusive rights to its use. Because a well-known name is a valuable asset and generates more sales than an unknown name, manufacturers zealously protect their trademarks. White-Westinghouse, for example, runs advertisements to remind people that Laundromat and Frigidaire are registered trademarks, not generic terms. When a name becomes too widely used, it no longer qualifies for protection under trademark laws. Cellophane, kerosene, linoleum, escalator, zipper, shredded wheat, trampoline, and raisin bran are just a few of the many brand names that have passed into the public domain, much to their creators' dismay.

References

1. Salmon, W.J., and Cmar, K.A. (May–June 1987). Private Labels Are Back in Fashion. *Harvard Business Review,* 99.
2. Alsop, R. (May 9, 1988). What's in a Name? Ask Supermarket Shoppers. *The Wall Street Journal,* 21.

Check the boxes in front of correct answers and then circle the numbers in front of questions whose answers are implied by the passage but not directly stated in it.

1. Which of the following is *not* a brand name?
   - ☐ a. Irish Spring
   - ☐ b. Dove
   - ☐ c. Caress
   - ☐ d. Lavender

2. Which of the following is *not* a brand symbol?
   - ☐ a. McDonald's golden arches
   - ☐ b. Shell's gas pumps
   - ☐ c. Pillsbury's doughboy
   - ☐ d. Prudential's rock

3. Which of the following is *not* a national brand?
   - ☐ a. Tide
   - ☐ b. Ann Page
   - ☐ c. Oldsmobile
   - ☐ d. Bic

4. The popularity of generic products declined in the 1980s because
   - ☐ a. consumers were disappointed by them.
   - ☐ b. inflation became less of a problem.
   - ☐ c. cents-off coupons produced competition.
   - ☐ d. all of the above

5. Which of the following is a trademark?
   - ☐ a. Betty Crocker
   - ☐ b. Zipper
   - ☐ c. Shredded Wheat
   - ☐ d. all of the above

6. ☐ T   ☐ F   A private brand is a brand that has legal protection so that its owner has exclusive rights to its use.

7. ☐ T   ☐ F   Manufacturers seek trademark protection for their brand names because it is difficult to think up good new brand names.

8. ☐ T   ☐ F   Brand names may be owned by manufacturers but not by wholesalers or retailers.

9. ☐ T   ☐ F   The image of Ronald McDonald is a brand symbol.

10. ☐ T   ☐ F   The brand name *Pepsi* has been so widely used that it no longer qualifies for protection under trademark laws.

EXERCISE 9.20   The Supreme Court

Above the west portico of the Supreme Court Building are inscribed the words EQUAL JUSTICE UNDER LAW. At the opposite end of the building, above the east portico, are the words JUSTICE THE GUARDIAN OF LIBERTY. These mottoes reflect the Court's difficult task: achieving a just balance among the values of freedom, order, and equality. Consider how these values came into conflict in two controversial issues the Court faced in recent years.

Abortion pits the value of order—the government's responsibility for protecting life—against the value of freedom—a woman's right to decide whether or not she will give birth. In the abortion cases beginning with *Roe* v. *Wade* (1973), the Supreme Court extended the right to privacy (an expression of freedom) to cover a woman's right to terminate a pregnancy.[1] The Court determined that at the beginning of pregnancy, a woman has the right to an abortion, free from government-imposed constraint. But the Court also recognized that toward the end of pregnancy, government interest in protecting the fetus's right to life normally outweighs a woman's right to abortion.

School desegregation pits the value of equality—equal educational opportunities for minorities—against the value of freedom—the right of parents to send their children to neighborhood schools. In *Brown* v. *Board of Education*,[2] the Supreme Court carried the banner of racial equality by striking down state-mandated segregation in public schools. This decision helped launch a revolution in race relations in the United States. The justices recognized the disorder their ruling would create, but in this case believed that equality clearly outweighed freedom. Twenty-four years later, the Court was still embroiled in controversy over equality when it ruled that race could be a factor in university admissions (to diversify the student body), in the *Bakke* case.[3] In securing the equality of blacks, the Court then had to confront the charge that it was denying the freedom of whites.

The Supreme Court makes national policy. Because its decisions have far-reaching impact on all of us, it is vital that we understand how it reaches those decisions. With this understanding, we can better evaluate how the Court fits within our model of democracy.

References

1. *Roe* v. *Wade*, 410 U.S. 113 (1973).
2. *Brown* v. *Board of Education of Topeka*, 347 U.S. 483 (1954).
3. *Regents of the University of California* v. *Bakke*, 438 U.S. 265 (1978).

Check the boxes in front of correct answers and then circle the numbers in front of questions whose answers are implied by the passage but not directly stated in it.

1. The issue of abortion pits the values of
   □ a. freedom and order.
   □ b. freedom and equality.
   □ c. equality and order.
   □ d. none of the above

2. The issue of desegregation pits the values of
   □ a. freedom and order.
   □ b. freedom and equality.
   □ c. equality and order.
   □ d. none of the above

3. A woman's right to terminate a pregnancy is
   □ a. guaranteed by the Supreme Court.
   □ b. guaranteed by the Constitution.
   □ c. an expression of freedom.
   □ d. an expression of equality.

4. The right of parents to send their children to neighborhood schools is
   □ a. an issue of freedom.
   □ b. an issue of order.
   □ c. denied by the Supreme Court.
   □ d. denied by the Constitution.

5. The *Bakke* case pitted the
   □ a. freedom of blacks against the equality of whites.
   □ b. freedom of blacks against the freedom of whites.
   □ c. equality of blacks against the equality of whites.
   □ d. freedom of whites against the equality of blacks.

6. □ T □ F In *Roe* v. *Wade* the Supreme Court determined that women have the right to abortion throughout pregnancy.

7. □ T □ F Until about forty years ago it was legal for states to segregate public schools.

8. □ T □ F The Justices of the Supreme Court did not consider whether their decision in *Brown* v. *Board of Education* would create disorder.

9. □ T □ F The Supreme Court has ruled that universities may not use applicants' race as a consideration in deciding whom they will admit to study for degrees.

10. □ T □ F The decisions of the Supreme Court are important because they affect all citizens of the United States.

EXERCISE 9.21   Stages of Dying

A dying person may experience several intense emotions. Swiss-born psychiatrist Elisabeth Kübler-Ross has theorized there are five typical stages of dying.

Denial ("No, not me")   At first knowledge that death is coming, a terminally ill patient rejects the news. The denial overcomes the initial shock and allows the person to begin to gather together his or her defenses. Denial, at this point, is a healthy defense mechanism. It can become distressful, however, if it is reinforced and encouraged by the relatives and friends of the dying patient.

Anger ("Why me?")   In the second stage, the dying person begins to feel resentment and rage about the fact of his or her death. The anger may be directed at the patient's family and medical staff, but there is very little they can do except to try to endure such encounters and comfort the patient to help him to arrive at the next stage.

Bargaining ("Yes, me, but . . .")   In this stage, a patient may try to bargain, usually with his or her God, for a way to reverse or at least postpone dying. The patient may promise, in exchange for recovery, to become devoted to good works or to see his family more. Or he may say, "Let me live long enough to see my grandchild born, or to see the spring again."

Depression ("Yes, it's me")   In the fourth stage, the patient gradually realizes the actual consequences. This may begin as grieving for the health that has been lost and then become anticipatory grieving for the loss—of friends, loved ones, life itself—that is to come. This is perhaps the most difficult time, and the dying person should not be left alone. Yet we should not try to cheer the patient up, for he or she must be allowed to grieve.

Acceptance ("Yes, me, and I'm ready")   In this last stage, the person has accepted the reality of his personal death: the moment is neither frightening nor painful, sad nor happy, but only inevitable. As the person waits for the end of life, he or she may ask to see fewer visitors, to begin to separate himself from other people, and perhaps to turn to one person for support.

Some of these stages may exist at the same time as others. Some may occur out of this order. Each stage may take days, or it may take only hours or even minutes.

Check the boxes in front of correct answers and then circle the numbers in front of questions whose answers are implied by the passage but not directly stated in it.

1. Denial may become distressful when
   - ☐ a. initial shock is overcome.
   - ☐ b. it is encouraged by relatives.
   - ☐ c. the news is rejected.
   - ☐ d. the healthiness of it is misunderstood.

2. Terminally ill people may direct anger at their
   - ☐ a. sons and daughters.
   - ☐ b. husbands and wives.
   - ☐ c. doctors and nurses.
   - ☐ d. all of the above

3. The purpose of bargaining is to
   - ☐ a. become devoted to good works.
   - ☐ b. spend more time with family members.
   - ☐ c. prolong life and postpone death.
   - ☐ d. improve one's relationship with God.

4. The most difficult stage is probably
   - ☐ a. denial.
   - ☐ b. anger.
   - ☐ c. bargaining.
   - ☐ d. depression.

5. Acceptance of the reality of death is
   - ☐ a. inevitable.
   - ☐ b. frightening.
   - ☐ c. painful.
   - ☐ d. all of the above

6. ☐ T   ☐ F   It is unhealthy for terminally ill people to deny that death is approaching.

7. ☐ T   ☐ F   The psychiatrist who proposed the five stages of dying was born in Switzerland.

8. ☐ T   ☐ F   A dying person may experience two or more of the stages at the same time.

9. ☐ T   ☐ F   Each stage lasts at least two days.

10. ☐ T   ☐ F   Dying people experience depression because they know that they are going to lose friends, loved ones—life itself.

EXERCISE 9.22   Pricing Strategies

Fine-tuning the price of a product may mean the difference between success and failure in a business. Companies use a variety of techniques to optimize their pricing decisions, four of which are described here: price lining, odd pricing, suggest pricing, and discount pricing.

Many companies follow a policy called **price lining,** offering their products at a limited number of set prices. For instance, companies marketing audio cassettes may offer a $6 line, a $9 line, and a $12 line. Price lining has two advantages: It simplifies the job of selling the products, and it makes the consumer's choice easier by limiting the number of alternatives.

In many industries, prices tend to end in numbers slightly below the next dollar figure, such as $3.95, $4.98, or $7.99. This method is known as **odd pricing,** or psychological pricing. The assumption here is that a customer sees $3.98 as being significantly lower than $4.00; thus, the company will sell more at only 2 cents less. Another rationale for this kind of pricing is that customers set price limits for themselves, defining how much they will pay for a given product. For example, a man may decide that $25.00 is the maximum that he will spend on a dress shirt. According to this reasoning, a price tag of $24.99 will appear to be safely within his range, while one of $25.00 may give him pause. Few studies have tested the effectiveness of such pricing, but those that have been done suggest that customers are more rational than psychological pricing assumes. Also, customers are usually aware that sales taxes, where they exist, raise the price of an item.

Some manufacturers of consumer goods advertise their merchandise at suggested retail prices, a practice known as **suggest pricing.** They may even stamp such a price on a product at the factory. Retailers have the choice of selling the goods at the suggested price or of selling for less and creating the impression that they are offering a bargain.

With **discount pricing,** companies offer different types of temporary price reductions, depending on the type of customer and the type of item being offered. A **trade discount** is offered by the producer to the wholesaler or retailer. An interior decorator, for example, may buy furniture from a manufacturer at a discount, then resell it to a client. A **quantity discount** is offered to buyers who order large quantities of a product. Theoretically, these buyers deserve a price break because they are cheaper to serve; they reduce the cost of selling, storing, and shipping products and of billing customers. A **cash discount** is a price reduction offered to people who pay in cash or who pay promptly.

Check the boxes in front of correct answers and then circle the numbers in front of questions whose answers are implied by the passage but not directly stated in it.

1. A family restaurant might price most meals at $7.99 and $9.99 to
   ☐ a. simplify selling meals.
   ☐ b. make choice easier for customers.
   ☐ c. compete with fast-food restaurants.
   ☐ d. both *a* and *b*

2. When a department store sells jeans for $25 and $35 but not $20 and $40, the store is using
   ☐ a. price lining.
   ☐ b. odd pricing.
   ☐ c. suggest pricing.
   ☐ d. discount pricing.

3. Some companies use odd pricing because they
   ☐ a. have researched its effectiveness.
   ☐ b. assume they will sell more products.
   ☐ c. have found that customers shop impulsively.
   ☐ d. believe it causes shoppers to overlook the sales tax.

4. A shop that usually sells ice cream cones for $1.50 sold them for $.99 for one week. This is an example of
   ☐ a. odd-even pricing.
   ☐ b. suggest pricing.
   ☐ c. discount pricing.
   ☐ d. cash discount.

5. Those who buy large quantities of a product reduce the seller's cost of
   ☐ a. storage.
   ☐ b. selling.
   ☐ c. billing.
   ☐ d. all of the above

6. ☐ T ☐ F   The price of $2.98 is not an odd price because it is an even number.

7. ☐ T ☐ F   The passage explains seven pricing techniques.

8. ☐ T ☐ F   A buyer must pay cash in order to receive a cash discount.

9. ☐ T ☐ F   A paint contractor who purchases hundreds of gallons of paint each year is likely to receive a trade discount and a quantity discount.

10. ☐ T ☐ F   When a product has a suggested price, manufacturers disapprove when retailers sell it for a lower or higher price.

EXERCISE 9.23   Compliance

Pressures to comply are quite common. For example, a stranger might ask you to yield a phone booth so he can make a call, a saleswoman might suggest that you buy a more expensive watch than you had planned on, or a co-worker might ask you for some money to buy a cup of coffee. What determines whether a person will comply with a request? Many factors could be listed, but three stand out as especially interesting. Let's briefly consider each.

The Foot-in-the-Door Effect   People who sell door-to-door have long recognized that once they get a foot in the door, a sale is almost a sure thing. To state the **foot-in-the-door** principle more formally, a person who agrees to a small request is later more likely to comply with a larger demand. Evidence suggests, for instance, that if someone asked you to put a large, ugly sign in your front yard to promote safe driving, you would refuse. If, however, you had first agreed to put a small sign in your window, you would later be much more likely to allow the big sign to be placed in your yard (Freedman & Fraser, 1966).

The Door-in-the-Face Effect   Let's say that a neighbor comes to your door and asks you to feed his dogs, water his plants, and mow his yard while he is out of town for a month. This is quite a major request—one that most people would probably turn down. Feeling only slightly guilty, you tell your neighbor that you're sorry but you can't help him out. Now, what if the same neighbor returns the next day and asks you if you would at least pick up his mail while he is gone. Chances are very good that you would honor this request, even if you might have resisted it otherwise.

Psychologist Robert Cialdini and his associates coined the term **door-in-the-face effect** to describe the reverse of the foot-in-the-door effect (Cialdini et al., 1975). On some occasions the best way to get a person to agree to a small request is to first make a major request. After the person has turned down the major request ("slammed the door in your face"), he or she may be more willing to agree to a lesser demand.

The Low-Ball Technique   Anyone who has purchased an automobile will recognize a third way of inducing compliance. Automobile dealers are notorious for convincing customers to buy a car by offering "low-ball" prices that undercut the competition. The dealer first gets the customer to agree to buy at an attractively low price. Then, once the customer is committed, various techniques are used to bump the price up before the sale is concluded. The **low-ball technique,** then, consists of getting a person committed to act and then making the terms of acting less desirable. Another example would be asking someone to loan you $5 and then upping it to $15. Or, you might ask someone if he or she would give you a ride to school in the morning. Only after the person has agreed would you tell her or him that you had to be there at 6 A.M.

Check the boxes in front of correct answers and then circle the numbers in front of questions whose answers are implied by the passage but not directly stated in it.

1. The foot-in-the-door effect predicts that if you lend somebody a dollar, you will later be likely to
   ☐ a. ask for your dollar back.
   ☐ b. ask the person to lend you a dollar.
   ☐ c. lend the same person five dollars.
   ☐ d. lend other people a dollar.

2. The door-in-the-face effect predicts that if you refuse to lend somebody your car, you may later be likely to
   ☐ a. lend the person bus fare.
   ☐ b. give the person a lift.
   ☐ c. help the person get a ride.
   ☐ d. any of the above

3. You would be low-balled if after you agree to pay $75 for a used VCR the salesperson tells you
   ☐ a. the VCR was priced at $95 yesterday.
   ☐ b. the price does not include free delivery.
   ☐ c. you must also pay $35 to have the VCR cleaned.
   ☐ d. videocassettes are on sale for $3 each.

4. The foot-in-the-door effect has long been recognized by
   ☐ a. clinical psychologists.
   ☐ b. door-to-door salespeople.
   ☐ c. shoe manufacturers.
   ☐ d. carpenters who install doors.

5. If after accepting a dinner invitation you are asked to bring with you a bottle of wine and a dessert, you are encountering the
   ☐ a. low-ball technique.
   ☐ b. foot-in-the-door effect.
   ☐ c. door-in-the-face effect.
   ☐ d. none of the above

6. ☐ T   ☐ F   The foot-in-the-door effect predicts that if you first agree to let somebody hug you, you are much more likely to later agree to let the person kiss you.

7. ☐ T   ☐ F   One way to get people to donate $10 to a cause is to ask them to donate $50 to the cause before requesting the $10 donation.

8. ☐ T   ☐ F   Automobile dealers are well known for using the foot-in-the-door technique.

9. ☐ T   ☐ F   When you first refuse to babysit friends' children for a weekend but later agree to look after them for two hours, you have responded to the door-in-the-face effect.

10. ☐ T   ☐ F   The door-in-the-face effect was first described in 1975.

EXERCISE 9.24 Role-Taking

Mead (1934) pointed out that a vital outcome of socialization is the ability to anticipate what others expect of us and to shape our own behavior accordingly. This capacity, he argued, is achieved by **role-taking**—pretending to take or actually taking the roles of other people, so that one can see the world and one's self from their viewpoints. In childhood we are able to internalize the expectations only of the **particular other**—specific other people such as parents. But as we grow older, we gradually learn to internalize the expectations of the **generalized other**, the attitudes and viewpoint of society as a whole. This internalized general concept of social expectations provides the basis for self-evaluation and hence for self-concept.

Mead showed how, as children progress through three stages of increasingly sophisticated role-taking, they gain a better understanding of themselves and of social life.

1. *Imitation*. Children under the age of about three lack a developed sense of self and so have difficulty distinguishing their roles from those of others. They merely mimic or imitate people in the immediate environment, such as family members, and they do so only occasionally and spontaneously—a gesture here, a word there. This is not really role-taking, but serves as preparation for it.

2. *Play*. After the age of about three, children begin to play at taking the roles of specific other people: they walk around in their parent's shoes; pretend to be an adult and scold a doll; or play "house," "doctors and nurses," and so on. By pretending to assume the roles of specific other people in this kind of play, children are taking the first steps in learning to see the world from a perspective that is not their own.

3. *Games*. By the early school years, children are ready to take part in organized games—preludes to the "game" of life—in which their roles are real and in which they must simultaneously take account of the roles and expectations of all the participants. A baseball pitcher, for example, must be aware not only of his or her own role requirements but also of the roles and likely responses of every other player. Very young children cannot play organized games: because they are still limited to their own perspective, they cannot grasp the role of other players, and thus cannot anticipate how others will respond to their actions.

Mead pointed out that socialization is never perfect or complete. He distinguished between what he called the "I" (the spontaneous, self-interested, impulsive, unsocialized self) and the "me" (the socialized self that is conscious of social norms, values, and expectations). The "I," he insisted, is never completely under the control of the "me." The socialized self is usually dominant, but we all have the capacity to break social rules and violate the expectations of others.

Reference

Mead, G.H. (1934). *Mind, self, and society: From the standpoint of a social behaviorist.* C.W. Morris (ed.). Chicago: University of Chicago Press.

Check the boxes in front of correct answers and then circle the numbers in front of questions whose answers are implied by the passage but not directly stated in it.

1. According to Mead, until children are about three years old, their behavior is
   ☐ a. controlled by parents.
   ☐ b. enjoyable to observe.
   ☐ c. imitative of family members.
   ☐ d. filled with spontaneous gestures.

2. The important development during the play stage is that children
   ☐ a. walk around in their parents' clothing.
   ☐ b. begin to see things from the perspective of others.
   ☐ c. play games such as "house" and "doctors and nurses."
   ☐ d. pretend to be adults, treating dolls as children.

3. The important development during the game stage is that children
   ☐ a. understand their role and the roles of others.
   ☐ b. learn to play baseball and other games.
   ☐ c. develop an unlimited understanding of others.
   ☐ d. become strong enough to compete in sports.

4. Mead called the attitudes of society as a whole the
   ☐ a. generalized other.
   ☐ b. particular other.
   ☐ c. "I."
   ☐ d. "me."

5. The socialized self that is conscious of social values and expectations is called the
   ☐ a. particular self.
   ☐ b. generalized self.
   ☐ c. "I."
   ☐ d. "me."

6. ☐ T ☐ F Very young children cannot play organized games because they cannot anticipate how others will respond to their actions.

7. ☐ T ☐ F Not everybody has the capacity to break social rules and violate the expectations of others.

8. ☐ T ☐ F Mead believed that socialization is complete by the time people graduate from high school.

9. ☐ T ☐ F The "I" first begins to come under the control of the "me" during the game stage.

10. ☐ T ☐ F Parents can promote the social development of their children by encouraging them to play games of various kinds.

EXERCISE 9.25   The Third World

Before considering the problems of the Third World, let us ask whether Africa, Asia, and Latin America can be <u>validly</u> and usefully lumped together as a single <u>entity</u>. Some experts prefer to speak of "the emerging nations" or "the less developed countries"—deliberately vague terms suggesting a <u>spectrum</u> of conditions ranging from near-hopeless poverty to moderate well-being. Others add a Fourth and even a Fifth World in order to distinguish among the less developed nations. Still, these countries do share important characteristics that make it valid—with reservations—to speak of them jointly.

First, the countries of the Third World have <u>virtually</u> all experienced political and/or economic domination, nationalist reaction, and a struggle for independence or <u>autonomy</u>. This shared past has given rise to a common consciousness and a widespread feeling of having been <u>oppressed</u> and <u>victimized</u> in their relations with Europe and North America. This outlook has been <u>nurtured</u> by a variety of nationalists, Marxists, and anti-<u>imperialist</u> intellectuals, who have argued forcibly that the Third World's problems are the result of past and present <u>exploitation</u> by the wealthy capitalist nations. Precisely because of their shared sense of past injustice, many influential Latin Americans identify with the Third World, despite their countries' greater <u>affluence</u>. Indeed, the term *Third World* was first widely used by Latin American intellectuals in the late 1950s, who picked up the term from a French scholar who <u>likened</u> the peoples of Africa, Asia, and Latin America to the equally diverse but no less oppressed and humiliated French third estate before the revolution of 1789. Later the term came into global use as a handy way of distinguishing Africa, Asia, and Latin America from the "first" and "second" worlds, the capitalist and Communist industrialized nations.

Second, a large majority of men and women in Third World countries still live in the countryside and depend on agriculture for a living. Agricultural goods and raw materials are still the primary exports. In Europe, North America, and Japan, by contrast, people live mainly in cities, depending chiefly on industry and urban services for employment.

Finally, the agricultural countries of Asia, Africa, and most of Latin America are united by awareness of their common poverty. By no means everyone in the Third World is poor; some people are quite wealthy. The average standard of living, however, is low, especially compared with that of people in the wealthy industrial nations, and massive poverty remains ever present.

Check the boxes in front of correct answers and then circle the numbers in front of questions whose answers are implied by the passage but not directly stated in it.

1. Third World countries have virtually all experienced
   ☐ a. economic expansion.
   ☐ b. nationalist reaction.
   ☐ c. easily won independence.
   ☐ d. a high standard of living.

2. The term *Third World* was popularized by
   ☐ a. Marxists.
   ☐ b. Latin American intellectuals.
   ☐ c. the French third estate.
   ☐ d. capitalists.

3. Which of the following is *not* part of the Third World?
   ☐ a. Peru
   ☐ b. India
   ☐ c. Russia
   ☐ d. Zambia

4. The "first world" does *not* include
   ☐ a. Canada
   ☐ b. Great Britain
   ☐ c. Spain
   ☐ d. Brazil

5. The "second world" includes
   ☐ a. Russia
   ☐ b. Argentina
   ☐ c. Japan
   ☐ d. New Zealand

6. ☐ T ☐ F   The Third World consists of countries in Africa, Asia, and Latin America.

7. ☐ T ☐ F   Since Japan is in Asia, it is a Third World country.

8. ☐ T ☐ F   A majority of Third World people are poor and live in the countryside.

9. ☐ T ☐ F   Third World countries are indebted to European and North American countries for helping them make economic and social progress.

10. ☐ T ☐ F   The Third World is sometimes called "the emerging nations" or "the less developed countries."

Defense Mechanisms

A normal way of coping with anxiety and frustration is to mobilize psychological defenses against the threat. These defensive tactics, though unconscious, are so common that they have been classified and named. You will recognize some of these defense mechanisms as ways you use to cope.

Repression is the forgetting of painful memories or frightening impulses. Material that is repressed is pushed out of consciousness so that the anxiety associated with it is lessened. If you have repressed the memory of your father's death, you cannot recall the details of the incident, although you may be aware that he is dead; you can thus avoid the pain and trauma you would experience in reliving the tragedy.

Displacement is the redirection of hostile feelings from an unsafe to a safe target. Anger that is displaced is anger that is directed not toward the person who caused it, but toward a second party. A child who is spanked by a parent may displace the anger and kick, not the parent, but the cat—an innocent second party. If your day at school has been upsetting, you may come home and yell at your younger brother (displaced aggression).

Rationalization is a way of explaining away all your difficulties in a fashion that protects your ego and self-esteem. You rationalize your failures by inventing logical excuses for them. Suppose you tried to win a contest but failed; what could you do to feel better? You could say, "I didn't want to win anyway"; "the contest was rigged"; "I didn't really try"; or, "the contest actually wasn't worth the effort." Each of these rationalizations serves to defend your ego and self-esteem against the embarrassment of failure.

Projection is a way of denying your own feelings and attitudes and attributing them to others ("projecting" them onto other people). To admit that you feel angry may make you anxious; to defend yourself against this anxiety, you may insist that others are angry at you, rather than the other way around.

Emotional insulation is a way of defending yourself against hurt by withdrawing your emotional investment from your work and relationships. Rather than risk great disappointments, you are cautious and more reserved, and you are careful not to let your hopes get too high. If you take no risks, if you are careful not to put your ego on the line, no one can hurt you. You withdraw into a protective shell to ward off frustration and disappointment.

Check the boxes in front of correct answers and then circle the numbers in front of questions whose answers are implied by the passage but not directly stated in it.

1. Defense mechanisms are
   - ☐ a. defensive tactics.
   - ☐ b. unconscious.
   - ☐ c. common.
   - ☐ d. all of the above

2. A grocer failed in business because he didn't have good business sense, but he claimed that he failed because of unfair competition. He used the defense mechanism of
   - ☐ a. repression.
   - ☐ b. displacement.
   - ☐ c. rationalization.
   - ☐ d. projection.

3. When people deny their own negative feelings but find those attitudes in others, they are using the defense mechanism of
   - ☐ a. repression.
   - ☐ b. displacement.
   - ☐ c. rationalization.
   - ☐ d. projection.

4. People who cannot recall the details of abuse they suffered as children use the defense mechanism of
   - ☐ a. repression.
   - ☐ b. displacement.
   - ☐ c. rationalization.
   - ☐ d. projection.

5. A man who when angry at his boss engages in arguments with his wife is probably using the defense mechanism of
   - ☐ a. repression.
   - ☐ b. displacement.
   - ☐ c. rationalization.
   - ☐ d. projection.

6. ☐ T ☐ F It is not normal to use defense mechanisms.

7. ☐ T ☐ F The defense mechanism of projection is used by a shopkeeper who cheats his customers because he believes they want to cheat him.

8. ☐ T ☐ F Rationalization protects the ego from embarrassment.

9. ☐ T ☐ F A man who does not ask women for dates because he fears they will turn him down uses the defense mechanism of emotional insulation.

10. ☐ T ☐ F The defense mechanism of repression is futile because it does not spare us from repeatedly experiencing the painful events of our lives.

EXERCISE 9.27   **The Maid of Orléans**

The ultimate French success rests heavily on the actions of an obscure French peasant girl, Joan of Arc, whose vision and work revived French fortunes and led to victory. A great deal of pious and popular legend surrounds Joan the Maid, because of her peculiar appearance on the scene, her astonishing success, her martyrdom, and her canonization by the Catholic church. The historical fact is that she saved the French monarchy, which was the embodiment of France.

Born in 1412 to well-to-do peasants in the village of Domrémy in Champagne, Joan of Arc grew up in a religious household. During adolescence she began to hear voices, which she later said belonged to Saint Michael, Saint Catherine, and Saint Margaret. In 1428 these voices spoke to her with great urgency, telling her that the dauphin (the uncrowned king Charles VII) had to be crowned and the English expelled from France. Joan went to the French court, persuaded the king to reject the rumor that he was illegitimate, and secured his support for her relief of the besieged city of Orléans.

Joan arrived before Orléans on April 28, 1429. Seventeen years old, she knew little of warfare and believed that if she could keep the French troops from swearing and frequenting whorehouses, victory would be theirs. On May 8, the English, weakened by disease and lack of supplies, withdrew from Orléans. Ten days later, Charles VII was crowned king at Reims. These two events marked the turning point in the war.

In 1430 England's allies, the Burgundians, captured Joan and sold her to the English. When the English handed her over to the ecclesiastical authorities for trial, the French court did not intervene. While the English wanted Joan eliminated for obvious political reasons, sorcery (witchcraft) was the ostensible charge at her trial. Witch persecution was increasing in the fifteenth century, and Joan's wearing of men's clothes appeared not only aberrant but indicative of contact with the devil. In 1431 the court condemned her as a heretic—her claim of direct inspiration from God, thereby denying the authority of church officials, constituted heresy—and burned her at the stake in the marketplace at Rouen. A new trial in 1456 rehabilitated her name. In 1920 she was canonized and declared a holy maiden, and today she is revered as the second patron saint of France. The nineteenth-century French historian Jules Michelet extolled Joan of Arc as a symbol of the vitality and strength of the French peasant classes.

The relief of Orléans stimulated French pride and rallied French resources. As the war dragged on, loss of life mounted, and money appeared to be flowing into a bottomless pit, demands for an end increased in England. The clergy and intellectuals pressed for peace. Parliamentary opposition to additional war grants stiffened. Slowly the French reconquered Normandy and, finally, ejected the English from Aquitaine. At the war's end in 1453, only the town of Calais remained in English hands.

Check the boxes in front of correct answers and then circle the numbers in front of questions whose answers are implied by the passage but not directly stated in it.

1. Joan did *not* hear the voice of
   - ☐ a. Saint Michael.
   - ☐ b. Saint Catherine.
   - ☐ c. Saint Margaret.
   - ☐ d. the Virgin Mary.

2. Joan believed France would win the war if soldiers
   - ☐ a. would put their faith in God.
   - ☐ b. ate better food to build their strength.
   - ☐ c. were kept from visiting whorehouses.
   - ☐ d. would bathe and wear clean uniforms.

3. Joan was believed to have contact with the devil because she
   - ☐ a. heard voices.
   - ☐ b. lived with swearing soldiers.
   - ☐ c. rejected Charles VII.
   - ☐ d. wore men's clothing.

4. Joan's trials were in
   - ☐ a. 1431 and 1456.
   - ☐ b. 1430 and 1431.
   - ☐ c. 1430 and 1456.
   - ☐ d. 1456 and 1920.

5. Joan was condemned as a heretic because she
   - ☐ a. had contact with the devil.
   - ☐ b. claimed direct inspiration from God.
   - ☐ c. wore men's clothing.
   - ☐ d. practiced witchcraft.

6. ☐ T ☐ F Joan's parents were rich merchants.

7. ☐ T ☐ F Joan was declared a saint in 1456.

8. ☐ T ☐ F The English withdrew from Orléans because they were overcome by superior French forces.

9. ☐ T ☐ F The dauphin was a prince—the son of a king.

10. ☐ T ☐ F Joan's great contribution was that she saved the French monarchy.

EXERCISE 9.28   **Listening**

When listening to someone, how much do you really hear and understand? Studies show that the average listener retains only *half* of what is said in a ten-minute oral presentation. Within forty-eight hours, that drops by half again. As a result, only about 25 percent of what is heard is understood, evaluated, and retained. Even worse, ideas may be distorted by as much as 80 percent as they travel through the chain of command in an organization (1).

Managers spend much of their time listening to problems, proposals, directives, orders, and so on. Employees, in turn, must listen to managers or supervisors explain changes in work procedures, schedules, and the like. If only one quarter of what people hear registers, is it any wonder that things can and do go wrong?

Listening with Empathy   Fortunately, listening is a skill that can be taught. One of the fundamentals of good listening is listening with empathy, that is, understanding what is being said from the speaker's point of view (2). Managers who are skilled in the art of good listening put aside their emotions, biases, and preconceptions and view problems from the employees' perspective.

Is emphathetic listening difficult? Psychologist Carl Rogers states that it takes courage to listen at this level. If you doubt this statement, try playing Rogers's communication game. In this game, only one person speaks at a time. The other person restates the speaker's ideas and feelings until the speaker is satisfied they have been heard correctly. This rule ensures that the listener really understands what the speaker is saying *from the speaker's point of view.* Most people are dismayed to find how easily they misinterpret or distort someone else's message.

Improving Listening Skills   According to Dr. Lyman K. Steil of Communication Consultants Associated and other communication experts, there are no hard and fast rules for developing listening skills. However, some general guidelines have been developed for teaching people to be better listeners.

1. *Develop listening responses.* Nodding one's head occasionally, remarking, "I see" or "I understand," indicate that the listener is paying attention and is actively involved in the conversation.

2. *Avoid prejudging the speaker.* A poor listener usually decides in advance that the topic is dull and tunes out the message after the first few sentences. A good listener may not be any more impressed with the topic but will still attempt to evaluate the concepts to determine if any can be used. In addition, a poor listener will be distracted by the speaker's delivery or appearance. A good listener focuses on the content and on learning what the speaker knows about the subject. On a one-to-one basis, a critical listener can bring a conversation to a quick end. Good listening means creating a climate of trust, mutual respect, and warmth.

3. *Don't anticipate.* Resist the temptation to finish a speaker's sentence or jump to conclusions when only part of the message has been given. The average person talks at about 125 words a minute but thinks four times faster. As a result, the listener has about 375 words of excess thinking capacity for every minute a person speaks (3). Give the speaker time to find the right words and to finish the message. Too often the conclusions we jump to are the wrong ones.

4. *Eliminate distractions.* A good listener creates a quiet, comfortable environment for listening. Closing a door, turning off noisy machinery, moving closer to the speaker, or changing to a quieter location can ensure that both sender and receiver can communicate well.

5. *Ask for clarification; restate important points.* Good listeners make sure they understand the terms and concepts the other person is using. One must not only be aware of the everyday meaning of words but also realize that each person has his or her own unique definitions associated with them. If there is confusion about what the speaker means, the listener can ask questions or restate what has been said until the points are clear.

One way to gain greater clarification of a message is to learn how to phrase questions. Questions can be either *open* or *closed.* Closed questions tend to elicit "yes" or "no" responses and yield a minimum of information. Open questions encourage more productive and detailed responses. For example, compare the closed question, "Do you like the new work schedule?" with the open question, "Tell me, what do you think about the new work schedule?"

6. *Be ready to give feedback.* When asked, a listener should give feedback as soon as possible. The response should be specific and framed in "I" statements. Instead of saying, "Your thinking is fuzzy here," the listener must pinpoint what needs to be done or changed. "I feel an important step has been overlooked. I suggest you check with inventory before planning that large an order."

References

1. Mundale, S. (Oct. 1980). Why More CEO's Are Mandating Listening and Writing Training. *Training/HRD*, 37–41.
2. Hulbert, J. (Feb. 1979). They Won't Hear You if You Don't Listen. *Administrative Management*, 57.
3. Ibid., p. 62.

Check the boxes in front of correct answers and then circle the numbers in front of questions whose answers are implied by the passage but not directly stated in it.

1. Within forty-eight hours after listening to a ten-minute speech, we have forgotten
   - ☐ a. 25 percent of what we heard.
   - ☐ b. 40 percent of what we heard.
   - ☐ c. 60 percent of what we heard.
   - ☐ d. 75 percent of what we heard.

2. *Empathy* is the ability to
   - ☐ a. see things from the other person's point of view.
   - ☐ b. teach others how to listen better.
   - ☐ c. learn how to listen without being distracted.
   - ☐ d. know what others will say before they say it.

3. Those who play Carl Rogers's communication game are usually dismayed to discover that they
   - ☐ a. don't let others finish what they want to say.
   - ☐ b. misinterpret or distort what others say.
   - ☐ c. cannot grasp the speaker's point of view.
   - ☐ d. are unable to communicate their ideas.

4. Which of the following is an open question?
   - ☐ a. Where do you go to school?
   - ☐ b. How can you improve your listening?
   - ☐ c. What grade did you get on your chemistry test?
   - ☐ d. Do you like your English teacher?

5. Which of the following is a closed question?
   - ☐ a. Do you want to improve your reading skills?
   - ☐ b. How can teachers help students learn?
   - ☐ c. What are your ten favorite movies?
   - ☐ d. Why is college tuition so expensive?

6. ☐ T   ☐ F   Listening is a skill that can be taught.

7. ☐ T   ☐ F   There are several hard and fast rules for developing listening skills.

8. ☐ T   ☐ F   The average listener thinks three times faster than the average speaker speaks.

9. ☐ T   ☐ F   When an employee and supervisor have a conversation, it is inadvisable for the employee to repeat or restate what the supervisor says.

10. ☐ T   ☐ F   Good listeners don't use the words *I* or *me* when they have conversations.

EXERCISE 9.29   **Career Planning**

The time to begin planning is as early as possible. A good way to start is to match your interests and skills with those required by various occupations or occupational areas. You can obtain help from your school's placement office and from a variety of publications: the *College Placement Annual* and the *Occupational Outlook Handbook* published by the U.S. Department of Labor, for example. Most people find that planning to enter a general occupational area is more effective than targeting a specific job.

You must, of course, satisfy the educational requirements for the occupational area you wish to enter. Early planning will give you the opportunity to do so. But those people with whom you will be competing for the better jobs will also be fully prepared. Can you do more?

The answer is yes. Corporate recruiters say that the following give job candidates a definite advantage:

- Work experience in cooperative work/school programs, during summer vacations, or in part-time jobs during the school year. Experience in the chosen occupational area carries the most weight, but even unrelated work experience is important.

- The ability to communicate well. Verbal and written communication skills are increasingly important in all aspects of business. Yours will be tested in your letters to recruiters, in your résumé, and in interviews. They will be of use throughout your career.

- Clear and realistic job and career goals. Recruiters feel most comfortable with candidates who know where they are headed and why they are applying for a specific job.

Here again, early planning can make all the difference in getting your goals together, in sharpening your communication skills (through elective courses, if necessary), and in obtaining solid work experience.

Letter and Résumé   Preparation again becomes important when it is time to apply for a position. Your college placement office and various publications (including such directories as *Standard & Poor's Register of Corporations* and *Thomas' Register*) can be helpful—in your task of finding firms to apply to for jobs. Help-wanted ads and employment agencies may also provide leads.

Your first contact with a prospective employer will probably be through the mail—in a letter expressing your interest in working for that firm. This letter should be clear and straightforward, and it should be cast in proper business-letter form. It (and any other letters that you write to potential employers) will be considered part of your employment credentials.

This first letter should be addressed to the personnel or human resources manager, by name if possible. You may include in this letter—very briefly—some information regarding your qualifications and your reason for writing to that particular firm. You should request an interview and, if the firm requires it, an employment application.

You may wish to include a copy of your résumé with your first letter (most applicants do so). In any case, you should already have prepared the résumé, which is a summary of all your employment credentials and capabilities. Your goal in preparing both the letter and the résumé is to leave the potential employer with the feeling that you are someone who deserves an interview.

The résumé should fit on a single sheet of standard letter paper. It should be carefully thought out and reworked as many times as necessary to get it right—to put your best foot forward. Your résumé should be <u>concise</u>, but everything important should be noted on it. You need not include explanations or details, because you will have an opportunity to discuss your qualifications in your interviews.

Figure 9.1 shows a typical résumé. Items that should be included are your name, address, and telephone number; your employment and/or career objectives; your educational background; your work experience; any awards you have won; and the principal activities you take part in outside of school or work. You may either include the names and addresses of references or add a note to the effect that references will be furnished on request. (If you do include your references, make sure you have their permission to do so.) You are not <u>obliged</u> to include personal data (such as age, marital status, and state of health). However, in some cases the omission of these data may raise questions in the minds of personnel managers.

FIGURE 9.1

A Résumé

MARIA GONZALEZ
612 Brookhaven St.
Dallas, TX 75233
(214) 339-2617

PERSONAL DATA
Single   Age: 24
Birthdate: March 3, 1968   Health: Excellent

EMPLOYMENT OBJECTIVE
An accounting position that will provide involvement in all facets of the accounting cycle.

EDUCATIONAL BACKGROUND
North Texas State University, Bachelor of Business Administration, May, 1990. Major in Management, Minor in Accounting. Grade point average: 3.4 based on a 4.0 scale.

El Centro Community College, Associate of Applied Science in Accounting, May 1988. Major emphasis on accounting and general business. Grade point average: 3.6 based on a 4.0 scale.

South Oak Cliff High School - High School Diploma, 1986

WORK EXPERIENCE
6/90 - Present: Accounting clerk for Murphy Manufacturing, Inc. Prepared customer invoices, accounts payable, and accounts receivable.
6/88 - 8/89:   Accounting clerk for Murphy Manufacturing, Inc. Prepared employee tax records and payroll information.
6/87 - 8/87:   General office clerk for Barton Foods Company. Prepared customer invoices, performed typing and receptionist duties.

EXTRA CURRICULAR ACTIVITIES
Outstanding Young Women of America, 1990
President of the Phi Beta Lambda chapter, North Texas State University
Member of the Future Accountants Club
Served as Youth Director for Underprivileged Children's Association in Denton, Texas

REFERENCES (by permission)

Dr. Harold Putter   Miss Sara Fleetwood   Mrs. Patti Church
Chairman,   Murphy Manufacturing, Inc.   Office Supervisor
Department of Accounting   1246 McKinney Avenue   Barton Foods Company
North Texas State University   Dallas, TX 75201   802 Houston Street
Denton, TX 76244

Check the boxes in front of correct answers and then circle the numbers in front of questions whose answers are implied by the passage but not directly stated in it.

1. You will probably *not* be able to locate a copy of the *Occupational Outlook Handbook* in
   - ☐ a. an office of the U.S. Department of Labor.
   - ☐ b. your college library.
   - ☐ c. a local bookstore.
   - ☐ d. your school's placement office.

2. Corporate recruiters do *not* claim that job candidates have an advantage if they have
   - ☐ a. work experience.
   - ☐ b. good communication skills.
   - ☐ c. realistic career goals.
   - ☐ d. high moral standards.

3. A letter you write expressing your interest in working for a firm should include all of the following *except*
   - ☐ a. information about your qualifications.
   - ☐ b. facts about your salary requirements.
   - ☐ c. your reason for writing to the firm.
   - ☐ d. a request for an interview.

4. Your résumé must include
   - ☐ a. references.
   - ☐ b. your age.
   - ☐ c. your marital status.
   - ☐ d. none of the above

5. A good résumé will
   - ☐ a. convince an employer you deserve an interview.
   - ☐ b. include at least three impressive references.
   - ☐ c. be neatly typed on two sheets of paper.
   - ☐ d. be handwritten by those with good handwriting.

6. ☐ T   ☐ F   When job applicants are equally qualified, the ones who have worked before have an advantage.

7. ☐ T   ☐ F   The computer and telephone have made it unnecessary for employees to have good writing skills.

8. ☐ T   ☐ F   Your résumé should include descriptions of the duties you performed on jobs you have had.

9. ☐ T   ☐ F   You should not give an employer the name of a reference unless you have permission to do so.

10. ☐ T   ☐ F   When you apply for jobs, you are not required to inform employers how old you are or whether you are married.

EXERCISE 9.30   Conflict

Conflict creates a special kind of frustration. When an individual must make a decision between *incompatible* or *contradictory* needs, desires, motives, wishes, or external demands, he or she experiences conflict. There are four basic forms of conflict, each with its own characteristics (Lewin, 1935).

Approach-Approach Conflicts   The simplest conflict comes from having to choose between two *positive* or desirable alternatives. Choosing between tutti-frutti-coconut-mocha-champagne-ice and orange-marmalade-peanut-butter-coffee-swirl at the ice-cream parlor may throw you into a temporary conflict, but if you really like both choices, your decision will be quickly made. Even when more important decisions are involved, **approach-approach conflicts** tend to be the easiest to resolve. The old fable about the mule who died of thirst and starvation while standing between a bucket of water and a bucket of oats is obviously unrealistic. When both alternatives are positive, the scales of decision are easily tipped one direction or the other.

Avoidance-Avoidance Conflicts   Avoidance conflicts are based on being forced to choose between two *negative*, or undesirable, alternatives. A person in an **avoidance conflict** is "caught between the devil and the deep blue sea," or "caught between the frying pan and the fire." In real life, avoidance conflicts involve choosing between things like birth control and religious belief, studying and failure, unwanted pregnancy and abortion, the dentist and tooth decay, a monotonous job and poverty.

Notice that these examples can only be defined as conflicts on the basis of an individual's own needs and values. If a woman wants to terminate a pregnancy and has no personal objection to abortion, she experiences no conflict. If she would not consider abortion under any circumstances, there is no conflict.

Approach-Avoidance Conflicts   Approach-avoidance conflicts are also difficult to resolve. Since people seldom escape them, they are in some ways more troublesome than avoidance conflicts. A person in an **approach-avoidance conflict** is "caught"—being simultaneously attracted to, and repelled by, the same goal or activity. Attraction keeps the person in the situation, but its negative aspects cause turmoil and distress. For example, a high school student arrives to pick up his date for the first time. He is met at the door by her father who is a professional wrestler—seven feet tall, 300 pounds, and entirely covered with hair. The father gives the boy a crushing handshake and growls that he will break him in half if the girl is not home on time. The student considers the girl attractive and has a good time. But does he ask her out again? It depends on the relative strength of his attraction and his fear. Almost certainly he will feel ambivalent about asking her out again, knowing that another encounter with her father is involved.

Ambivalence (mixed positive and negative feelings) is a central characteristic of approach-avoidance conflicts. Ambivalence is usually translated into *partial approach* (Miller, 1944). Since our student is still attracted to the girl he may spend time with her at school and elsewhere, but may not actually date her again. Some more realistic examples of approach-avoidance conflicts are: planning marriage to someone your parents strongly disapprove of, wanting to be an actor but suffering stage fright, wanting to buy a car but not wanting to be tied to monthly payments, wanting to eat when overweight, and wanting to go to school but hating to study. Many of life's important decisions have approach-avoidance dimensions.

In reality, conflicts are rarely as clear-cut as those described. People in conflict are usually faced with several dilemmas at once, so several types of conflict are superimposed and intermingled. The fourth type of conflict moves us closer to this realistic state of affairs.

Double Approach-Avoidance Conflicts   You are offered two jobs, one with good pay but poor hours and dull work, the second with interesting work and excellent hours but low pay. Which do you select? This situation is more typical of the choices we must usually make. It offers neither completely positive, nor completely negative, alternatives. It is, in other words, a **double approach-avoidance conflict,** since each alternative has both positive and negative qualities.

When faced with double approach-avoidance conflicts, people tend to **vacillate,** or waver, between the alternatives. Just as you are about to choose one such alternative, its undesirable aspects tend to loom large so you swing back toward the other choice. If you have ever been romantically attracted to two people at once, each having qualities you like and dislike, then you have probably experienced vacillation.

On a day-to-day basis, most double approach-avoidance conflicts are little more than an annoyance. When they involve major life decisions, such as choice of a career, school, mate, job, whether to have children, and so forth, they add significantly to the amount of stress experienced.

References

Lewin, K.A. (1935). *A Dynamic Theory of Personality*. New York: McGraw-Hill.
Miller, N.E. (1944). Experimental Studies of Conflict. In *Personality and the Behavior Disorders*, Vol. I. J.McV. Hunt (ed.). New York: Ronald Press, 431–465.

Check the boxes in front of correct answers and then circle the numbers in front of questions whose answers are implied by the passage but not directly stated in it.

1. People experience an approach-avoidance conflict when they want to
   ☐ a. go swimming rather than hiking.
   ☐ b. buy a sweater rather than jeans.
   ☐ c. visit Disney World while in Florida.
   ☐ d. own a new car but not have car payments.

2. The need to decide whether to have an abortion is *not* a conflict for women who
   ☐ a. do not object to abortion.
   ☐ b. would not consider having an abortion.
   ☐ c. both *a* and *b*
   ☐ d. none of the above

3. A double approach-avoidance conflict is one in which
   ☐ a. two alternatives are both positive and negative.
   ☐ b. two alternatives are doubly negative.
   ☐ c. one alternative is both positive and negative.
   ☐ d. one alternative is doubly negative.

4. Most double approach-avoidance conflicts
   ☐ a. cause great mental anguish.
   ☐ b. are small annoyances.
   ☐ c. should be ignored.
   ☐ d. are sources of unnecessary stress.

5. Which of the following types of conflict is usually the easiest to resolve?
   ☐ a. approach-approach
   ☐ b. avoidance-avoidance
   ☐ c. approach-avoidance
   ☐ d. double approach-avoidance

6. ☐ T ☐ F   Those who must work at boring, low-paying labor or go hungry experience an avoidance-avoidance conflict.

7. ☐ T ☐ F   A person forced to choose which of two desirable cars she will purchase experiences an approach-approach conflict.

8. ☐ T ☐ F   The conflicts in our everyday lives are rarely as clear-cut as those described in the passage.

9. ☐ T ☐ F   To be romantically attracted to two people at the same time, both of whom have likable and unlikable qualities, is to experience an approach-avoidance conflict.

10. ☐ T ☐ F   Approach-avoidance conflicts involve superimposed and intermingled conflicts.

EXERCISE 9.31　　**Stages of Relationships**

We have all been conscious of changes in relationships from initial attraction to some permanent or semipermanent bond. Moreover, we know that some relationships never get anywhere, some reach a level of stability for an extended period, and some deteriorate. The stages that relationships go through have been given different labels according to who is discussing the process. In this section we consider four stages in developing a relationship. In each case we identify it with the various labels that have been used for that stage. Each of these stages need not be identifiable as a separate step, nor is it absolutely necessary that a relationship pass through the steps in this order. We believe that an analysis of these stages will deepen your understanding of the nature of relationships.

Sampling (also called "initiating" and "auditioning")
This first stage contains aspects of the selection process. As we begin a relationship, we try to find out what we have in common with the other person. If a person shows desirable traits or behaviors, we pursue that person. If a person is undesirable for some reason, the relationship is terminated or held at a particular level. In other words, in the acquaintance stage people make decisions about whether they will find a deeper relationship profitable.

Bargaining (also called "exploring")　　[During] this first stage in a relationship . . . people determine the kinds of rewards they may expect to get from the relationship and the kinds of costs that will be incurred. In this stage people get information about each other and build images based upon this information. Tom finds that if he spends his time and money a certain way, he will be rewarded. Tom takes the time to take Phyllis to a museum. If Phyllis does not seem to care about what they see, if Phyllis cannot share in a discussion of what they see, or if Phyllis does not show any appreciation of the time Tom is taking, the cost will exceed the reward. If Tom does not get any (or too few) of the needed or expected rewards, he may feel that his total expenditure in time, energy, and money has been wasted. Tom will stop taking Phyllis to museums and, unless he still believes that some potential for reward exists, will probably stop seeing Phyllis altogether.

Bargaining also takes place in same-sex relationships. Tom sees a potential friendship developing with George because both like to play racquetball. But if George cannot get enough free time to play with Tom, or if George can play only at hours when Tom cannot, or if George is too poor or too good a player to make an enjoyable game, or if their games are about equal but Tom just does not get the pleasure he expects, the racquetball friendship will not develop, will stagnate, or will deteriorate.

Commitment (also called "integrating and revising" and "intensifying")　　This is the stage in a relationship at which a person gives up other relationships in favor of a particular one. Individuals get together frequently for long periods. During this stage they seldom see the other's flaws or they are willing to ignore them. This is considered a very "euphoric" stage. Also during this stage people may develop their own language, pet names for each other, "in" jokes, and the like. Later in this stage a certain amount of evaluation takes place. The question of whether the relationship is a permanent one is considered. Jack and Margaret go out a few times and enjoy themselves. Each is benefiting from the relationship. The relationship has progressed so well and the rewards have been so high that they begin to spend even more time together. Although other relationships may be maintained during this time (Margaret continues to go jogging with Andrea), relationships of the same kind will be limited (Jack was also dating Nancy, but no longer).

Institutionalization (also called "bonding")   It is in this stage of the relationship that two people formally ratify their commitment. This stage is not really a process but an event. In a male–female relationship, this stage is most often marked by marriage. In another kind of relationship, it could be marked by signing a contract, by forming a partnership, or by any other act that is appropriate for that particular relationship.

But what happens after bonding? In real life people seldom live happily ever after. The stability of relationships, especially intimate ones, is under constant pressure, and, just as a relationship can *build*, so can it *deteriorate*. The three stages of deterioration that we identify incorporate the material found in most analyses.

Reduction of Tolerance (also called "differentiating" and "circumscribing")   In this stage people begin to change their orientation from *we* to *I*. "Touchy" subjects begin to limit the amount of sharing of personal feelings and ideas. The relationship begins to show much less open discussion, and people begin to have more unresolved conflicts.

Drifting Apart (also called "stagnating" and "avoiding")
During this second stage people begin to lose interest in the opinions and feelings of the other, even on important ideas and issues. Conversation gravitates toward small talk, gossip, and other "safe" communication. Soon the people begin to avoid each other. They seek out other company to share the interests and activities that are important to them. In this stage people cease being "best friends." There need not be any hostility between the people; if anything, this stage is likely to be marked by gross indifference.

Ending   In this stage one or both parties seek to bring a formal end to the relationship. Again, like bonding, this is not as much a process as an event.

Movement through these stages can be very quick, and it is easy for people to miss the signs of deterioration.

Check the boxes in front of correct answers and then circle the numbers in front of questions whose answers are implied by the passage but not directly stated in it.

1. According to the passage, relationships have
   ☐ a. seven stages.
   ☐ b. six stages.
   ☐ c. five stages.
   ☐ d. four stages.

2. The second stage of a relationship is called
   ☐ a. bargaining.
   ☐ b. commitment.
   ☐ c. institutionalization.
   ☐ d. reduction of tolerance.

3. The third stage of a relationship is called
   ☐ a. commitment.
   ☐ b. institutionalization.
   ☐ c. reduction of tolerance.
   ☐ d. drifting apart.

4. The fourth stage of a relationship is called
   ☐ a. ending.
   ☐ b. bonding.
   ☐ c. deterioration.
   ☐ d. institutionalization.

5. The fourth stage of a relationship does *not* include
   ☐ a. institutionalization.
   ☐ b. reduction of tolerance.
   ☐ c. drifting apart.
   ☐ d. ending.

6. ☐ T ☐ F During the first stage of a relationship, we try to find out what we have in common with the other person and to determine the kinds of rewards we might get from spending more time with him or her.

7. ☐ T ☐ F During the second stage of a relationship, people start spending much time together, and they tend to overlook each other's shortcomings.

8. ☐ T ☐ F "Bonding" may occur in a relationship between a man and a woman but not in a relationship between two men or two women.

9. ☐ T ☐ F The last stage of a relationship is called "deterioration."

10. ☐ T ☐ F Relationships deteriorate in a three-stage process: (1) reduction of tolerance, (2) drifting apart, and (3) ending.

Topics

A **topic** is something dealt with in writing or conversation; it is the person, place, or thing that is the subject of a discussion.

Topics in Textbooks

Topics in American history include Thomas Jefferson, Pearl Harbor, and civil rights. Those who study physics learn about topics such as energy, chain reactions, and Newton's laws of motion. Topics in psychology textbooks include anxiety, dreams, drug abuse, emotions, and intelligence. Textbooks list topics in their indexes.

Efficient reading includes identifying the topics of paragraphs and longer passages. Underline the word that is the topic of the following paragraph.

> There are three basic types of love. Agape is the selfless and nonsexual love for others that inspires devotion to high principles; it is the type of love to which Jesus referred when he said, "Love one another." The second type of love, philia, is the affection we have for close friends and family members who are not the object of our sexual desire. Finally, eros is the love characterized by sexual attraction that, in our society, is the basis for romance and marriage.

You should have underlined *love*. This paragraph explains three types of love; *love* is the topic of the paragraph.

Exercises for Topics

Exercises 10.2 through 10.5 provide practice in locating topics in textbook passages. Before you do those exercises, review the characteristics of topics by doing Exercise 10.1. If you do the exercises in this chapter thoughtfully and carefully, you will improve a skill that will help you when you do other exercises in *RSVP* and when you read textbooks for your college courses.

EXERCISE 10.1   Topics in Lists

Check the word that is the topic for each list. For instance, check *Coins* in the first list because pennies, nickels, dimes, and quarters are all coins.

1. ☐ Pennies
   ☐ Nickels
   ☐ Dimes
   ☐ Coins
   ☐ Quarters

2. ☐ Hate
   ☐ Emotions
   ☐ Envy
   ☐ Fear
   ☐ Love

3. ☐ Stores
   ☐ Groceries
   ☐ Bakeries
   ☐ Pharmacies
   ☐ Florists

4. ☐ Spaghetti
   ☐ Lasagna
   ☐ Fettucini
   ☐ Pasta
   ☐ Linguini

5. ☐ Letter
   ☐ Writing
   ☐ Newspaper
   ☐ Magazine
   ☐ Book

6. ☐ Entertainment
   ☐ Television
   ☐ Movies
   ☐ Circuses
   ☐ Theater

7. ☐ Steam
   ☐ Energy
   ☐ Atomic
   ☐ Electricity
   ☐ Gasoline

8. ☐ May
   ☐ June
   ☐ Women
   ☐ April
   ☐ May

9. ☐ Second
   ☐ Minute
   ☐ Day
   ☐ Time
   ☐ Hour

10. ☐ Beef
    ☐ Meat
    ☐ Lamb
    ☐ Pork
    ☐ Veal

11. ☐ Nails
    ☐ Hardware
    ☐ Hammer
    ☐ Hinge
    ☐ Screws

12. ☐ Fowl
    ☐ Chicken
    ☐ Turkey
    ☐ Duck
    ☐ Quail

13. ☐ Milk
    ☐ Coffee
    ☐ Beverages
    ☐ Soda
    ☐ Tea

14. ☐ Cars
    ☐ Airplanes
    ☐ Trains
    ☐ Buses
    ☐ Vehicles

15. ☐ Sandals
    ☐ Shorts
    ☐ T-shirt
    ☐ Bikini
    ☐ Clothes

16. ☐ Ballet
    ☐ Sculpture
    ☐ Arts
    ☐ Painting
    ☐ Opera

17. ☐ Eyes
    ☐ Lips
    ☐ Nose
    ☐ Face
    ☐ Chin

18. ☐ Pounds
    ☐ Yards
    ☐ Cups
    ☐ Measures
    ☐ Feet

19. ☐ Seattle
    ☐ Boston
    ☐ Chicago
    ☐ Cities
    ☐ Memphis

20. ☐ Novel
    ☐ Poem
    ☐ Essay
    ☐ Drama
    ☐ Literature

21. ☐ Spain
    ☐ Europe
    ☐ Germany
    ☐ France
    ☐ Italy

EXERCISE 10.2 **Topics in Paragraphs**

Underline the topic of each paragraph. A topic is usually stated in one word in the first sentence of a paragraph, but it is sometimes stated in more than one word or in a sentence other than the first.

1

George Sand (1804–1876), a strong-willed and gifted woman, defied the narrow conventions* of her time in an unending search for self-fulfillment. After eight years of unhappy marriage in the provinces, she abandoned her dullard of a husband and took her two children to Paris to pursue a career as a writer. There she soon achieved fame and wealth, eventually writing over eighty novels on a variety of romantic and social themes. All were shot through with a typically romantic love of nature and moral idealism. George Sand's striking individualism went far beyond her flamboyant preference for men's clothing and cigars and her notorious affairs with the poet Alfred de Musset and the composer Frédéric Chopin, among others. Her semi-autobiographical novel *Lélia* was shockingly modern, delving deeply into her tortuous quest for sexual and personal freedom.

2

In basic terms, the theory of supply and demand holds that when people want a good or service very much, they will be willing to pay a higher price for it; and when the price rises, manufacturers will be willing to supply it in greater quantity. People will usually have to pay more for something they want that's in short supply (as anyone who's tried to buy a shovel immediately after a heavy snowfall knows); but if the product is widely available, the sellers will have to settle for lower prices. In other words, supply and demand are continuously reacting to one another, and the balance between them at any given moment is reflected by the current price on the open market. Thus the price of a product may drop, not because a businessperson is trying to lure customers away from the competition, but because consumer demand for the product has fallen off.

3

Whereas race refers only to physical characteristics, the concept of ethnicity refers to cultural features that may be handed down from one generation to the next through the socialization process. These features may include language, religion, national origin, dietary practices, a sense of common historical heritage, or any other distinctive cultural trait. Many groups, such as American blacks or Indians, are both racially and ethnically distinct from most people in their society. Such groups are regarded as doubly "different." In other cases, ethnic groups cannot be distinguished from the bulk of the population by their physical characteristics. German- and Polish-Americans, for example, are physically indistinguishable, but members of the two groups may form distinct subcultures based on their different ethnic backgrounds.

* Words underscored in blue are defined in the Master Vocabulary List on pages 413–425, and the exercise on page 58 is based on these words.

EXERCISE 10.3   **Topics in Paragraphs**

Underline the topic of each paragraph. A topic is usually stated in one word in the first sentence of a paragraph, but it is sometimes stated in more than one word or in a sentence other than the first.

1

Atoms are ageless. Atoms in your body have existed since the beginning of time, cycling and recycling among innumerable forms, both nonliving and living. When you breathe, for example, only part of the atoms that you inhale are exhaled in your next breath. The remaining atoms are taken into your body to become part of you, and they later leave your body by various means. You don't "own" the atoms that make up your body; you borrow them. We all share from the same atom pool as atoms forever migrate around, within, and throughout us. So some of the atoms in the nose you scratch today could have been part of your neighbor's ear yesterday! Not only are we all made of the same *kinds* of atoms, we are also made of the *same* atoms— atoms that cycle from person to person as we breathe, sweat, and vaporize.

2

The most obvious fact about notions of female attractiveness is that there are few if any universal standards. Some people regard the shape and color of the eyes as the main underline{determinant} of beauty; others are more concerned about the formation of the mouth, nose, or ears. In some societies small, slim women are admired, but there is a strong cross-cultural tendency for men to prefer fat women; in some African societies the sexy woman is one who is positively underline{obese}. The Masai of eastern Africa prefer women with small breasts, whereas the Apache prefer women with very large breasts. In many tropical societies women do not cover their breasts, but this does not mean that the men are in a constant state of underline{erotic} underline{frenzy}. The breasts are simply not considered a sexual stimulus at all, and attention may focus instead on the legs, underline{buttocks}, back, or elsewhere.

3

Curtis paid Tony four unfiltered Camel cigarettes for a fresh slice of soap weighing less than an ounce. Tony added the four cigarettes to another six he had been saving and paid Morley ten cigarettes for an egg. This could have been a scene in a World War II prison camp, where cigarettes became money among prisoners. If cigarettes can be used in place of dollar bills, then what is money? Anything may be used as money, as long as it is acceptable to everyone as money and everyone regards it as a medium of exchange for goods and services. Throughout history, many things have served as money. American Indians used underline{wampum} beads made of polished shells strung together. Other cultures have used salt, cattle, chickens, shells, rocks, coconuts, and precious metals such as gold.

EXERCISE 10.4 **Topics in Paragraphs**

Underline the topic of each paragraph. A topic is usually stated in one word in the first sentence of a paragraph, but it is sometimes stated in more than one word or in a sentence other than the first.

1

We usually think of the school as being mainly concerned with teaching skills and knowledge, and this is certainly one of its major functions. But the schools in every society also engage in outright indoctrination in values. We may find this fact more readily apparent in societies other than our own—until we consider the content of civics classes or the daily ritual of the Pledge of Allegiance. The school socializes not only through its formal academic curriculum but also the "hidden curriculum" implicit in the content of school activities, ranging from regimented classroom schedules to organized sports. Children learn that they must be neat and punctual. They learn to sit still, keep quiet, wait their turn, and not be distracted from their work. They learn that they should respect and obey without question the commands of those who have social authority over them.

2

Many contributed to the steady advance of science in the nineteenth century. In 1808, John Dalton, an English chemist, formulated the atomic theory. In 1831, another English chemist, Michael Faraday, discovered the principle of electromagnetic induction on which the electric generator and electric motor are based. In 1847, Hermann von Helmholtz, a German physicist, formulated the law of conservation of energy, which states that the total amount of energy in the universe is always the same; energy that is used up is not lost but is converted into heat. In 1887, another German physicist, Heinrich Hertz, discovered electromagnetic waves, which later made possible the invention of radio, television, and radar. In 1869, Dmitri Mendeleev, a Russian chemist, constructed a periodic table for the elements that helped make chemistry more systematic and mathematical. In 1861, Louis Pasteur, a French scientist, proved that diseases were caused by microbes and devised vaccines to prevent them.

3

Sports announcing is highly competitive, and years of dedicated effort must be invested before there is a likelihood of significant reward. Despite this, the attraction of spending a career in close association with the world of sports motivates scores of young people to undertake the struggle. If you are determined to become a professional sports announcer despite the stiff competition and the long apprenticeship, weigh carefully the words of the late Russ Hodges: (1) You must love sports and broadcasting and commit yourself to both. (2) You must truly believe that you will be successful. (3) You should educate yourself for a different career just in case you are one of the ninety-five in a hundred who do not succeed in sports announcing.

EXERCISE 10.5   **Topics in Paragraphs**

Underline the topic of each paragraph. A topic is usually stated in one word in the first sentence of a paragraph, but it is sometimes stated in more than one word or in a sentence other than the first.

1

News, some journalists say, is something that steps beyond the commonplace, the usual. As John Bogart of the *New York Sun* said in 1830, "When a dog bites a man, that's not news because it happens so often, but if a man bites a dog, that is news." Turner Catledge of the *New York Times* suggested that "News is anything you didn't know yesterday." To David Brinkley of ABC News, "News is the unusual, the unexpected. Placidity is not news. If an airplane departs on time, it isn't news. If it crashes, regrettably, it is."

2

In the past, it was to people's economic advantage to have children. Sons could become hands on the farm or apprentices in a trade; daughters could relieve some of the drudgery of the mother's housework and marry men who could provide additional help and income to the family. Today, however, children are anything but an economic asset. Every few years some organization or other calculates the cost of raising a child. The amount can be staggering, especially if college tuition is part of the package. Clearly, a child does not enhance a couple's financial status. Sometimes, people also have negative emotional and physical reactions to becoming parents—depression, resentment, guilt, fatigue, marital difficulties.

3

If the education of children in the eighteenth century was poor, the treatment of criminals was appalling. Whether an individual was imprisoned for unpaid debts or for banditry or murder, prison conditions differed little. Prisoners were often starved or exposed to disease, or both. In many Continental countries, where torture was still legal, prisoners could be subjected to brutal interrogation or to random punishment. In 1777, English reformer John Howard published a report on the state of prisons in England and Wales: "The want of food is to be found in many country gaols. In about half of these, debtors have no bread, although it is granted to the highwayman, the housebreaker, and the murderer; and medical assistance, which is provided for the latter, is withheld from the former." Torture was illegal in England, except in cases of treason, but prison conditions were often as harmful to the physical and mental health of inmates as torture was.

Main Ideas and Details

Chapter 10 explains that a topic is the person, place, or thing that is the subject of a discussion. A topic is also an essential part of a main idea.

Main Ideas

A **main idea** is a statement about the specific way in which a topic is discussed. For instance, the topic *love* can be discussed in many ways, including the following:

- Why people fall in *love*
- How to know if you are in *love*
- Ways to express your *love*
- The *love* of parents for their children

These are four main ideas about *love*—four specific ways in which love can be discussed.

The main idea of the following paragraph is printed in boldface in the first sentence.

> There are **three basic types of love.** Agape is the selfless and nonsexual love for others that inspires devotion to high principles; it is the type of love to which Jesus referred when he said, "Love one another." The second type of love, philia, is the affection we have for close friends and family members who are not the object of our sexual desire. Finally, eros is the love characterized by sexual attraction that, in our society, is the basis for romance and marriage.

A main idea may be located in the first, last, or any other sentence of a paragraph. The main idea of the following paragraph is printed in boldface in the second sentence.

> For love to develop, two people must first establish rapport—a warm relationship characterized by ease of communication and mutual understanding. Rapport is most likely to develop between people

who have similar social, cultural, religious, and educational backgrounds; it is the first step of the **four-stage process through which love develops.** Rapport leads to self-revelation, in which two people reveal to each other more about themselves than they ordinarily reveal. Self-revelation may lead to the third stage—mutual dependency, in which two people become dependent on one another as <u>confidants</u>* and for doing things together. The circle is complete when mutual dependency leads to need fulfillment, in which people satisfy each other's need for someone to love.

Love is the topic of both of these paragraphs; however, they have very different main ideas, and their main ideas are located in different places in the paragraphs.

Details

Main ideas in textbooks are usually accompanied by **details,** which are explanations, examples, or other supporting information about a main idea. The relations between main ideas and details may be shown by listing details under main ideas, as in the following example:

Three Types of Love

1. Agape is selfless, nonsexual love for others that inspires devotion to high principles.

2. Philia is affection for friends and family members.

3. Eros is love characterized by sexual attraction that is the basis for romance and marriage.

The summary below shows the relations between the main idea and details in the paragraph about the four-stage process through which love develops.

Stages Through Which Love Develops

1. Rapport—two people establish a warm relationship characterized by ease of communication and mutual understanding.

2. Self-revelation—they reveal more about themselves than they usually do.

3. Mutual dependency—they depend on each other as confidants and for doing things together.

4. Need fulfillment—they satisfy each other's need for someone to love.

Exercises in this chapter, Chapter 12, and Chapter 21 provide practice in locating and listing details.

---

* Words underscored in blue are defined in the Master Vocabulary List on pages 413–425, and the exercise on page 58 is based on these words.

Help for Finding Details

College textbooks use various techniques to help you locate the details in paragraphs and longer selections, including (1) words in italics or boldface, (2) numbers, (3) bullets, and (4) statements in introductions.

1. Words printed in italics or boldface may name details. Words printed in boldface name the details that are discussed in the following passage.

Grammar

Grammar deals with three major components of language: phonology, syntax, and semantics.

Phonology refers to the sounds we make when we speak and how we use those sounds to produce meaning by placing them into the form of words. Speakers of English use just forty-six basic phonemes to produce words, while the basic phonemes of other languages range in number from a mere fifteen to as many as eighty-five. The differences in phonemes underlie one reason why people have difficulty in learning other languages: For example, to the speaker of Japanese, a language that does not have an "r" phoneme, English words such as "roar" present some difficulty.

Syntax refers to the rules that indicate how words are joined together to form sentences. Every language has intricate rules that guide the order in which words may be strung together to communicate meaning. English-speakers have no difficulty in knowing that "Radio down the turn" is not an appropriate sequence, while "Turn down the radio" is. Moreover, the importance of appropriate syntax is demonstrated by the changes in meaning that stem from modifications in the order of words in the following three sentences: "John kidnapped the boy," "John, the kidnapped boy," and "The boy kidnapped John."

The third major component of language is semantics. **Semantics** refers to the rules governing the meaning of words and sentences of language. Semantic rules allow us to use words to convey the most subtle of nuances. For instance, we are able to make the distinction between "The truck hit Laura" (which we would be likely to say if we had just seen the vehicle hitting Laura) and "Laura was hit by a truck" (which we would probably say if asked why Laura was missing class while she recuperated).

Despite the complexities of language, most people learn its grammar effortlessly and are able to communicate without referring to a complicated set of rules.

Notice that the three details, which are three components of language, are printed in boldface.

2. Arabic numerals, such as *1, 2,* and *3,* or number words such as *first, second,* and *third,* may indicate details. A combination of numerals and italics is used to indicate details in the following passage.

Normal Childhood Problems

Child specialists Chess, Thomas, and Birch (1965) have listed a number of difficulties experienced at times by almost every child. These can be considered normal reactions to the unavoidable stress of growing up.

1. All children experience occasional *sleep disturbances*, including wakefulness, frightening dreams, or a desire to get into their parents' bed.

2. *Specific fears* of the dark, dogs, school, or of a particular room or person are also common.

3. Most children will be *overly timid* at times, allowing themselves to be bullied by other children into giving up toys, a place in line, and the like.

4. Temporary periods of *general dissatisfaction* may occur during which nothing pleases the child.

5. Children also normally display periods of *general negativism* marked by tantrums, refusal to do anything requested, or a tendency to say no on principle.

6. Another normal problem is *clinging*, in which children refuse to leave the side of their mothers or to do anything on their own.

7. Development does not always advance smoothly. Every child will show occasional *reversals* or *regressions* to more infantile behavior.

An additional problem common to the elementary school years is *sibling* rivalry. Where there is more than one child in a family, it is normal for a certain amount of jealousy, rivalry, and even hostility to develop between brothers and sisters.

Numbers such as *first* and *second* are used to help you locate the details in the following passage. Underline the numbers in the passage to emphasize how many characteristics of professions are stated.

Professions

Professions are distinguished from other occupations by several characteristics. First, the skill of professionals is based on systematic, theoretical knowledge, not merely on training in particular techniques. Second, professionals have considerable autonomy over their work. Their clients are presumed to be incompetent to make judgments about the problems with which the profession is concerned: you can give instructions to your hairdresser or tailor but cannot advise a doctor or lawyer on matters of medicine or law. Third, professionals form associations that regulate their profession's internal affairs and represent its interests to outside bodies. Fourth, admission to a profession is carefully controlled by the existing members. Anyone can claim to be a salesperson or a carpenter, but someone who claims to be a surgeon or a professor without having the necessary credentials is an impostor. Becoming a professional involves taking an examination, receiving a license, and acquiring a title, and this process is usually regulated by the professional association concerned. Fifth, professions have a code of <u>ethics</u> that all their members are expected to <u>adhere</u> to.

You should have underlined the words *first, second, third, fourth,* and *fifth.*

3. Bullets may indicate details. Bullets are dots or squares that are used to draw attention to items in a list. Square bullets indicate the details in the following passage.

Emotional Health

There are many exceptions to any rule about emotional health, of course, but most authorities agree that emotionally healthy people have at least the following characteristics:

- They are able to understand reality and deal with it <u>constructively</u>.
- They can adapt to reasonable demands for change.
- They have a reasonable degree of personal <u>autonomy</u>.
- They can cope with stresses.
- They have concern for other people.
- They have an ability to love.
- They are able to work productively.
- They act in ways that meet their basic needs.

It is important to remember that our emotional health is not a <u>static</u> condition; it is a dynamic process. Our level of emotional health varies slightly day by day.

Notice that bullets give prominent emphasis to the eight characteristics of emotionally healthy people.

4. Introductory statements often give information about details. An introduction may state the number of details in a passage, or it may name the details. For example, following is the introduction to the passage entitled "Grammar," on page 157.

Grammar

Grammar deals with three major components of language: phonology, syntax, and semantics.

This introduction states that there are three details in "Grammar," and it names them: phonology, syntax, and semantics.

EXERCISE 11.1 Main Ideas and Details

Each problem in this exercise contains one main idea and four details. Check the sentence or phrase in each problem that states the main idea and underline the topic.

1. ☐ Interferes with communication
   ☐ Causes hearing loss
   ☐ Negative effects of noise
   ☐ Induces anxiety, stress, and fright
   ☐ Can lead to heart disease, colitis, and ulcers

2. ☐ Don't smoke cigarettes.
   ☐ Engage in regular exercise.
   ☐ Sleep seven to eight hours nightly.
   ☐ Use these strategies for healthy living.
   ☐ Maintain your proper weight.

3. ☐ Tell off-color jokes.
   ☐ Discuss politics and religion.
   ☐ Bite your nails and pick your nose.
   ☐ Avoid these annoying habits on the job.
   ☐ Seldom say "thank you" or give compliments.

4. ☐ Feels unprepared for taking tests
   ☐ Sees tests as difficult and threatening
   ☐ Anticipates failing tests
   ☐ Fears or dislikes the teacher
   ☐ Causes of test anxiety

5. ☐ High level of specialization in jobs
   ☐ Some characteristics of a bureaucracy
   ☐ Formal pattern for delegating authority
   ☐ Departments organized according to their function
   ☐ Formal relations between supervisors and workers

6. ☐ A sore that does not heal
   ☐ Danger signals of cancer
   ☐ Noticeable change in a wart or mole
   ☐ Change in bowel or bladder habits
   ☐ Unusual bleeding or discharge

7. ☐ Desire to find employment and acquire land
   ☐ Belief that they would find social equality
   ☐ Reasons immigrants came to the United States
   ☐ Read advertisements that encouraged immigration
   ☐ Discouragement with conditions in homeland

8. ☐ Half of new mothers have difficulty nursing.
   ☐ Some women are unable to breast-feed after their first delivery.
   ☐ A mother's breasts may be inflamed.
   ☐ The mother may take medications that are dangerous to the baby.
   ☐ There are good reasons for not breast-feeding.

EXERCISE 11.2 **Main Ideas and Details**

Read "Dreams" and answer the questions that follow it.

Dreams

Most psychologists agree that dreams have four easily recognized characteristics. First of all, they are made up of a succession of usually vivid and colorful *visual images*. Second, dreams are *fantastic* in that the space-time relationships of waking consciousness are distorted. Time may speed up or slow down, one scene may shift quickly into another without regard for logical relationships, and normally distinct concepts are condensed into unusual images. In the example above, a bowl of Jell-O, a staircase, and an algebra teacher are woven into one theme. The third characteristic of dreams is that they are often charged with *emotion*. The emotions of dreams can range from the intensely pleasurable, as in sexual dreams, to the intensely frightening, as in nightmares of being helplessly pursued. Finally, dreams have a *delusional quality*. That is, dreams are products of our imagination, yet we believe them to be real when they occur (Hobson & McCarley, 1977).

Reference

Hobson, J.A., and McCarley, R.W. (1977). The Brain as a Dream State Generator: An Activation-Synthesis Hypothesis of the Dream Process. *American Journal of Psychiatry, 134* (12), 1335–1348.

1. What is the topic? _____

2. What is the main idea?

   _____

3. Check the items in the following list that help determine the number of details in the passage.
   ☐ An introductory statement
   ☐ Words printed in italics or boldface
   ☐ Numbers such as *1, 2,* and *3*
   ☐ Numbers such as *first, second,* and *third*
   ☐ Bullets

4. How many details are in the passage? _____

5. Write the first detail on the following lines.

   _____

   _____

   _____

EXERCISE 11.3   **Main Ideas and Details**

Read "Political Participation" and answer the questions that follow it.

Political Participation

One way to understand the low rate of political participation in America is to study which groups in the population are more likely to vote than others. The widely accepted differences among groups include the following:

- Young people are less likely to vote than middle-aged and older people.

- Whites are more likely to vote than blacks and Hispanics.

- College graduates are more likely to vote than people who attended college but did not graduate, who are in turn more likely to vote than people with only a high school education or less.

- Southerners are less likely to vote than other Americans.

- Men are more likely to vote than women.

- People with jobs are more likely to vote than the unemployed.

- People who have lived in one place for a long time are more likely to vote than those who have moved recently.

- Married people are more likely to vote than singles.

It is much easier to list these differences in voter participation than it is to explain them.

1. What is the topic? _____

2. What is the main idea?

   _____

3. Check the items in the following list that help determine the number of details in the passage.
   ☐ An introductory statement
   ☐ Words printed in italics or boldface
   ☐ Numbers such as *1, 2,* and *3*
   ☐ Numbers such as *first, second,* and *third*
   ☐ Bullets

4. How many details are in the passage? _____

5. Write the first detail on the following lines.

   _____

   _____

© 1992 by Houghton Mifflin Company

EXERCISE 11.4 **Main Ideas and Details**

Read "Corrections" and answer the questions that follow it.

Corrections

Corrections are the <u>sanctions</u> and other measures that society applies to convicted criminals—in the United States, primarily imprisonment, probation, and parole. Ideally, corrections serve several distinct purposes:

1. *Retribution*. Corrections serve to punish the offender, applying revenge on behalf of both the victim and society as a whole.

2. *Deterrence*. Through punishment, corrections serve both to deter the offender from <u>deviating</u> again, and to scare others who might be tempted into crime.

3. *Incapacitation*. By imposing restrictions on the freedom of the offender, corrections help prevent that person from committing further crimes, at least for the duration of the restrictions.

4. *Rehabilitation*. Corrections may serve to reform the offender by providing the skills and attitudes that make return to a law-abiding life possible and more attractive.

For most adults convicted of the serious crime-index offenses, corrections are likely to include imprisonment. This was not always the case, for prisons are a relatively recent <u>innovation</u>. Until two centuries ago, convicts were more likely to be executed, tortured, deported, or exposed to public ridicule in the <u>stocks</u>.

1. What is the topic? _____

2. What is the main idea?

   _____

3. Check the items in the following list that help determine the number of details in the passage.
   ☐ An introductory statement
   ☐ Words printed in italics or boldface
   ☐ Numbers such as *1, 2,* and *3*
   ☐ Numbers such as *first, second,* and *third*
   ☐ Bullets

4. How many details are in the passage? _____

5. Write the first detail on the following lines.

   _____

   _____

EXERCISE 11.5   **Main Ideas and Details**

Read "India's Legacies" and answer the questions that follow it.

India's Legacies

India's most enduring legacies are the three great religions that flowered in the sixth and fifth centuries B.C.: Hinduism, Jainism, and Buddhism. One of the modern world's largest religions, Hinduism holds that the *Vedas*, or hymns in praise of the Aryan gods, are sacred revelations, and that these revelations prescribe the caste system. Religiously and philosophically diverse, Hinduism assures that there are many legitimate ways to worship Brahma, the supreme principle of life. India's best-loved hymn, the *Bhagavad Gita*, guides the Hindu in a pattern of life in the world and of release from it.

Jainism derives from the great thinker Vardhamana Mahavira (ca 540–468 B.C.), who held that only an ascetic life leads to bliss and that all life is too sacred to be destroyed. Nonviolence is a cardinal principle of Jainism. Thus, a Jain who wishes to do the least violence to life turns to vegetarianism.

Mahavira's contemporary, Siddhartha Gautama (ca 563–483 B.C.), better known as "Buddha," was so deeply distressed by human suffering that he abandoned his Hindu beliefs in a search for ultimate enlightenment. Meditation alone, he maintained, brought that total enlightenment in which everything is understood. Buddha developed the "Eightfold Path," a series of steps of meditation that could lead to *nirvana*, a state of happiness attained by the extinction of self and human desires. Buddha opposed all religious dogmatism and insisted that anyone, regardless of sex or class, could achieve enlightenment. He attracted many followers, and although Buddhism split into two branches after his death, Buddhist teachings spread throughout India to China, Japan, Korea, and Vietnam. Buddhism remains one of the great Asian religions, and in recent times has attracted adherents in the West.

1. What is the topic? _____

2. What is the main idea? _____

3. Check the items in the following list that help determine the number of details in the passage.
   □ An introductory statement
   □ Words printed in italics or boldface
   □ Numbers such as *1, 2,* and *3*
   □ Numbers such as *first, second,* and *third*
   □ Bullets

4. How many details are in the passage? _____

5. Write the first detail on the following lines. _____

   _____

EXERCISE 11.6 **Main Ideas and Details**

Underline the main ideas in the following paragraphs. Then, write the topics and details on the lines.

Water in itself has no nutritional value. Yet it is perhaps the most important of all food components! Why? A major reason is that water is the <u>medium</u> both for transporting <u>nutrients</u> to the cells of the body and for removing cellular waste products. In addition, water acts as a medium for digestion, is the body's temperature regulator, serves to cushion vital organs, and lubricates the joints. Finally, water and some of the chemicals it carries are responsible for bodily structure: The cells in our bodies contain fluid, and there is fluid around the cells too.

Topic: _____

1. _____

   _____

2. _____

   _____

3. _____

   _____

4. _____

5. _____

6. _____

7. _____

   _____

The bulk of the fresh water is frozen in icecaps or hidden in underground <u>aquifers</u>, so less than 1 percent of all the earth's water is available at the surface for human use—and much of this is in the "wrong" place. Yet modern industrial societies require huge amounts of water for domestic, agricultural, and industrial purposes: it takes 120 gallons of water to put an egg on the breakfast table, 15,000 gallons to grow a bushel of wheat, and 60,000 gallons to produce a ton of steel. American society consumes enormous quantities of water—more than 2,000 gallons a day per person, which is more than three times as much as the Japanese use.

Topic: _____

1. _____

   _____

2. _____

   _____

3. _____

   _____

4. _____

   _____

   _____

EXERCISE 11.7   Main Ideas and Details

Underline the main ideas in the following paragraphs. Then, write the topics and details on the lines.

Problems like these are resolved when you have money, a token of wealth with three main functions. First, money is a *medium of exchange*, a tool for simplifying transactions between buyers and sellers. With money in your pocket, you can go to a travel agent and get a ticket; the travel agent can give the money to the airline, which uses it to meet expenses. Second, money also functions as a *measure of value*, so you don't have to negotiate the relative worth of dissimilar items every time you buy something, as you would if you were bartering milk for airline tickets. The value of the ticket is stated in dollars, and your resources are measured in the same terms. Because of this common denominator, you can easily compare your ability to pay with the price of the item. Third, money serves as a *store of value*. Unlike many goods, it will keep. You can put it in your pocket until you need it, or you can deposit it in a bank.

Merchants increasingly used the convenient and portable paper money as a medium of exchange. The popularity of paper money also gave rise to the new profession of counterfeiting; Chinese counterfeiters risked their heads, since those inept or unlucky enough to be caught were decapitated. Paper money in turn gave rise to a system of credit and banking that enabled merchants to deposit money, take out loans, and invest in commercial ventures. Facilitated by the new monetary and banking systems, trade burgeoned so much that the Sung government derived more revenue from taxes on trade than from the traditional land tax.

Topic: _____

1. _____

_____

_____

2. _____

_____

_____

3. _____

_____

_____

Topic: _____

1. _____

_____

2. _____

_____

3. _____

_____

_____

4. _____

_____

_____

_____

EXERCISE 11.8 **Main Ideas and Details**

Underline the main ideas in the following paragraphs. Then, write the topics and details on the lines.

As actual death approaches, people are likely to feel increasingly drowsy and may be quite unaware of what is going on around them. Drugs, the disease, and the psychological distancing done by the patient tend to contribute to drowsiness. Only about 6 percent of dying patients are conscious shortly before death, and the moment of death is rarely distressful. There is even some evidence that as death approaches, the brain releases a chemical that makes the moment of death pleasant instead of painful. For most people, death comes as they would wish it—quickly, painlessly, and peacefully.

Theories abound concerning what happens when we die. Most religions build their philosophies on the issue of death and its consequences. Some promise a better life after death, in a wonderful place—a heaven with streets of gold and pearls for some Christians and Jews, a land of green meadows and running water for desert Muslims—if adherents behave according to the rules of their group and their god(s). Other religions teach that everyone is growing toward godhood in this life, and that we are born again and again until we reach that perfection. Some philosophers say that we cannot possibly know what happens after death, and that we can only judge whether life is or is not worth living according to the rewards we find or make in this life.

Topic: _____

1. _____

_____

2. _____

_____

3. _____

_____

_____

Topic: _____

1. _____

_____

_____

_____

2. _____

_____

_____

3. _____

_____

_____

4. _____

_____

_____

EXERCISE 11.9   Main Ideas and Details

Underline the main ideas in the following paragraphs. Then, write the topics and details on the lines.

What effect does divorce have on children? For most children, the experience is very trau-matic. Extreme anger, regression to earlier forms of behavior, and physical symptoms such as asthma are not uncommon. Younger children especially seem to blame themselves; older adolescents are more often angry or ashamed. For the first few months most children wish the separation could be repaired; they want the father or mother to rejoin the household. It helps if parents can explain that the child did not cause the divorce; often, children feel that something they did divided their parents.

Topic: _____

1. _____

   _____

2. _____

   _____

3. _____

   _____

4. _____

   _____

5. _____

   _____

6. _____

   _____

7. _____

   _____

Children may get hurt in three kinds of situations. Most injuries happen when a child's skills are inadequate for safe use of a product. The two-year-old on a bicycle and the ten-year-old on a minibike are likely to get hurt. In other accidents, as children are doing something they know how to do, their skills suddenly fail them, and they get hurt. For example, a child riding a bicycle suddenly loses control—perhaps skids on sand or a slippery patch or has a seizure—and falls, breaking a bone. Finally, injuries also happen when an object suddenly fails. Bicycles malfunction; toys and pieces of furniture collapse or break, and injure children.

Topic: _____

1. _____

   _____

   _____

2. _____

   _____

   _____

3. _____

   _____

Major and Minor Details

Chapter 11 introduces paragraphs that have one level of details. However, since passages often contain more than one level of details, it is necessary to distinguish between major and minor ones.

Major details are explanations, examples, or other supporting information about a main idea, and **minor details** are explanations, examples, or other supporting information about a major detail. For instance:

> My best friends are Ruby, Rita, and Rhoda, who is an excellent cook.

In this sentence, the main idea is "my best friends," the major details are "Ruby," "Rita," and "Rhoda," and the minor detail is the statement about Rhoda ("who is an excellent cook").

Minor Details

The word *minor* is often used to mean "not very important," as in "I have a minor head cold." However, *minor* in the term *minor detail* is used to explain a relationship among details, not to identify whether details are important or unimportant. A minor detail in one context may be a major detail in other contexts. For instance, *history* and *chemistry* are minor details in the following outline.

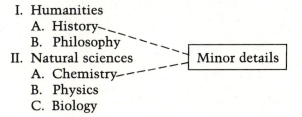

Some College Subjects

I. Humanities
   A. History
   B. Philosophy
II. Natural sciences
   A. Chemistry
   B. Physics
   C. Biology

Minor details

Whereas *history* and *chemistry* are minor details labeled by capital letters in this context, they are major details labeled by Roman numerals in the following outline.

Some College Subjects

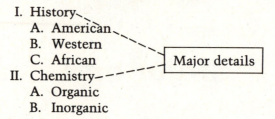

   I. History
      A. American
      B. Western
      C. African
  II. Chemistry
      A. Organic
      B. Inorganic

Major details

Keep in mind that the terms *major detail* and *minor detail* are used simply to explain a relationship in a specific context, not to identify whether the details are important or unimportant—a minor detail in one context may be a major detail in other contexts.

Details in Outlines

An **outline** is a well-organized summary of information, such as the outline on page 171, which summarizes the information in the following passage.

Romantic and Mature Love

Sexual attraction is the basis for romantic love and mature love—two very different forms of love.

Romantic lovers unrealistically idealize one another, and they attempt to possess each other completely. When they are apart, they suffer real pain because they feel incomplete when they are not with their lovers. Romantic lovers expect to feel love and passion only for each other, and they tend to be jealous of one another.

Mature lovers, on the other hand, completely accept their lovers as they are—they don't idealize them. They allow each other freedom to grow and develop potential to the fullest, and they feel complete when they are separated from each other. Though they are sexually faithful to one another, they experience and enjoy deep affection for others who are close to them. Within a relationship based on mature love, sex is a means of expressing intense caring, acceptance, and intimacy.

Compare this passage to the outline on page 171 before you do the exercises in this chapter.

Outlines

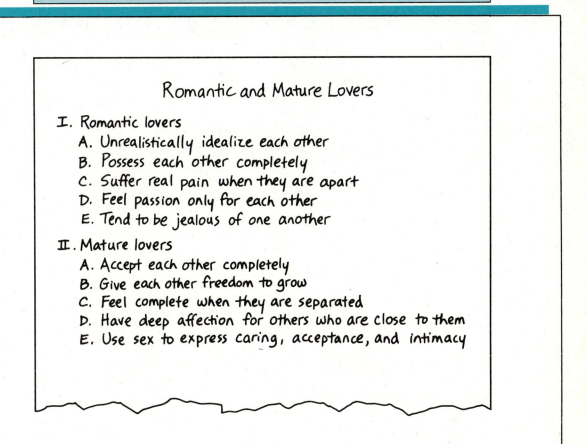

Romantic and Mature Lovers

I. Romantic lovers
   A. Unrealistically idealize each other
   B. Possess each other completely
   C. Suffer real pain when they are apart
   D. Feel passion only for each other
   E. Tend to be jealous of one another

II. Mature lovers
   A. Accept each other completely
   B. Give each other freedom to grow
   C. Feel complete when they are separated
   D. Have deep affection for others who are close to them
   E. Use sex to express caring, acceptance, and intimacy

This is an outline of the passage entitled "Romantic and Mature Love," on page 170; it is a well-organized summary that shows the relationships among the major and minor details in the passage.

Outlines prepared in the traditional format have the following characteristics:

- The title states the topic or main idea.
- Major details are labeled with Roman numerals.
- Minor details are labeled with capital letters.

Exercises in this chapter provide practice in making outlines in the traditional format.

EXERCISE 12.1 Exercise

Make an outline of the following passage on the lines at the bottom of this page.

The physical benefits of exercise are well known. Exercise strengthens the heart and lungs, improves endurance, increases flexibility of the joints, improves digestion and elimination, and even reduces menstrual discomfort in many women. However, the psychological benefits are not familiar to many college students. Studies have found that even a short walk can relieve anxiety. In addition, exercise reduces free-floating* hostility, improves concentration and alertness, and reduces symptoms of depression.

Title: _____

   I. _____

      A. _____

      B. _____

      C. _____

      D. _____

      E. _____

  II. _____

      A. _____

      B. _____

      C. _____

      D. _____

*Words underscored in blue are defined in the Master Vocabulary List on pages 413–425, and the exercise on page 59 is based on these words.

EXERCISE 12.2 **Families**

Make an outline of the following passage on the lines at the bottom of the page.

A **nuclear family** consists of a married couple and their children. Most people are born into a nuclear family—their family of <u>orientation</u>—and then go on to establish a nuclear family of their own—their family of <u>procreation</u>. The only possible members of a *family of orientation* are a mother, father, brothers, and sisters. Your *family of procreation* may include your husband or wife, sons, and daughters.

Exactly who is a member of an **extended family** differs from country to country. In the United States the extended family is usually considered to include children, parents, and other relatives who live with them in the same house or very near by.

Title: _____

I. _____

    _____

   A. _____

    _____

   B. _____

    _____

II. _____

   A. _____

   B. _____

   C. _____

    _____

EXERCISE 12.3   Daydreams

Make an outline of the following passage on the lines at the bottom of this page.

Two of the most common daydream "plots" are the conquering hero and the suffering martyr themes. In a conquering hero fantasy, the daydreamer is a famous, rich, or powerful person: a star, athlete, musician, famous surgeon, brilliant lawyer, or magnificent lover. Themes such as these seem to reflect mastery needs and escape from the frustrations and compromises of everyday life. Suffering martyr daydreams are built around feelings of being neglected, hurt, rejected, or unappreciated by others. In suffering martyr fantasies, some event occurs that causes others to regret their actions and to realize what a wonderful person the daydreamer was all along. At one time or another, just about everyone has felt misunderstood or unappreciated. These feelings seem to underlie suffering martyr daydreams.

Title: _____

   I. _____

      A. _____

        _____

      B. _____

        _____

  II. _____

      A. _____

        _____

      B. _____

        _____

EXERCISE 12.4   **The Presidency**

Make an outline of the following passage on the lines at the bottom of this page.

The formal requirements for those seeking the presidency are not particularly difficult to meet. The Constitution says that to be president a citizen must be "natural born," thirty-five years of age or older, and a resident within the United States for fourteen years. Of course, many other conditions also have to be met before a person can realistically hope to be president of the United States. For a candidate to have a chance, he must be male, white, and Christian (until recently, Protestant). He must be nominated by the Republicans or Democrats. And his political beliefs must be in the mainstream. Unusual or extreme ideas are unlikely to attract a plurality of the voters. These restrictions eliminate major segments of the population from serious consideration, regardless of their abilities.

Title: _____

I. _____

    A. _____

    B. _____

    C. _____

II. _____

    A. _____

    B. _____

    C. _____

    D. _____

EXERCISE 12.5   Packaging

Make an outline of the following passage on the lines at the bottom of this page.

The packaging of products you purchase serves several important purposes. Packaging around such items as stereo receivers and television sets protects them from damage and makes them easier to ship, and some packaging around food and drugs protects them from tampering. The packaging around many products makes them easier for storekeepers to display, more attractive to customers, and more difficult for shoplifters to take. Packaging also often provides a convenience to customers. Dispenser packages make products such as dishwashing detergent easier to use, and plastic trays <u>facilitate</u> heating frozen food without dirtying a pan.

Title: _____

    I. _____

        A. _____

        B. _____

   II. _____

        A. _____

        B. _____

  III. _____

  IV. _____

   V. _____

  VI. _____

        A. _____

        B. _____

EXERCISE 12.6   The Ego-Defense Mechanisms

Make an outline of the following passage on a sheet of notebook paper. Use the following Roman numerals and capital letters in your outline: I, A, B, C, II, A, B, III, A, B, C.

The Ego-Defense Mechanisms

As the "executive" of the personality, the ego strives to direct behavior in ways that satisfy the id, the superego, and the demands of reality. In attempting to achieve this goal, the ego develops several defense mechanisms. These **ego-defense mechanisms** are unconscious strategies used by the ego to shield itself from threatening perceptions, feelings, and impulses. The defense mechanisms help keep the demands of the id and the dictates of the superego under control. In doing so, they reduce feelings of anxiety and keep other feelings, such as guilt, conflict, and anger, from overwhelming the ego. However, the ways of behaving and viewing the world that result from these mechanisms are not always effective or realistic. The defense mechanisms can be divided into three groups: (1) the behavior-channeling defense mechanisms, (2) the primary reality-distorting mechanisms, and (3) the secondary reality-distorting mechanisms.

Behavior-Channeling Defenses

The three behavior-channeling defenses are *identification*, *displacement*, and *sublimation*. These mechanisms direct behavior in ways that protect the person from conflict, anxiety, or harm. For the most part, they produce realistic behavior that the person feels is moral.

Identification involves attempting to resolve conflicts about one's behavior by identifying with another person who appears successful, realistic, and moral—trying to act as much like that person as possible. Freud regarded identification as a relatively healthy defense mechanism. Conflicts about behavior are generally accompanied by anxiety. By resolving conflicts, identification also reduces anxiety.

Displacement directs aggressive behavior away from someone or something that has aroused anger toward someone against whom it is both safe and morally acceptable to aggress. For example, a man who has been angered by his boss might fear being hostile toward him and might therefore honk his horn at a fellow commuter on the way home, shout at his wife, ridicule his son, or kick his dog. In all of these instances, he is displacing aggression in a way that he feels is safe and acceptable.

Sublimation entails expressing drives for pleasure or aggression in socially acceptable ways. In this way, the id obtains partial satisfaction while the superego's dictates are followed. For example, a person might sublimate his sexual drives into painting highly respectable representations of nudes. Aggressive drives might be channeled into studying military history or playing contact sports. Freud felt that sublimation was extremely important for civilized existence and social achievement.

Primary Reality-Distorting Defenses

One of the most basic ways the ego protects itself from feelings or perceptions that cause anxiety is simply not to feel or perceive them. The two defense mechanisms that protect the ego by keeping threatening feelings or perceptions out of awareness are *repression* and *denial*. They are called primary reality-distorting mechanisms because they are the first line of defense. They protect the ego from even being aware of threats.

Repression entails blocking from awareness unacceptable unconscious drives such as sexual feelings or impulses, aggressive thoughts or wishes, or feelings of guilt emanating from the superego. For example, a person who feels guilty for cheating on an exam may simply repress these feelings and not consciously experience them.

Denial is the defense mechanism used to keep threatening perceptions of the external world, rather than internal drives and feelings, out of awareness. For example, a person living in California may simply refuse to admit that earthquakes threaten his life and home, or a smoker may deny that cigarettes are hazardous to her health.

Secondary Reality-Distorting Defenses

Repression and denial simply push threatening feelings and perceptions out of awareness. However, other defense mechanisms often are called into play following denial or repression (White & Watt, 1981). The three secondary reality-distorting mechanisms we will discuss are *projection, reaction formation,* and *rationalization.*

Projection involves perceiving personal characteristics in other people that you cannot admit in yourself. For example, a man might repress his own sexual feelings toward his brother's wife and then project those feelings onto her. Thus, the man will perceive that his brother's wife is sexually interested in him. Another common example is for people to project feelings of anger felt toward others onto those other people. A student who is angry with her roommate might project her anger and perceive the roommate as angry or hostile.

Reaction formation is consciously feeling or acting the strong opposite of one's true unconscious feelings because the true feelings are threatening. For example, a girl who hates her father may repress those feelings and consciously experience strong feelings of affection for him instead. These feelings are due to reaction formation.

Rationalization, a very common defense mechanism, involves generating a socially acceptable explanation for behavior that may be caused by unacceptable drives. For example, a person may rationalize aggression by saying that another person deserved to be punished or harmed. A man may rationalize sexually harassing a woman by telling himself that she really wants to have sex with him, even if she does not admit it.

Reference

White, R.W., and Watt, N.F. (1981). *The Abnormal Personality*. New York: Wiley.

Expository Patterns

As a college student you will read and study many textbooks that contain **exposition**—writing that gives explanations and information. Exposition in textbooks very often:

- defines words
- explains methods
- describes sequences
- present lists of various kinds

This chapter explains how to identify these expository patterns in the textbooks you study for your college courses.

Definitions

Each college subject has its own **terminology**—words or phrases that have specific meanings within that subject. For example, *depression* is a term used with different meanings in the study of meteorology, business, and psychology. In meteorology, it specifies a condition that is associated with low barometric pressure. In business *depression* means "a period of low employment, wages, and prices," and in psychology it refers to feelings of hopelessness and inadequacy. Sometimes terms are phrases of two or more words. For instance, the phrase *fruits of a crime* is used in law and criminology to refer to anything that comes into a criminal's possession as the result of a crime. Additional examples of terminology for college subjects are listed on page 49.

In textbooks, terms are often explained using definitions and examples. A **definition** is a statement of the meaning of a word; the definition of *beverage* is "a liquid for drinking." An **example** is something selected to show the general characteristics of whatever is named by a term; examples of beverages include milk, orange juice, coffee, and beer.

The following excerpt from an English textbook illustrates the way in which terminology is often defined.

Idioms

Idioms, groups of words that together establish an idiosyncratic* meaning, are often illogical if examined word for word. For example, *break it up*, commonly understood to mean "stop fighting," does not make sense when examined one word at a time. *Break*, to split into two or more pieces, creates a visual image of fighters separating. *It*, though indefinite, clearly refers to the implied subject, *fight*. *Up* defies explanation unless it is considered part of the idiom *break up*. Other unanalyzable idioms include *pick up* (*the house*), *take a shower*, *fall in love*, and *catch a cold*. Such idioms have developed along with our language, and although they may not make literal sense, they are understood.

This paragraph states the definition of the *idioms* and gives several examples of the term.

Methods

Methods are the procedures or processes used to do something. Some textbooks are devoted almost entirely to explaining the ways things are done—textbooks for mathematics and foreign language courses, for instance. *RSVP* explains methods for improving vocabulary, reading, study, and test-taking skills.

The following excerpt from a human relations textbook explains how to write affirmations.

Affirmations

When you want to take control of your self-esteem, focus self-talk on your positive thoughts. Learn how to write *affirmations* for each of your goals. Affirmations are self-talk statements declaring your goals and the qualities you want to develop. When creating your personal and professional affirmations, be sure to follow these guidelines:

1. Begin each affirmation with a first-person pronoun, such as *I*, or *my*.

2. Use a present-tense verb, such as *am, have, feel, create, approve, do,* or *choose*.

3. Describe the end results you want to achieve. Be sure to phrase the statement *toward* where you want to go, not away from what you don't want. Say, "I am a slim, trim 120 pounds," as opposed to "I am losing 30 pounds."

Write affirmations for different facets of your personal and professional life, such as "I do my own thinking and make my own decisions," "I am filled with a feeling of quiet calmness," and "I am an

* Words underscored in blue are defined in the Master Vocabulary List on pages 413–425, and the exercise on page 59 is based on these words.

© 1992 by Houghton Mifflin Company

employee who is able to be a strong team member." Put your affirmations on three-by-five-inch index cards and attach them to your bathroom mirror, refrigerator, car dashboard, desk blotter, and so on. Your brain is like a computer. It will put out exactly what you put in. If you put positive self-talk in, positive behavior will result.

Some textbooks also give information about methods that are used by professionals. For instance, the following passage from a psychology textbook explains methods psychologists use to study the development of metamemory. The purpose of the explanation is to inform you about methods psychologists use, not to train you in how to do the things that practicing psychologists do.

Metamemory

The development of memory strategies is only part of a growing competence in memory and reasoning. In the middle childhood years, children also begin to reflect on their own memory and reasoning skills. **Metamemory,** or knowledge about memory—knowing how much one can remember, how long it takes to commit something to memory, and the like—is the term used to define this capacity.

How do psychologists study the development of metamemory? One way is to determine what people of different ages know about the limits of their memory capacity. For example, in a typical study an experimenter placed two pictures of common objects in front of subjects ranging in age from 5 to 20 years. The subjects were asked if they thought they would be able to name the objects in the pictures *after* the experimenter covered them up. The experimenter continued with this procedure, gradually increasing the number of pictures from 2 to 10. On each trial the subjects guessed whether they could remember the objects, while the experimenter tested their actual ability to do so. When did the subjects realize the limits of their memory capacity? The children under 7 years of age consistently overestimated their ability to remember the pictures. They often thought that they could recall many more pictures than they were capable of remembering. But by 9 or 10 years of age, the children gave realistic estimates of what they could remember. In fact, children of this age estimated what they could remember about as accurately as the 20-year-old subjects (Flavell & Wellman, 1976).

Reference
Flavell, J.H., and Wellman, H.M. (1976). Metamemory. In R.V. Kail and J.W. Hagen (eds.). *Memory in Cognitive Development*. Hillsdale, NY: Erlbaum.

Sequences

A **sequence** is the order in which things follow each other in time, space, rank, or some other dimension.

Time sequences are explained in many textbooks, including those used to study history. To think intelligently about the history of the United States, for instance, it is necessary to understand the order in which presidents were in office and the sequence in which major wars were fought.

This type of sequence is called *time sequence, chronological sequence,* or *temporal sequence*—all three terms have the same meaning.

Spatial sequences are important in the study of such subjects as astronomy and geography. For instance, those who know the order of planets in space know that a rocket flying away from Earth must pass the orbits of Mars and Jupiter before reaching Saturn.

In *hierarchical sequences,* items are arranged by complexity, importance, or rank. In biology, for instance, forms of life are organized in hierarchical sequence, beginning with the least complex and advancing to the most complex. In this arrangement of animal life, the one-celled protozoa are at the bottom, and apes are very near the top of the hierarchy.

Sequences are often indicated by dates or other numbers, as in the following example.

Changes Time Brings

Many of the changes time brings have more to do with the way you look than with the way you feel. At age 30, you'll have a few lines on your forehead. At age 40, you'll find "crows' feet" (from squinting) at the corners of your eyes and arcs (from smiling) linking your nostrils to the sides of your mouth. At age 50, the lines will look more pronounced, and the skin at your cheeks may sag; and at age 60, excess skin and fat deposits may form bags under your eyes. At age 70, your skin will be rougher; your face will be wrinkled; and after seven decades of gravity's pull, your ear lobes will be ¼ inch longer than when you were 20 years old.

Reference
Groch, J., and Winter, R. (May 1984). Biological markers. *American Health.*

This passage describes a time sequence—the physical changes that occur at ages 30, 40, 50, 60, and 70.

Sequences are also often indicated by the words *stages, steps,* and *phases.* Read the following passage and underline the names of the stages of courtship.

Courtship

How can people make sure they're marrying someone truly compatible? One way is by taking plenty of time to get to know the other person. Social scientists have noted that courting couples seem to go through three stages. First, in what's called the "stimulus stage," each person tries to measure his or her own good and bad qualities against those of the other; people tend to be drawn to others who seem to have about the same assets and liabilities as themselves (for example, people who are about equally good-looking or popular). Next, in the "value stage," the couple look for compatible beliefs, attitudes, and interests to support their initial attraction. But it isn't until they get to the "role stage" that they reveal to each other how they handle responsibility, react to disappointment, and cope with a wide variety of life situations. The key to compatibility is to be sure you've arrived at this last stage before you think seriously about marrying each other. Those who marry during this stage are less likely to be unpleasantly surprised than those who <u>impulsively</u> marry on short acquaintance.

You should have underlined "stimulus stage," "value stage," and "role stage."

Lists

A **list** is a presentation of a series of items of any kind; it is by far the most common pattern used in textbooks. Very often a list contains one of the following types of information.

causes	criteria	theories	characteristics
effects	purposes	categories	kinds
reasons	factors	advantages	differences
functions	types	disadvantages	similarities

Following are two passages that contain lists. The first passage gives a list of *norms*, or standards.

Eye Contact

In our society there are three basic *norms*, or standards, by which we judge eye contact. For one thing, when we communicate with others, we expect them to look at us; we consider people to be rude if they don't look at us when we talk with them. We also interpret sustained eye contact as an invitation to communicate. Some students avoid eye contact with their teachers because they fear teachers may ask them a question or invite them to make a contribution to class discussions. Finally, depending on the situation, we often understand eye contact to indicate physical attraction. When members of the opposite sex linger while gazing into our eyes at a party, we assume there is something about our appearance that appeals to them.

This passage presents a list of three norms for eye contact.

Norms for Eye Contact

1. We consider people rude if they don't look at us when we talk with them.

2. We interpret sustained eye contact as an invitation to communicate.

3. We often understand eye contact to indicate physical attraction.

The second example presents a list of *theories*.

Dreams

People are generally puzzled by their dreams, and many theories have tried to explain the functions of dreams. Early theorists felt that dreams helped to eliminate mental tensions that had built up during the day. Freud stated that the purpose of dreaming is to satisfy a wish. He felt that dreams guard your sleep; they enable you to carry out impulses, unfulfilled during the day, that might have disturbed your sleep. Carl Jung is believed to have analyzed over 100,000 dreams. He felt that you dream about things that you are lacking in your waking life. Another common theory of dreams states that their function is simply that of problem solving. Dreaming may be a continuation of thinking about your daily problems. A dream may show you how to deal with your needs and wishes.

This passage contains a list of four theories about dreams.

Theories About Dreams

1. They help eliminate mental tensions that build up during the day.

2. They satisfy wishes and enable us to carry out unfulfilled impulses (Freud).

3. They are about things we lack in our waking life (Carl Jung).

4. They help us solve problems and show us how to deal with our needs and wishes.

These examples show lists of norms and theories; however, expository passages may also present lists of causes, effects, factors, purposes, advantages, and many other kinds of information.

EXERCISE 13.1   Romantic Love

Read "Romantic Love" and then answer the questions at the bottom of the page.

Romantic Love

Romantic love is a noble ideal, and it can certainly help provide a basis for the spouses to "live happily ever after." But since marriage can equally well be founded on much more practical considerations, why is romantic love of such importance in the modern world? The reason seems to be that it has the following basic functions in maintaining the institution of the <u>nuclear family</u> (Goode, 1959):

1. *Transfer of loyalties.* Romantic love helps the young partners to loosen their bonds with their family of <u>orientation</u>, a step that is essential if they are to establish an independent nuclear family. Their total <u>absorption</u> in one another <u>facilitates</u> a transfer of commitment from existing family and kin to a new family of <u>procreation</u>.

2. *Emotional support.* Romantic love provides the couple with emotional support in the difficulties that they face in establishing a new life on their own. This love would not be so necessary in an extended family, where the relatives are able to confront problems cooperatively.

3. *Incentive to marriage.* Romantic love serves as bait to lure people into marriage. In the modern world, people have considerable choice over whether they will get married or not. A contract to form a lifelong commitment to another person is not necessarily a very tempting proposition, however: to some, the prospect may look more like a noose than like a bed of roses. Without feelings of romantic love, many people might have no incentive to marry.

To most of us, particularly to those who are in love, romantic love seems to be the most natural thing in the world, but it is a purely cultural product, arising in certain societies for specific reasons. In a different time or in a different society, you might never fall in love, nor would you expect to.

Reference
Goode, W.J. (1959). The Theoretical Importance of Love. *American Sociological Review,* 24, 38–47.

1. Write the word missing from the following revised title for the passage:

   "_____ Romantic Love Is Important"

2. Check the statement that best describes the passage and write an answer to the question that follows the statement.
   - ☐ *It defines words.* What words does it define?
   - ☐ *It explains a method.* What are the steps of the method?
   - ☐ *It describes a sequence.* What are the items in the sequence?
   - ☐ *It presents a list.* What are the items in the list?

EXERCISE 13.2   The Black Death

Read "The Black Death" and then answer the questions at the bottom of the page.

The Black Death

In 1291 Genoese sailors had opened the Straits of Gibraltar to Italian shipping by defeating the Moroccans. Then, shortly after 1300, important advances were made in the design of Italian merchant ships. A square rig was added to the mainmast, and ships began to carry three masts instead of just one. Additional sails better utilized wind power to propel the ship. The improved design permitted year-round shipping for the first time, and Venetian and Genoese merchant ships could sail the dangerous Atlantic coast even in the winter months. With ships continually at sea, the rats that bore the disease spread rapidly beyond the Mediterranean to Atlantic and North Sea ports.

Around 1331 the bubonic plague broke out in China. In the course of the next fifteen years, merchants, traders, and soldiers carried the disease across the Asian caravan routes until in 1346 it reached the Crimea in southern Russia. From there the plague had easy access to the Mediterranean lands and western Europe.

In October 1347, Genoese ships brought the plague to Messina, from which it spread throughout Sicily. Venice and Genoa were hit in January 1348, and from the port of Pisa the disease spread south to Rome and east to Florence and all Tuscany. By late spring, southern Germany was attacked. Frightened French authorities chased a galley bearing the disease from the port of Marseilles, but not before plague had infected the city, from which it spread to Languedoc and Spain. In June 1348, two ships entered the Bristol Channel and introduced it into England. All Europe felt the scourge of this horrible disease.

1. Write another title for the passage.

   _____

2. Check the statement that best describes the passage and write an answer to the question that follows the statement.
   □ *It defines words.* What words does it define?
   □ *It explains a method.* What are the steps of the method?
   □ *It describes a sequence.* What are the items in the sequence?
   □ *It presents a list.* What are the items in the list?

EXERCISE 13.3 **Conversations**

Read "Conversations" and then answer the questions at the bottom of the page.

Conversations

How do you go about striking up a conversation with strangers? For some people the advice given in this next section will be second nature. For those who find starting conversations difficult, however, the following suggestions for <u>initial</u> <u>interaction</u> with a stranger may be some of the most important information in this chapter.

1. *Formally or informally introduce yourself.* Start a conversation with a person by introducing yourself (or by getting someone else to introduce you). For example, "Hi, my name is Gordon. What's yours?" may sound trite, but it works. Or you might have a friend introduce you by saying, "Doris, I'd like you to meet my friend Bill. Bill, Doris is Susan's sister."

2. *Refer to the physical <u>context</u>.* One of the safest ways of starting a conversation is by referring to some aspect of the physical context. Certainly, one of the oldest and most effective of these is a comment about the weather: "This is awful weather for a game, isn't it?" Other contextual references include such statements as "They've really decorated this place beautifully," "I wonder how they are able to keep such a beautiful garden in this climate?" and "Doesn't it seem stuffy in here?"

3. *Refer to your thoughts or feelings.* A very direct way to make contact is by commenting on what you are thinking or feeling at the moment: "I really like parties, don't you?" or "I live on this floor too—do these steps bother you as much as they do me?"

4. *Refer to the other person.* "I don't believe I've ever seen you— have you been working here long?" "President and Mrs. Phillips have sure done a lovely job of remodeling this home. Did you ever see it before the renovation?"

None of these statements is particularly threatening, so if the person you want to meet feels the same way about you, chances are he or she will respond pleasantly.

1. Write a title that better describes the information in the passage.

_____

2. Check the statement that best describes the passage and write an answer to the question that follows the statement.
   ☐ *It defines words.* What words does it define?
   ☐ *It explains a method.* What are the steps of the method?
   ☐ *It describes a sequence.* What are the items in the sequence?
   ☐ *It presents a list.* What are the items in the list?

EXERCISE 13.6   **News**

Read "News" and then answer the questions at the bottom of the page.

News

Doris A. Graber has argued that five criteria are used most often for choosing news stories, and all are related to popular appeal rather than political significance (1). First, the content of stories must have a *high impact* on the audience. The kidnapping of a local child will usually be more interesting than the deaths of many unknown persons far away. Second, interest will be heightened if a story deals with "natural or man-made *violence, conflict, disaster,* or *scandal*" (2). People find events of this sort endlessly fascinating in real life as well as in the world of fiction.

Familiarity is the third element of newsworthiness. The more the public knows about famous people and institutions, the more they want to know. Thus established politicians and celebrities receive more coverage than persons who have not yet found a way to public prominence. Fourth, the public likes *novel* and *up-to-date* stories. Interest can wane quickly. Finally, *local events* are generally more newsworthy than stories from far away. As Graber points out, this kind of interest is what keeps small town newspapers and local television alive. Local can be an elastic term, however. Washington and Hollywood have become so familiar that they may seem local to the regular TV viewer.

References
1. These factors are discussed in Graber, D. (1984). *Mass Media and American Politics.* 2nd ed. Washington, DC: Congressional Quarterly Press, 78–79.
2. Ibid., p. 78.

1. Write the word missing from the following revised title for the passage:

   "_____ for Choosing News Stories"

2. Check the statement that best describes the passage and write an answer to the question that follows the statement.
   ☐ *It defines words.* What words does it define?
   ☐ *It explains a method.* What are the steps of the method?
   ☐ *It describes a sequence.* What are the items in the sequence?
   ☐ *It presents a list.* What are the items in the list?

EXERCISE 13.7   The Looking-Glass Self

Read "The Looking-Glass Self" and then answer the questions at the bottom of the page.

The Looking-Glass Self

Charles Horton Cooley (1864–1929) was an American economist turned social psychologist. He held that self-concepts are formed early in childhood and then reevaluated throughout life whenever a person enters a new social situation.

The central concept in Cooley's theory is the **looking-glass self**—a self-concept <u>derived</u> from a social "mirror" in which we can observe how others react to us. Our concept of ourselves is derived from this reflection, for we learn from other people's responses to us whether we are attractive or ugly, popular or unpopular, respectable or <u>disreputable</u>. According to Cooley (1902), the process of developing the self involves three steps.

1. *Imagining our own appearance.* First, we imagine what appearance and personality we present to others. We may imagine ourselves as witty, intelligent, slim, helpful, or perhaps as something quite the opposite.

2. *Interpreting others' reactions.* Second, we imagine how others judge the appearance and personality that we think we present. Do they really see us the way we imagine we appear, or are they receiving a different impression?

3. *Developing self-concept.* Third, we use our interpretation of others' judgments to develop feelings about ourselves. If the image we find in the social mirror is favorable, our self-concept is <u>enhanced</u>; if the image is unfavorable, our self-concept is diminished.

Of course, people may misjudge the way others see them. All of us make misinterpretations at times, and some people <u>habitually</u> misjudge the opinion of others and have unrealistically high or low self-concepts as a result. But whether our reading of the image in the "looking glass" is accurate or not, it is through this interpretation that we learn our identity. There can be no self without society, no "I" without a corresponding "they" to provide our self-image.

1. Write the word missing from the following revised title for the passage:

   "_____ in the Process of Developing the Self"

2. Check the statement that best describes the passage and write an answer to the question that follows the statement.
   □ *It defines words.* What words does it define?
   □ *It explains a method.* What are the steps of the method?
   □ *It describes a sequence.* What are the items in the sequence?
   □ *It presents a list.* What are the items in the list?

EXERCISE 13.8   Intimate Relationships

Read "Intimate Relationships" and then answer the questions.

Intimate Relationships

Relationships can end because a couple was mismatched to start with, or because the association did not <u>evolve</u> and <u>thrive</u> over time—usually some of both. It's tempting to consider relationships that fail as mistakes. But sometimes a perfectly good relationship at the time may outlive its usefulness if partners grow apart from each other.

Sometimes it's hard to know where you stand in a relationship. Consider your partner's words as well as deeds, in making an assessment. Intimacy implies trust but neither blind trust nor a <u>compulsive</u> need for absolute certainty work well. Make your feelings known, and expect <u>reciprocal</u> openness. Beyond that, nagging attempts to <u>extract</u> confessions of love, for example, merely drive a partner away. When <u>ethical</u>, emotional, and practical considerations suggest a parting of the ways, bear in mind the following:

1. Give the relationship an honest decent chance before you break it up. You can then make a cleaner break, have fewer doubts, and feel less guilt.

2. Be fair and honest. You owe it to yourself and to your friend, lover, or spouse to learn something from the experience so you don't repeat the same mistakes in the next relationship.

3. Be tactful and <u>compassionate</u>. Your freedom from a burdensome relationship need not be gained at the cost of damaging another person's self-esteem. Rather than dwelling on the partner's short-comings, emphasize your mutual lack of fit and admit your own contributions to the problem.

4. If you are the rejected one, give yourself time to resolve the bitterness you are apt to feel. Then be forgiving. As in response to other losses, you will need to go through a process of "mourning." You may first feel disbelief ("This can't be happening to me"), then anger, then sadness, and finally acceptance. Despite all the romantic talk about "one and only" loves, you actually have many potential candidates with whom you can establish intimate relationships.

1. Write a title that better describes the information in the passage.

   _____

2. Check the statement that best describes the passage and write an answer to the question that follows the statement.
   - ☐ *It defines words.* What words does it define?
   - ☐ *It explains a method.* What are the steps of the method?
   - ☐ *It describes a sequence.* What are the items in the sequence?
   - ☐ *It presents a list.* What are the items in the list?

EXERCISE 13.9   Human Population

Read "Human Population" and then answer the questions at the bottom of the page.

Human Population

No human population is ever completely stable. Some populations grow and others decline. The size of some populations changes rapidly, while that of others changes much more slowly. Some populations have a high proportion of young people; others, of old people. These and other population characteristics are the result of social and environmental processes that can be analyzed through the science of **demography,** the study of the size, composition, distribution, and changes in human population.

Population growth or decline in a given society is affected by three factors: the birth rate, the death rate, and the rate of migration into or out of the society. The **birth rate** (or "fertility" rate) is the annual number of births per thousand members of a population. In the impoverished Asian country of Bangladesh, for example, the birth rate is high, 43 per thousand; in Canada it is low, 15 per thousand. The **death rate** (or "mortality" rate) is the annual number of deaths per thousand members of a population. In Bangladesh the death rate is high, 17 per thousand, while in Canada it is comparatively low, 7 per thousand. The **migration rate** is the annual difference between the number of immigrants (people entering) or emigrants (people leaving) per thousand members of the population.

Changes in population size are measured by the **growth rate,** the difference between the number of people added to, and the number of people subtracted from, a population, expressed as an annual percentage. The average world growth rate at the moment is about 1.7 percent per year. The United States now has a relatively low annual growth rate of 0.7 percent. . . .

1. Write a title that better describes the information in the passage.

   _____

2. Check the statement that best describes the passage and write an answer to the question that follows the statement.
   □ *It defines words.* What words does it define?
   □ *It explains a method.* What are the steps of the method?
   □ *It describes a sequence.* What are the items in the sequence?
   □ *It presents a list.* What are the items in the list?

EXERCISE 13.10   **Sports**

Read "Sports" and then answer the questions at the bottom of the page.

Sports

Like any other institution, sport serves various functions for the social system as a whole. Among the functions that have been identified are the following:

1. *Leisure activities.* Sport provides organized leisure activities for the population—a useful function in a society where people have a good deal of free time.

2. *Physical exercise.* Sport encourages people to engage in vigorous physical activity, which is important in a society where people get little exercise.

3. *Role models.* Sport provides, through famous athletes, role models whose skills and determination are held up for public emulation.

4. *Outlet for energies.* Sport may act as a "safety valve" for spectators and participants, allowing them to express aggressive or competitive energies in a generally harmless way.

5. *Reinforcement of values.* Sport serves to reinforce many of the basic values of society, such as teamwork, competition, discipline, and obedience to rules.

Changes in sport, like those in any other institution, parallel changes in the wider society. Until about a hundred years ago, Americans' favorite sports were such activities as foot racing, boat racing, cockfighting, hunting, and fishing; the large-scale spectator sports of football, baseball, hockey, and basketball were virtually unknown, and became popular only as the nation was transformed from a predominantly rural, agricultural society into an urban, industrial one.

1. Write the word missing from the following revised title for the passage:

   "_____ of Sports"

2. Check the statement that best describes the passage and write an answer to the question that follows the statement.
   ☐ *It defines words.* What words does it define?
   ☐ *It explains a method.* What are the steps of the method?
   ☐ *It describes a sequence.* What are the items in the sequence?
   ☐ *It presents a list.* What are the items in the list?

Visual Material

Most textbooks contain visual information as well as verbal information. The verbal information is conveyed in words, and the visual information is presented in a variety of ways including photographs, diagrams, graphs, tables, and charts.

This chapter explains how to interpret pictures, graphs, charts, diagrams and other **visual material.**

Cartoons

A **cartoon** is a drawing depicting a humorous situation, often accompanied by a caption. Textbook authors use cartoons to make amusing comments or to provoke thought about topics in their books. For example, the cartoon below is used in a popular sociology textbook to make a satiric comment on a serious discussion about sexual harassment and date rape.

Interpret a cartoon by studying the drawing and reading the caption to decide whether it is amusing to you. Then try to figure out how the cartoon is related to a topic in the text.

"I know you expect something in return for the movie, the flowers, and the dinner. Wait here and I'll get you a receipt."

© 1986 Artemis Cole

Photographs

Photographs are sometimes used primarily to decorate a book. However, they are usually used for one or more of the following purposes:

- to show the characteristics of something
- to illustrate or elaborate on a point made in the text
- to arouse an emotional response

The photograph below shows the characteristics of something. By studying the photograph you can learn that cumulus clouds are the bright, billowy ones, and by reading the caption you can learn how cumulus clouds are formed.

A cumulus cloud above the Henry Mountains in Utah. Such clouds form in upward-flowing air currents.   © Tad Nichols

The following photograph arouses an emotional response and illustrates a point made in a sociology text. When you examine the photograph, you may feel pity, compassion, sadness, disgust, anger, rage, or some other emotion. If you then read the caption, you will learn that the photograph was selected to illustrate an important point about people's willingness to help strangers.

Interpret a photograph by studying it to understand what it depicts and to experience whether it arouses an emotional response in you. Then read the caption to learn additional information about whatever is depicted in the photograph or to learn why the photograph was included in your textbook.

Bystander apathy, or the unwillingness of bystanders to "get involved" in the problems of others, is especially common in cities and other crowded environments. People are reluctant to interpret a situation as an emergency unless "someone else" does so first, with the result that they all tend to ignore the problem.   © Charles Gatewood / THE IMAGE WORKS

Circle Graphs

A **circle graph** is a drawing in which a circle is divided into segments to show the sizes of the parts that make up a whole. Circle graphs are also sometimes called pie graphs or pie charts. The segments of the circle (or pieces of the pie) are usually given different colors or designs. In the graphs below, the segments are white, blue, and striped.

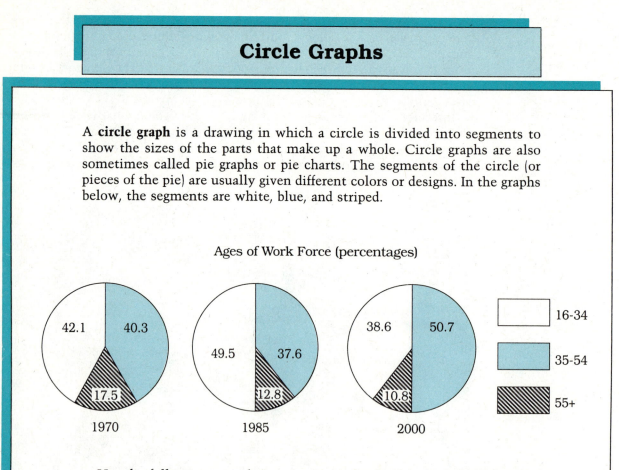

Ages of Work Force (percentages)

Use the following procedure to interpret the data in these circle graphs:

1. *Read the title.* What information is presented in the graphs?

2. *Read the labels.* What is represented by each of the three circle graphs?

3. *Read the key.* What is represented by the white, blue, and striped areas?

4. *Compare the data.* Which age category of workers is shown to decrease most between 1985 and 2000?

5. *Decide the important point.* What is the most important point made by the data in the circle graphs?

The answers to the questions are (1) ages of the work force; (2) the years 1970, 1985, and 2000; (3) white represents ages 16–34, blue represents ages 35–54, and stripes represent ages 55 and older; (4) ages 16–34; (5) in the year 2000 half the workers will be ages 35–54, or in 2000 61.5 percent of workers will be 35 or older compared with 50.4 percent in 1985.

Exercise 14.1 on page 206 provides additional practice in interpreting data presented in a circle graph.

Bar Graphs

A **bar graph** is a drawing in which the lengths of parallel bars are used to show differences in amounts. The information from the top to bottom of a bar graph is on the vertical axis, and the information from left to right is on the horizontal axis.

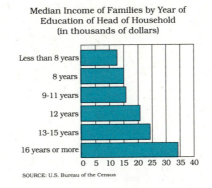

Median Income of Families by Year of
Education of Head of Household
(in thousands of dollars)

SOURCE: U.S. Bureau of the Census

Use the following procedure to interpret the data in this bar graph:

1. *Read the title.* What information is presented in the graph?

2. *Study the vertical axis and the horizontal axis.* What information is presented on the vertical axis (top to bottom) and the horizontal axis (left to right)?

3. *Compare the data.* How much greater is the median income of families in which the head of household has 16 or more years of education compared with families in which the head of household has 12 years of education?

4. *Decide the important point.* What is the most important point made by the data in the graph?

The answers to the questions are (1) median income of families by years of education of head of household; (2) years of education is on the vertical axis and dollars in thousands is on the vertical axis; (3) about $13,000; (4) the more years of education of the head of household the larger the median annual family income.

Exercise 14.2 on page 207 provides additional practice in interpreting data presented in a bar graph.

Line Graphs

A **line graph** is a drawing in which lines are used to show increases or decreases in amounts. The information from top to bottom is on the vertical axis, and the information from left to right is on the horizontal axis.

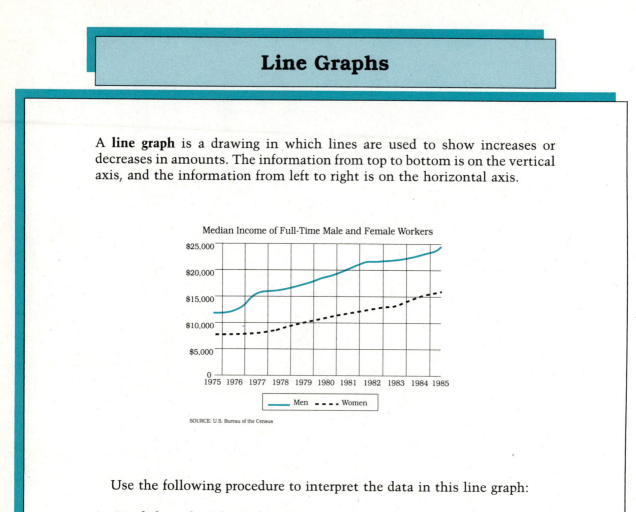

Median Income of Full-Time Male and Female Workers

SOURCE: U.S. Bureau of the Census

Use the following procedure to interpret the data in this line graph:

1. *Read the title.* What information is presented in the graph?

2. *Study the vertical and horizontal axes.* What information is on the vertical axis (top to bottom) and the horizontal axis (left to right)?

3. *Read the key.* What is represented by the dotted line and solid lines?

4. *Compare the data.* From 1980 to 1985 did the difference between the median income increase, decrease, or stay about the same?

5. *Decide the important point.* What is the most important point made by the data in the graph?

The answers are (1) median income of full-time male and female workers; (2) dollars in thousands and years; (3) females and males; (4) the difference was about $8,000 in both 1980 and 1985; (5) women's earnings have changed little in relation to the earnings of men.

Exercise 14.3 on page 208 provides additional practice in interpreting data presented in a line graph.

Tables

A **table** is a systematic listing of statistical information that is presented in orderly columns and rows to facilitate comparisons among data. The table below has three columns and six rows. The columns read from top to bottom (the first column is a list of degrees), and the rows read from left to right beginning with "Business, 12%, 33%" and ending with "Medicine, 16%, 32%."

**Percentages of Advanced Degrees
Earned by Women in Selected Disciplines**
(Source: U.S. Department of Education)

Degree	1975–1976	1986–1987
Business	12%	33%
Computer science	15	29
Dentistry	4	24
Engineering	4	13
Law	19	40
Medicine	16	32

Use the following procedure to interpret the data in this table:

1. *Read the title.* What information is presented in the table?

2. *Read the column headings.* What information is presented in the second and third columns of the table?

3. *Compare the data.* What is the conspicuous difference between the percentages of degrees earned by women in 1986–1987 compared with 1975–1976?

4. *Decide the important point.* What is the most important point made by the data in the table?

The answers to the questions are (1) the percentages of advanced degrees earned by women in selected disciplines; (2) percentages for 1975–1976 and 1986–1987; (3) percentages are greater for 1986–1987; (4) a larger percentage of advanced degrees was earned by women in 1986–1987 than in 1975–1976, but most advanced degrees were earned by men.

Exercise 14.4 on page 209 provides additional practice in interpreting data presented in a table.

Classification Charts

A **classification chart** is a well-organized summary of information about two or more persons, places, or things that are similar or different in two or more ways. As in tables, information is presented in orderly columns and rows to facilitate comparisons. The columns read from top to bottom, and the rows read from left to right. The classification chart below is a summary of information about reading.

Four Purposes of Reading

Purpose of Reading	Examples of Materials	Reading Rate in Words per Minute (wpm)	Percent of Comprehension
To analyze and evaluate	An insurance contract or a poem	100–125 wpm	100%
To study for tests	Textbooks and library materials	125–225 wpm	80%–100%
For enjoyment and information gathering	Newspapers, magazines, and paperback books	225–350 wpm	60%–80%
To locate specific facts	Cookbooks and automobile manuals	350–600 wpm	50%–60%

Use the following procedure to interpret this chart:

1. *Read the title.* What information is presented in the chart?

2. *Study the columns and rows.*
   a. What information is presented in the third column (up and down)?
   b. What information is presented in the last row (left to right)?

3. *Compare the information.*
   a. What reading rate is used to study for tests?
   b. What is the level of comprehension when reading for enjoyment?
   c. What are examples of materials that are read to locate specific facts?

The answers to the questions are (1) four purposes for reading; (2a) reading rate in words per minute; (2b) information about reading to locate specific facts; (3a) 125–225 wpm; (3b) 60%; (3c) cookbooks and automobile manuals.

Exercise 14.5 on page 210 provides additional practice in interpreting information presented in a comparison chart.

Process Charts

A **process chart,** or flowchart, is a drawing in which information is enclosed within geometric figures that are arranged to show how someone or something progresses through the steps of a process. Process charts take many different forms. The steps in the process chart below are organized into three stages.

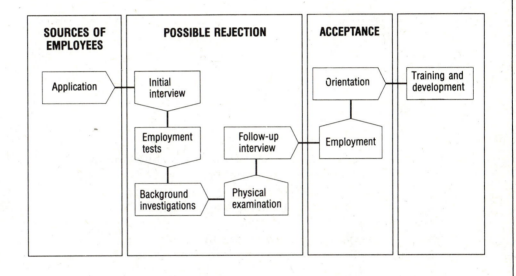

Use the following procedures to interpret the information in this process chart:

1. *Read the title.* What information is presented in the chart?

2. *Survey the chart.* How many steps are in the process? How many steps are in the second stage of the process?

3. *Determine the process.*
   a. What is the first step in the employment process?
   b. What are the first three steps during which a job applicant might be rejected?
   c. What step immediately follows employment?

The answers to the questions are (1) the employment process; (2) nine; three (3a) application; (3b) initial interview, employment tests, and background investigations; (3c) orientation.

Exercise 14.6 on page 211 provides additional practice in interpreting information presented in a process chart.

Diagrams

A **diagram** is a drawing that explains something by depicting its characteristics or by outlining its parts and showing the relationships among them. The following diagrams show the characteristics of three kinds of crosses.

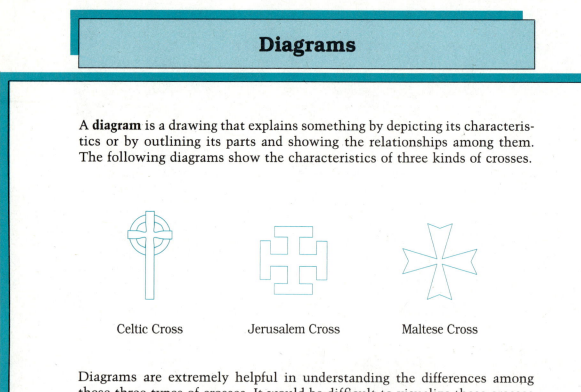

Celtic Cross   Jerusalem Cross   Maltese Cross

Diagrams are extremely helpful in understanding the differences among these three types of crosses. It would be difficult to visualize these crosses from their definitions alone: A *Celtic cross* is an upright cross with a circle around the intersection of the bars; a *Jerusalem cross* is a cross with four arms, each terminating in a crossbar; and a *Maltese cross* is a cross with arms that look like arrowheads pointing inward.

Diagrams *(continued)*

The following diagram outlines the parts of something—in this case, teeth—and shows the relationships among the parts.

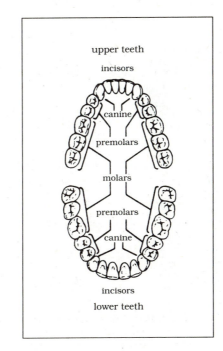

Diagrams that show relationships among parts often provide the answers to numerous questions. For example, the diagram above provides answers to these and other questions:

1. How many molars do adults have?

2. How many canine teeth do adults have?

3. How many incisors do adults have?

4. Where are premolars located in relation to other teeth?

5. What is the name of the upper-front teeth?

6. What is the name of the teeth in the back of the mouth?

The answers to the questions are (1) twelve, (2) four, (3) eight, (4) between the canines and the premolars, (5) incisors, (6) molars.

Exercise 14.7 on page 212 provides additional practice in interpreting a diagram.

EXERCISE 14.1   Circle Graph

Use the suggestions on page 198 to interpret the data in the following circle graphs and to answer the questions that follow them.

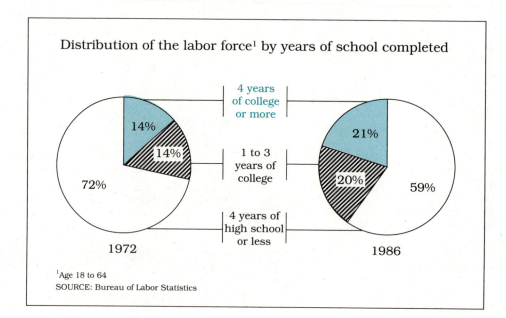

Distribution of the labor force[1] by years of school completed

4 years of college or more

1 to 3 years of college

4 years of high school or less

1972   1986

[1]Age 18 to 64
SOURCE: Bureau of Labor Statistics

1. Which category of the labor force decreased between 1972 and 1986?

   _____

2. Which category of the labor force increased most between 1972 and 1986?

   _____

3. What percentage of the labor force had completed at least one year of college in 1986?

   _____

4. Workers with four years of high school or less decreased at the rate of about 1 percent each year. If this trend continues, what percentage of the labor force will have four years of high school or less in the year 2000?

   _____

5. What is the most important point made by the data in the graphs?

   _____

EXERCISE 14.2 **Bar Graph**

Use the suggestions on page 199 to interpret the data in the following bar graph and to answer the questions that follow it.

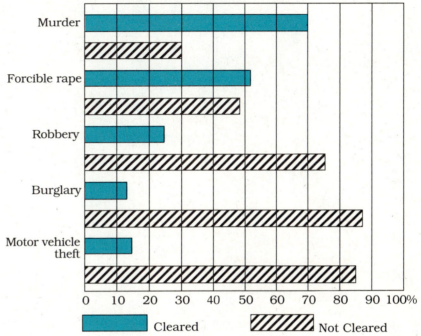

Percentages of crimes in five catagories that are cleared and are not cleared by arrest

SOURCE: Crime in the United States: Uniform Crime Reports (Washington, D.C.: Government Printing Office, 1979), p. 178

1. What is the only crime for which a majority of incidences are cleared by arrest?

   _____

2. For what crime are approximately an equal number of incidences cleared and not cleared by arrest?

   _____

3. Approximately _____ percent of robbery cases are cleared by arrest.

4. Approximately _____ percent of burglary and motor vehicle theft cases are not cleared by arrest.

5. What is the most important point made by the data in the graph?

   _____

EXERCISE 14.3   **Line Graph**

Use the suggestions on page 200 to interpret the data in the following line graph and to answer the questions that follow it.

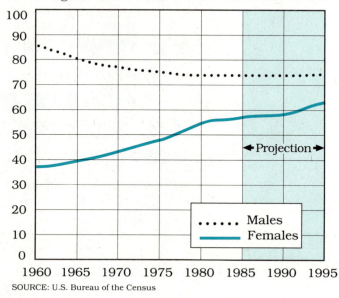

Percentages of males and females in the labor force

SOURCE: U.S. Bureau of the Census

1. In 1960 _____ percent of males were in the labor force.

2. It is projected that in 1995 _____ percent of males will be in the labor force.

3. In 1960 _____ percent of females were in the labor force.

4. It is projected that in 1995 _____ percent of females will be in the labor force.

5. What is the most important point made by the data in the graph?

_____

_____

EXERCISE 14.4   **Table**

Use the suggestions on page 201 to interpret the data in the following table and to answer the questions that follow it.

Additional Years United States Males May Expect to Live
(life expectancy)

Age	Never Smoked Regularly	Cigarettes Smoked by Daily Amount			
		1–9	10–19	20–39	40+
25	48.6	44.0	43.1	42.4	40.3
30	43.9	39.3	38.4	37.8	35.8
35	39.2	34.7	33.8	33.2	31.3
40	34.5	30.2	29.3	28.7	26.9
45	30.0	25.9	25.0	24.4	23.0
50	25.6	21.8	21.0	20.5	19.3
55	21.4	17.9	17.4	17.0	16.0
60	17.6	14.5	14.1	13.7	13.2
65	14.1	11.3	11.2	11.0	10.7

Source: Hammond study. Reprinted by permission of Public Health Service, Department of Health, Education, and Welfare.

1. Comparing men age 25 who never smoked regularly to men age 25 who smoked five cigarettes a day, how many additional years can the non-smokers expect to live?

   _____

2. Comparing men age 45 who never smoked regularly to men age 45 who smoked ten cigarettes a day, how many additional years can the non-smokers expect to live?

   _____

3. Comparing men age 25 who never smoked regularly to men age 65 who never smoked regularly, how many additional years can the men age 65 expect to live?

   _____

4. What is the most important point made by the data in the table?

   _____

EXERCISE 14.5   **Classification Chart**

Use the suggestions on page 202 to interpret the information in the following classification chart and to answer the questions that follow it.

Behaviors Exhibited by Nonassertive, Assertive, and Aggressive Persons

	Nonassertive Person	Assertive Person	Aggressive Person
In conflict situations	Avoids the conflict	Communicates directly	Dominates
In decision-making situations	Allows others to choose	Chooses for self	Chooses for self and others
In situations expressing feelings	Holds true feelings inside	Open, direct, honest, while allowing others to express their feelings	Expresses feelings in a threatening manner; puts down, inhibits others
In group meeting situations	Indirect, unclear statements: "Would you mind if . . ."	Direct, clear, "I" statements: "I believe that . . ."	Clear, but demeaning "you" statements: "You should have known better . . ."

1. In conflict situations, _____ people avoid the conflict.

2. In decision-making situations, _____ people choose for themselves and others.

3. In situations that call for expressing feelings, _____ people put down and inhibit others.

4. In group meeting situations, _____ people make indirect and unclear statements.

5. This classification chart appears in a human relations textbook. Which of the three types of people described in the chart do you suppose the authors believe behave most appropriately and constructively?

_____

EXERCISE 14.6   **Process Chart**

Use the suggestions on page 203 to interpret the information in the following chart of the check-clearing process and to answer the questions.

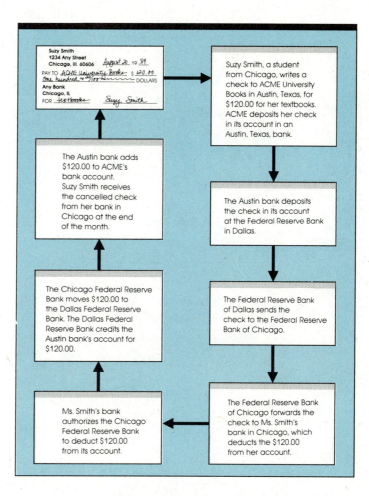

Match the following questions with the answers lettered *a* through *d* at the bottom of this page.

_____ 1. Who received the check from the Austin bank?

_____ 2. Who received it from the Dallas Federal Reserve Bank?

_____ 3. Who received it from the Chicago Federal Reserve Bank?

_____ 4. Who received $120 from the Chicago Federal Reserve Bank?

_____ 5. Who added $120 to ACME's bank account?

a. ACME's Austin bank   c. Chicago Federal Reserve Bank
b. Dallas Federal Reserve Bank   d. Suzy Smith's Chicago bank

EXERCISE 14.7   Diagram

Use the suggestions on pages 204–205 to interpret the following diagrams and to answer the questions that follow them.

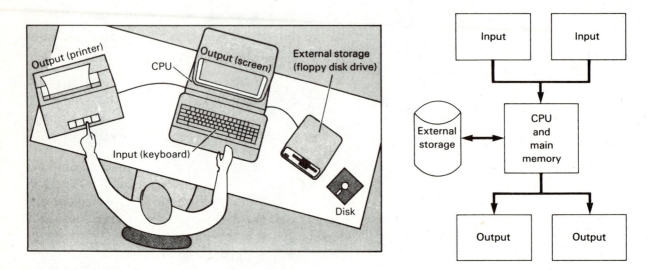

The parts of a computer are input/output (I/O) devices, central processing unit (CPU), external storage, and main memory.

1. Give an example of an input device.

   _____

2. Give two examples of an output device.

   _____

3. Give an example of equipment used for external storage.

   _____

4. What are I/O devices?

   _____

5. What is located in the central processing unit?

   _____

6. In what part of a computer are data probably processed?

   _____

Critical Reading

Critical reading is reading that is done for the purpose of judging the merits or faults of written material. What are the merits and faults of the following note that an eight-year-old sent to her uncle?

> Dear Unkle Jim,
>
> Thank you for the tois.
>
> Luv,
>
> Debbie

Reading critically, you might conclude that the girl who wrote this note has good social skills—it is appropriate to thank gift givers and to express affection to close relatives. Debbie's third-grade teacher, on the other hand, might judge from the note that she should give the child help to improve her spelling.

Criteria, or standards, for evaluating material vary with the type of writing. For example, the following are some criteria that can be used to judge the merits of a newspaper report about a "miracle" drug.

- Is the source a university or drug company?
- Was the research done on humans or only on animals?
- Who conducted the research?
- What was the source of the funding for the research?
- Are side effects of the drug reported?

Distinctive criteria, or standards, are used to evaluate poetry, drama, novels, biographies, cookbooks, and other forms of writing.

This chapter explains the criteria for critical reading that are most useful to college students. These criteria provide answers to the following questions about written material:

- Is it authoritative?
- Is it complete?
- Is it factual?
- Is it logical?
- Is it manipulative?
- Is it slanted?

The following discussions explain some ways to decide the answers to these questions.

Is It Authoritative?

Writing is **authoritative** when it is written by an expert in the subject it is about. When trial lawyers write books about trying cases in courts of law, their books are authoritative. However, when trial lawyers write books about subjects on which they are not experts, their books are not authoritative.

A writer might be an authority on one aspect of a subject but not on another aspect of the same subject. A trial lawyer might be an authority on trying criminal cases but not civil ones; a physics professor might be an authority on biophysics but not astrophysics. Within each subject, distinctions are also often made between "authorities" and "leading authorities." Among all the authorities on a subject, a few are usually more esteemed and considered to be the outstanding or leading experts in a field.

Very often authoritativeness is the primary consideration college instructors use when selecting textbooks. If you have difficulty understanding a book that you are required to read, one reason might be that your instructor selected the book because it is authoritative and not because it is easy to read.

It is frequently impossible for the average reader to determine whether an author is qualified to write about a subject. As a result, we ordinarily rely on the reputations of publishers to help us form judgments about the authoritativeness of the information in books, magazines, and newspapers. For instance, you are more likely to believe a report about a miracle drug if you read about it in *Newsweek* magazine than if you read about it in the kind of newspaper that is sold at grocery store checkout counters. You know that *Newsweek* has a reputation for publishing reliable information and that tabloid newspapers have a reputation for publishing sensational stories.

College textbooks are written by authorities on their subjects, and they are read by similar authorities before they are published; your teachers consider the textbooks that they assign to be authoritative. However, textbooks are seldom the most authoritative sources of information because they are usually secondary sources rather than primary ones. A **primary source** is a firsthand source; a **secondary source** is a source that gives information about a primary source. For example, the text of a speech given by Abraham Lincoln is a primary source of information about what he said, but a summary of the speech in a history textbook is a secondary source about what he said. Textbooks are authoritative secondary sources for students who, in a term of college study, have insufficient time to locate and read all the relevant primary sources.

Exercise 15.1, on page 220, provides practice in evaluating the authoritativeness of various sources.

Is It Complete?

Textbooks seldom provide complete information about the topics discussed in them; the discussions in textbooks are usually brief summaries of large bodies of literature. For example, a thirty-page chapter about the origins of English words in an English textbook does not give complete information about the topic. Hundreds of books and articles have been written about the origins of English words.

Sometimes, of course, textbooks do provide complete information about topics. A two-page discussion in an English textbook about how to use commas correctly is likely to be complete information about this topic; so is a four-page discussion in a mathematics textbook about how to solve a specific type of problem.

However, for the most part, textbooks are not complete. An instructor selects a textbook because it is complete enough to teach a specific course, not because it includes everything that is known about the topics discussed in it. One characteristic of a good textbook is that it is complete enough for the specific purpose it was written to serve.

Exercise 15.2, on pages 221–222, provides practice in evaluating the completeness of written material.

Is It Factual?

Facts are things that are known to be true or that are regarded, as a result of observation, as true. For example, it is known to be true that John F. Kennedy was president of the United States from 1961 until 1963—this is a fact. The first law of thermodynamics, which states that energy cannot be created or destroyed, is *also* regarded as true. There is no certain proof that the law is true, but as a result of their observations, scientists regard it as true—so it is also a fact.

Facts are different from **opinions,** which are viewpoints, beliefs, and judgments. Equally knowledgeable and informed people who agree about facts may argue or debate about opinions. For example, informed people do not argue about when John F. Kennedy was president, but they may debate whether he was one of our greatest presidents.

Since experts' opinions vary, it is often wise to make decisions only after learning the opinions of several authorities. For example, if a physician tells you that you must have an operation to relieve abdominal pain, you would be wise to consult with other doctors to determine whether they agree with this opinion. Another doctor might know of a treatment that would relieve your condition without the need for surgery.

Educated people also sometimes disagree about facts. To accept the facts of a discipline, it is necessary to understand and accept the methodology the discipline uses to make observations and establish facts. For example, sociologists have established the fact that the death penalty is not a deterrent to crime. However, many educated and informed people believe that the death penalty does help prevent crime; they do not understand or accept the methods sociologists use to make observations and establish facts.

Exercise 15.3, on page 223, provides practice in distinguishing between facts and opinions.

Is It Logical?

A logical argument is one that is arrived at by using sound reasoning procedures, such as those in this well-known example.

> *All men are mortal.*
> *Socrates is a man.*
> *Therefore, Socrates is mortal.*

This ancient example of logical reasoning states: All men must eventually die; Socrates is a man; therefore, he must eventually die.

Sometimes, unfortunately, writers use illogical reasoning to gain support for their arguments or conclusions. Five unsound arguments, or fallacies, are so commonly used that they have been given names: hasty generalization, the either-or fallacy, attack on the person fallacy, appeal to pity, and appeal to ignorance.

1. A **hasty generalization** is a conclusion drawn from too small a sample or from a sample that is not likely to be typical.

> Three New York City police officers were found guilty of taking cocaine from drug dealers and selling it to drug addicts; from this we can see that the police department is corrupt from top to bottom.

The conclusion that a police department of several thousand officers is corrupt throughout is not justified by the fact that three officers have been found guilty of unethical behavior.

2. The **either-or fallacy** is an illogical argument in which we are asked to believe that there are only two extreme possibilities, when there are in fact additional alternatives.

> Since she received very low grades on her midterm examinations, she must either quit her job or drop out of college.

There are more alternatives than the ones stated in this sentence. The student could work fewer hours each week; she could devote more of her free time to studying; or she could drop one course rather than all of them. This type of fallacy is also sometimes called the black-or-white fallacy or a false dilemma.

3. In the **attack on the person fallacy,** a person's conclusion is ignored and he or she is discredited instead.

> He claims that we are doing an ineffective job of educating children, but he has no right to criticize teachers because he has never spent even an hour trying to teach a classroom full of students.

The claim that teachers are ineffective in their efforts should be considered on its own merits; it is irrelevant that it was stated by a person who is not himself a teacher.

4. When the **appeal to pity** is used, a person seeks agreement with a conclusion by asking for sympathy rather than by presenting evidence that supports the conclusion.

> It is true that he brutally murdered his wife in a fit of rage, but he must not be sent to prison because a prison term will deprive his teenage sons of their father during the years that they need him most.

The reason given for not imprisoning the man is irrelevant; prison terms for brutal murderers are not decided on the basis of whether they have teenage sons.

5. In the **appeal to ignorance,** the person who states a conclusion asks those who oppose the conclusion to disprove it.

> I say that almost all firearms in this country are owned by law-abiding citizens. If you can't prove that I'm wrong, I must be right.

This kind of argument is invalid because it is the responsibility of a person who states a conclusion to demonstrate that the conclusion is true. The fact that you cannot prove that most firearms *are not* owned by law-abiding citizens does not prove that they *are* owned by law-abiding citizens.

Exercise 15.4, on page 224, provides practice in distinguishing among these five types of illogical arguments.

Is It Manipulative?

Manipulation is the use of shrewd means to persuade readers to hold certain opinions or to take specific actions. Manipulative methods of persuasion differ from illogical arguments in that manipulation is usually used intentionally whereas fallacious arguments are often used unintentionally by those who are unfamiliar with the rules of logical argumentation.

About fifty years ago the techniques of manipulation were given catchy names and popularized as propaganda techniques. The following paragraphs describe the six most commonly used of these strategies: glittering generalities, name calling, transfer, testimonial, plain folks, and bandwagon.

1. **Glittering generalities** are words or phrases used to arouse a favorable response when describing a product, a policy, or a person. For instance, facial make-up might be described as "all natural, hypoallergenic, in colors that will dazzle and capture him." Political candidates are often promoted as standing for "freedom," "democracy," "a drug-free society," "law and order," "civil rights," or "the American way."

2. **Name calling** is associating an unfavorable label with something to create a negative impression of it. Hubert Humphrey failed to win the Democratic nomination for president in a campaign in the 1960s in part because of a belittling slogan devised by his opponents—"Dump the Hump." Sometimes the unfavorable label is implied rather than directly stated. For instance, those who oppose abortion have taken the label "pro-life," implying that those who support women's right to abortion are "pro-death" or "anti-life."

3. **Transfer** is a technique in which a product or idea is associated with something that is known to be viewed favorably. Beer manufacturers do not sell beer using television commercials that show an overweight man drinking beer alone in front of a television set; they show fit young men enjoying beer together after athletic competition or men and women at a party or picnic having a good time and drinking beer. When a Republican presidential candidate praises remarks made by Democrats such as Franklin D. Roosevelt and Harry S Truman, he intends Democratic voters to associate these popular former Democratic presidents with his Republican candidacy.

4. A **testimonial** is a statement made by a famous or respected person in favor of or against something. When celebrities appear in television commercials asking viewers to buy a product, use a service, or contribute to a charitable cause, they are giving testimonials.

5. **Plain folks** is a technique used when an idea or product is associated with "ordinary" people or the things that "ordinary" people do. Politicians who usually wear suits and neckties are often photographed in shirt-sleeves or sportswear just before elections; the informal attire suggests that we should vote for them because they are ordinary people—just like us. Household products such as laundry detergent and toilet tissue are sold using commercials that feature actors who look like us or people we know.

6. **Bandwagon** is a way of soliciting support for a product or viewpoint by creating the impression that everyone, or practically everyone, uses the product or holds the opinion. An advertising campaign on some radio stations warned homeowners that they should not be the last on their block to convert their heating systems from oil to gas. Young men sometimes resort to the bandwagon strategy in attempting to persuade young women to be more sexually intimate than they are inclined by telling them that "everybody does it." Gas companies and young men are trying to get homeowners and young women to "jump on the bandwagon."

Exercise 15.5, on page 225, provides practice in distinguishing among these six types of manipulative methods of persuasion.

Is It Slanted?

Writing is **slanted** when it is intended to convince readers of a particular opinion. The words writers use to describe an event can influence readers' attitudes. "He gave her a juicy kiss" creates a much more favorable impression than "He slobbered all over her when he kissed her."

Writers also influence readers' thoughts by the conclusions they choose to state. Compare the following statements.

- Some high schools provide students with birth-control devices.
- Some high schools encourage sexual promiscuity by providing students with birth-control devices.
- Some high schools help prevent unwanted pregnancies and the spread of AIDS and venereal diseases by providing students with birth-control devices.

The first statement presents a fact but does not include information that might convince readers to hold a particular opinion about whether high schools *should* provide students with birth-control devices. The other two statements are slanted. The second sentence is worded so that it might convince some readers that high schools should not provide students with contraceptives, while the third sentence might persuade some readers that high schools provide a valuable service when they make birth-control devices available to students.

Writing can also be slanted by omitting information that might encourage readers to hold an opinion other than the one the writer wants them to hold. For example, if writers want readers to have the opinion that high schools should not provide students with contraceptives, they will omit all information that might encourage readers to hold an opposing view. This type of slanting is sometimes called **card stacking.**

Exercise 15.6, on page 226, provides practice in identifying writing that is slanted.

EXERCISE 15.1 **Authoritativeness**

Read "Is It Authoritative?" on pages 214–215. Then check the boxes in front of the sources of information that are most authoritative for the stated purposes.

1. Which of the following is the most authoritative source of information about the religious beliefs of ancient Egyptians?
   ☐ a. a novel about Cleopatra's love affairs
   ☐ b. an article in the *New York Times*
   ☐ c. an article in a standard encyclopedia

2. Which of the following is the most authoritative source of information about the requirements for graduating from your college?
   ☐ a. a textbook about studying in college
   ☐ b. the catalogue or bulletin for your college
   ☐ c. a book from the United States Department of Education

3. Which of the following is the most authoritative source of information about an astronaut's experiences in outer space?
   ☐ a. a report in the *Washington Post* newspaper
   ☐ b. notes in the astronaut's personal diary
   ☐ c. an article in *Newsweek*

4. Which of the following is the most authoritative source of information about the effects of smoking on health?
   ☐ a. a statistical report by the surgeon general
   ☐ b. a college health education textbook
   ☐ c. warnings printed on cigarette packs

5. Which of the following is the most authoritative source of information about the correct spellings of English words?
   ☐ a. an English composition textbook
   ☐ b. a spelling or vocabulary book
   ☐ c. a standard desk dictionary

6. Which of the following is the most authoritative source of information about President George Bush's appearance when he gave a speech?
   ☐ a. a video recording of the speech
   ☐ b. a word-for-word transcript of the speech
   ☐ c. an eyewitness report of somebody who heard it

7. Which of the following is the most authoritative source of information about this year's federal income taxes?
   ☐ a. a business or finance textbook
   ☐ b. the opinions of an accountant
   ☐ c. current publications of the Internal Revenue Service

EXERCISE 15.2 **Completeness**

Read "Is It Complete?" on page 215. Then compare the following textbook excerpts and decide which excerpt is more complete. Then answer the questions that follow the second passage.

Establishing Credit

After examining a credit-scoring chart, most college-age people wonder if they will ever get credit when they need it. There are five ways to prove, to a limited extent, that you have the ability to manage credit.

1. *Act on some factors* you can control.* Establish both a checking and a savings account. Avoiding overdrafts on a checking account and making regular deposits to a savings account may be good financial management, but the lender wants only to know that you *have* a checking and a savings account.

2. *Visit a local retail establishment.* Tell them that your intention is to establish a credit rating, and request an account. A local retailer is more likely to open a limited account if you visit the store in person and dress neatly. Once the account is open, use it to make a few purchases for which you typically use cash. When the bill arrives, pay it promptly and in full. Presto, a credit history is established.

3. *Request and acquire an oil company credit card.* Although more difficult to obtain than a local retail credit account, these are not impossible to get. Should one company refuse, apply at another, as scoring systems differ. Again, use the credit sparingly once obtained and repay promptly.

4. *Apply for a bank credit card.* Most bank card companies have a program of test credit for people without an extensive credit history. The limit on credit purchases may be $50 or $300, but once again the opportunity then exists to establish a credit rating. Later you can request an increase in the credit limit.

5. *Ask a bank for a small short-term cash loan.* Putting these funds into a savings account at the bank will almost guarantee that you will make the required three or four monthly payments. Also, the interest charges on the loan would be partially offset by the interest earned on the savings.

The Keys to Establishing a Good Credit Rating

There are good reasons to establish and maintain a solid credit record even if you don't plan to use it much. But getting credit to start with may be difficult, particularly for young people, minorities, and women

* Words underscored in blue are defined in the Master Vocabulary List on pages ■■■–■■■, and the exercise on page 59 is based on these words.

who want credit in their own right. Yet just about anyone can get credit if she or he meets some basic requirements and has the patience to argue the case with enough creditors. The question to answer is, Would you lend yourself money?

Your record at a credit bureau is a <u>crucial</u> item in obtaining credit. It's a good idea to check your credit history periodically at various credit bureaus to be sure it is accurate.

Besides maintaining a good credit bureau record, there are some specific things you can do to help establish a good credit history:

1. Open both a checking account and a savings account.

2. Establish credit with a department store. Department store credit is often easier to obtain than bank credit, and many creditors look favorably on that type of credit when judging your application.

3. Take out a small installment loan from a bank and pay it back promptly. Some creditors look for evidence that you can successfully handle different types of credit.

4. Do not borrow from a small-loan company if you can help it. Its rates are likely to be high, but more important, listing a small-loan company as a credit reference could hurt you in obtaining other credit.

5. If a bank or a major department store offers you a credit card, take it. Use it to help establish a credit history.

6. Obtain credit from organizations that report to credit bureaus—banks, large department stores, and the like. Many small stores, American Express, and the oil companies do not routinely report their accounts to credit bureaus.

7. Don't apply for credit too often in a six-month period. If you're turned down, that fact often stays on your credit record. Creditors may judge you unfavorably.

8. Pay all bills promptly, including those from utility companies. Although utilities do not report their customers' accounts to credit bureaus, your promptly paid receipts may persuade <u>prospective</u> creditors to take a chance with you.

9. If you are married and have a joint credit account, make sure that it's reported to the credit bureau in both your names. If you're a woman, the accounts should be reported in your given name—Mary Smith, for example, not Mrs. John Smith.

Be <u>wary</u> of organizations that claim they can help improve your credit rating or can help you get credit. They have no special relationship with any credit bureau.

Write answers to the following questions.

1. Which passage is more complete?

2. List four suggestions or types of information in the more complete passage that are not included in the other passage.

EXERCISE 15.3   **Factuality**

Read "Is It Factual?" on pages 215–216. Then, on the lines provided, write **F** in front of facts and **O** in front of opinions.

_____   1. The death penalty is an effective deterrent to crime.

_____   2. The death penalty is used in several states of the United States.

_____   3. John F. Kennedy was the first president to make extensive use of television to communicate with the American public.

_____   4. Franklin Roosevelt was one of the three greatest presidents we ever had.

_____   5. Vermont is the state with the smallest black population.

_____   6. The state of Vermont has no ocean coastline.

_____   7. Vermont is the most beautiful New England state.

_____   8. Pictures of men and women engaging in sexual intercourse are pornographic.

_____   9. Laws prohibit young children from attending public screenings of pornographic movies.

_____   10. Mount Rainier, in Washington State, is 14,410 feet high.

_____   11. It is worth a trip to Washington State just to visit Mount Rainier.

_____   12. Some women work as firefighters.

_____   13. Female police officers are as able in their work as male police officers.

_____   14. More Americans have been killed by privately owned firearms than by all the wars the United States has fought.

_____   15. Americans' right to own firearms must not be restricted in any way.

_____   16. Some of Jesus' teachings were not original; they had been introduced earlier by others.

_____   17. Jesus lived about two thousand years ago.

_____   18. Jesus has had a more positive influence on humankind than any other person who ever lived.

EXERCISE 15.4 Fallacies

Read "Is It Logical?" on pages 216–217. Then, on the lines provided, write the letters **a, b, c, d,** or **e** to indicate the fallacy used in each statement.

a. hasty generalization
b. either-or fallacy
c. attack on the person fallacy
d. appeal to pity
e. appeal to ignorance

_____   1. If he doesn't eat more fruit and vegetables and exercise regularly he must prepare to die at an early age.

_____   2. Your honor, I beg you to have mercy on me for killing my parents; I'm an orphan now!

_____   3. The teachers at my school are rude; one of them practically knocked me down in the hallway, and he didn't even say, "Excuse me."

_____   4. I'm convinced that there is intelligent life on other planets in the universe, and if you can't prove that there isn't, that shows that I'm right.

_____   5. Of course he advocates that the government should pay medical bills—he's a communist, like his father.

_____   6. I know that I don't deserve a passing grade for your course, but I had a bad cold during most of the term and I had a hard time concentrating because my father was sick and my grandmother died. My car broke down, too.

_____   7. If you're not my friend, you're my enemy.

_____   8. I don't care if she does have a doctoral degree in nutrition, I don't take advice about diet from overweight people who eat snack foods such as potato chips, ice cream, and pizza.

_____   9. I say that there is a God, and if you disagree with me, prove that there is no God.

_____   10. Women are more considerate and loving than men; my mother and my wife are the only two truly considerate and loving people I've ever known.

EXERCISE 15.5 **Manipulation**

Read "Is It Manipulative?" on pages 217–218. Then, on the lines provided, write the letters **a, b, c, d, e,** or **f** to indicate the manipulative technique used in each statement.

a. glittering generalities
b. name calling
c. transfer
d. testimonial
e. plain folks
f. bandwagon

_____ 1. I didn't want to get involved in taking drugs, but everybody I knew was doing it and I always did what my friends did.

_____ 2. Our spaghetti sauce is made by one of Rome's most famous chefs using the finest Italian tomatoes and herbs from our own garden.

_____ 3. Michael Jackson appeared in a television commercial to promote his own line of clothing.

_____ 4. Every year newspapers publish photographs of former president Jimmy Carter in work clothing as he joins with other volunteers to convert dilapidated buildings into desirable housing for the poor.

_____ 5. Women like him because he's tall and handsome, wears stylish clothing, drives a Mercedes-Benz, and takes them to the best restaurants and clubs.

_____ 6. They claim to protect the rights of the needy, but I say they prevent the state from administering justice to Nazis, welfare cheats, and child molesters.

_____ 7. Drug users tend to be depressed, anxious, and alienated; and they almost always have a poor self-image.

_____ 8. Most homes have a microwave oven; don't be the last on your block to enjoy the latest kitchen technology.

_____ 9. My dentist is pretty and gentle, and she always has a smile and a kind word.

_____ 10. You know that if I can raise a large family on a small budget, keep clean clothes on four young children, and put three wholesome meals on the table every day that I will vote the way you'd vote if you were in Congress.

EXERCISE 15.6   Slant

Read "Is It Slanted?" on pages 218–219 before you answer the following questions.

1. Check the statement in each of the following pairs of statements that is slanted to create a more favorable opinion.

   a. ☐ He told an outrageous lie.
       ☐ He stated the facts incorrectly.

   b. ☐ She is determined to succeed.
       ☐ She is a very pushy person.

   c. ☐ He is a slow worker.
       ☐ He is thorough at whatever he does.

   d. ☐ She has many weird notions.
       ☐ She has many original ideas.

   e. ☐ They like to talk.
       ☐ We can't get them to shut up.

2. Following are eight types of written material. Check the boxes in front of the four types that are *most likely* to be slanted.

   ☐ An advertisement for a vacation to Mexico
   ☐ A news article in *Time*
   ☐ A chapter in a chemistry textbook
   ☐ A tobacco company's report about the effects of smoking
   ☐ A magazine article opposing abortion
   ☐ An entry about the moon in an encyclopedia
   ☐ An autobiography of a movie star
   ☐ A manual about how to care for an automobile

3. Following are eight characteristics of a student. Check the boxes in front of the four statements you would expect to find in a favorable letter of reference written by the student's teacher.

   ☐ He was frequently late to class.
   ☐ He was never absent from class.
   ☐ He made interesting contributions to class discussions.
   ☐ He turned in his term paper two weeks late.
   ☐ His term paper was outstandingly good.
   ☐ He laughed at errors made by less able students.
   ☐ He smokes two packs of cigarettes a day.
   ☐ He is hardworking and trustworthy.

Four

The Study Program: Preparing for Tests

In college, test scores are used to compute final course grades, and final course grades are used to compute grade point averages. As a result, the students who graduate from college are the ones who do well on tests.

Some students have difficulty when they take tests because they prepare for them by reading and rereading rather than by studying. **Reading** is the process people use to understand information presented in writing; **studying,** in contrast, is the process they use to learn and remember information. Chapters 9–15 explain some methods that will improve your reading skills. This part of *RSVP*, Chapters 16–22, explains how to study for tests. Studying involves the following procedures:

- Taking good class notes
- Surveying before studying
- Marking books
- Making notes from textbooks
- Reciting and reviewing from notes

These procedures are explained in the next seven chapters. Chapters 1, 2, and 3 also include suggestions that can help you study for tests.

The Study Process

Studying involves deciding what to learn and then doing what is necessary to acquire the skills or to remember the information that is needed to answer test questions correctly. This chapter provides an overview of the procedures for effective studying that are summarized in "The Study Process" on page 230 and explained in detail in Chapters 17–22.

Take Good Class Notes

It is essential for you to have good notes about what your teachers say in your classes. During class meetings your teachers will explain information in required course reading material that they know is difficult for many students to understand, and provide important information that is not printed in course textbooks. They will also give hints about what you should study when you prepare for tests. You need records of these kinds of information if you want to do your best when you take tests.

Methods for taking good notes are explained in Chapter 17, which begins on page 235.

Survey Before You Read

For most of your courses, you will need to learn information in textbooks. **Textbooks** are books that are used to study college subjects, such as the books teachers assign for psychology, business, and chemistry courses.

Survey your books when you purchase them at the beginning of each term and then survey each chapter before you read it. A **survey of a book** includes reading the introduction and table of contents at the beginning of the book and examining the glossary, index, and other material at the end of the book. A **survey of a chapter** involves reading the introduction, headings, and closing summary. It takes only a few minutes to survey a chapter, but this is time well spent because it provides background information that increases your reading comprehension. The methods for surveying are explained in Chapters 18 and 19.

The Study Process

Use the following procedures to learn information and skills for college tests.

1. Take good class notes (see Chapter 17).

2. Survey before you read (see Chapters 18 and 19).

3. Mark your books (see Chapter 20).

4. Make notes from textbooks (see Chapter 21).

5. Anticipate test questions.
   - Use your class notes as a guide.
   - Use helps provided in textbooks.
   - Attend test reviews.
   - Talk with teachers' former students.
   - Examine teachers' past tests.
   - Learn "easy" information.

6. Recite and review (see Chapter 22).

Mark and Make Notes from Textbooks

One of the best-known facts about human learning is that information is easier to learn when it is organized in a meaningful way. Figures 16.1 and 16.2 illustrate how to organize information in a textbook by marking it and summarizing it in well-organized notes. The skills you developed when you studied topics, main ideas, and details in Chapters 10, 11, and 12 will help you learn how to mark and make notes from textbooks when you study Chapters 20 and 21.

Anticipate Test Questions

The questions that appear on college tests tend to emphasize the information that is most important for students to know. Therefore, if you anticipate test questions, you will study the things that are most important for you to learn. Use the following six suggestions to help you anticipate test questions.

1. Use class notes as a guide. The notes you take in class will usually be your best source of information about test questions. When you study your notes, give special attention to four types of information.

FIGURE 16.1

An Example of
Highlighting

Conflict

We encounter conflict when we must choose between two or more alternatives. There are three basic types of conflict: approach-approach, avoidance-avoidance, and approach-avoidance.

The **approach-approach conflict** is the need to choose between two attractive alternatives. The need to choose between vacationing in England or France is an example of an approach-approach conflict. This type of conflict is resolved when one possibility becomes more attractive than the other. If a vacation in England will include visits with friends and the trip to France will not, then England may become the more attractive choice.

The **avoidance-avoidance conflict** exists when you must choose between two *un*attractive alternatives. An example is the need to decide whether you will have a tooth pulled or have root canal work done on it. This type of conflict is resolved when one possibility becomes more *un*attractive than the other. If having a tooth pulled becomes more unattractive, you may choose to have root canal work done on the tooth.

The **approach-avoidance conflict** is present when one possibility or goal is both attractive and unattractive. The pursuit of a college degree is an approach-avoidance conflict for many students. It is attractive because a college degree may lead to better job opportunities in the future. But it is unattractive because it requires students to study hard and to take courses that they may prefer not to take. This type of conflict is often resolved unsatisfactorily. For instance, many students resolve their conflict about college study by dropping out of college. Later many of these people regret that they did not stay in school and earn a college degree.

FIGURE 16.2

Notes for the
Passage in
Figure 16.1

Types of Conflict

Approach-approach – when I must choose between two
attractive alternatives. (EX) Vacation in England or France.
Resolved when one choice becomes more attractive.
Avoidance-avoidance – when I must choose between two
unattractive alternatives. (EX) Have a tooth pulled or have root
canal work. Resolved when one choice becomes more unattractive.
Approach-avoidance – when one possibility is both attractive
and unattractive. (EX) College study is attractive and
unattractive. Often not satisfactorily resolved (many
students drop out of college and later regret it).

- Information you copied from the chalkboard
- Information teachers said is important or difficult to learn
- Information teachers stated while reading directly from their notes
- Information about topics that are also discussed in required course reading material

Mark these types of information so that you don't overlook them when you study. You might draw a star or write *Important* in the margin next to the information, or you might mark it with yellow or pink highlighting ink so it will stand out when you prepare for tests (see pages 273–275).

2. Use textbook helps. Use learning goals, review questions, lists of terminology, and exercises and problems in your textbooks to help you anticipate test questions.

- **Learning goals** and **review questions** give information about what students are expected to learn in a textbook. Therefore, when a chapter begins with learning goals or ends with review questions, make certain that you have achieved the goals or can answer the questions.
- The meaning of course **terminology** is usually tested in many questions on college tests. As a result, it is essential that you make certain you know all of the terminology listed at the end of chapters or printed in italics or boldface within chapters.
- When instructors ask you to do **exercises** or solve **problems** in a textbook, they will also usually require you to do similar exercises or to solve similar problems on tests. Therefore, when you take a test, be prepared to do any kinds of exercises or to solve any types of problems that are in the course textbook.

These features of textbooks are explained in detail in Chapters 18 and 19.

3. Attend test reviews. Some instructors give reviews for tests during class or at special times outside of class. Attend reviews, take complete notes, and learn everything you are told to learn. Teachers who give reviews want you to learn what is most important for you to know; they want to help you do your best. Take full advantage of the help they give.

4. Talk with teachers' former students. If at all possible, ask former students of your instructors how to study for tests. Teachers' testing methods seldom change much from year to year. As a result, students who studied with your teachers in the past have answered test questions very much like the ones you will answer. Students who received good grades for the courses you are taking know things that may be very useful to you. They may be eager to explain to you the methods that they used to earn good grades.

5. Examine teachers' past tests. Some teachers give students tests to keep, and some schools place past tests on file for students to examine. Ask your instructors' former students if they have copies of tests you may examine, and if your teachers' tests are on file, locate them and study them.

Also, analyze the questions on the first test you take for a course; they will give you hints about the types of things to learn for subsequent tests. For instance, if the questions on a first test are mostly about little facts in a textbook, that teacher's other tests are also likely to focus on the same kinds of facts—study them for the next test.

6. Learn "easy" information. Some students believe incorrectly that if information is easy for them to understand, they know it. However, the difference between understanding and knowing is the difference between reading and studying. Reading is done to understand information; studying is done to remember and recall it.

You have no doubt understood everything you have read about how to study in *RSVP*. However, you cannot recall most of the information in this book unless you have studied it. For instance, without looking back at Chapter 3, on a sheet of notebook paper try to list the methods it suggests you use to concentrate for longer periods. Unless you studied Chapter 3, or looked back at it, you were probably not able to list accurately the eight basic suggestions it gives for increasing concentration.

When you study for tests, make certain that you learn easy-to-understand information. It is extremely disappointing to lose points on tests for failure to learn information that you could have learned easily.

Recite and Review

Many students try to learn information in books and notes by reading and rereading it. These students believe incorrectly that reading and studying are the same process.

It is true that books must be read to study them; however, books may be read *without* studying them! Reading is the process that is used to understand information that is presented in writing. It involves such activities as locating the main ideas and the details that are related to them. Studying, on the other hand, is the process that is used to decide what to learn and to remember and recall information. Studying involves using the procedures already outlined in this chapter plus reciting and reviewing.

When you want to remember and recall information, you must recite and review it. **Reciting** is the act of repeating information silently or aloud until you can recall it without reading it. Most information stays in your memory only about 20 seconds unless you recite it. (See the discussion about memory on page 116.) **Reviewing** is the repetition that is essential for learning. Much of what we learn is soon forgotten unless we review it. If you find that you do not remember information that you study for tests, you probably do not review sufficiently. You will remember best what you review most. Chapter 22 explains how to recite and review.

EXERCISE 16.1   Anticipating Test Questions

Write the name of the most difficult course you are taking on the line.

_____

Check the items in the following list that can help you anticipate test questions for this course.

- ☐ The teacher writes important information on the chalkboard.
- ☐ The teacher sometimes mentions that specific information is important or difficult to learn.
- ☐ The teacher discusses topics in class that are also discussed in the course textbook.
- ☐ There are learning goals at the beginning of textbook chapters.
- ☐ Terminology is listed at the end of textbook chapters or printed in italics or boldface in the chapters.
- ☐ There are review questions, exercises, or problems at the end of textbook chapters.
- ☐ The teacher gives test reviews.
- ☐ I know some of the teacher's former students who can tell me how to study for the teacher's tests.
- ☐ Tests the teacher gave in the past are available for me to examine.
- ☐ I have already taken one of the teacher's tests and examined it to figure out what kinds of questions might be on the next test.

Take Good Class Notes

Within two days after a lecture you will have forgotten about three-fourths of what you heard, and within a week you will have forgotten virtually all that was said during the lecture. If you don't have written records of what your teachers say in class, you will not be able to prepare for tests by studying what they taught you during class meetings.

Class notes usually include explanations about complicated course material, important facts that are not stated in required reading material, and hints about what to study for tests. They are usually the best source of help for understanding course subject matter and for deciding what to study for tests. Attend classes faithfully to take complete and well-organized notes about the explanations, facts, and hints you will need to do your best when you take examinations.

Use An Appropriate Notebook

It is essential that you have a notebook that makes it easy for you to keep notes for each class completely separate from the notes for your other classes. For example, notes for a biology, a math, and an English course should be kept in three separate sections of a notebook. If you mix your notes for one class with your notes for another class, your notes will not be properly organized when you study them to prepare for tests.

There are suggestions for purchasing a notebook on pages 9–10, and "How to Organize Class Notes" on page 236 includes advice for organizing notebooks.

Improve Your Listening

Suggestions for improving your ability to listen to lectures are summarized in "How to Improve Listening" on page 240. The first suggestion in the list is to read or skim information about the lecture topic in the course textbook immediately before class. It is especially important to use this suggestion when teachers tell you to read about lecture topics before class and when

How to Organize Class Notes

These are methods that you should definitely use.

- Take notes on 8½- by 11-inch notebook paper so that all the information about topics is usually on one page rather than on two or three pages.

- Write your name, address, and telephone number in the front of your notebook so it can be easily returned to you if you lose it.

- Keep assignments for all classes in a special assignment section of your notebook so you'll be less likely when you study to overlook assignments buried in notes.

- Start each day's notes on a new sheet of paper, and begin them with a heading that includes the date and course name or course number. The date is essential for putting notes back in correct sequence when they become mixed up, for verifying that notes are complete, and for finding where to begin studying when teachers announce that tests cover material in notes beginning on a particular date.

- Leave at least one blank line before each main idea.

- Make diagrams and other drawings large, and skip lines before and after them.

You may also find that these strategies are helpful.

- Keep notes in a ring binder and use dividers to separate the notes for each class.

- Punch holes in papers instructors hand out and insert them in your ring binder for safe keeping.

- Write only on one side of each piece of paper so you can see all your notes when you spread them out on a desk to study them.

- Number each page so you can easily put notes back in correct order if you remove them from your ring binder.

you have difficulty understanding what teachers say during lectures. If at all possible, do the reading just before class so it will be fresh in your mind as you listen to the lecture.

In addition, before you go to a class, take care of any physical needs that may become sources of discomfort and interfere with your concentration. You may need to use the rest room, have a drink of water, or eat something if you are likely to become hungry before class is over. Dress so you can remove clothes if a classroom is too warm or put on clothes if it is too cold. If you wear a shirt or blouse under a sweater or jacket, you can take off the sweater if you become too warm or put on the jacket if you become too cold.

Sit where you can see your teachers clearly because their gestures, facial expressions, and eye movements often convey important information.

- *A gesture may supplement words.* For instance, an instructor may point at the chalkboard to emphasize something written there that she wants you to understand or know.

- *A facial expression may contradict words.* An instructor may say "This is easy," but a playful expression on his face may suggest that he is teasing and wants you to understand the opposite—"This is very difficult."

- *A gesture or facial expression may suggest what you are to do.* A teacher may stop talking and raise her eyebrows, suggesting that she is ready to answer your questions, or she may purse her lips or give some other signal when opening a book of poetry to indicate that she wants complete silence before she reads aloud from the book.

- *Eye movements may indicate that important information is being given.* Instructors often glance at their notes because they want you to record important information that is written in them.

When a classroom is very large, try to sit in the front and center of the room. In any event, select a seat from which you can't see out a window and which is away from any student who distracts you.

Finally, avoid worrying and daydreaming during lectures—they will distract you from listening. There is nothing you can do about a problem while you are in a classroom listening to a lecture; worrying will not solve the problem but it will prevent you from taking good lecture notes. Therefore, when a problem comes into your mind, write it on your list of things to do, tell yourself to stop worrying and to pay attention to the lecture, and deal with the problem after class.

Take Well-Organized Class Notes

Take well-organized class notes by using the format illustrated in Figure 17.1 on page 239 or any of the note-taking methods discussed on pages 299–306. The suggestions in "How to Organize Class Notes" on page 236 apply no matter what note-taking method you use.

Notice that the class notes illustrated in Figure 17.1 emphasize the relations between major thoughts and details.

- Major thoughts stand out clearly. In Figure 17.1, major thoughts are preceded by a line with no writing on it, they are written to the left side of the page, and they are underlined.

- Details are listed under major thoughts in an orderly fashion. In Figure 17.1, some details are preceded by numbers and others are preceded by stars.

Of course, the notes you take under pressure during a class are not likely to be as neatly written and tidy as the notes in Figure 17.1.

Many experienced students favor the Cornell System, which is a variation of the traditional note-taking format. To use the Cornell System, draw a vertical line two and a half inches from the left edge of each sheet of notebook paper, as illustrated below.

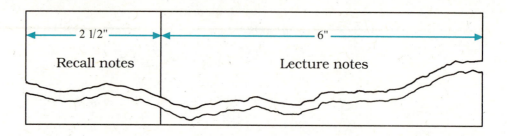

Record class notes in the space to the right of the vertical line and write words, phrases, or questions to assist you in learning the information in your notes in the space to the left of the vertical line. The Cornell System is explained in detail by Walter Pauk in *How to Study in College*, Fourth Edition (Boston: Houghton Mifflin, 1989).

Summarize What Teachers Say

When you take class notes, summarize what teachers say; do not attempt to write down what they say word for word. It is impossible to record teachers' words exactly because they usually speak at the rate of about 125 to 150 words per minute, but you can probably write no more than 25 to 30 words a minute. Therefore, you must learn to summarize what teachers say in your own words.

Adapt to Each Teacher

The suggestions in this chapter pertain to teachers who give well-organized lectures; however, some instructors give disorganized lectures, some ramble from topic to topic, and some refer to the course textbook while they lecture.

- When you have teachers who give *disorganized* lectures, leave the left pages of your notebook blank and after class rewrite notes on the blank left pages.
- When you have teachers who *ramble* from topic to topic without explaining how the topics are related, take the most complete notes you can about each topic they discuss.
- When you have teachers who *read* from the course textbook, follow along in your copy of the textbook; mark the points they emphasize and cross out the information they tell you is not important.

It is your responsibility as a student to adapt to the instructional methods your teachers use.

Study Skills 101, 9/14/92   Shepherd

Taking Good Class Notes

Five characteristics of good notes
1. Written on 8½-by-11-inch notebook paper.
2. Heading includes name or number of course, teacher's name, date, and lecture topic.
3. Major details stand out clearly.
4. Minor details are listed neatly under major details.
5. They summarize what teachers say.

How to improve listening
★ Eliminate environmental distractions. (Ex) Don't sit near windows or annoying classmates.
★ Eliminate physical distractions.
    1. Visit rest room before class.
    2. Eat before class so you won't get hungry.
    3. Dress so you won't be too warm or cold.
★ Eliminate internal distractions. (Ex) Don't think about what you'll do after class.

Hints for taking and studying notes
★ Read about lecture topics before classes.
★ Mark things written on chalkboards and about which teachers give study hints for special attention when studying.
★ Review notes as soon after class as possible.
★ Study notes thoroughly before tests.

FIGURE 17.1
Well-Organized Class Notes

Listen for Major Thoughts

During lectures, make it your goal to find major thoughts and to make them stand out clearly in your notes. Some teachers directly state important thoughts by using phrases such as "Now I'm going to discuss . . ." and "My next point is . . ." Instructors also use pauses and repetition to emphasize major thoughts in their lectures. If they pause while lecturing, this is often

How to Improve Listening

Use these suggestions when you listen to classroom lectures.

1. Just before class, read or skim the information about the lecture topic in the course textbook.

2. Eliminate distractions.
   - Sit where you have a good view of the teacher and where you can't see out a window.
   - Don't sit near students who distract you.
   - Keep only paper, pen, and other essential materials on your desk.
   - Eat before class so you won't be hungry during class.
   - Dress in layers so you can remove clothing if you become warm or put on clothing if you become cold.

3. Keep your eyes on the teacher as he or she speaks because gestures, facial expressions, and eye movements may often convey important information.

4. Sit using good posture.

5. Listen to find the answers to the following questions and use the answers to make good notes:
   - What topic should I use as the heading for my notes?
   - In what format should I record notes?
   - What major thought should I write in my notes?
   - How many details should I list?

6. Ask the teacher for clarification when you are not certain you understood what was said.

a clue that students should write down what they said just before the pause or what they will say after it. When teachers repeat statements, it is usually a definite hint that you should record the repeated information in your notes.

Listen for Details

Many lecturers make it clear how many details to list under major thoughts by making statements such as the following.

- Sociologists identify *four* types of families.
- There are *five* steps in the selling process.
- Let's examine *three* tragic effects of the Civil War.

When instructors make statements such as these, it is clear exactly how many details to list.

In other instances, teachers make it clear that students should list details but not how many of them to list. For instance, an instructor may say, "I'm going to talk about some of the problems involved in starting a small business." In this case, students should write "Problems with starting a small business" as a major thought in their notes and then prepare to list the problems. However, they will not know how many problems there are until the teacher states them.

Details often supply the following kinds of information:

causes	criteria	theories	characteristics
effects	purposes	categories	kinds
reasons	factors	advantages	differences
functions	types	disadvantages	similarities

When teachers use these and similar words during lectures, they are hints about the kinds of details to list in your notes.

Watch the Chalkboard

All your teachers were students at one time, and as students they learned that the information *their* teachers wrote on chalkboards was very often used as the basis for test questions. Many of your teachers assume that you also have figured out that you should copy and learn anything written on the board. Many of them believe that they are announcing a test question to you whenever they write on a chalkboard.

Therefore, include in class notes everything your teachers write on the chalkboard and mark it for special attention when you study. You might draw a star or write *Important* in the margin next to the information, or you can mark it with yellow or pink highlighting ink so you will not overlook it when you study for a test.

Some of the types of information instructors write on chalkboards include:

- Tables, charts, and diagrams
- Mathematical formulas
- Important terminology
- People's names and dates

Make diagrams and other drawings large and set them off in your notes with plenty of space before and after them.

Listen for Study Hints

Instructors often inform students about what material is especially important to learn by making statements such as the following:

- This is very important.
- I'll probably ask a test question about this.
- You must be able to do these kinds of problems.
- This confuses some students—don't let it confuse you.

When teachers make such statements, write them in your notes and mark the information to which they pertain for special attention in the same way you mark the information you copy from the chalkboard.

Some of your instructors will give reviews for tests during class or at special times outside of class. Attend reviews, take complete notes, and learn everything that you are told to learn. Teachers who give reviews want to focus your attention on learning what is most important; take advantage of the help they give you. When instructors don't give test reviews, ask them what to study; it is reasonable for you to assume that your teachers want you to know what you should learn.

Take Complete Notes

When you are aware that you have missed information during a lecture, leave a blank space in your notes. Also place a question mark (?) or some other symbol in the margin next to information that you do not understand or that you believe you may have recorded incorrectly. When the time is appropriate, raise your hand and ask the question that will help you to make your notes complete or accurate. Or improve your notes after class by talking with the teacher, by talking with a classmate who takes good notes, or by studying required reading material.

It is extremely important for you to attend all of your classes so you will have a complete set of notes. If you are absent from a class, you have no alternative but to copy the notes taken by one of your classmates. Unfortunately, though, the notes that are useful to your fellow students may not be very helpful to you. Therefore, when you copy notes, make certain you completely understand them by having the person who took them carefully explain what they mean.

Copy notes before or after class, not during it. Students who copy notes during class miss two lectures—the one they are copying and the one their teacher gives while they are copying.

"How to Take Complete Class Notes," on page 243, summarizes procedures to ensure that your notes are complete.

Review Notes After Class

Notes taken in September may contain information that you need to learn for a test in November. If you don't understand your notes in September, you won't understand them in November when you study for a test. Therefore, during the first free time you have following a lecture, reread your notes to make certain that you understand them and that they are complete.

Change your notes in any way that makes them easier to understand. Correct misspelled words, fill in missing information, and make other changes that improve them.

How to Take Complete Class Notes

- Attend *all* lectures.
- Include everything that teachers write on the board and mark it for special attention when you study.
- Include everything that teachers say after glancing at their notes.
- Mark for special attention material in notes teachers say is important or difficult to learn.
- Record examples exactly as they are given so you will recognize them if they show up in test questions.
- Include all definitions of terminology; in many subjects a large portion of test questions directly or indirectly test students' knowledge of terminology.
- When you miss information, leave a blank space for it in your notes. After class find out what you missed and write it in your notes where it belongs.
- Take notes until the very end of class. Instructors often rush to cover a great deal of information during the last few minutes of a class session.
- Build note-taking speed by using simplified handwriting and abbreviations.
- Avoid recopying your notes; it is easy to make errors and lose information when you recopy notes.
- Copy notes from a classmate if you must be absent.

Study Notes Before Tests

It is almost always essential to study class notes thoroughly before tests. If your class notes do not help you do well on tests, either you have taken poor notes or your instructor did not give helpful lectures. Improve your note-taking by following the suggestions in this chapter and the suggestions on how to study class notes on page 320.

Build Note-Taking Speed

Lecturers usually speak at the rate of about 125 to 150 words per minute, but students take notes at the rate of only about 25 to 30 words per minute. Therefore good class notes are summaries rather than word-for-word records of teachers' statements.

Note-taking requires the ability to write quickly and neatly, but there are very few first-year college students who use a fast, neat method for writing class notes. If you want to write notes more quickly and neatly, you may benefit from an experience reported by Walter Pauk in his book, *How to Study in College.*

> The breakthrough in my own notetaking came when I saw an instructor write on a blackboard using a modified printing style. Her writing was not only surprisingly rapid, but also amazingly clear. I immediately began to write in a similar style—without needing practice at all. I believe anyone can adopt this style, and use it to write neatly and clearly.

Here is how the individual letters are formed in this modified printing style:

a b c d e f g h i j k l m n o p q r s t u v w x y z

And here is the style as used in a paragraph:

There are four advantages to using this modified printing style. First, it is faster than cursive writing; second, it is far neater, permitting easy and direct comprehension; third, it saves time by precluding rewriting or typing; and fourth, it permits easy and clear reforming of letters that are ill-formed due to haste.

Even today, I almost always write this way because the style is the easiest, swiftest, and neatest of any I've tried.

Practice writing class notes more neatly and rapidly by using Professor Pauk's simplified method of handwriting. You may also write faster by using symbols of the type listed in "Symbols for Building Note-Taking Speed" on page 245 and abbreviations of the following kinds:

1. Use standard abbreviations: *pp.* (pages), *etc.* (and so on), *e.g.* (for example), *i.e.* (that is).

2. Use standard abbreviations without periods: *NY* (New York), *ex* (example), *mph* (miles per hour), *p* (page).

3. Use first letters of words: *subj* (subject), *psy* (psychology), *chap* (chapter), *ques* (question).

4. Omit vowels: *bldg* (building), *hdbk* (handbook), *wk* (week), *yr* (year).

Symbols for Building Note-Taking Speed

Symbol	Meaning	Example of Its Use
&	and	Bring a pen & pencil.
#	number	He gave his S.S. #.
%	percent	Only 41% voted for him.
$	money	She earns a lot of $.
@	at	He bought 2 shirts @ $20 each.
?	question	The ? was never answered.
'	feet	There are 5,280' in a mile.
"	inches	She's 5' 6½" tall.
×	by	The room is 10' × 14'.
=	equals	A kilo = 2.2 pounds.
≠	not equal to	He's ≠ to the task.
∴	therefore	I think, ∴ I am.
∵	because	She smiles ∵ she's happy.
. . .	and so on	We ate, sang, danced . . .
>	greater than	His taxes are > than hers.
<	less than	His income is < than hers.
w/	with	Wine improves w/age.
w/o	without	He's never w/o a kind word.

5. Add *s* to abbreviations to form the plural: *subjs* (subjects), *hdbks* (handbooks), *chaps* (chapters), *yrs* (years).

6. Use Arabic numerals: 7/4/1776 (July 4, 1776), 2 (two), 4th (fourth), $15 million (fifteen million dollars).

The best abbreviations for you to use in class notes are the ones you understand. Be careful not to use an abbreviation such as *comp* and later find yourself unable to remember if it stands for companion, comparative, compensation, complete, compose, composition, compound, comprehensive, or one of the many other words that begin with *comp*.

Finally, do not slow yourself down by worrying a great deal about spelling when you take class notes. You are the only one who will read your notes; you can correct misspelled words after class.

EXERCISE 17.1   **Abbreviations and Symbols**

Rewrite the following sentences using abbreviations and symbols for the words printed in boldface. If you do not know the standard abbreviation, make up an abbreviation of your own.

1. **Seventy-five percent** of the students earned **less than one hundred dollars** last month.

    _____

2. He **could not answer** the **professor's question.**

    _____

3. She is **five feet four and one-half inches** tall.

    _____

4. They lived **two thousand years before the birth of Christ.**

    _____

5. We drove **fifteen miles north** of **New York City.**

    _____

6. Read the **first twenty pages** of **Chapter Ten.**

    _____

7. His acting was **without equal.**

    _____

8. Our debts are **greater than** our income.

    _____

9. The dance floor measures **twenty feet by forty-five feet.**

    _____

10. The **United States of America** entered **World War II** on **December 7, 1941.**

    _____

EXERCISE 17.2 **Abbreviations**

Write abbreviations for the following common words. If you do not know the standard abbreviation, make up an abbreviation of your own.

1. Mister	_____	21. minute	_____
2. miles per hour	_____	22. week	_____
3. Senior	_____	23. month	_____
4. Junior	_____	24. year	_____
5. Doctor	_____	25. inch	_____
6. Professor	_____	26. foot	_____
7. pages	_____	27. and so on	_____
8. for example	_____	28. example	_____
9. page	_____	29. building	_____
10. handbook	_____	30. weeks	_____
11. following	_____	31. mile	_____
12. company	_____	32. ounce	_____
13. incorporated	_____	33. pound	_____
14. corporation	_____	34. quart	_____
15. chapter	_____	35. gallon	_____
16. without	_____	36. Street	_____
17. equal	_____	37. Avenue	_____
18. number	_____	38. Boulevard	_____
19. money	_____	39. Road	_____
20. second	_____	40. Highway	_____

EXERCISE 17.3   Summarizing

Write summaries of the following statements.

1. Write class notes on paper that measures 8½ by 11 inches rather than on paper of a smaller size, such as 5- by 8-inch paper.

    _____ *Write notes on 8½" × 11" paper.* _____

2. Major thoughts should stand out clearly in notes, and details should be listed neatly under them; however, they need not be labeled with Roman numerals, capital letters, and Arabic numerals in the traditional outline format.

    _____

    _____

3. Each day's notes should have a heading that includes the name or number of the course, the date, the teacher's name, and the lecture topic. For example: Introduction to Psychology; September 22, 1992; Professor Martin; Freud's Theory of Personality.

    _____

    _____

4. All your teachers were students at one time, and as students they learned that the information *their* teachers wrote on chalkboards was very often used as the basis for test questions. Many of your teachers assume that you also have figured out that you should copy and learn anything written on the board. Many of them believe that they are announcing a test question whenever they write on a chalkboard. Therefore, include in class notes everything your teachers write on the chalkboard and mark it for special attention when you study.

    _____

    _____

5. If you believe you write too slowly, you can increase the speed with which you take class notes by using fewer lines, curves, and flourishes in your writing and by using abbreviations (such as "eq" for *equation*) and symbols (such as "%" for *percent*).

    _____

    _____

EXERCISE 17.4 **Rating Lecturers**

Write the names of two of your lecture courses above the columns on the right. Then rate lecturers in each category, using 100 (perfect), 90–99 (excellent), 80–89 (good), 70–79 (satisfactory), 60–69 (poor), 0–59 (unacceptable).

1. _____   2. _____

1. Gives well-organized lectures

2. States main ideas clearly

3. Usually identifies the number of minor details to include in a list

4. Pauses to give me time to write

5. Repeats important statements so I can get them in my notes

6. Makes me feel free to ask questions so my notes will be complete

7. Makes good use of the chalkboard

8. Informs me what is most important to learn

9. Seems very interested in the subject matter of the course

10. Explains difficult ideas and concepts so they are easy for me to understand

Totals

Divide totals by 10 to find averages.

Averages

EXERCISE 17.5   Rating Class Notes

Write the names of the same lecture courses you wrote in Exercise 17.4 above the columns on the right. Then rate your notes for the courses in each category, using 100 (perfect), 90–99 (excellent), 80–89 (good), 70–79 (satisfactory), 60–69 (poor), 0–59 (unacceptable).

1. _____   2. _____

1. I read about lecture topics before class when lectures are difficult to understand.

   _____   _____

2. I begin each day's notes with a complete heading.

   _____   _____

3. Main ideas stand out clearly.

   _____   _____

4. Minor details are listed under main ideas, and they are often numbered.

   _____   _____

5. My notes summarize rather than repeat word for word what the teacher said.

   _____   _____

6. My notes include everything written on the chalkboard, marked for special attention when I study for tests.

   _____   _____

7. My notes include study hints, and the information to which they pertain is marked for special attention when I study for tests.

   _____   _____

8. I ask questions when I need to make my notes complete.

   _____   _____

9. I practice new ways to write faster when I take notes.

   _____   _____

10. I review my notes as soon after class as possible.

   _____   _____

Totals   _____   _____

Divide totals by 10 to find averages.

Averages   _____   _____

Compare your ratings for lecturers in Exercise 17.4 with those for your notes to determine whether there are relationships between them. For instance, if you rated a lecturer for a course high, did you rate your class notes for the course high also?

Survey Textbooks

If you are a full-time college student, you will usually need to read, study, and learn the information in five or more textbooks each term. This may seem like an impossible task, but it isn't—thousands of college students do it every year. The first step in studying your textbooks is to survey them soon after you purchase them.

Read "How to Survey a Textbook" on page 252 before you read the discussions that follow.

The Title Page

Begin a survey by reading the **title page.** It gives exact information about the title of a book, the author or authors, the publisher, and the city in which the book was published. The title page is usually the second or third page in a book. When the title of a book is not followed by an edition number, it is the first edition; and when more than one city is listed on a title page, the book was published in the first city listed. There is a title page in Exercise 18.1 on page 254.

The Copyright Page

After you have read the title page, read the page that follows it—the copyright page. A **copyright page** tells when a book was published. When more than one year is listed in the copyright information, the book was published in the most recent year listed. For example, if the years 1992, 1988, and 1984 are listed, the book was published in 1992. The years 1988 and 1984 refer to earlier editions of the book.

The copyright year tells you whether the information in a book is sufficiently up-to-date for your purposes. For instance, if you want to learn about the current tax laws of the United States, you will want to read a book with a very recent copyright date. On the other hand, if you want to learn how to give a speech, a book published ten years ago may give information that is sufficiently up-to-date for this purpose. There is information from a copyright page in Exercise 18.2 on page 255.

How to Survey a Textbook

Before you read a textbook, examine the features in the front and back of the book.

1. Survey the front of the book.
   - Read the **title page** to learn the title, author (or authors), and publisher of the book.
   - Read the **copyright page** to find out the year the book was published.
   - Read the **table of contents** to get an overview of the organization of the book and the major topics discussed in it.
   - Read the **preface** or **introduction** to find out whether it describes special features that are provided in the book to help students learn.

2. Survey the back of the book.
   - Determine whether the last chapter is followed by an **appendix;** if it is, find out what is in the appendix.
   - Check to see if there is a **glossary** at the end of the book or if there are short glossaries in each chapter.
   - Determine whether **references** are listed at the end of the book or at the end of each chapter.
   - Determine whether there is an **index** at the end of the book or if the book has a subject index *and* a name index.

The Table of Contents

Continue your survey by reading the **table of contents,** which provides an overview of the organization of a book and the major topics discussed in it. When a table of contents does not follow the copyright page, look for it following the preface or introduction. There is part of a table of contents in Exercise 18.3 on page 256.

The Preface or Introduction

A **preface** or an **introduction** explains why a book was written; it usually presents information about the purpose, philosophy, or contents of a book, and it often describes special features that are provided to help students learn information in the book. These opening remarks are usually located on pages following the table of contents, but sometimes they appear before it. Most books have either a preface or an introduction; some books have both. Part of a preface appears in Exercise 18.4 on page 257.

The Appendix

An **appendix,** which contains supplementary material, is usually located immediately after the last chapter. An appendix in a chemistry textbook may present an overview of the mathematics it is important to know in chemistry, and an appendix in an English textbook may explain how to punctuate and capitalize when writing. However, many textbooks have no appendix. There is part of an appendix in Exercise 18.5 on page 258.

The Glossary

A **glossary** is an alphabetically arranged list of important words and their definitions. When a glossary is included in a book, it is usually located after the last chapter or after the appendix. A textbook that has no glossary at the end may have short glossaries at the end of each chapter. There is part of a glossary in Exercise 18.6 on page 259.

The References

The **references,** a **bibliography,** or **notes** are lists of publications and other sources that an author quotes from or refers to in a book. References are usually listed at the end of a textbook, following the glossary or last chapter. When they are not at the end of a book they may be listed at the end of each chapter. Textbooks for subjects such as English, speech, and mathematics usually have no references. There are references in Exercise 18.7 on page 260.

The Index

An **index** is an alphabetically arranged list of subjects and the numbers of the pages on which the subjects are discussed in a book. When an index is included in a book, it is on the very last pages.

Some books have two indexes: a **subject index** and a **name index,** or author index. When a name index (or author index) is included in a book, it is located before the subject index. If you do not find the name of a person in an index, look to see if the book has a name index. For instance, if you do not find Sigmund Freud listed in the index of a psychology textbook, look for his name in the name index or author index. There is part of a name index in Exercise 18.8 on page 261 and part of a subject index in Exercise 18.9 on page 262.

EXERCISE 18.1   Title Page

Answer the questions that follow the title page from *Business*.

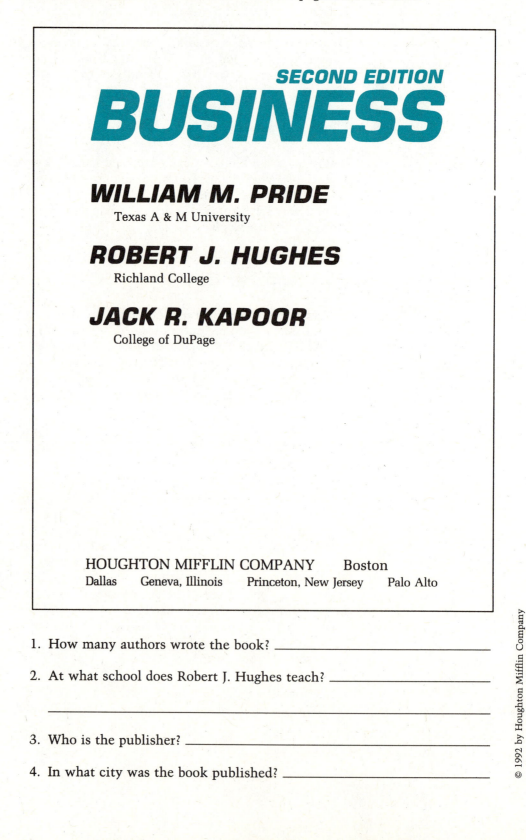

1. How many authors wrote the book? _____

2. At what school does Robert J. Hughes teach? _____

   _____

3. Who is the publisher? _____

4. In what city was the book published? _____

EXERCISE 18.2   **Copyright Page**

Answer the questions that follow the copyright information from *Business*.

Copyright © 1988 by Houghton Mifflin Company. All rights reserved.

No part of this work may be reproduced or transmitted in any form or by any means, electronic or mechanical, including photocopying and recording, or by any information storage or retrieval system, without the prior written permission of Houghton Mifflin Company unless such copying is expressly permitted by federal copyright law. Address inquiries to Permissions, Houghton Mifflin Company, One Beacon Street, Boston, MA 02108.

Printed in the U.S.A.

Library of Congress Catalog Card Number: 87-80200
ISBN: 0-395-35674-1

8987-VH-ABCDEFGHIJ

1. In what year was the book published? _____

2. If people want permission to reproduce passages in *Business,* to what address should they write to request it?

_____

_____

_____

EXERCISE 18.3   Table of Contents

Answer the questions that follow part of the table of contents from *Business*.

CONTENTS

1. What is the title of the first chapter? _____

_____

2. On what page is there a chapter review? _____

EXERCISE 18.4 **Preface**

Answer the questions that follow part of the preface from *Business*.

PREFACE

The American system of business is no mere abstraction. It's a network of real people—millions of individuals seeking challenges, opportunities, and excitement through participation in business. Professors and students of business are an important part of this network. The time they invest jointly in examining the business system today bears directly on the success of the business system tomorrow.

Accordingly, we believe that professors and students deserve the best textbook available, one that is current, dynamic, and interesting—just like business itself. We have developed *Business, Second Edition*, to meet this challenge. Along with its comprehensive instructional package, *Business* provides instructors with the opportunity to present business fundamentals effectively and efficiently. For their part, students will enjoy the *Business* experience and will be well prepared for further study in a variety of business fields.

The second edition of *Business* covers new topics, presents expanded coverage of important issues, focuses on small as well as large businesses, provides thorough career information, and contains numerous pedagogical aids. The comprehensive ancillary package includes *Microstudy Plus*, a new self-help computer-aided instructional diskette, and *Business Video File*, a free series of twenty-four videos—one for each chapter and the Appendix. Here are several distinctive features of *Business, Second Edition*, and the instructional package that accompanies it.

1. What challenge was the book developed to meet? _____

_____

2. List three of the five improvements introduced in the second edition of *Business*.

_____

_____

_____

EXERCISE 18.5 Appendix

Answer the questions that follow part of the appendix from *Business*.

APPENDIX
Careers in Business

As you look ahead to your own career, you are probably interested in the effects that these employment trends will have on employment and employment opportunities.

- Jobs in service industries will account for an increasing proportion of total employment.

- Training—and retraining—will become increasingly important, as firms require their employees to understand and utilize the latest technology. Good jobs will generally require strong educational qualifications.

- Automation of factories and offices will create new types of jobs. Many of these will be computer-related. In some cases, employees will be able to complete assignments at home on remote computer terminals.

- The number of women in the workforce, the number of two-income families, and the number of older workers will increase. There will be greater emphasis on job sharing, flexible hours, and other innovative work practices to accommodate employees' special circumstances.

What, exactly, will the jobs be? A 1986 survey by *Scholastic Update* indicates that computer service technicians will be in greatest demand, followed closely by legal assistants. Those college graduates with majors in computer science, accounting, business, marketing, and economics will also be in high demand according to human resource experts. There will be fewer manufacturing jobs, and those that remain will require "high-tech" skills.

1. Why will the retraining of employees become increasingly important?

   _____

2. Which two occupations are expected to be in greatest demand in the future?

   _____

   _____

EXERCISE 18.6 **Glossary**

Answer the questions that follow part of the glossary from *Business*.

GLOSSARY

absolute advantage the ability to produce a specific product more efficiently than any other nation (23)

accessory equipment standardized equipment used in a variety of ways to carry out production or office activities within a firm (12)

accounts receivable turnover a financial ratio that is calculated by dividing net sales by accounts receivable; measures the number of times a firm collects its accounts receivable in one year (19)

acid-test ratio a financial ratio that is calculated by dividing the sum of cash, marketable securities, accounts receivable, and notes receivable by current liabilities (19)

Active Corps of Executives a group of active managers who counsel small-business owners on a volunteer basis (4)

ad hoc committee a committee created for a specific short-term purpose (6)

administrative law the regulations created by government agencies that have been established by legislative bodies (21)

administrative managers managers who are not associated with any specific area but who provide overall administrative guidance and leadership (5)

advertising a paid, nonpersonal message communicated to a selected audience through a mass medium (14)

advertising media the various forms of communication through which advertising reaches its audience (14)

affirmative action program a plan designed to increase the number of minority employees at all levels within an organization (2)

assets the things of value that a firm owns (19)

authoritarian leader one who holds all authority and responsibility, with communication usually moving from top to bottom (5)

authority the power, within the organization, to accomplish an assigned job or task (6)

boycott a refusal to do business with a particular firm (10)

boycotts in restraint of trade agreements between competitors not to sell to or buy from a particular entity (22)

brand a name, term, symbol, design, or any combination of these that identifies a seller's products and distinguishes them from competitors' products (12)

brand advertising *see* selective advertising

brand mark the part of a brand that is a symbol or distinctive design (12)

brand name the part of a brand that can be spoken (12)

1. What is an ad hoc committee? _____

_____

2. What are assets? _____

_____

3. What is a boycott? _____

_____

EXERCISE 18.7   References

Answer the questions that follow notes from *Business.*

NOTES

CHAPTER 1

[1]Based on information from Bro Uttal, "Compaq Bids for PC Leadership," *Fortune,* September 29, 1986, pp. 30–32; Joel Kotkin, "The 'Smart Team' at Compaq Computer," *Inc.,* February 1986, p. 48; Paul Duke, Jr., "Compaq to Introduce Two Computers Using Intel's State-of-the-Art 386 Chip," *The Wall Street Journal,* September 9, 1986; Jo Ellen Davis, "Compaq Still Confounds Its Skeptics," *Business Week,* March 3, 1986, p. 99. [2]*Fortune,* September 29, 1986, p. 6. [3]*Ibid.,* p. 7. [4]Adapted from "The Origins of Enterprise in America," Exxon U.S.A., third quarter 1976, pp. 8–11.

CHAPTER 2

[1]Based on information from William R. Doerner, "Pullout Parade," *Time,* November 3, 1986, p. 32+; Miriam Horn, "Hassle Factor Hits Home," *U.S. News & World Report,* October 20, 1986, p. 46; Elizabeth Weiner and Steve Mufson, "All Roads Lead Out of South Africa," *Business Week,* November 3, 1986, p. 24; Wayne Svoboda, "The Big Pullout Goes On," *Time,* December 1, 1986, p. 39; and "The Big Guys Pull Out," *Fortune,* November 24, 1986, p. 10. [2]Colgate-Palmolive Company, *Annual Report,* 1981, p. 26. [3]Robert Kreitner, *Management,* 3rd ed. (Boston: Houghton Mifflin, 1983), p. 68. [4]*Ibid.* [5]John L. Hysom and William J. Bolce, *Business and Its Environment* (New York: West, 1983), p. 270. [6]"In Reagan's Lap: New Taxes," *U.S. News & World Report,* October 20, 1986, p. 8. [7]Stanley N. Wellborn, "Pouring Lead from the Tap," *U.S. News & World Report,* November 24, 1986, p. 70. [8]Roul Tunley, "Is Your Water Safe?" *Reader's Digest,* November 1986, p. 232. [9]*The World Almanac and Book of Facts* (New York: Newspaper Enterprise Association, 1983), p. 800. [10]"A Smokestack Alert," *U.S. News & World Report,* May 5, 1986, p. 8. [11]"The Nation Awakes to a New Danger, *U.S. News & World Report,* February 28, 1983, p. 28. [12]"Engineers' Duty to Speak Out," *The Nation,* June 28, 1986, p. 880.

CHAPTER 3

[1]Based on information from Kevin Maney, "Business of Pro Sports: Money the Great Equalizer," *USA Today,* March 23, 1987, p. 11C; Richard Rescigno, "Not Quite a Layup," *Barron's,* November 17, 1986, p. 22; "From the Backboards to the Big Board," *Fortune,* December 22, 1986, p. 8; and "Celts Score on the Big Board," *Time,* December 15, 1986, p. 61. [2]*U.S. News & World Report,* January 16, 1984, p. 65. [3]"Converse Trying a Full Court Press in Athletic Shoes," *Business Week,* May 7, 1984, p. 52. [4]*Fortune,* April 30, 1984, p. 270. [5]*Fortune,* July 8, 1985, p. 22.

CHAPTER 4

[1]Based on information from A. Jay Higgins, "When You Care Enough to Send the Very Wittiest," *Bangor Daily News,* February 14–15, 1987, p. W1; Lynnell Mickelson, "Condolences on Your Pantyhose," *Detroit Free Press,* February 22, 1985, pp. B1–2; and Amanda Troy Segal, "Wild Cards," *Savvy,* August 1984, p. 44. [2]U.S. Small Business Administration, Washington, D.C., September 1984. [3]*Ibid.* [4]According to the Office of Advocacy, U.S. Small Business Administration, there were 668,904 new incorporations in 1985. [5]*Ibid.* [6]*USA Today,* February 24, 1986, p. 2B. [7]Joshua Hyatt, "Too Hot to Handle," *Inc.,* March 1987, p. 58. [8]This section draws heavily from *The Pitfalls of Managing a Small Business* (New York: Dun & Bradstreet, 1976) and from a brochure published by the National Federation of Independent Business. [9]*A Report of the Committee on Small Business,* House of Representatives, Ninety-Ninth Congress, January 2, 1987, p. 22. [10]*Ibid.* [11]*Hearings on Job Creation and Small Business,* part 1, p. 310. [12]*USA Today,* February 10, 1986, p. 4E. [13]*Ibid.* [14]*USA Today,* February 10, 1986, p. 6E.

---

1. In Chapter 1, who published the article referred to in the fourth note?

_____

2. In Chapter 2, who wrote the book referred to in the third note? _____

_____

3. In Chapter 3, to which magazine do the fourth and fifth notes refer?

_____

EXERCISE 18.8   Name Index

Answer the questions that follow part of the name index from *Business*.

NAME INDEX

AAMCC, 400
AAMCO Transmissions, 113
A&P, 394
A&W Root Beer, 363
Action Instruments, 152
Action Packets, Inc., 491
Adams, Cindy, 344
Adline, 13
Advertising Age, 536
Aetna Life and Casualty, 193, 242, 525
Aiken, Howard, 603
Air Florida System, Inc., 171
Air Line Pilots Association, 309
Akers, John, 37
Alcoa, 524
All American Telephone, 524
Allegheny, 671
Allen-Bradley Canada Ltd., 207
Allstate Insurance Company, 339, 536–537
Alza Corp., 550
Americana Encyclopedia, 395
American Airlines, 6, 193, 664, 671
American Can Co., 243, 377
American Dairy Association, 418
American Data Systems, 105
American Express, 86, 627
American Motors, 20, 142, 218, 704
American Red Cross, 133
American Telephone & Telegraph Co. (AT&T), 48, 77, 92, 93, 166, 339, 570, 627, 659

Amway, 383
Anderson, Warren M., 62
Apache Petroleum Company, 66
Apple Computer, 4, 8, 98, 102, 107, 135, 136, 321, 603, 604, 610, 621
Ardman, Perri, 96–97
Ariel, Gideon, 105
Arthur Andersen & Co., 569
Arthur Young & Co., 569
Ash, Mary Kay, 439
Association of American Railroads, 418
AT&T, *see* American Telephone & Telegraph Co.
Atari, 321
Atlantic Monthly, 252
Atlantic Richfield, 268
ATR Wire and Cable Company, 142
Avia, 93
Avis, 148, 400
Avon, 382, 383, 395

Babbage, Charles, 601
Bailes, Harold R., 105
Baldwin Ice Cream, 27
Bally Manufacturing Company, 266
BankAmerica, 446
Bank of America, 212, 471
Barron's, 524
Baskin-Robbins, 113, 120
Beatrice Foods, 186
Bell, W., 394
Bell Telephone Laboratories, 263

Benetton, 686–687
Berg, Paul, 629
Bergerac, Michael, 156
Bertelsmann, 701
Best Products, 344
Bethlehem Steel, 165, 229
Better Business Bureau (BBB), 46
Bing, Dave, 27
Bing Steel, 27
Birch, David, 8
Bird, Larry, 67
Bissaker, Robert, 600
Black & Decker, 244
Block, H.&R., 400
Boaz, Joyce, 96–97
Boesky, Ivan, 57
Bolles, Richard, 275
Borman, Frank, 6
Boston Celtics, 66
Bowen, Otis R., 558–559
Bowmar, 46
Braniff Airlines, 309
Bricklin, Daniel, 608
Brik Pac, Inc., 377
Britannica Encyclopedia, 395
Bristol-Myers Company, 254
Brown-Forman Distillers, 89
Burger King, 119, 133, 397
Business Insurance, 526
Business Roundtable, 670, 672
Business Week, 526, 616

1. On what pages are there references to the Avis car rental company?

   _____

2. On what page is there a reference to Howard Aiken? _____

3. On what pages are there references to AT&T? _____

   _____

EXERCISE 18.9 Subject Index

Answer the questions that follow part of the subject index from *Business*.

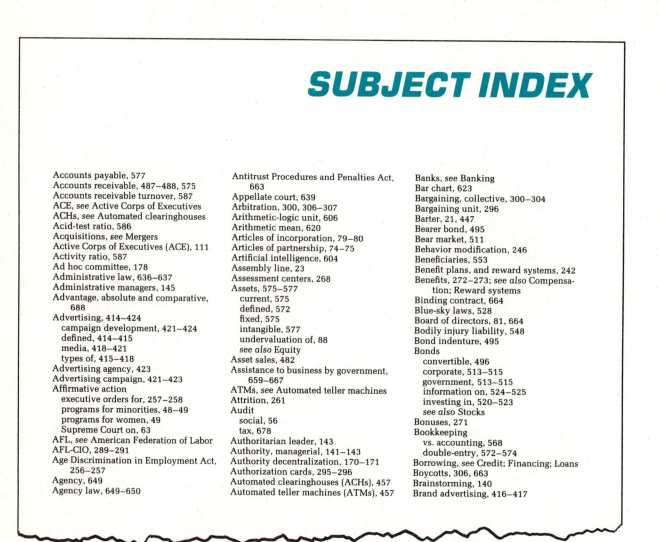

SUBJECT INDEX

Accounts payable, 577
Accounts receivable, 487–488, 575
Accounts receivable turnover, 587
ACE, *see* Active Corps of Executives
ACHs, *see* Automated clearinghouses
Acid-test ratio, 586
Acquisitions, *see* Mergers
Active Corps of Executives (ACE), 111
Activity ratio, 587
Ad hoc committee, 178
Administrative law, 636–637
Administrative managers, 145
Advantage, absolute and comparative, 688
Advertising, 414–424
 campaign development, 421–424
 defined, 414–415
 media, 418–421
 types of, 415–418
Advertising agency, 423
Advertising campaign, 421–423
Affirmative action
 executive orders for, 257–258
 programs for minorities, 48–49
 programs for women, 49
 Supreme Court on, 63
AFL, *see* American Federation of Labor
AFL-CIO, 289–291
Age Discrimination in Employment Act, 256–257
Agency, 649
Agency law, 649–650

Antitrust Procedures and Penalties Act, 663
Appellate court, 639
Arbitration, 300, 306–307
Arithmetic-logic unit, 606
Arithmetic mean, 620
Articles of incorporation, 79–80
Articles of partnership, 74–75
Artificial intelligence, 604
Assembly line, 23
Assessment centers, 268
Assets, 575–577
 current, 575
 defined, 572
 fixed, 575
 intangible, 577
 undervaluation of, 88
 see also Equity
Asset sales, 482
Assistance to business by government, 659–667
ATMs, *see* Automated teller machines
Attrition, 261
Audit
 social, 56
 tax, 678
Authoritarian leader, 143
Authority, managerial, 141–143
Authority decentralization, 170–171
Authorization cards, 295–296
Automated clearinghouses (ACHs), 457
Automated teller machines (ATMs), 457

Banks, *see* Banking
Bar chart, 623
Bargaining, collective, 300–304
Bargaining unit, 296
Barter, 21, 447
Bearer bond, 495
Bear market, 511
Behavior modification, 246
Beneficiaries, 553
Benefit plans, and reward systems, 242
Benefits, 272–273; *see also* Compensation; Reward systems
Binding contract, 664
Blue-sky laws, 528
Board of directors, 81, 664
Bodily injury liability, 548
Bond indenture, 495
Bonds
 convertible, 496
 corporate, 513–515
 government, 513–515
 information on, 524–525
 investing in, 520–523
 see also Stocks
Bonuses, 271
Bookkeeping
 vs. accounting, 568
 double-entry, 572–574
Borrowing, *see* Credit; Financing; Loans
Boycotts, 306, 663
Brainstorming, 140
Brand advertising, 416–417

1. On what page is *ad hoc committee* explained? _____

2. How many types of *assets* are explained in the text? _____

3. On what pages are *boycotts* discussed? _____

4. How many pages are devoted to *advertising*? _____

EXERCISE 18.10   **Survey of a Textbook**

When you do this exercise, use a textbook you are studying for another course; if you have no other textbook, answer the questions by referring to *RSVP*.

1. Title _____

2. Author(s) _____

3. Publisher _____

4. Date of publication _____

Check the items that pertain to the textbook you are surveying.

Table of Contents
☐ It provides an outline of the topics in the textbook.
☐ It shows that the book is divided into parts or sections.

Preface or Introduction
☐ It states for whom the book is intended.
☐ It describes special features provided to help students learn.

Appendix
☐ There is an appendix.
☐ It contains useful or interesting information.
☐ There is no appendix.

Glossary
☐ It is at the end of the book.
☐ There is a short glossary in each chapter.
☐ There is no glossary.

References, Bibliography, or Notes
☐ They are listed at the end of the book.
☐ They are listed at the end of each chapter.
☐ There are no references, bibliography, or notes.

Index
☐ There is a subject index *and* a name (or author) index.
☐ There is only one index.
☐ There is no index.

EXERCISE 18.11   **Survey of a Textbook**

When you do this exercise, use a textbook other than the one you used for Exercise 18.10.

1. Title _____

2. Author(s) _____

3. Publisher _____

4. Date of publication _____

Check the items that pertain to the textbook you are surveying.

Table of Contents
☐ It provides an outline of the topics in the textbook.
☐ It shows that the book is divided into parts or sections.

Preface or Introduction
☐ It states for whom the book is intended.
☐ It describes special features provided to help students learn.

Appendix
☐ There is an appendix.
☐ It contains useful or interesting information.
☐ There is no appendix.

Glossary
☐ It is at the end of the book.
☐ There is a short glossary in each chapter.
☐ There is no glossary.

References, Bibliography, or Notes
☐ They are listed at the end of the book.
☐ They are listed at the end of each chapter.
☐ There are no references, bibliography, or notes.

Index
☐ There is a subject index *and* a name (or author) index.
☐ There is only one index.
☐ There is no index.

Survey Chapters

Most students read a chapter in a textbook by turning to the first page and reading through to the last one. This is *not* an efficient way to read and study the chapters in textbooks. Experienced students know that it is more effective to survey a chapter before reading it. When you survey a chapter, you learn things that make it possible for you to read the chapter with greater understanding. Read "How to Survey a Chapter" on page 266 and scan the textbook chapter on pages 383–412 before you read the discussions that follow.

Title and Introduction

Begin a survey by reading the chapter title and the introduction to the chapter. The title and introduction should summarize what the chapter is about, and an introduction may state the main purpose of the chapter. Whether an introduction to a chapter is short or long, read it carefully as part of your survey.

Learning Goals

Textbook chapters sometimes begin with a list that explains what you should learn as you read and study them. The list may have a heading such as "Learning Goals," "Learning Objectives," "Performance Goals," "Study Guides," or "Chapter Preview." When a chapter begins with **learning goals,** read them as part of your survey and make certain you have achieved the goals in the list before you take a test on the chapter. When you study chapters using learning goals as a guide, your attention will be focused on learning what you are supposed to learn.

Headings

Continue your chapter survey by reading the **headings** to learn what topics are discussed in the chapter. Textbook designers use a variety of methods to show the relationships among headings.

© 1992 by Houghton Mifflin Company

How to Survey a Chapter

Use the following steps to survey a chapter before you read and study it.

1. Survey the beginning of a chapter.
    -   Read the **title** and **introduction** to learn the topic and purpose of the chapter.
    -   If there are **learning goals** at the beginning of the chapter, read them to find out what you are supposed to learn when you study the chapter.

2. Survey the body of the chapter.
    -   Read the **headings** throughout the chapter to find out what topics are discussed in it.
    -   Examine graphs, diagrams, pictures, cartoons, and other **visual material** in the chapter.
    -   Scan any **inserts** or **marginal notes.**

3. Survey the end of the chapter.
    -   If there is an easy-to-understand **summary** at the end of the chapter, read it to get a quick overview of the important information or ideas discussed in the chapter.
    -   If **terminology** is listed at the end of the chapter, read it to find out what new words you are supposed to learn when you study the chapter.
    -   If there are **review questions** at the end of the chapter, read them to get an idea of the types of questions you may have to answer about chapter content when you take a test.
    -   If there are **exercises** or **problems** at the end of the chapter, read them to understand what skills you are expected to learn when you study the chapter.

-   The size of a heading indicates its importance; the larger the heading, the more important it is.
-   A heading in boldface or a special color (such as red or blue) is more important than a heading of the same size that is not in boldface or a special color.
-   A heading printed above a paragraph is more important than a heading printed on the first line of a paragraph.

Textbooks often have headings in addition to major headings and sub-headings. The hints in the list above will help you to understand the relative importance of headings in books that have three, four, or more types of headings.

Visual Material

Textbooks for natural sciences, social sciences, business and many other college subjects include photographs, graphs, and diagrams to summarize or illustrate information. Use the methods explained in Chapter 14 to examine visual material when you survey a chapter.

Inserts

An **insert** is material set off from the rest of the information in a textbook by using lines or by printing it on a shaded background of light blue, yellow, gray, or some other color. Inserts serve a variety of purposes: they can discuss timely issues, explain ways information in a text may be put to practical use, or provide students with opportunities to test themselves. "How to Survey a Chapter" on page 266 is an example of an insert.

Marginal Notes

Some textbooks print definitions of terms and other information in margins. Figure 19.1 on page 268 shows a portion of a business textbook with a learning objective and the definition of a term printed in the margin. "Learning Objective 6" is printed at the place where the information needed to achieve the objective is located, and the term *robotics* is defined in the margin next to the place where it is first used in the book.

Summary

A chapter **summary** provides a quick overview of the information explained in the chapter; therefore, when a textbook chapter ends with a summary, read the summary *before* you read the chapter. The only time it is not helpful to read a summary before reading a chapter is when it is difficult to understand because it includes many technical words whose meanings you will not know until you read the chapter.

Terminology

At the end of chapters there is often a list of the important terminology, or words, used in the chapter. Terminology may be listed under a heading such as "Key Terms," "Important Words," "Key Concepts," or "Terms Used in This Chapter." When there is a list of terminology at the end of a chapter, study it before you read the chapter. Also, learn the meanings of *all* the words in the list before you take a test on the chapter; in many college courses a majority of test questions directly or indirectly test students' understanding of subject terminology.

If there is no list of terms at the beginning or end of a chapter, scan the pages of the chapter to locate important words introduced in it; they are likely to be printed in italics, boldface, or a special color. In *RSVP* terminology is printed in boldface, and it is defined in the glossary.

also increase customer satisfaction, prevent product-safety problems, and decrease costs by reducing the size of the facility's scrap heap.

Automation and Robotics

Learning Objective 6
Understand the increasing role of automation and robotics in production processes

Automation, a development that is revolutionizing the work place, is the total or near-total use of machines to do work. The rapid increase in automated procedures in recent years has been made possible by the microprocessor, a silicon chip one-quarter-inch square that does the electronic switching work of 100,000 vacuum tubes. Microprocessors have led to the production of desk-top computers for offices, where clerical tasks, information retrieval and storage, and interoffice communications are being transformed. In factories, computers are being used in robots and in flexible manufacturing systems.

Robotics

robotics the use of programmable machines to perform a variety of tasks by manipulating materials and tools

Robotics is the use of programmable machines to perform a variety of tasks by manipulating materials and tools.[5] Robots work quickly, accurately, and steadily. They are especially effective in tedious assembly-line jobs and for handling hazardous materials. To date the automotive industry has made the most extensive use of robotics, but robots have also been used to mine coal, inspect the inner surfaces of pipes, assemble computer components, provide certain kinds of patient care in hospitals, and clean and guard buildings at night. It is estimated that more than 30,000 robots will be functioning in U.S. businesses by the 1990s.

FIGURE 19.1
Marginal Notes in a Textbook

Review Questions

A chapter may end with a list of questions that summarizes what you should learn in the chapter. This list may have a heading such as "Questions," "Exercises," "Discussion Questions," or "Review Questions." When there are **review questions** at the end of a chapter, read them before you read the chapter. Also, make certain that you can answer the questions before you take a test on the chapter.

Exercises and Problems

Some textbooks provide exercises or problems to help in learning **skills,** which are abilities acquired through practice. Writing error-free prose, solving mathematical problems, speaking foreign languages, and performing scientific experiments are a few of the skills taught in colleges.

It is often necessary to do more **exercises** or **problems** than a teacher requests. For instance, when a mathematics textbook provides forty problems of a specific type, a teacher may assign only twenty of them. However, some students may need to do twenty-five, thirty, or all forty problems.

If you are an accomplished athlete, musician, dancer, or writer, you know that long hours of practice are necessary to acquire a skill. Do the exercises and problems in your textbooks to give yourself the practice you need to develop the abilities taught in your college courses.

EXERCISE 19.1   **Building High Self-Esteem**

This is the first in a series of five exercises for applying study skills to the textbook chapter entitled "Building High Self-Esteem," which is on pages 383–412 in the appendix.

1. This exercise is for surveying the chapter.

2. Exercise 20.10 on pages 297–298 is for marking information in the chapter.

3. Exercise 21.10 on page 316 is for making notes on information in the chapter.

4. Exercise 22.4 on page 328 is for reciting the information in your notes.

5. Exercise 23.2 on page 337 is for answering test questions about the information you recited.

Survey the textbook chapter on pages 383–412 by removing this page from the book and answering the following questions.

1. What is the **title** of the chapter?

   _____

2. **Learning goals** are listed under the heading "Chapter Preview." What is the sixth learning goal?

   _____

3. According to the two-paragraph **introduction,** what is the importance of high self-esteem?

   _____

   _____

4. The first **major heading** in the chapter is "Self-Esteem Defined" on page 384. What are the other three major headings in the chapter?

   _____

   _____

5. "How Your Self-Esteem Develops" on page 386 is the first **subheading** following the major heading "Self-Esteem Defined" on page 384. Beginning on page 387, check the headings in the following list that have the same level of importance as "How Your Self-Esteem Develops."

   ☐ Childhood
   ☐ Adolescence
   ☐ Adulthood
   ☐ Characteristics of People with High Self-Esteem

□ Self-Esteem and Success at Work
□ Your Self-Esteem Influences Your Behavior
□ Maltz Discovers the Power of Self-Esteem
□ The Power of Expectations
□ Your Own Expectations
□ The Expectations of Others
□ Mentors
□ How to Build Your Self-Esteem
□ Accept the Past, Change the Future
□ Your Organization Can Help

6. Write an answer to one of the questions in the "Thinking/Learning Starters" on page 392.

_____

_____

_____

7. What is the purpose of the **photograph** on page 386?

_____

_____

_____

8. Read the **summary** on pages 406–407. Does it provide an easy-to-understand overview of the chapter?

_____

9. How many **key terms** are listed at the end of the chapter?

_____

What is the definition of *mentors* given on page 398?

_____

_____

_____

10. Read the "Review Questions" and list three of the characteristics asked for in the fourth question.

_____

_____

_____

EXERCISE 19.2   ## Surveying a Chapter in Your Textbook

When you do this exercise, use a textbook you are studying for another course you are taking or have taken.

1. Textbook title   _____

2. Chapter title   _____

3. Number of pages in the chapter   _____

4. Check the statements that are true about the chapter.

☐ The **title** states what the chapter is about.
☐ The **introduction** states the purpose of the chapter.
☐ There are **learning goals** at the beginning of the chapter.
☐ **Headings** summarize the topics that are discussed in the chapter.
☐ There are bar **graphs** or line graphs in the chapter.
☐ There are diagrams, cartoons, or other drawings in the chapter.
☐ There are photographs in the chapter.
☐ There is a **summary** at the end of the chapter.
☐ The summary is easy to read and understand.
☐ There is a list of **terminology** at the end of the chapter.
☐ Terminology is printed in boldface, italics, or a special color in the chapter.
☐ There are **review questions** at the end of the chapter.
☐ There are **exercises** or **problems** at the end of the chapter.

EXERCISE 19.3   **Surveying a Chapter in Your Textbook**

When you do this exercise, use a textbook other than the one you used for Exercise 19.2.

1. Textbook title _____

2. Chapter title _____

3. Number of pages in the chapter _____

4. Check the statements that are true about the chapter.

- ☐ The **title** states what the chapter is about.
- ☐ The **introduction** states the purpose of the chapter.
- ☐ There are **learning goals** at the beginning of the chapter.
- ☐ **Headings** summarize the topics that are discussed in the chapter.
- ☐ There are bar **graphs** or line graphs in the chapter.
- ☐ There are diagrams, cartoons, or other drawings in the chapter.
- ☐ There are photographs in the chapter.
- ☐ There is a **summary** at the end of the chapter.
- ☐ The summary is easy to read and understand.
- ☐ There is a list of **terminology** at the end of the chapter.
- ☐ Terminology is printed in boldface, italics, or a special color in the chapter.
- ☐ There are **review questions** at the end of the chapter.
- ☐ There are **exercises** or **problems** at the end of the chapter.

Mark Your Books

One of the best-known facts about human learning is that information is easier to learn when it is organized in a meaningful way. Most successful college students organize information they want to learn from their books by marking it and by then using their marks as a guide for summarizing the information into study notes.

Figures 20.1 and 20.2 on page 274 illustrate how markings are used as a guide in making notes.

Reasons for Marking Books

If you were told in high school that you must not write in books, you may wonder why marking textbooks is an essential skill for efficient college study. The main reason is that when you mark a book in the way explained in this chapter, you make a permanent record of the information you want to learn from that book. On the other hand, when you do not mark a book as you read it, you must reread it to find the information you need to learn.

Some students resist writing in their books because they cannot, or fear they cannot, resell marked books. This is a foolish way to economize. Textbooks are expensive, but they are a small part of the cost of attending college in comparison to tuition, housing, food, transportation, and other expenses. Virtually all successful students mark their books because it saves them valuable study time.

The only students who do not need to mark their books are the ones who make good notes as they read. If you make well-organized summaries of the information in your books as you read them, you do not need to underline, highlight, or write in your books.

Underline or Highlight

To **underline** is simply to draw lines under words; it is usually done with a pen, using a ruler as a guide. Many students prefer to highlight rather than underline because highlighting can be done neatly without using a

FIGURE 20.1

A Highlighted
Textbook Passage

Steps in the Selling Process

Many businesses have as their primary function the selling of a product or service; selling may be viewed as a four-step process.

First, the selling business wants to find buyers. Buyers are attracted to a product or service through advertising, the availability of the product or service, or the efforts of salespeople. Department stores find buyers by advertising and by being located where customers shop. Encyclopedias are often sold through advertising and the efforts of salespeople.

After potential buyers have been found, a product or service must be presented in the most attractive and convincing way possible. Expensive perfume is offered for sale in attractive and expensive-looking bottles. Low-cost vacation trips are sold in offices that convince customers they will receive a bargain; it would not be convincing to sell low-cost travel in an office that is decorated with rare objects of art and expensive furniture.

Once buyers have been found and the product or service has been presented in an attractive and convincing way, the salesperson must create the customer's desire to buy. This is usually achieved by persuading customers that their lives will be better when they make a purchase. Another technique salespeople use is to establish rapport with customers so they buy because they like the salesperson rather than because they need or want what they purchase.

The final step in the selling process is to close the sale. Once the customer has the desire to buy, the salesperson will do something to motivate the customer to put out money for a purchase. A clothing salesperson might ask, "Will you take the brown sweater or the blue one?" A travel salesperson might close a sale by asking, "Shall I book you hotel rooms in London, Paris, and Rome, or have you decided not to stop in Paris?"

FIGURE 20.2

Notes for the
Passage in
Figure 20.1

Steps in the Selling Process

1. Find buyers. (EX) Advertise and locate stores where customers shop.

2. Present the product or service attractively and convincingly. (EX) Sell perfume in expensive-looking bottles.

3. Create the customers' desire to buy (by persuading them that the purchase will make their lives better).

4. Close the sale. (EX) Say, "Will you take the brown sweater or the blue one?"

ruler. To **highlight** is to mark words using a felt-tipped pen that contains watercolor ink. Yellow and pink are the most popular colors. In this book I use *underline* to mean "underline" or "highlight."

Light blue is used to indicate highlighting in the passage in Figure 20.1.

When you use the guidelines that are summarized in "How to Mark Books" on page 276, you may find that it sometimes seems impossible to follow the second guideline—"Do not mark too much." However, there are at least three ways to avoid excessive underlining. First, it is sometimes better to underline only key words that identify major details than to underline information about major details. For instance, if a page in a human anatomy textbook describes all the bones in the hand and arm, underline the names of the bones but not the information about them. Later, use the underlining as a guide for making notes. The following discussion explains two other ways you can reduce the amount of underlining in your books.

Numbers and Vertical Lines

It is often more appropriate to number details rather than to underline them. For example:

Brain Death

In the past, a person was considered dead when he or she stopped breathing and the heart ceased to beat. Today, however, medical technology* is able to maintain the heartbeat and respiration in people who would otherwise be dead. As a result, in 1968 a committee of the Harvard Medical School offered a definition of death based on the concept of brain death. A person would be considered dead if he or she was ①unreceptive and unresponsive; ②was in an irreversible coma; ③did not move or did not breathe when off a mechanical respirator; ④had no reflexes; and ⑤had a flat electroencephalogram (EEG), indicating no brain waves. That definition is now widely accepted medically, and a number of states have written it into law.

If the five details in this passage were underlined, the entire last half of the paragraph would be underlined.

In addition, vertical lines are useful for a variety of purposes, including marking definitions and examples.

Colloquialisms

The term **colloquial** is defined by *The American Heritage Dictionary* as "characteristic of or appropriate to the spoken language or writing that seeks its effect; informal in diction or style of expression." Colloquialisms are not "incorrect" or "bad" English. They are the kinds of words people, educated and uneducated alike, use when they are speaking together informally. Their deliberate use in writing conveys the impression of direct and intimate conversation. To achieve this effect you might use contractions (don't, wasn't, hasn't) or clipped words (taxi, phone).

---

* Words underscored in blue are defined in the Master Vocabulary List on pages 413–425, and the exercise on page 60 is based on these words.

How to Mark Books

Use the following guidelines when you mark, underline, or highlight your books.

- **Read a section before you mark it.** If you mark as you read, you may mark information that you later decide is not especially important.

- **Do not mark too much.** If almost everything on a page is marked, it is the same as if nothing were marked. As a general rule, don't underline more than 20 percent of the information on a page. For instance, if there are 40 lines of print on the pages of a book, don't underline more than about 8 lines on a page. Avoid excessive underlining by numbering details and by using vertical lines to mark information that you might otherwise underline.

- **Mark information that will help you make notes.** The purpose of marking a book is to make a permanent record that will help you later make notes for learning information.

- **Make major details stand out.** You use major details to make well-organized notes, and it is almost always important to learn them.

- **Mark definitions of terminology.** On many college tests 70 percent of questions directly or indirectly test students' knowledge of terminology.

- **Mark examples.** Learn the examples included in your books so you will recognize them if they are used in test questions.

On page 275, "def" is used as an abbreviation for "definition," and "Ex" is an abbreviation for "Examples."

In the following example, "Imp't" is used as an abbreviation for "Important," to draw attention to information a reader decided is especially important.

The Family

The family is without doubt the most significant single agent of socialization in all societies. One reason for the importance of the family is that it has the main responsibility for socializing children in the crucial early years of life. The family is where children establish their first emotional ties, learn language, and begin to internalize cultural norms and values.

Some students write asterisks (*) next to information they decide is especially important and question marks (?) next to material that is unclear to them. Write any symbols or words in your books that help you to learn the information in them.

Many scholars write comments in the margins of books as they study them. For example, if while reading a statement written by Carl Jung, students of psychology recall that Sigmund Freud expressed a similar point of view, they may write "Freud agrees" in the margin. You, too, may interact with the authors of your books by writing whatever comments you want in the margins of the books you own.

Helps for Finding Details

Authors and editors provide five helps for locating details to mark in textbooks: (1) words in italics or boldface, (2) numbers, (3) bullets, (4) statements in introductions, and (5) subheadings. The first four of these helps are explained on pages 157–159 in Chapter 11, "Main Ideas and Details."

The following passage illustrates how subheadings help locate the major details in a passage.

Reasons for Using Credit

Consumers borrow because they need money for emergencies, because they want to enjoy the good life, and for a variety of other reasons.

Emergencies   Consumers use credit to pay for unexpected expenses, such as emergency medical services or auto repairs.

Early Consumption and Convenience   Buying a color television on credit allows consumers immediate home use of the product and the convenience of not having to carry large sums of money.

"The Good Life"   An increasing number of younger persons (nearly two-thirds of the people under twenty-five) use credit as a tool for personal money management. Such credit users seem to want to have now what it took their parents perhaps twenty years to acquire.

Debt Consolidation   Many consumers who have difficulty making credit repayments turn to a **debt-consolidation loan.** Here the borrower exchanges several smaller debts with varying due dates and interest rates for one payment, which is usually lower in amount than the payments on the other debts combined. For the privilege of "consolidating" all debts into one, the consumer is charged a substantial interest rate (perhaps 28 percent) and the term of the loan is lengthened.

Identification   For many activities, such as renting an automobile or cashing a check, consumers often need to show one or two credit cards for identification.

Notice that the subheadings make it clear that there are five reasons people use credit.

© 1992 by Houghton Mifflin Company

EXERCISE 20.1 **SQ3R**

Use the introduction and subheadings to guide you in marking the following passage.

The SQ3R Study Method

An excellent set of suggestions for effective studying is to be found in the *SQ3R Study Method* designed by Francis Robinson at Ohio State University. The five steps are *Survey, Question, Read, Recite,* and *Review.* Each is described briefly here.

Survey To survey a chapter, begin by reading the various headings and subheadings. In this way you learn generally what the chapter is about, and you know what to expect. Skim some of the first sentences and look at any pictures, tables, or graphs. If there is a summary, read it as part of your survey, because it will give you the important points of the chapter. The survey technique increases your ability to understand and learn new material.

Question Some textbooks have lists of questions at the beginning or end of each chapter. If a book has them, use them and try to answer them. Try to think about the material and ask yourself questions about it. Asking questions is a way of actively taking part in the learning process. Active participation is a key to learning. Questions also are ways of testing yourself to see what you have learned.

Read The next step is to read. Read carefully and try to answer the questions that you have asked yourself. Make sure that you read everything—tables, graphs, and captions as well as the main text. Students often say, "I forget what I read as soon as I put the book down." So read to remember by telling yourself to remember. Notice particularly any words or phrases that are italicized, because authors use italics to point out important terms, concepts, and principles.

Recite Recitation is an important part of effective studying. Recite, not just in class periods, but to yourself by recalling what you have read. Recitation takes a lot of effort, for it is easy just to read and put the book away. Try to recall main headings and main ideas. For example, what does SQ3R stand for? As you read, stop several times and recite to yourself the major points that are being presented in the text. Recitation is important because it helps prevent forgetting by forcing you to keep your attention on the task.

Review The fifth step in the SQ3R technique is to review. Review is important for remembering. The best times for review are right after first studying and again just before a test. Most good students try to get one or two reviews in between. These reviews include rereading and recitation.

EXERCISE 20.2   Conversation

Use the numbers and words printed in italics to guide you in marking the
following passage.

Effective Conversationalists

Effective conversationalists are likely to share at least the following
five characteristics.

1. *Effective conversationalists have quality information.* The key to
solid, stimulating conversation is to have information that others
value. In a recent study Claire Brunner and Judy Pearson found that
men in particular judge others as competent communicators on the
basis of their knowledge.[1] In late September before the 1988 general
election I was with a group of people, one of whom had just finished
conducting a major opinion poll on a political issue. For an hour
that person was the center of attention. Why? Because she had
information that people wanted to hear about.

    Although you cannot be an expert in every area, the more you
know, the greater the chance that you will be a good conversation-
alist. Do you read at least one newspaper a day (not just the comics
or the sports)? Do you read at least one news or professional magazine a week? Do you watch television documentaries and news
specials as well as entertainment and sports programs? Do you engage knowledgeable people in conversation on topics about which
they have expert information? Do you go to the theater, concerts,
and so on? If you answered no to all of these questions, you probably
do not have much to contribute to social conversations. Only when
you expose yourself to a broad array of information experiences can
you develop ideas that others will find interesting and provide grist
for the conversation mill.

2. *Effective conversationalists enjoy the give-and-take of informal
discussion.* The best conversations usually occur when people enjoy interacting. Do you enjoy listening to the ideas presented by
others? Do you like to comment on, discuss, and even disagree with
what they say? If you do, then you probably enjoy the conversations
you have. In addition, those you converse with can sense this enjoyment through the nonverbal messages you send.

3. *Effective conversationalists ask good questions.* There are times
when you will be the center of attention, when the conversation
will focus on your ideas. Many times, however, the quality of your
conversation will depend on how well you can draw out the other
person. Even when you are the major source of information in a
conversation, you want other people to react to the issue being
discussed. To do this you need to develop your skill as a questioner.

4. *Effective conversationalists listen to others' ideas.* A conversation
represents an interaction between people, not a one-way broadcast.
Although some people regard a conversation as successful when
they do all the talking, effective conversations are characterized by

the development of shared meaning. In a normal conversation, then, you can expect to be the listener at least half the time.

5. *Effective conversationalists work to increase their skill.* You improve by being willing to take every opportunity to engage in conversation with others about current events, art, social problems, and other issues that go beyond the easy topics of sports, television, and gossip. As you progress you will find your conversations becoming more interesting, <u>provocative</u>, and stimulating.

Reference

1. Brunner, C., and Pearson, J. (Nov. 1984). *Sex differences in perceptions of interpersonal communication competence.* Paper presented at the annual meeting of the Speech Communication Association, Chicago, IL.

EXERCISE 20.3   **Altruism**

Use the introduction, headings, and words printed in italics to guide you in marking the following passage.

Altruism

Although we read frequently about people's indifference to others in trouble, and experiments have shown that individuals in groups are often reluctant to take action in an emergency, we must remember that almost every day, individuals do perform acts of genuine heroism. In Europe, during the Second World War, many people put their lives in jeopardy to help Jews escape from the Nazis. In the 1960s hundreds of young American men and women participated in voter registration drives in the Deep South, at great personal risk. Frequently we read of people who rush into burning buildings or jump into deep water to rescue someone in danger. Why are some people more likely to help than others? The reasons vary, depending on the particular situation. Three approaches to explaining altruism are reviewed by Middlebrook (1974): a normative explanation, a cost analysis, and the influence of moods and feelings.

The Normative Explanation   During socialization, children learn the rules of appropriate conduct, which include two norms of helping behavior. The first is the *norm of social responsibility*, which states that people should help others who need help because it is the right thing to do. Studies have shown that people will be helpful if they see another person helping someone else (Bryan & Test, 1967), because observing this behavior makes the social responsibility norm salient. However, research has shown that this norm is not a strong determinant of helping behavior (Berkowitz, 1972). The second norm, called the *norm of reciprocity*, holds that people should treat others as the others have treated them. This means that we help the person who previously did a favor for us, and if a person has denied us help in the past, we deny it to that person when he or she needs it. Gouldner (1960) suggested that this is a universal norm, and many subsequent studies have demonstrated the norm of reciprocity (Kahn & Tice, 1973).

The Cost Analysis Approach   The *cost analysis* approach holds that helping behavior is most likely to occur when the rewards for helping outweigh the costs. Costs would be the negative consequences and rewards the positive consequences to the individual. Darley and Latané (1970) have shown that the relative cost of the help requested influences the incidence of helping. Ninety-three of their social psychology students went out on the streets of New York and made a number of different requests of passersby. They found that what was asked made a significant difference as to whether or not people complied with the request. For example, people were much more likely to give change for a quarter (73 percent) than to tell their name (39 percent), which involves a certain personal risk in a large metropolis.

Thus, the number of people complying decreases as the costs of helping increase.

Helping is much less likely to occur if it involves the threat of danger. In large cities, such as New York, people may be <u>inhibited</u> from helping because of urban crime statistics, which lead to lack of trust in others. This theory was illustrated in a study that compared helping behavior in New York City with that of individuals in several small towns in New York State. The investigators, working singly, rang doorbells, asking the occupants if they could use the telephone. In the city, 75 percent of the residents did not open their doors, whereas in the small towns, about 75 percent admitted the strangers (Altman, Levine, Nadien & Villena, unpublished, in Milgram, 1970).

The Mood Approach   The third, or *mood*, approach suggests that moods and feelings influence the extent to which people are willing to help others. A person in a good mood is more likely to offer assistance or act in a generous manner to others than is a person in a bad mood (Berkowitz, 1972; Rosenhan, Underwood & Moore, 1974). Helping others also minimizes one's feelings of guilt. If you have wronged someone, you may want to make it up by doing something nice for the person. Feelings of <u>equity</u> might also cause you to correct a wrong, even if you are not responsible for it; for seeing someone unjustly hurt disturbs your belief that the world is a fair place. Sympathy—<u>compassion</u> for an injured person—may also stimulate helping behavior.

References

Berkowitz, L. "Social Norms, Feelings, and Other Factors Affecting Helping and Altruism." In *Advances in Experimental Social Psychology.* Vol. 6. Ed. L. Berkowitz. New York: Academic Press, 1972, pp. 63–108.

Bryan, J., and M. Test. "Models and Helping: Naturalistic Studies in Aiding Behavior." *Journal of Personality and Social Psychology,* 6 (1967), 400–407.

Darley, J., and B. Latané. "Norms and Normative Behavior: Field Studies of Social Interdependence." In *Altruism and Helping Behavior: Social Psychological Studies of Some Antecedents and Consequences.* Eds. J. Macaulay and L. Berkowitz. New York: Academic Press, 1970, 83–101.

Gouldner, A.W. "The Norm of Reciprocity: A Preliminary Statement." *American Sociological Review,* 25 (1960), 161–178.

Kahn, A., and T. Tice. "Returning a Favor and Retaliating Harm. The Effects of Stated Intentions and Actual Behavior." *Journal of Experimental Social Psychology,* 9 (1973), 43–56.

Middlebrook, P.N. *Social Psychology and Modern Life.* New York: Knopf, 1974.

Milgram, S. "The Experience of Living in Cities." *Science,* 167 (1970), 1461–1468.

Rosenhan, D.L., B. Underwood, and B. Moore. "Affect Moderates Self-gratification and Altruism." *Journal of Personality and Social Psychology,* 30, No. 4 (1974), 546–552.

EXERCISE 20.4   Adversity

Use the subheadings to guide you in marking the following passage.

Coping with Adversity

When people believe they have been wronged, they are likely to behave in one of three ways: <u>passively</u>, aggressively, or <u>assertively</u>.

Passive Behavior   When people behave passively, they do not try to influence the behavior of others. People who behave passively are reluctant to state opinions, share feelings, or assume responsibility for their actions. Thus, they often submit to the demands of others, even when doing so is inconvenient or against their best interests.

For example, when Bill uncrates the new color television set he purchased at a local department store, he notices a large, deep scratch on the left side of the cabinet. If he behaved passively, Bill would be angry about the scratch, but he would keep the set and do nothing to influence the store clerk from whom he purchased it to replace it.

Aggressive Behavior   When people behave aggressively, they lash out at the source of their discomfort with little regard for the situation or for the feelings of those they are attacking. Unfortunately, too many people confuse aggressiveness with assertiveness. Unlike assertiveness, aggressive behavior is judgmental, <u>dogmatic</u>, fault-finding, and <u>coercive</u>.

To exemplify aggressive behavior and to extend the contrast we are making, let's return to Bill's problem. If Bill behaved aggressively, after discovering the scratch on the cabinet of his new television set, he might <u>brashly</u> display his anger. He might storm back to the store, loudly demand his money back, and accuse the clerk of intentionally selling him damaged merchandise. During his <u>tirade</u>, he might threaten the store with a lawsuit. Such aggressive behavior might or might not get Bill a new television set; it would certainly damage the interpersonal relationships he had with those to whom he spoke.

Assertive Behavior   When people behave assertively, they state what they believe to be true for them, describe their feelings fully, give good reasons for their beliefs or feelings, suggest the behavior or attitude they think is fair, avoid exaggerating for dramatic effect, and take responsibility for their actions and feelings without personal attacks on others. If Bill behaved assertively, he would be angry about bringing home a damaged set—the feeling of anger is common to each of these three contrasting response behaviors. The difference between assertive behavior and the other two response styles is not the feeling but the behavior of the person as a result of that feeling. If Bill responded assertively, he might call the store and ask to speak to the clerk from whom he had purchased the set. When the clerk answered, Bill would describe his anger that resulted from discovering a large scratch on the cabinet when he uncrated the set. He would then say that he was calling to find out what to do to return the damaged set and get a new one.

While both the aggressive and the assertive behaviors might achieve Bill's purpose of getting a new television set, the assertive behavior would achieve the same result at lower emotional costs to both Bill and those with whom he talked.

In order to emphasize the contrast among the response styles, let's examine another situation in which the issue is the quality of an interpersonal relationship. Betty works in an office with both male and female employees. Whenever the boss has an especially interesting job to be done, he assigns it to a male employee whose desk is next to Betty's. The boss has never said anything to Betty or to the male employee that would indicate that the boss thinks less of Betty or her ability. Nevertheless, Betty is hurt by the boss's behavior.

If Betty behaved passively, she would say nothing to the boss. If Betty behaved aggressively, she would call her boss on his behavior by saying something like "Why the hell do you always give Tom the plums and leave me with the garbage! I'm every bit as good a worker and I'd like a little recognition!"

In contrast, if Betty behaved assertively, she would go back to the boss's office and describe his behavior and her feelings about that behavior to him. She might say, "I don't know whether you are aware of it, but during the last three weeks every time you had a really interesting job to do, you gave the job to Tom. To the best of my knowledge, you believe that Tom and I are equally competent—you've never given me any evidence to suggest that you thought less of my work. But when you 'reward' Tom with jobs that I perceive as plums and continue to offer me routine jobs, it really hurts my feelings. Do you understand my feelings about this?"

If you were Betty's boss, which of her responses would be most likely to achieve her goal of getting better assignments? Probably the assertive behavior. Which of her responses would be most likely to get her fired? Probably the aggressive behavior. Which of her behaviors would be least likely to "rock the boat"? Undoubtedly the passive behavior—but then she would continue to get the boring job assignments.

To be assertive, then, you should (1) identify what you are thinking or feeling and (2) state it in the most interpersonally sound way possible.

You must also understand that being assertive may not achieve your goals. Every skill we have discussed in this section is designed to increase the chances of interpersonal effectiveness. But there will still be times when what you attempt won't work or may even backfire. Just as with self-disclosure and describing feelings, being assertive involves risks. For instance, in the preceding example Betty's boss might become so defensive that he fires Betty. But if being treated unfairly is a concern to Betty—and I believe it should be—then Betty can accept the risk of such an undesirable outcome, knowing that if she uses the skill properly, getting fired would be very unlikely. If you are truly assertive and not aggressive, you are far more likely to achieve your goals than you would be if you behaved in some other way.

EXERCISE 20.5   Spoken Language

Use the subheadings and words printed in boldface to guide you in marking the following passage.

Components of a Spoken Language

Although it is not the only form of language, the oral or spoken form is by far the most common. The world's many cultures are united by the use of a rich variety of spoken languages. A spoken language has three major components: *phonology, syntax*, and *semantics*. Each component makes a distinct contribution to the sentences we speak and understand. The components do not operate in isolation, however. Rather, they function together to form the grammar of a language. By **grammar,** we mean the set of rules that allow us to speak and comprehend our language.

Phonology

Phonology refers to the study of how sounds are combined to produce words and sentences. Although you may think of words as the smallest units of sound, they are actually formed from a smaller class of sounds known as phonemes. A **phoneme** is the smallest unit of sound in a spoken language that influences the comprehension and production of a larger unit, such as a word. There are approximately 45 distinct phonemes in English that correspond roughly to the consonants and vowels of the alphabet. They must be combined with one another to produce generally recognizable sounds. In the English language, phonemes include such sounds as the *t* at the beginning of *tea* and the *k* at the beginning of *key* (Dale, 1976). You might note that *tea* and *key* sound exactly the same except for the initial *t* and *k* of each word. The difference in the meaning of *tea* and *key* is expressed through a single phoneme at the beginning of each word. This is the primary function of phonemes: they are sounds that help us distinguish the meaning of one word from another.

The smallest *meaningful* elements of a spoken language are **morphemes.** Words are morphemes, though not all words are single morphemes. When a speaker uses the word *pictures*, for example, he or she is actually using two morphemes. One is *picture* and the other is the plural ending *s*. The first morpheme tells us that the speaker is referring to a drawing or photograph. The second morpheme tells us that the speaker is referring to more than one object. The plural ending *s* is a morpheme because it adds new information, and thus new meaning, to the speaker's utterance.

Other examples of morphemes include suffixes, such as *ing*, and prefixes, such as *anti*. The importance of suffixes and prefixes can be shown by considering the difference between *run* and *running*, or *establishment* and *antiestablishment*. In each case, the addition of the suffix or prefix produces a change in meaning.

Phonology is important because it allows us to distinguish between acceptable and unacceptable words. For example, each of the following sequences of letters is probably unfamiliar to you, but you can use your knowledge of English to determine which one is actually a word:

kferg
knout
kbear

The sequences beginning with *kf* and *kb* can be ruled out because you know intuitively that English words do not begin with these letters. The sequence *knout* is a possibility because English permits *kn* at the beginning of words (such as in *knight* and *knot*). Incidentally, *knout* is an English word for a whip with long leather thongs.

Syntax

Syntax is the set of rules that determines how morphemes are combined to form grammatically correct sentences. All languages have rules specifying what is and is not an acceptable sentence. Consider the following two sentences:

The boy ran away.
Boy the ran away.

Adult speakers of English know that the first sentence is grammatically correct and that the second is incorrect. The rules of English do not permit a noun phrase (*the boy*) to be formed by placing the article (*the*) after the noun (*boy*).

It is worth noting, however, that syntactic rules are arbitrary. English generally does not allow the adjective to follow the noun, but other languages, such as Spanish and French, do. Furthermore, even within cultures, certain dialects use syntactic rules that differ from the standard form (Labov, 1970). Psychologists must be aware of this point when assessing the syntactic skills of individuals from communities that have substantial non-standard dialects, such as some black or Hispanic communities (Baratz, 1970).

Semantics

As we noted earlier, **semantics** is the study of how meaning is expressed through words and sentences. Meaning is a very complex aspect of language. Words, for example, can refer to concrete objects (such as *ball* or *horse*), to abstract qualities (such as *beauty* and *love*), and to relationships among objects (such as *more* or *better*). In addition, some words can have both a *denotative* and a *connotative* meaning. The denotative meaning of a word is its literal meaning; the connotative meaning of a word is its emotional or affective meaning. For example, the literal or dictionary meaning of *house* and *home* is about the same: they both can be defined as a building in which people live, or a residence for human beings. But the connotative meanings are slightly different. The word *home* conjures up an image of a warm, relaxing, and pleasant place, whereas *house* seems to be a more impersonal term.

But the complexity of word meaning does not end at the level of individual words. Meaning is often determined by subtle differences in the way something is said, or even the context in which it is said. If, for example, a policeman stops you for speeding and says, "May I see your license, please," you would be foolish to interpret the remark as a polite inquiry. It is a command, not a question, as you would soon find out if you answered, "No." The role of contextual meaning in particular, and the social uses of language more generally, form a special branch of semantics known as *pragmatics* (Macauley, 1980).

In summary, the three major components of a spoken language are phonology, syntax, and semantics. They operate together to form the grammar of a language; that is, the set of rules that allow us to produce and comprehend the words and sentences we know. In the following section, we will consider the question of how people learn these rules or, to put it more directly, how a spoken language develops.

References

Baratz, J.D. (1970). Teaching reading in an urban Negro school system. In F. Williams (Ed.), *Language and poverty*. Chicago: Markham.

Dale, P. (1976). *Language development: Structure and function.* New York: Holt, Rinehart & Winston.

Labov, W. (1970). The logic of nonstandard English. In F. Williams (Ed.), *Language and poverty*. Chicago: Markham.

Macauley, R.K. (1980). *Generally speaking: How children learn language.* Rowley, MA: Newbury House.

EXERCISE 20.6   **Personal Space**

Use the numbers and boldface to guide you in marking the following passage.

Personal Space

An interesting aspect of social behavior is the effort people expend to regulate the space around their bodies. Each person has an invisible "spatial envelope" that defines his or her **personal space** and extends "I" or "me" boundaries past the skin. Maintaining and regulating personal space directly affects many social interactions. There are unspoken rules covering the interpersonal distance considered appropriate for formal business, casual conversation, waiting in line with strangers, and other situations. The study of rules for the personal use of space is called **proxemics** (Hall, 1974).

The existence of personal space and the nature of proxemics can be demonstrated by "invading" the space of another person. The next time you are talking with an acquaintance, move closer and watch the reaction. Most people show immediate signs of discomfort and step back to reestablish their original distance. Those who hold their ground will turn to the side, look away, or position an arm in front of themselves as a kind of barrier to intrusion. If you persistently edge toward your subjects, you should find it easy to move them several feet from their original positions. Conventions governing comfortable or acceptable distances vary according to relationships as well as activities. Hall (1966) identifies four basic zones (listed distances apply to North American culture):

1. **Intimate distance.** For most American adults the most private personal space extends about 18 inches out from the skin. Entry within this space is reserved for special people or circumstances. Lovemaking, comforting others, cuddling children, and massage all take place within this space. So does wrestling!

2. **Personal distance.** This is the distance maintained in comfortable interaction with friends. It extends from about 1½ to 4 feet from the body. Personal distance basically keeps people within "arm's reach" of each other.

3. **Social distance.** Impersonal business and casual social gatherings take place in a range of about 4 to 12 feet. This distance eliminates most possibilities of touching and formalizes conversation by requiring greater voice projection. "Important people" in many offices use the width of their imposing desks to maintain social distance while conducting business.

4. **Public distance.** When people are separated by more than 12 feet, interactions take on a decidedly formal quality. People look "flat," and the voice must be raised. Formal speeches, lectures, business meetings, and the like are conducted at public distance.

Because of the consistencies of spatial behavior in our culture, you can learn much about your relationship to others by observing the distance you most comfortably hold between yourselves. Watch for this dimension in your daily social activities.

EXERCISE 20.7 **Advertising**

Use the subheadings and Figure 20.3 to guide you in marking the following passage.

Advertising Media

The **advertising media** are the various forms of communication through which advertising reaches its audience. They include newspapers, magazines, television, radio, direct mail, and outdoor displays. Figure 20.3 shows how businesses <u>allocate</u> their advertising <u>expenditures</u> among the various media. The *print media*—which includes newspapers, magazines, direct mail, and billboards—account for about 49 percent of all advertising expenditures. The *electronic media*—television and radio—account for about 28 percent.

FIGURE 20.3

Advertising Expenditures by Media

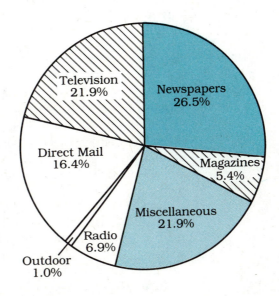

Newspapers   Newspaper advertising accounts for about 27 percent of all advertising expenditures. More than half is purchased by <u>retailers</u>.

Newspaper advertising is used so extensively by retailers because it is reasonable in cost. Furthermore, it provides only local coverage, so advertising dollars are not wasted in reaching people who are outside the store's market area. It is also <u>timely</u>. Ads can usually be placed the day before they are to appear, and their effectiveness can be measured easily.

There are some drawbacks, however, to newspaper advertising. For one, it has a short life span; newspapers are generally read through once and then discarded. Color reproduction in newspapers is usually poor, so most ads must be run in black and white. Finally, marketers cannot target specific markets through newspaper ads, except with regard to geographic area.

Magazines   The advertising revenues of magazines have been climbing dramatically since 1976. In 1985 they reached $5.1 billion, or about 5.4 percent of all advertising expenditures.

Advertisers can reach very specific market segments through ads in special-interest magazines. A boat manufacturer has a ready-made consumer audience in those who subscribe to *Yachting* or *Sail*. Producers of cameras and photographic equipment advertise primarily in *U.S. Camera* or *Popular Photography*. A number of more general magazines like *Time* and *Cosmopolitan* publish regional editions, which provide advertisers with geographic segmentation as well.

Magazine advertising is more prestigious than newspaper advertising, and it provides high-quality color reproduction. In addition, magazine advertisements have a longer span than those in other media. Issues of *National Geographic*, for example, may be retained for months or years by subscribers, and the ads they contain are viewed over and over again.

The major disadvantages of magazines are high cost and lack of timeliness. Magazine ads—especially full-color ads—are expensive, although the cost per reader may compare favorably with that of other media. And, because magazine ads must normally be prepared more than a month in advance, they cannot be adjusted to reflect the latest market conditions.

Direct Mail   Direct-mail advertising is promotional material that is mailed directly to individuals. Direct mail is the most selective medium: mailing lists are available (or can be compiled) to reach almost any target market from airplane enthusiasts to zoologists. The effectiveness of direct-mail advertising can be measured easily because recipients either buy or don't buy the product that is advertised.

But the success of direct-mail advertising depends on appropriate and current mailing lists. A direct-mail campaign may fail if the mailing list is outdated and the mailing does not reach the right people. In addition, this medium is relatively costly. Nevertheless, direct-mail advertising expenditures amounted to more than $15 billion in 1985 or about 16.4 percent of the total.

Outdoor Advertising   Outdoor advertising consists of short promotional messages on billboards, posters, and signs and in skywriting. In 1985 outdoor advertisers spent $945 million, or approximately 1 percent of total advertising expenditures, on outdoor advertising.

Sign and billboard advertising allows a focus on a particular geographic area, and it is fairly inexpensive. However, because most of it is directed toward a mobile audience (and the advertising on buses and taxis is itself mobile), the message must be limited to a few words. The medium is especially suitable for products that lend themselves to pictorial display.

Television   Television is the newest advertising medium, and it ranks second only to newspapers in total revenue. In 1985, 21.9 percent of advertising expenditures went to television. Approximately 98 percent of American homes have at least one television set, which is used an average of seven hours each day.[1] Television obviously provides a massive market for advertisers.

© 1992 by Houghton Mifflin Company

Television advertising is the primary medium for larger firms whose objective is to reach national or regional markets. A national advertiser may buy *network time*, which guarantees that its message will be broadcast by hundreds of local stations that are affiliated with the network. And both national and local firms may buy *local time* on a single station that covers a particular geographic selling area.

Advertisers may *sponsor* an entire show, alone or with other sponsors. Or they may buy *spot time* for a single 10-, 20-, 30-, or 60-second commercial during or between programs. To an extent, they may select their audience by choosing the day of the week and the time of day when their ads will be shown. Budweiser advertises its beer and Noxzema advertises its shaving cream during the TV football season because the majority of viewers are men, who are likely to use these products.

Television advertising rates are based on the number of people who are expected to be watching when the commercial is aired. During the 1984 Summer Olympics in Los Angeles, a 30-second network commercial cost as much as $250,000. ABC, which had exclusive television rights, sold well over $600 million worth of advertising for the Games.

Unlike magazine advertising, and perhaps like newspaper ads, television advertising has a short life. If a viewer misses a commercial, it is missed forever. Viewers may also become indifferent to commercial messages. Or they may use the commercial time as a break from viewing, thus missing the message altogether. (Remote-control devices make it especially easy to banish at least the sound of commercials from the living room.)

Radio   Advertisers spent about $6.5 billion or 7 percent of the total on radio advertising in 1985, up from $4.7 billion in 1982. Like magazine advertising, radio advertising offers selectivity. Radio stations develop programming for—and are tuned in by—specific groups of listeners. There are almost half a billion radio sets in the United States (about six per household), which makes radio the most accessible medium.

Radio can be less expensive than other media. Actual rates depend on geographic coverage, the number of commercials contracted for, the time period specified, and whether the station broadcasts on AM, FM, or both. Even small retailers are able to afford radio advertisements.

Reference
1. *Chicago Sun-Times*, January 25, 1984, pp. 1, 26.

Television

Use the dates to guide you in marking the following passage.

Television

The histories of radio and television are closely intertwined. The three major television networks were radio networks first, and the same companies that developed home radio and pioneered commercial broadcasting developed television.

Early in the 1920s, such corporations as General Electric and RCA allocated small budgets for experiments with television. The idea seemed far-fetched and futuristic to many in the industry, but research was authorized in the hope that it would eventually pay off. General Electric employed an inventor, Ernst Alexanderson, to work on the problem, and by 1927 he had developed a workable system. However, it was not to be the system that the industry finally adopted.

Even though the country had entered the age of corporate research and development, a lone inventor played a key role. Gutenberg had put together a workable printing system; Morse had made the telegraph a reality; Edison and Armat had perfected the motion picture; Marconi had developed a practical wireless; and Armstrong had developed FM broadcasting (over which television signals are broadcast). Incredibly, television too was invented independently by a genius working in isolation on a shoestring budget. A boy named Philo T. Farnsworth, who was in high school in the remote community of Rigby, Idaho, astounded his science teacher when he showed him drawings of a workable television system. The year was 1922, and Farnsworth had single-handedly solved the problems in sending and receiving television signals. By 1930 Farnsworth had patented his device. Vladimir Zworykin, an engineer employed by RCA, had been working on a similar system but had not patented it. At age twenty-four, Philo Farnsworth forced the corporate giant to meet his terms in order to obtain the rights to manufacture the system. Early television sets used his basic designs.

The Early Broadcasts   The earliest experimental television sets used tiny screens, about three by four inches. Cameras were crude and required intense lighting. People who appeared on the screen had to wear bizarre purple and green makeup to provide contrast for the picture. Nevertheless, in 1927, a picture of Herbert Hoover, then secretary of commerce, appeared on an experimental broadcast.

By 1932 an experimental TV station, complete with studio and transmitting facilities, had been built in the Empire State Building. RCA set aside a million dollars to develop and demonstrate television. In 1936 it began testing the system, broadcasting two programs a week. Before World War II, a few people in the New York area had TV receivers in their homes. The medium was set to take off.

But the new industry was about to be nipped in the bud. The Japanese attacked Pearl Harbor in December 1941, and the war effort monopolized the country's attention. All the electronics manufacturers

© 1992 by Houghton Mifflin Company

turned to producing for the armed forces, and not until 1945 did these companies return to making products for the civilian market. In the immediate postwar years, however, television stations were quickly established in many major cities, and the public began to buy sets as fast as they could be manufactured. TV had become a medium for home use.

The Big Freeze   From 1948 through 1952, the Federal Communications Commission ordered a "freeze" on the issuance of licenses and construction permits. It wanted to study thoroughly the broadcasting situation and allocate appropriate frequencies to TV, FM radio, and other forms of broadcasting. As a result, many American cities could not receive television until after the freeze was lifted.

During the freeze, the FCC developed a master plan that still governs TV broadcasting today. The system prevents one television station from interfering with the broadcast of another. Thus the chaos that characterized early radio broadcasting was avoided. When the freeze was lifted in 1952, television spread quickly throughout the United States. Soon television was so successful that social commentators often spoke of the "television generation." Most Americans born after World War II never knew a world without television. The medium is presumed to have shaped their lives in significant ways.

The Coming of Color   Color television got off to a slow start, although there was much talk about it as early as the 1940s. The networks and manufacturers struggled to perfect a system for transmitting and receiving color pictures, but the quality of early color transmission was uneven at best. There were other problems as well. Many black-and-white sets could not receive pictures transmitted in color. The FCC insisted that the system for color transmission be such that black-and-white television sets could still receive a picture (though not in color). Add to these problems the need to produce a color television set within the financial means of large numbers of people, and the slow development of color is not surprising.

In 1953 the FCC approved RCA's system of color television. Although the system produced crude colors, it did allow existing black-and-white sets to receive programs. The networks exercised a great deal of caution in delivering color broadcasts, however. At first they broadcast only a few programs in color. By 1967, though, most network programs were in color, and even local stations began to produce programs in color. All the black-and-white cameras had to be phased out, and new technicians trained. But the industry made the transition to the new technology smoothly. By 1986, over 91 percent of those homes with a receiver had color television, and it seemed that nearly all American homes would have a color set by the end of the decade.

Today television is the most popular mass medium of all. Many families own several sets, and audiences for some programs run into the tens of millions. Television viewing averages over seven hours daily per TV household. Color has all but replaced black and white. Cable television is commonplace and is challenging the dominance of the medium by the three major networks. Satellites in space relay programs coming from all parts of the world.

EXERCISE 20.9   **The Infection Chain**

Use the subheadings and Figure 20.4 to guide you in marking the following passage.

The Infection Chain

To understand how pathogens cause infection, let us look closely at Figure 20.4, which illustrates the chain reaction that spreads infection. The infection chain is the way pathogens pass between human beings.

First of all, an *infectious agent*, or pathogen, must be present. The pathogen grows in a place, called a *reservoir*, where the conditions for its reproduction are <u>optimal</u>. The pathogen leaves the reservoir through what is called a *portal of exit*. The pathogen then moves by some *means of transmission* to a person (*host*) who is <u>susceptible</u> to it. The pathogen enters the host through a *portal of entry*, usually a body opening, and may or may not multiply further. If not extinguished within the host, it may exit through the same or a different portal. For example, an organism taken in through the respiratory tract may exit through the same portal by means of a cough or sneeze. Or the portals of entry and exit may differ: an organism that enters by mouth may exit through the bowel.

Each link is essential to the chain. If the chain is broken at any point, by chance or because of deliberate <u>intervention</u>, the pathogen is <u>inactivated</u>. Let us examine each link in more detail.

FIGURE 20.4

The Infection Chain

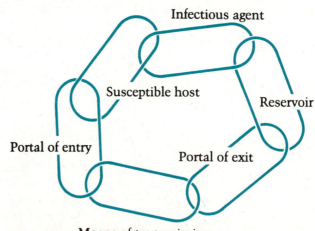

Infectious Agents   There are six types of infectious agents or pathogens: bacteria, viruses, fungi, protozoa, parasitic worms, and rickettsia. These infectious agents are present in the environment and on and within the bodies of people and animals. How to prevent and control infection depends largely on the type of infectious agent.

The Reservoir   The reservoir is the place where infectious agents or pathogens multiply. Common reservoirs are water, food, body tissues, <u>excreta</u> and fluids, and contaminated objects such as basins, equipment, and dressings.

In order to multiply, microorganisms need one or more of a variety of conditions: the presence or absence of oxygen, light or darkness, <u>compatible</u> temperature, moisture, and some form of nourishment. A pH (acid-base balance) above 5, slightly alkaline, promotes the growth of many pathogens.

Portal of Exit When body tissue <u>harbors</u> the organism, a pathway for pathogens to leave the body, a portal of exit, can be identified. Pathogens may exit through the <u>orifices</u> of the respiratory tract in the form of secretions, the <u>gastrointestinal</u> tract in the form of <u>vomitus</u> or <u>feces</u>, or the <u>genitourinary</u> tract in the form of urine. Wound drainage and blood can also provide a portal of exit. If the reservoir is outside the body, the portal exit is the point at which the organism leaves the food, water, or other substance.

Means of Transmission As we shall see, the means of transmission, or means by which pathogens move from one person to another, is the link in the infection chain at which intervention is often most effective. We will discuss this concept later in relation to isolation technique.

Some pathogens can be transmitted by only one means. Others use more than one means of transmission. In general, there are four routes of transmission.

Contact, the first route, may be *direct* or *indirect.* Direct contact is a means of transmission with particular <u>pertinence</u> for nurses who provide hygienic care or perform procedures. Touching another person is a way to transmit pathogens by direct contact. Transmission of pathogens by *droplet*—the projection of moisture by coughing or sneezing—is also considered direct contact. Indirect contact is transmission of a pathogen on linen or equipment that has been contaminated. Carrying a stethoscope that has not been cleaned between patients is a <u>breach</u> of proper technique.

Pathogens are also transmitted by *vehicles*—substances in or on which they are conveyed. Food and water serve as vehicles for some organisms. "Food poisoning" is an infection caused by the bacteria staphylococcus and transmitted by the vehicle of spoiled food. Blood can also serve as a <u>vehicle</u> for the spread of certain pathogens. An example is the virus that causes hepatitis B or serum hepatitis, which can be transmitted in blood transfusions.

Pathogens can also be *airborne,* carried on dust particles surrounded by moisture and suspended in the air. Pathogens projected by a sneeze can become attached to dust particles and remain airborne.

Finally, pathogens can be transmitted by <u>vectors</u>. Common vectors are insects and animals such as birds, rats, or mosquitoes. Turtles are no longer sold in pet stores because they often carry the infection-producing bacteria salmonella. Rat-control measures have greatly reduced the incidence of vector-transmitted infections.

Portal of Entry The pathogen enters the body of a *susceptible host* through a portal of entry. Any of the *orifices* or openings of the body, such as those of the respiratory, gastrointestinal, and genitourinary tracts, can serve as portals of entry. Skin that is no longer <u>intact</u>

is an important portal of entry. Even small skin <u>abrasions</u> may serve as portals of entry, as can larger wounds and decubitus ulcers (pressure sores).

The Susceptible Host   The person in whom the organism is present is called the host. In some persons the pathogens never reach a high enough level to cause an active infection, but are harbored and can be passed along to someone else. Such a person is called a *carrier.* One famous carrier was a food handler, later nicknamed "Typhoid Mary," who caused numerous cases of typhoid fever in people to whom she served food but who never developed the disease herself.

For a person to become ill, not only must the strain be <u>virulent</u> to that person, but also the host must be susceptible. Some people are more susceptible to infection than others, for one or a number of reasons which will be mentioned later.

EXERCISE 20.10   **Building High Self-Esteem**

This is the second in a series of five exercises for applying study skills to the textbook chapter entitled "Building High Self-Esteem," which is on pages 383–412 in the appendix.

1. Exercise 19.1 on page 269–270 is for surveying the chapter.

2. This exercise is for marking information in the chapter.

3. Exercise 21.10 on page 316 is for making notes on information in the chapter.

4. Exercise 22.4 on page 328 is for reciting the information in your notes.

5. Exercise 23.2 on page 337 is for answering test questions about the information you recited.

Use the suggestions earlier in this chapter and the ones below to guide you as you mark the textbook chapter on pages 383–412.

Use This Help to Guide You in Marking	Mark Information That Answers These Questions
1. The term *self-esteem* printed in boldface on page 385.	What is *self-esteem?*
2. The heading "How Your Self-Esteem Develops" on page 386 and the three subheadings that follow it: "Childhood" (page 387); "Adolescence" (page 388); and "Adulthood" (page 389).	How does self-esteem develop in childhood, adolescence, and adulthood?
3. The heading "Characteristics of People with High Self-Esteem" on page 390 and the list of six characteristics printed in italics following the heading.	What are the characteristics of people with high self-esteem?
4. The heading "Self-Esteem and Success at Work" on page 393.	How does self-esteem affect success at work?
5. The term *failure syndrome* printed in boldface on page 394.	What is the *failure syndrome?*
6. The heading "The Power of Expectations" on page 396 and the two subheadings that follow it: "Your Own Expectations" (page 396) and "The Expectations of Others" (page 397).	How is your behavior affected by your own expectations and by the expectations others have for you?
7. The term *self-fulfilling prophecy* printed in boldface on page 396.	What is a *self-fulfilling prophecy?*
8. The term *Pygmalion effect* printed in boldface on page 397.	What is the *Pygmalion effect?*

9. The heading "Mentors" and the term *mentors* printed in boldface on page 398.

What is a *mentor?*

10. The list numbered 1 through 7 on page 399.

What are the criteria for selecting a mentor?

11. The heading "How to Build Your Self-Esteem" on page 400 and the subheadings that follow it on pages 401–405.

What are the five strategies for building self-esteem?

12. The term *affirmations* printed in boldface on page 403.

What are *affirmations?*

13. The list numbered 1, 2, and 3 on page 403.

What are the guidelines for writing affirmations?

14. The heading "Your Organization Can Help" on page 405.

How can organizations help workers build high self-esteem?

Make Notes from Books

The first way to organize information in a textbook is to mark it using the methods explained in Chapter 20. The second way is to make notes on the information.

Good notes will help you learn. In order to make notes, you must think about what you read and restate it in your own words. In many instances, you will learn information as you process it in this way. Also, since notes are summaries, you will have much less to learn when you study from notes than when you study directly from textbooks. Finally, when you make notes, you don't need to learn information exactly as it is presented in a book—you can rearrange it in formats that make it easier for you to learn.

Examine the examples of notes on pages 300–306 before you read the following discussion.

Notes on Cards

Most students make notes on notebook paper, but some very successful students prefer to study from notes written on index cards. Whether you use notebook paper or cards, make notes using the procedures in "How to Make Textbook Notes" on page 300.

Figure 21.1 on page 300 illustrates how to make notes on 3- by 5-inch cards.

- Write a descriptive title on the blank side of a card.
- Write details on the back of the card upside down in relation to the title on the front.

When you make notes in this way, the information on the back of the cards is in the proper position for reading when you turn the cards over.

There are four advantages of making notes on 3- by 5-inch cards rather than on notebook paper. *First*, since the cards are small, they require you to summarize and condense information. *Second*, cards make it easy to integrate class notes and textbook notes, because you can copy information in your class notes onto related textbook notes so that all the information about a topic is in one place for efficient study. *Third*, cards make it possible

How to Make Textbook Notes

Use the underlining and other marks you made in your textbook to guide you in making notes on a passage.

- Decide what format you will use for the notes (see pages 300–306).
- Begin the notes with a title that accurately describes the information you want to learn.
- Make the major details stand out in your notes.
- Include some minor details.
- Include examples, because they help in understanding and learning information and because they may appear in test questions.

FIGURE 21.1

Notes on an Index Card

Factors in Mate Selection

1. Age - Husbands tend to be about two years older
2. Social class - Mates tend to be from the same class and to share tastes and interests
3. Religion - Mates tend to share the same faith
4. Education - Mates generally have similar educational levels
5. Racial and ethnic background - People tend to marry within their own groups; interracial marriages are rare
6. Propinquity - People tend to marry those who live near them

to separate information that you have learned from information that you have not learned. By separating "learned" notes from "unlearned" notes, you can readily direct your attention toward studying information that you have not yet learned. *Fourth,* cards are convenient to study at times when studying from a notebook is inconvenient. You can study notes on cards while walking from class to class or even while standing on a bus; notes on notebook paper are inconvenient to study at such times.

Major and Minor Details

Comparison of Computers and People

Computers

1. Speed — calculate and organize information quickly
2. Accuracy — virtually eliminate errors people often make
3. Neatness — produce printed material that is neater than most handwritten and typed material
4. Logic — require users to be analytical and logical in giving instructions

People

1. Judgement — know when to ask for help and when to wait for missing information
2. Flexibility — anticipate and respond to change
3. Intuition — deal with problems using insight acquired through experience
4. Feeling — are creative because they approach problems with eagerness, curiosity, excitement, and other emotions
5. Knowledge — understand what they are doing, whereas computers do not

When you make textbook notes, first consider whether you should prepare them so that major and minor details stand out, as you learned to do when you studied Chapters 11 and 12. The notes above have the following characteristics:

- The title describes the content of the notes and is written in the center of the page.
- A line is left blank before each major detail.
- Minor details are indented and listed neatly under major details.

Exercises 21.1, 21.2, and 21.3 provide practice in making textbook notes that give prominence to major and minor details.

Paragraph Summaries

Ways to Extend Life

<u>Don't Smoke or Drink</u> On the average, those who smoke cigarettes live five fewer years than people who don't smoke. Excessive drinking damages the liver and kidneys, and drunkenness is a major factor in automobile accidents.

<u>Eat Wisely</u> Eat fruit, vegetables, whole-grain cereals, nonfat milk products, and fish and poultry (rather than red meats and eggs). Limit intake of sugar and salt, and don't overeat — the fatter people are, the more likely they are to die.

<u>Keep Active</u> Exercise benefits the cardiovascular, respiratory, muscular, skeletal, digestive, and other systems. Frequent sexual activity maintains the capacity for sexual response, and intellectual activity promotes intellectual development in old age.

<u>Reduce Stress</u> Stress increases blood pressure and quickens the heart rate.

When you decide you cannot organize information in notes that emphasize major and minor details, it may be appropriate to make notes in paragraph summaries. The paragraph summary notes above have the following characteristics:

- The title describes the content of the notes and is written in the center of the page.
- A line is left blank before each paragraph.
- Each paragraph is indented.
- Each paragraph begins with an underlined title, which is the topic of the paragraph.

Exercise 21.4 provides practice in making textbook notes in the paragraph summary format.

Definitions of Terminology

Types of Religion

Supernaturalism	Belief that supernatural forces influence human events for good or bad. (Ex) A rabbit's foot can protect one from harm.
Animism	Belief that active, animate spirits operate in people, animals, rivers, mountains, or weather.
Theism	Belief in gods who are powerful, interested in human affairs, and worthy of worship.
Polytheism	Belief in a number of gods.
Monotheism	Belief in one supreme being. (Ex) Judaism, Christianity, and Islam.

On many college tests, 70 percent or more of the questions directly or indirectly test knowledge of terminology; therefore, it is extremely important for you to learn the terminology that is defined in your textbooks. The definitions-of-terminology notes above have the following characteristics:

- Terms are written on the left side of the page.
- Definitions and examples are written on the right side of the page.
- A line is left blank before each new term.

The definitions are statements about the meanings of the terms, while the examples illustrate general characteristics of the terms.

Exercise 21.5 provides practice in making textbook notes in the definitions-of-terminology format.

Classification Charts

The Psychosexual Stages (Freud)

Stage	Age	Characteristics
Oral	Birth to 1 year	Gets pleasure from mouth by sucking, eating, biting, and chewing.
Anal	1 year to 3 years	Gets pleasure from holding and letting go of body waste.
Phallic	3 years to 6 years	Derives pleasure from own primary sex organs.
Latency	6 years to about 11 years	Denies attraction for parent of opposite sex and identifies with parent of the same sex.
Genital	Adolescence	Experiences the awakening of sexuality and desire for heterosexual love.

Classification charts are useful for organizing information that explains how two or more persons, places, or things are alike or different in two or more ways. The chart above summarizes Sigmund Freud's theory about the psychosexual stages of human development, which is explained in many psychology textbooks. The information is summarized under headings that explain the two ways in which the stages differ from one another: "Age" and "Characteristics." The notes also emphasize the sequence in which the stages occur.

When you have difficulty making good notes, ask this question: "Does this information explain how two or more persons, places, or things are alike or different in two or more ways?" If the answer to this question is yes, make notes in a classification chart.

Exercises 21.6 and 21.7 provide practice in making textbook notes in classification charts.

Time Lines

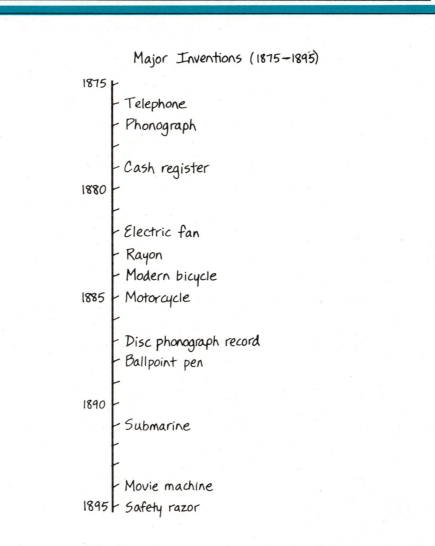

Major Inventions (1875–1895)

1875 —
— Telephone
— Phonograph

— Cash register
1880 —

— Electric fan
— Rayon
— Modern bicycle
1885 — Motorcycle

— Disc phonograph record
— Ballpoint pen

1890 —

— Submarine

— Movie machine
1895 — Safety razor

A time line is useful when you want to learn the chronological sequence of events. To prepare a time line, draw a line and mark it off in equal time intervals. In the example above, a line is marked off in five-year intervals; however, in other time lines the intervals may represent one week, one month, one year, one hundred years, or any other period.

After you have marked off the interval on the time line, write events in the places where they belong. In the example above, "Cash register" is written on the line before 1880 because it was invented in 1879, and "Motorcycle" is written next to 1885 because it was invented in 1885.

The major advantage of time lines is that they make it easy to visualize the passage of time between events. For example, the time line above makes it easy to visualize that ten years passed between the invention of the phonograph (1887) and the disc phonograph record (1887).

Exercise 21.8 provides practice in making notes in a time line.

Maps

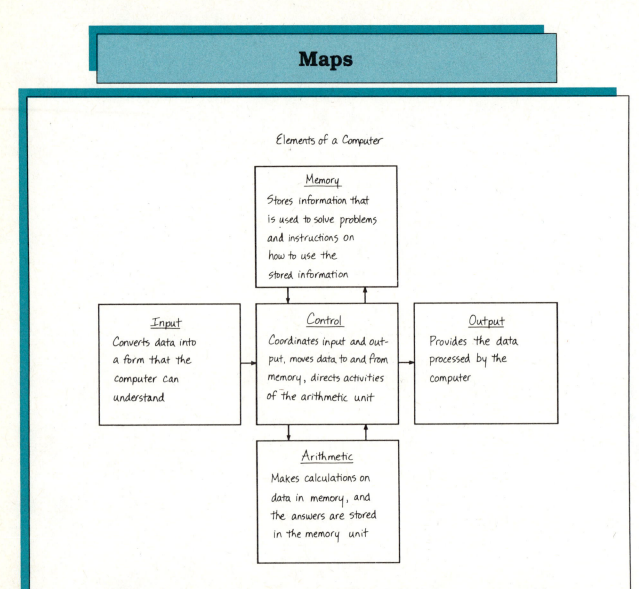

Elements of a Computer

Memory
Stores information that is used to solve problems and instructions on how to use the stored information

Input
Converts data into a form that the computer can understand

Control
Coordinates input and output, moves data to and from memory, directs activities of the arithmetic unit

Output
Provides the data processed by the computer

Arithmetic
Makes calculations on data in memory, and the answers are stored in the memory unit

Maps used when traveling show the relations among places; maps used for notes show the relations among ideas, information, and concepts. In **maps,** information enclosed within squares, circles, or other forms is connected by lines or arrows to information enclosed within other forms to indicate how the information is interrelated.

In the map above, descriptions of the elements of a computer are enclosed within rectangles, which are connected by arrows to show how the elements of a computer are interrelated. For example, one arrow between "Input" and "Control" indicates that data flow from input to control, but not from control to input. On the other hand, two arrows between "Memory" and "Control" indicate that data flow back and forth between memory and control.

Exercise 21.9 provides practice in making a map.

EXERCISE 21.1   **"The SQ3R Study Method" (page 278)**

Make index card notes for the passage named above. Write your notes on the form below. See pages 300 and 301 for examples of the types of notes you are to make.

EXERCISE 21.2   **"Effective Conversationalists"** (pages 279–280)

Make notes that show major and minor details for the passage named above. See page 301 for an example of the type of notes you should make.

EXERCISE 21.3   "Altruism" (pages 281–282)

Make index card notes for the passage named above. Write your notes on the form below. See pages 300 and 301 for examples of the types of notes you should make.

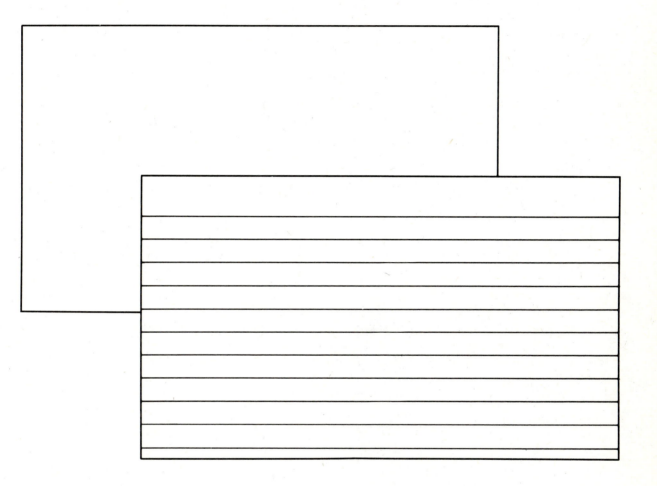

EXERCISE 21.4   **"Coping with Adversity" (pages 283–284)**

Make paragraph summary notes for the passage named above. See page 302 for an example of the type of notes you should make.

EXERCISE 21.5 **"Components of a Spoken Language"** (pages 285–287)

Make definition-of-terminology notes for the passage named above. See page 303 for an example of the type of notes you should make.

EXERCISE 21.6   "Personal Space" (page 288)

Make notes in a classification chart for the passage named above. See page 304 for an example of the type of notes you are to make.

Zones of Personal Space

Zone	Distance	Use
Intimate	Up to 18"	

EXERCISE 21.7 "Advertising Media" (pages 289–291)

Make notes in a classification chart for the passage named above. See page 304 for an example of the type of notes you are to make.

Advertising Media

Media	Expenditure	Advantages	Disadvantages
Newspapers	27 %		

EXERCISE 21.8   **"Television" (pages 292–293)**

Make time-line notes for the passage named above. See page 305 for an example of what you are to do.

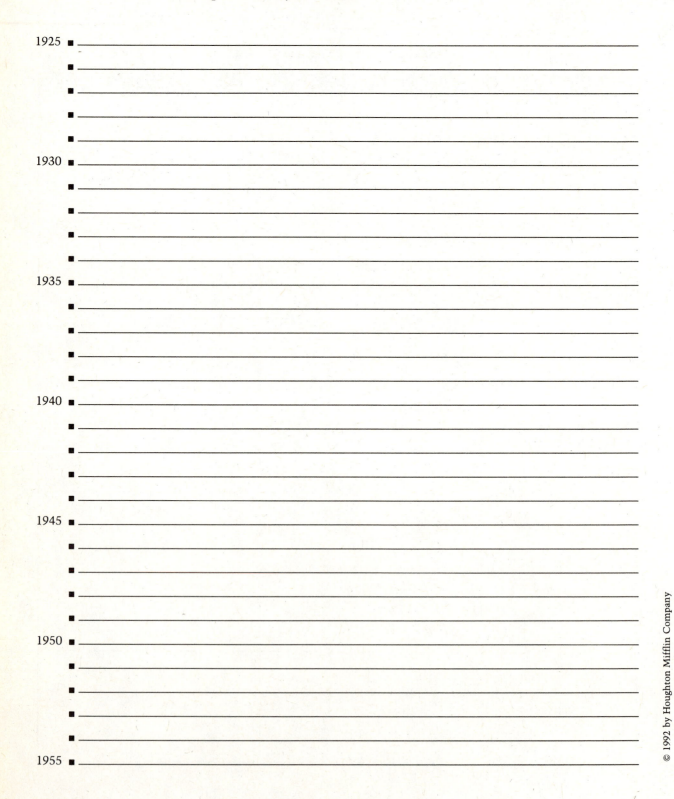

1925 ■ _____

■ _____

■ _____

■ _____

■ _____

1930 ■ _____

■ _____

■ _____

■ _____

1935 ■ _____

■ _____

■ _____

■ _____

1940 ■ _____

■ _____

■ _____

■ _____

1945 ■ _____

■ _____

■ _____

■ _____

■ _____

1950 ■ _____

■ _____

■ _____

■ _____

1955 ■ _____

EXERCISE 21.9   "The Infection Chain" (pages 294–296)

Make notes in a map for the passage named above. See page 306 for an example of the type of notes you are to make.

The Infection Chain

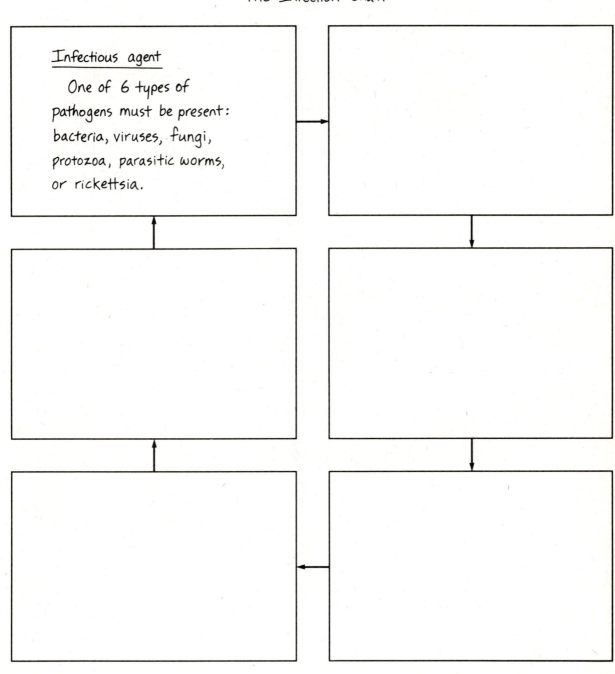

Infectious agent

One of 6 types of pathogens must be present: bacteria, viruses, fungi, protozoa, parasitic worms, or rickettsia.

EXERCISE 21.10   **Building High Self-Esteem**

This is the third in a series of five exercises for applying study skills to the textbook chapter entitled "Building High Self-Esteem," which is on pages 383–412 in the appendix.

1. Exercise 19.1 on pages 269–270 is for surveying the chapter.

2. Exercise 20.10 on pages 297–298 is for marking information in the chapter.

3. This exercise is for making notes on information in the chapter.

4. Exercise 22.4 on page 328 is for reciting the information in your notes.

5. Exercise 23.2 on page 337 is for answering test questions about the information you recited.

Use the marks you made when you did Exercise 20.10 and the guidelines on page 300 to make notes on the information in the textbook chapter on pages 383–412. Use the following fourteen titles as headings for your notes, which you may write on index cards or on notebook paper. The numbering below corresponds to the numbering in Exercise 20.10 on pages 297–298.

1. *Self-esteem*

2. Development of self-esteem

3. Characteristics of people with high self-esteem

4. How self-esteem affects success at work

5. The *failure syndrome*

6. How behavior is affected by expectations

7. *Self-fulfilling prophecy*

8. The *Pygmalion effect*

9. *Mentors*

10. Criteria for selecting a mentor

11. Strategies for building self-esteem

12. *Affirmations*

13. Guidelines for writing affirmations

14. How organizations help workers build high self-esteem

Recite and Review

The final and most important step in the study process is to recite and review. Most information stays in your memory only about 20 seconds unless you recite it! See the discussion about sensory, short-term, and long-term memory on page 116.

Reciting is the act of repeating information silently or aloud to learn and remember it. Students who recite information rather than read and reread it do better on tests because reciting gives them practice in answering test questions. For instance, when students recite the information in their biology notes, they practice answering questions that might be on their biology test. However, when students simply read and reread their biology notes, they do not practice answering biology test questions.

Reviewing is the repeated reciting of information that is necessary to keep from forgetting it.

This chapter explains how to recite and review, and it contains suggestions that may be of help to you when you have difficulty learning by reciting and reviewing. "How to Recite and Review" on page 318 and "Helps for Learning" on page 321 summarize the advice that is given in the following discussions.

Recite, Don't Memorize

Actors memorize their parts in plays to speak them word for word, but students recite to learn and remember information, not to memorize it. When a student needed to learn the information in Figure 22.1, on page 319, she recited it in the way outlined in Figure 22.2, also on page 319. Compare the example of recitation in Figure 22.2 with the notes in Figure 22.1 to notice that they are different in several respects.

- First, the student organized her thoughts by naming the three types of advertising.

- Second, she did not recite the information about the three types of advertising in the same sequence in which it is listed in her notes.

- Third, the explanations she gave while reciting are not word-for-word duplications of statements in the notes.

- Fourth, the examples she gave while reciting are not identical to examples in the notes.

> ### How to Recite and Review
>
> Organize the information you want to learn into notes that have descriptive titles and the other characteristics explained in Chapter 21.
>
> - Read the title of the information to be learned and turn the title into a question.
> - Try to answer the question silently or aloud to yourself without reading your notes.
> - Read the information in your notes to make certain that you recited it correctly; if you did not, reread the information and then immediately try to recite it again.
> - Continue in this way until you have thoroughly learned everything you want to learn at least twenty-four hours before a test.

She recited correctly, showing that she had learned the information in the notes, not that she had merely memorized the words.

When you recite, keep in mind that there is *not* a one-to-one relationship between the amount of information to learn and the amount of time needed to learn it. For instance, if you must learn the meanings of sixty terms for a psychology test, you may learn thirty of them in an hour. However, it might take you two or three hours to learn the remaining thirty terms because some of them may have meanings that are especially difficult for you to understand or remember.

Review Frequently

Reviewing is necessary because we tend to forget 30 to 40 percent of what we learn within twenty-four hours of learning it. For example, after reciting for an hour, a student had learned the information on twenty of eighty cards he had prepared to study for a physics test. However, when he reviewed the twenty "learned" cards the next day, he discovered that he had forgotten information on six of them. What happened to him is what happens to most of us; we tend to forget 30 to 40 percent of what we learn within twenty-four hours after we learn it.

It is essential that you schedule review for several short study sessions rather than for one or two long study sessions (see page 22).

1. To review notes on cards, maintain a deck of "learned" cards and a deck of "unlearned" cards. Then each time you recite:

- Begin by reviewing the deck of "learned" cards. If you have forgotten information on a card, put it in the "unlearned" deck.
- Recite the "unlearned" cards, attempting to move as many as you can into the "learned" deck.

FIGURE 22.1

Notes Used for Reciting

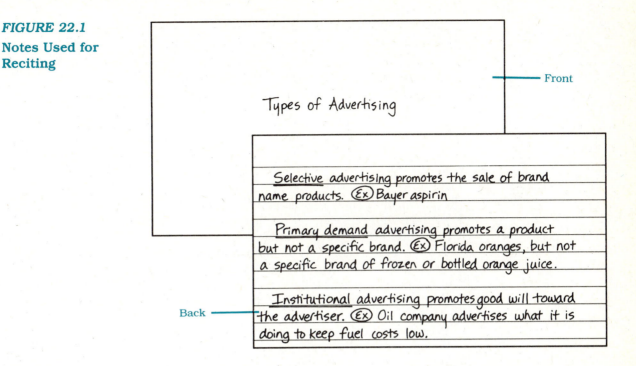

Front

Types of Advertising

Selective advertising promotes the sale of brand
name products. (Ex) Bayer aspirin

Primary demand advertising promotes a product
but not a specific brand. (Ex) Florida oranges, but not
a specific brand of frozen or bottled orange juice.

Institutional advertising promotes good will toward
the advertiser. (Ex) Oil company advertises what it is
doing to keep fuel costs low.

Back

FIGURE 22.2

Recitation of the Information in Figure 22.1

A student read the title on the front of the card in Figure 22.1 and changed it into the following question:

What types of advertising are there?

She then answered her question by reciting the information on the back of the card in the following way:

- Primary demand, selective, and institutional advertising
- Primary demand advertising sells a product without trying to sell any particular brand-name product . . . sells things made out of cotton without selling specific products, such as Arrow shirts or Cannon towels.
- Selective advertising is used to sell specific brand-name products, such as Cannon towels and Skippy peanut butter.
- Institutional advertising tries to increase good will toward the advertiser . . . as when Mobil Oil sponsors a movie on public television.

Continue in this way until you can accurately recite all the information twenty-four hours after you have moved all the cards to the "learned" deck.

2. To review notes on notebook paper, place checks in pencil next to information as you learn it. Then, each time you recite:

- Begin by reviewing checked information and erase checks next to information you have forgotten.

■ Recite the information that is not checked, attempting to place checks next to as much of it as you can.

Continue in this way until you can accurately recite all the information twenty-four hours after you have placed pencil checks next to all the information.

Prepare Class Notes for Reciting

If you make textbook notes on 3- by 5-inch cards, prepare class notes for reciting by summarizing them on cards. Then, organize the cards so that the ones about a topic that is in textbook notes *and* class notes are together. Reciting is more efficient when class notes and textbook notes about a topic are together rather than in different places.

If you make class notes in the traditional format that is illustrated on page 239, highlight the major headings in your notes and use them to stimulate recall. For instance, if "Types of Advertising" is a topic in the notes, highlight these words and use them for reciting in the way shown in Figures 22.1 and 22.2 on page 319.

If you make class notes using the Cornell System, explained on page 238, write key terminology and descriptive titles in the wide left margin of your notes; use the terms and titles in the left margin to stimulate recall of the information in your notes.

Walk to Aid Learning

When I was a college student, I told a friend that I was having extreme difficulty learning information for a test. She suggested that I might benefit from the advice her drama coach gave her that she could learn parts in plays more quickly if she studied them while walking rather than while sitting. I did what she recommended and found that I learned information more quickly when I recited it while walking outside rather than while sitting at a desk. When you have difficulty learning material, experiment to find out whether you learn more efficiently while walking than while sitting.

Write to Aid Learning

Writing is used to learn many of the skills that are taught in colleges, such as the skills you need to solve mathematical problems and to translate a foreign language into English. You can also use writing to learn information of the kind that is usually recited silently or aloud. If you have difficulty learning material by reciting it, try writing it on paper. Some students report that writing provides them with the additional reinforcement they need to learn and remember some kinds of information.

Listen to Aid Learning

Some students find that the most efficient way for them to learn is to listen to information they have recorded on audiocassettes. They say that this is a time-saving way for them to study because they can listen to their

> ### Helps for Learning
>
> When you have difficulty learning information by reciting and reviewing, try one or more of the following.
>
> - Schedule many short recitation sessions over a long period rather than a few long recitation sessions close to each other.
> - Recite while walking outside rather than while sitting inside.
> - Recite by writing on paper rather than by repeating information silently or aloud to yourself.
> - Record the hard-to-learn information on audiocassettes and recite it after you have listened to it enough times to learn it.
> - Use mnemonic acronyms, mnemonic sentences, and visualizations, which are explained on pages 321–324.

recorded notes even while they are walking or driving. Following are some of the ways students report using audiocassettes to help them in their course work.

- A man who has a job that requires him to spend much time driving records his class notes and listens to them as he drives from place to place. He checks his learning by turning off his cassette player, reciting what he heard, and replaying the material to make certain he has recited it correctly.
- A young woman had a great deal of difficulty understanding essays, short stories, and other literature she was required to read for an English course. When she recorded the selections and listened to them, her understanding of them increased dramatically.
- A young man who couldn't find the errors in his written work when he proofread it recorded what he wrote and found that he was able to spot his mistakes when he listened to what he had written as he played it back on an audiocassette player.

Many students learn material they recorded by listening to it over headphones as they walk from place to place.

Use Mnemonics

Mnemonic (ni-mon'ik) means "to help the memory." The rhyming jingle "*i* before *e* except after *c*" is a **mnemonic device** for remembering a spelling principle. This section explains three types of mnemonic devices that are helpful for learning information: acronyms, sentences, and visualizations.

1. A mnemonic *acronym* is a word made from the first letters of words you want to recall. One of the best-known mnemonic acronyms is *HOMES*, which is used to recall the names of the Great Lakes.

H	Huron
O	Ontario
M	Michigan
E	Erie
S	Superior

H recalls *Huron, O* recalls *Ontario,* and so on.

RICE is a mnemonic acronym used by medical students to recall the treatment for sudden, painful injuries to muscles or joints.

R	Rest
I	Ice
C	Compress
E	Elevate

R recalls *rest, I* recalls *ice,* and so on. The treatment is to *rest* the injured part, to apply *ice* for ten minutes at a time, to *compress* the muscle or joint by wrapping it in a reasonably snug elastic bandage, and to *elevate* the injured part above the level of the heart. Mnemonics such as *RICE* are passed on among medical students in much the same way nursery rhymes are passed on among children.

Figure 22.3 shows where a mnemonic device may be placed on the front of a 3- by 5-inch card. The acronym *SIP* may be used to recall the three types of advertising summarized in Figure 22.1 on page 319: *S* recalls *selective* advertising, *I* recalls *institutional* advertising, and *P* recalls *primary demand* advertising.

2. A *mnemonic sentence* is a sentence made of words that begin with the same letters as the first letters of words you want to recall. Following is a well-known mnemonic sentence.

My Very Earthy Mother Just Served Us Nine Pizzas.

The first letters of the words in this sentence are the same as those of the first names of the planets, starting with the one nearest the sun (Mercury) and proceeding to the one farthest from the sun (Pluto).

M	Mercury
V	Venus
E	Earth
M	Mars
J	Jupiter
S	Saturn
U	Uranus
N	Neptune
P	Pluto

Mnemonic sentences are particularly useful for learning information in a specific sequence. For instance, the acronym *HOMES* may be used to recall the names of the Great Lakes, but the following sentence may be used to remember the names of the Great Lakes in correct sequence going from west to east.

She Must Have Eaten Onions.

FIGURE 22.3
A Mnemonic Device on an Index Card

```
┌─────────────────────────────────────────┐
│                                           │
│         Types of Advertising              │
│                                           │
│                                           │
│                                           │
│                                           │
│                              SIP  ────── Mnemonic
│                                           acronym
└─────────────────────────────────────────┘
```

The first letters of the words in this sentence are the same as the first letters of the names of the Great Lakes in correct sequence from west to east.

S	Superior
M	Michigan
H	Huron
E	Erie
O	Ontario

Mnemonic sentences are also useful when the first letters of words to be recalled do not spell a word. The following sentence is used to remember the four sections of a symphony orchestra.

Sinners **W**ill **B**e **P**unished.

The first letters of the words in this sentence are the same as the first letters of the names of the sections of a symphony orchestra.

S	String section
W	Woodwind section
B	Brass section
P	Percussion section

Invent your own mnemonic sentences when you want to learn information in a specific sequence and when the first letters of words you want to remember do not spell a word.

3. A *visualization* is anything that can be visualized, or pictured in the mind, to aid the recall of information. Visualizations are usually examples, and this is one reason I suggest in Chapter 21 that you include examples in the notes you make for information in textbooks.

A student devised the following visualizations to learn three types of social mobility for his sociology course.

Types of Social Mobility	**Visualizations**
Horizontal (from one status to a similar status)	I changed jobs from pumping gas to parking cars.
Vertical (from one status to a higher or lower status)	I changed jobs from parking cars to being a management trainee for an insurance company.
Intergenerational (when the status of family members changes from one generation to another)	My grandfather was a laborer, but my father supervises skilled factory workers.

The student used these visualizations to help him understand, remember, and recall the three types of social mobility.

Experiment with mnemonic acronyms, mnemonic sentences, and visualizations. You are likely to find that one of these memory-aiding devices is more helpful to you than the others.

EXERCISE 22.1   **Mnemonic Devices**

Do these problems to practice making the three types of mnemonic devices.

Acronym

There are four major types of wounds: (1) a *laceration* is a tear, (2) an *incision* is a cut, (3) a *crush* is an injury caused by pressure, and (4) a *puncture* is a wound caused by piercing.

Use the first letters of the italicized words to write an acronym for remembering the four types of wounds.

_____

Sentence

There are four major categories of drugs: (1) *depressants*, which slow body functions, (2) *stimulants*, which speed up body functions, (3) *hallucinogens*, which cause people to see or hear things that are not actually present, and (4) *marijuana*, which produces various effects.

Write a mnemonic sentence in which the first letters of the words are the same as the first letters of the names of the four major types of drugs.

_____

Visualization

On page 288 there is a passage that describes four zones of private space. Read the passage and then devise visualizations for remembering the differences among the four zones.

1. Intimate distance   _____

   _____

2. Personal distance   _____

   _____

3. Social distance   _____

   _____

4. Public distance   _____

   _____

EXERCISE 22.2   ## Mnemonic Devices

Do these problems to practice making the three types of mnemonic devices.

Acronym

The Swiss psychiatrist Elisabeth Kübler-Ross has promoted the theory that there are five emotional stages through which people pass when they learn they are about to die: (1) denial, (2) anger, (3) bargaining, (4) depression, and (5) acceptance.

Use the first letters of these words to write a nonsense word that can be used to remember the names of the stages in the correct sequence.

_____

Sentence

Abraham Maslow theorized that there are five needs in the hierarchy of human needs, which are fulfilled in the following sequence: (1) physiological needs, (2) safety needs, (3) social needs, (4) esteem needs, and (5) self-actualization needs.

Write a mnemonic sentence in which the first letters of the words are the same as the first letters of the names of the human needs arranged in the correct sequence.

_____

_____

Visualization

On page 99 there is a passage that explains three types of advertising. Read the passage and then devise visualizations for remembering the differences among the three advertising categories.

1. Selective advertising _____

_____

2. Primary demand advertising _____

_____

3. Institutional advertising _____

_____

EXERCISE 22.3   **Mnemonic Devices**

Do these problems to practice making the three types of mnemonic devices.

Acronym

A microbiology textbook explains three measures that can be taken to reduce the incidence of rabies: (1) *immunize* more dogs and cats, (2) enforce *leash* laws, and (3) *educate* the public about the dangers of rabies.

Use the first letters of the italicized words to write a word for remembering the three measures for reducing rabies.

_____

Sentence

Following are the six principal components of soil: (1) air, (2) humus, (3) mineral salts, (4) water, (5) bacteria, and (6) rock particles.

Write a mnemonic sentence in which the first letters of the words are the same as the first letters of these six ingredients of soil: A, H, M, W, B, and R.

_____

_____

Visualization

On pages 283–284 there is an explanation of three methods of coping with adversity. Read about the methods and then devise visualizations for remembering the differences among them.

1. Passive behavior   _____

   _____

2. Aggressive behavior   _____

   _____

3. Assertive behavior   _____

   _____

EXERCISE 22.4   **Building High Self-Esteem**

This is the fourth in a series of five exercises for applying study skills to the textbook chapter entitled "Building High Self-Esteem," which is on pages 383–412 in the appendix.

1. Exercise 19.1 on pages 269–270 is for surveying the chapter.

2. Exercise 20.10 on pages 297–298 is for marking information in the chapter.

3. Exercise 21.10 on page 316 is for making notes on information in the chapter.

4. This exercise is for reciting the information in your notes.

5. Exercise 23.2 on page 337 is for answering test questions about the information you recited.

Use the suggestions in this chapter to recite, review, and learn the information in the notes you took for Exercise 21.10. Use the following questions to stimulate your recall of the information.

1. What is self-esteem?

2. How does self-esteem develop in childhood, adolescence, and adulthood?

3. What are the characteristics of people with high self-esteem?

4. How does self-esteem affect success at work?

5. What is the failure syndrome?

6. How is my behavior affected by my expectations and by the expectations others have for me?

7. What is a self-fulfilling prophecy?

8. What is the Pygmalion effect?

9. What is a mentor?

10. What are the seven criteria for selecting a mentor?

11. What are the five strategies for building self-esteem?

12. What are affirmations?

13. What are the three guidelines for writing affirmations?

14. How can organizations help workers build high self-esteem?

Five

The Study Program: Taking Tests

329

Teachers of most college courses are required to give tests and to consider test scores when they assign final course grades for students. It is the responsibility of teachers to give tests, and most of them take that responsibility seriously.

Some instructors give only a midterm and a final examination; students who do poorly on one of these tests usually receive low final course grades. Other teachers give many tests because they want to make certain that students learn what they teach and to give them chances to earn good course grades even if they do not do well on one or two tests. When you have teachers who give many tests, keep in mind that they are trying to help you to learn and to do your best in their courses.

Considering the importance test scores have in determining course grades, it is surprising that schools give little attention to teaching students how to do their best when they take tests. But test-taking is a skill that can be learned in the same way the skills of reading and writing are learned. The final six chapters of *RSVP* explain basic methods for taking any test and specific strategies for answering true-false, multiple-choice, matching, fill-in, and essay questions.

Basic Test-Taking Methods

Chapters 16–22 explain what to do *before* you take tests; this chapter suggests what you should do *while* you take them. "How to Take a Test" on page 332 summarizes methods that apply to all tests. Specific strategies for answering true-false, multiple-choice, matching, fill-in, and essay questions are explained in Chapters 24–28.

Reduce Your Test Anxiety

Test anxiety is uneasiness or apprehension students experience because they need to take a test. The physical symptoms of test anxiety include excessive sweating, discomfort in the stomach, headaches, rapid heartbeat, and shortness of breath.

Since anxiety results from fear, you can usually avoid test anxiety by preparing thoroughly for tests, using the methods explained in Chapters 16–22. If you are well prepared for a test, you will not have much to fear. It is also important to arrive at tests well rested and without rushing. You will not do your best on a test if you are tired or if you have created unnecessary anxiety for yourself by rushing into the test room at the last minute.

In addition, knowing and using good test-taking procedures will help you to reduce test anxiety. Anxiety directs thoughts *inward*, to think about discomfort; but good test-taking methods direct thoughts *outward*, to think about answering test questions correctly. If you use the methods explained in this chapter and in Chapters 24–28 when you take tests, you will be so busy in the worthwhile pursuit of answering questions correctly that your mind will probably not turn to futile thoughts of fear of taking tests.

If you become excited during a test, keep in mind that it is normal to be excited and that excitement can help you do your best, in the same way it helps athletes do their best during athletic competition. You may also find that the following exercise helps you to relax when you are anxious.

1. Without actually smiling, relax your face and feel yourself smiling on the inside.

2. Take a very deep breath—a breath so deep that you imagine it reaches to the soles of your feet.

3. Then, still smiling inside, let your breath out very slowly.

How to Take a Test

- Reduce anxiety by reminding yourself that you studied thoroughly before the test and you know how to use good test-taking strategies.
- Survey the test to learn what types of questions you must answer, whether questions are printed on both sides of each page, and where you must write your answers.
- Read the directions carefully and follow them exactly.
- Listen attentively to everything the teacher says before and during the test.
- Plan your test-taking time so you will answer all the questions you know in case time runs out.
- Answer the easiest questions first.
- Answer all the questions unless you are instructed not to.
- Check your answers, but be careful not to change correct answers to incorrect answers.
- Don't let other students see your answers. (You may be accused of cheating.)
- When a test is returned, study your incorrect answers to learn how you might do better on the next test the teacher gives.

If you cannot conquer test anxiety by using these methods, seek professional help. Many colleges have counselors who provide assistance to students who experience acute and disabling test anxiety.

Survey Tests

Before you answer any questions on a test, survey it to learn what types of questions you must answer, whether questions are printed on one or both sides of each page, and where you must write your answers.

Then read the test directions; they may be different from what you expect. For example, students usually expect that they are to answer all questions on tests; however, the directions for the essay test in Figure 23.1 instruct students to answer only two of the four questions. Students who answer all four questions make a serious mistake because they will not receive credit for their answers to the third and fourth questions (and their answer to the third or fourth question might be better than their answer to the first or second question).

FIGURE 23.1
An Essay Test

> Test: Mass Communication
>
> Answer any two of the following four questions. Each answer has a value of 50 points. You have 50 minutes to write your answers.
>
> 1. What part should the media play in changing the public's attitudes and opinions?
> 2. Compare the importance of movies as a mass medium in the 1940s to their importance today.
> 3. What issues and problems would each of the following disciplines emphasize in studying mass communication: psychology, sociology, and linguistics?
> 4. What questions and issues are of concern when studying broadcasting from a content point of view?

Listen to Everything Teachers Say

It is absolutely essential to listen attentively to everything that teachers say on test days. Before tests they often explain directions that give students difficulty, and during tests they sometimes warn students about typographical errors on tests.

Also, when there are only a few students left in a test room, instructors sometimes answer questions or make comments that help the remaining students give a correct answer to a difficult question. If you leave a test room before the end of a test period, you may miss information other students received and used to answer a question correctly.

Plan Test-Taking Time

Since there is often too little time to answer all test questions, you must plan how to use the available time. Allocate your test-taking time by finding the answers to the following questions.

- How many questions must I answer?
- How many points is each question worth?
- How much time do I have to answer the questions?

For example, a student took a psychology test with the following directions: "You have 50 minutes to answer 25 multiple-choice questions (2 points each) and 5 short-answer questions (10 points each)." He computed that the multiple-choice questions had a value of 50 points ($2 \times 25 = 50$) and the short-answer questions had a value of 50 points ($10 \times 5 = 50$). Therefore, he allotted twenty-five minutes for answering the multiple-choice questions and twenty-five minutes for answering the short-answer questions (about one minute for each multiple-choice question and about five minutes for each short-answer question).

Answer the Easiest Questions First

After you have planned how to use your test-taking time, determine which questions are easiest to answer and answer these questions first. There are at least three benefits to answering the easiest questions before answering the more difficult ones.

- *You will answer all the questions you can answer correctly*, in case time runs out before you answer all the questions. When test-taking time is limited, do not waste it trying to answer questions that you will almost certainly answer incorrectly.

- *You might think of answers* to some of the difficult questions. During the time it takes you to answer other questions, you will often remember answers to questions that you could not answer the first time you read them.

- *You might find answers* to some of the difficult questions. True-false and multiple-choice questions are sometimes interrelated, so that one question suggests the correct answer to another question. As you take tests look for information in questions that can help you select a correct answer to another question that you were unable to answer the first time you read it.

When you answer true-false or multiple-choice questions, read each question twice, then either answer it or move on to the next question. When you have read each question twice and answered as many as you can, reread the first unanswered question twice again and answer it or move on to the next unanswered question. Work through the test in this way as many times as necessary to select an answer to each question.

Check the time every ten minutes to make certain that you are answering questions at the rate that will help you get the highest possible score. During the last minute or two of the test period, mark some answer for each question. For instance, you might mark all unanswered true-false questions true, and you might mark *c* or some other letter for all unanswered multiple-choice questions.

Usually Answer All Questions

Give an answer to every question on a test unless you are specifically told not to answer all questions, as on an essay test (see Figure 23.1 on page 333). When you do not know an answer to a true-false or a multiple-choice question, guess the answer unless you are told that you will be severely penalized for incorrect answers.

When you guess the answer to a true-false question, you have a 50 percent chance of guessing the correct answer. There is a 50 percent chance the answer is true and a 50 percent chance the answer is false. When you guess the answer to a multiple-choice question with four answers (*a, b, c,* and *d*), you have a 25 percent chance of guessing the correct answer. There is a 25 percent chance the answer is *a*, a 25 percent chance the answer is *b*, and so on.

Check Your Answers

As you know, you should always carefully check your answers before you hand a test back to a teacher. However, when you check answers to true-false and multiple-choice questions, be slow to change them. If you are certain you answered a question incorrectly, cross out the incorrect answer and write the correct one. However, do not change an answer simply because you are nervous. Students who change answers because they are nervous about their original answers tend to change correct answers to incorrect answers!

When you change answers on tests, cross out the original answers but leave them visible so that when teachers review test answers in class you can analyze whether you changed correct answers to incorrect ones. By using this procedure you will soon learn whether you should change answers only when you are absolutely certain that you have written incorrect ones.

Ignore Other Test-Takers

Do you ever worry that students who finish a test before you may receive higher grades than you? If so, there is no need to have this concern. Some of the people who finish tests quickly do receive high test grades, but others complete tests quickly because they do not know the answers to many questions. Many of the students who receive high test grades use every minute of test-taking time to make certain that their answers are correct. Therefore, when you take a test, ignore other students and concentrate on answering questions correctly.

Also, if a classmate should ever ask you to share answers to test questions, don't do so. If another student is poorly prepared for a test, do not let this be your problem. If you let another student read your test answers, you may be accused of cheating; those who allow others to read their answers are as guilty of cheating as those who read them! Cheating in college is a serious offense that could result in disciplinary action or dismissal. Therefore, during tests, sit so other students cannot see your answers (and so you cannot see their answers).

Learn from Incorrect Responses

Test-taking is a skill, and skills are improved by making mistakes and learning not to make them. For instance, if you are a good automobile driver, you have learned not to make the mistakes you made while you were learning to drive. Similarly, you may become an expert test-taker by learning not to make the mistakes that you now make when you take tests.

When tests are returned to you, analyze them to understand why you answered questions incorrectly. You may decide that you did not plan test-taking time carefully enough or that you did not review class notes as much as you should have. You may also find it helpful to discuss your incorrect test answers with classmates and instructors. Use what you learn from your analyses and discussions to do better when you take future tests.

EXERCISE 23.1 **Planning Test-Taking Time**

Practice planning test-taking time by answering the following questions.

1. You have fifty minutes to solve ten mathematical problems, which have a value of 10 points each. How many minutes should you spend solving each problem?

    _____

2. You have one hundred minutes to answer four essay questions. One answer has a value of 40 points and three answers have a value of 20 points each. How many minutes should you plan to spend answering the 40-point question?

    _____

    How many minutes should you plan to spend answering each of the 20-point questions?

    _____

3. You have sixty minutes to answer twenty-five multiple-choice questions and ten short-answer questions. The multiple-choice questions have a value of 2 points each, and the short-answer questions have a value of 5 points each. How many minutes should you plan to spend answering the twenty-five multiple-choice questions?

    _____

    How many minutes should you plan to spend answering each short-answer question?

    _____

EXERCISE 23.2   **Building High Self-Esteem**

This is the fifth in a series of five exercises for applying study skills to the textbook chapter entitled "Building High Self-Esteem," which is on pages 383–412 in the appendix.

1. Exercise 19.1 on pages 269–270 is for surveying the chapter.

2. Exercise 20.10 on pages 297–298 is for marking information in the chapter.

3. Exercise 21.10 on page 316 is for making notes on information in the chapter.

4. Exercise 22.4 on page 328 is for reciting the information in your notes.

5. This exercise is for answering test questions about the information you recited.

You may take a true-false, multiple-choice, and short-answer test your instructor distributes, or you may answer some of the following questions.

15-Point Questions

Check the boxes in front of the *two* questions in the following list that your instructor requests you to answer. Each correct answer has a value of 15 points.

- ☐ 1. What is self-esteem?
- ☐ 2. What is the failure syndrome?
- ☐ 3. What is the Pygmalion effect?
- ☐ 4. What are the guidelines for writing affirmations?

35-Point Questions

Check the boxes in front of the *two* questions in the following list that your instructor requests you to answer. Each correct answer has a value of 35 points.

- ☐ 5. How does self-esteem develop in childhood, adolescence, and adulthood?
- ☐ 6. What are the characteristics of people with high self-esteem?
- ☐ 7. What are the criteria for selecting a mentor?
- ☐ 8. What are the strategies for building self-esteem?

EXERCISE 23.3   **Rating Your Test-Taking Methods**

Analyze whether you used effective test-taking methods when you did Exercise 23.2. Put checks in the boxes in front of the following statements that correctly describe the methods you used when you took the test.

☐ I prepared for the test using the methods that are explained in Chapters 16–22 of *RSVP*.

☐ Before I answered any questions, I surveyed the test to learn what types of questions I would answer, whether questions were printed on both sides of pages, and where to write answers.

☐ I read the test directions and followed them exactly.

☐ I listened attentively to everything the instructor said before and during the text.

☐ I planned my test-taking time carefully so I was able to answer all the questions for which I knew answers.

☐ I checked the time every ten minutes to make certain that I would answer questions at the rate that would help me get the highest possible score.

☐ I answered the easiest questions first.

☐ I picked up extra points by correctly guessing the answers to some questions.

☐ I double-checked my answers after I wrote them.

☐ I was careful not to let any classmate see my answers during the test.

☐ When the test was returned, I studied my incorrect answers to learn how I might do better on the next test.

If there is a statement you did not check, use it as a hint to improve your performance the next time you take a test.

True-False Questions

True-false questions are statements that test-takers must decide are either true or false. They are well suited for testing whether students have learned facts such as the following.

☐ T   ☐ F   The United States entered World War II in 1941.

The United States either entered World War II in 1941 or it did not. It did; the statement is true.

True-false questions are easy for teachers to write and grade, and students can answer them in a very short time. As a result, true-false questions appear frequently in tests for psychology, history, business, and other college courses for which instructors want to determine whether students have learned factual information.

Assume Statements Are True

When you answer true-false questions on college tests, mark *true* those statements that you know are true and mark *false* those that you know are false. When you are uncertain whether a statement is true or false, assume it is true. The reason for assuming that statements are true is that there is a definite *tendency* for true-false tests to include more true statements than false ones. As a result, when you guess the answer to a true-false question, you are more likely to guess the correct answer if you guess it is true.

However, keep in mind that a true-false statement is false if any part of it is false. For example,

☐ T   ☐ F   George Washington, Benjamin Franklin, and Abraham Lincoln were presidents of the United States.

This statement is false because Benjamin Franklin was not a president of the United States.

"How to Answer True-False Questions" on page 340 summarizes the suggestions in the following discussion.

How to Answer True-False Questions

Answer all questions that you know are true or false. When you are uncertain whether a question is true or false, use the following hints to help in locating statements that are likely to be false.

- Questions that contain extreme modifiers such as *always, all, only,* and *never* tend to be false.
- Questions that state a reason tend to be false (and they often contain the words *reason, because,* or *since*).

When you are uncertain whether a statement is true or false, guess that it is true.

Extreme Modifiers

Extreme modifiers are words such as *always, all, only,* and *never;* they tend to appear in false statements. On the other hand, statements that include **qualifiers** such as *some, frequently, many,* and *sometimes* tend to be true. Compare the following statements.

☐ T   ☐ F   **All** businesses adopt and use new technology.

☐ T   ☐ F   **Many** businesses adopt and use new technology.

The first statement is false, but the second statement is true. All businesses do not adopt and use new technology, but many of them do.

Compare the following false and true statements, paying attention to the words printed in boldface.

False Statements

1. Parents **always** love their children.

2. **All** children love chocolate.

3. The **only** reason people work is to earn money.

4. Men are **never** nurses.

5. **Nobody** reads dictionaries for pleasure.

True Statements

1. Parents **usually** love their children.

2. **Many** children love chocolate.

3. A **major** reason people work is to earn money.

4. Men are **seldom** nurses.

5. **Few** people read dictionaries for pleasure.

The false statements in the left column contain extreme modifiers such as *always* and *all,* which do not allow for exceptions. Following are more examples of extreme modifiers.

Extreme Modifiers Often in False Statements

all	none	best	absolutely
always	never	worst	absolutely not
only	nobody	everybody	certainly
invariably	no one	everyone	certainly not

The true statements in the right column contain qualifiers such as *usually* and *many*, which allow for exceptions. Following are more examples of qualifiers.

Qualifiers Often in True Statements

usually	frequently	often	sometimes
some	seldom	many	much
probably	a majority	apt to	most
might	a few	may	unlikely

Some students have difficulty deciding which words are extreme modifiers. If you have this problem, keep in mind that an extreme modifier is simply a qualifier that identifies the greatest degree and does not allow for exceptions, such as *always*. In contrast, *usually*, *frequently*, and *often* are not extreme modifiers—they are qualifiers that allow for exceptions.

Though true-false statements that contain extreme modifiers tend to be false, they can, of course, be true. For instance,

☐ T   ☐ F   Identical twins are **always** the same sex.

This statement is true; if twins are not the same sex, they are not identical.

Reasons

True-false questions that state reasons tend to be false, either because they state an incorrect reason or because they do not state all the reasons. For instance,

☐ T   ☐ F   The **reason** the government protects consumers is that consumer lobbyists fought for this protection.

This statement is false because it states an incomplete reason. The government protects consumers as a result of the actions of *many* groups and individuals who were not or are not necessarily lobbyists. Though we tend to think of the consumer movement as a new force in our society, it has been very strong since the 1880s, and it was not started by lobbyists.

The following true-false questions illustrate that the statement of a reason does not have to contain the word *reason*.

☐ T   ☐ F   The government protects consumers **because** lobbyists fought for this protection.

☐ T   ☐ F   **Since** consumer lobbyists fought to protect consumers, the government now protects them.

The words *because* and *since* indicate that these true-false questions state reasons.

True-false questions that state reasons can, of course, be true. For instance,

☐ T   ☐ F   Stores make much use of newspaper advertising because it is low in cost and has a high impact on consumers.

This statement is true—it gives two of the reasons stores use newspaper advertising.

The following exercises provide practice in learning how to select correct answers to true-false questions; the answers to the questions in the exercises are correct according to the sources upon which they are based. Use what you learn by doing the exercises to answer more true-false questions correctly on college tests.

EXERCISE 24.1   **True-False Questions**

The following statements are true, except for those that have an extreme modifier or that state a reason. Check **T** for true statements and **F** for false statements. When you check **F**, underline the word in the statement that indicates it is false.

1. ☐ T ☐ F   Young people tend to consider as necessities many products that adults categorize as luxuries.

2. ☐ T ☐ F   Criminologists are concerned only with the reasons people commit crimes and not with what happens to people after they are imprisoned.

3. ☐ T ☐ F   We do not know for certain what causes lightning.

4. ☐ T ☐ F   Men seem to fall in love more quickly and easily than women.

5. ☐ T ☐ F   Laws do nothing to diminish discrimination because it is not possible to legislate morality.

6. ☐ T ☐ F   All people are psychologically mature at age eighteen.

7. ☐ T ☐ F   The right hemisphere of the brain is believed to be the center for nonverbal reasoning.

8. ☐ T ☐ F   The reason for underlining textbooks is that, if they are underlined, students do not need to make notes on the information in them.

9. ☐ T ☐ F   The halo effect refers to the tendency always to rate individuals positively.

10. ☐ T ☐ F   Joggers can maintain the same physical fitness as runners by jogging the same distances that runners run.

11. ☐ T ☐ F   Since markup pricing complicates the process of deciding what prices to charge for products, retailers do not use it often.

12. ☐ T ☐ F   In the past, population growth was sometimes controlled by killing newborn babies.

EXERCISE 24.2   **True-False Questions**

The following statements are true, except for those that have an extreme modifier or that state a reason. Check **T** for true statements and **F** for false statements. When you check **F**, underline the word in the statement that indicates it is false.

1. ☐ T ☐ F International trade is not vital to our economy because we are the world's leading economic and military power.

2. ☐ T ☐ F In American society, people tend to marry others who are much like themselves with regard to age, social class, education, and so on.

3. ☐ T ☐ F Prejudice is based only on fear, ignorance, and cultural conditioning.

4. ☐ T ☐ F During the Civil War, more northern soldiers died from diseases or accidents than from combat.

5. ☐ T ☐ F Psychologists have shown that all six-year-olds can perform the thinking skills needed to learn to read.

6. ☐ T ☐ F College graduates usually earn more money than high school graduates.

7. ☐ T ☐ F People who divorce and remarry are more likely to divorce than people who marry for the first time.

8. ☐ T ☐ F The reason tropical Africa has a very good agricultural economy is that it has a very long growing season.

9. ☐ T ☐ F The decision to commit suicide is never made suddenly or impulsively.

10. ☐ T ☐ F Gambling is usually more profitable to organized crime than either prostitution or drugs.

11. ☐ T ☐ F The Old Testament does not report an incident in which a woman was put to death for sleeping with a man other than her husband.

12. ☐ T ☐ F It makes sense to choose a college major in the same field as one's intended career, because most graduates are employed in the general field of their college major.

EXERCISE 24.3   **True-False Questions**

The following statements are true, except for those that have an extreme modifier or that state a reason. Check **T** for true statements and **F** for false statements. When you check **F**, underline the word in the statement that indicates it is false.

1. □ T   □ F   The United States has one of the most severe systems for punishing criminals in the civilized world.

2. □ T   □ F   Highly talented people always have highly positive self-concepts.

3. □ T   □ F   Of the slaves who were taken from Africa, approximately 6 percent were brought to the United States.

4. □ T   □ F   The population is increasing rapidly in less developed countries of the world because of the high birthrates in those regions.

5. □ T   □ F   People are more likely to be murdered in their homes by somebody they know than on the streets by a stranger.

6. □ T   □ F   Women seem to fall out of love more quickly and with less difficulty than men.

7. □ T   □ F   Colorblindness is a vision problem of men, but never of women.

8. □ T   □ F   Average weekly movie attendance in the United States dropped from 90,000,000 in the 1940s to 22,500,000 in the 1980s.

9. □ T   □ F   There are almost as many independent nations in Africa as there are states in the United States.

10. □ T   □ F   Churchmen formed the only substantial block of white Southerners who criticized slavery during the years before the Civil War.

11. □ T   □ F   Since women have less education than men, they earn less money than men.

12. □ T   □ F   Sleep was not scientifically investigated until recently because there was no interest in this subject until after World War II.

EXERCISE 24.4 **True-False Questions**

The following statements are true, except for those that have an extreme modifier or that state a reason. Check **T** for true statements and **F** for false statements. When you check **F**, underline the word in the statement that indicates it is false.

1. □ T □ F The reason Napoleon sold Louisiana to the United States was that he feared we would take it by force.

2. □ T □ F It is healthy for us to express our anger.

3. □ T □ F Most human behavior is learned.

4. □ T □ F Stock certificates must be issued by all corporations.

5. □ T □ F People judge others on traits they are born with, such as height, skin color, hairiness, and nose shape.

6. □ T □ F Psychologists agree that our value systems are always formed by the time we are six years old.

7. □ T □ F Drug pushers usually become members of criminal organizations because they themselves are addicted and need a source of drugs.

8. □ T □ F Today, retail stores are staffed largely by part-time sales workers.

9. □ T □ F The lack of black police officers is due to the fact that there is discrimination against well-qualified black applicants for positions in the police force.

10. □ T □ F Almost all jobs contain some dreary activities.

11. □ T □ F Employers provide orientation for new employees only.

12. □ T □ F There are at least 7,000 people in the United States over one hundred years old.

Multiple-Choice Questions

Multiple-choice questions are incomplete statements followed by possible ways to complete them, or they are questions followed by possible answers. The incomplete statement or question that begins a multiple-choice question is called the **stem,** and the choices for answers are written so that one is the correct answer and the others are **distractors.**

1. United States senators serve
   □ a. two-year terms.
   □ b. four-year terms.
   □ c. six-year terms.
   □ d. eight-year terms.

In this example, the stem is "United States senators serve." The question is written with the intention that students who know the correct answer will select *c* (six-year terms), while other students will be distracted and select one of the distractors—*a*, *b*, or *d*.

Popularity of Multiple-Choice Questions

There are at least three reasons multiple-choice questions are popular among college teachers.

- They can be used to test all aspects of students' knowledge and their ability to reason using information they have learned.
- When answers are recorded on answer sheets, multiple-choice answers are easy to grade.
- Students with poor writing ability are not penalized when they answer multiple-choice questions (as they may be when they are required to give written answers to questions).

For these reasons, you will probably take many multiple-choice tests during your college career.

Eliminate the Distractors

Multiple-choice questions are prepared by first writing a stem and the correct answer. For instance,

2. A speech that has as its purpose to inform how to plan a successful party must use
   ☐ a. exposition.
   ☐ b.
   ☐ c.
   ☐ d.

After putting this much on paper, the question writer then fills in the distractors and decides where to locate the correct answer. As a result, the test-taker's job is to analyze multiple-choice questions to eliminate distractors and in this way to locate the correct answer that was "hidden" by the question writer.
   One way to eliminate distractors is to analyze a multiple-choice question as though it is a series of true-false questions. For instance,

☐ T   ☐ F   United States senators serve two-year terms.

☐ T   ☐ F   United States senators serve four-year terms.

☐ T   ☐ F   United States senators serve six-year terms.

☐ T   ☐ F   United States senators serve eight-year terms.

Most multiple-choice questions are actually a series of true-false statements, only one of which is true. When you answer a multiple-choice question, analyze it to eliminate distractors and to select as the correct answer the choice that makes the stem a true statement.
   When you have difficulty eliminating the distractors in a multiple-choice question, analyze it for the clues to correct answers and incorrect answers. "How to Answer Multiple-Choice Questions" on page 349 summarizes suggestions that are explained in detail in the following discussion.

"All of the Above"

When "all of the above" is a choice in a multiple-choice question, it tends to be the correct answer. Check the correct answer to the following question.

3. Teenage love involves
   ☐ a. sexual attraction.
   ☐ b. crushes.
   ☐ c. a search for identity.
   ☐ d. all of the above

You should have checked *d*; it is the correct answer.
   The question could, of course, have been written so that "all of the above" is not the correct answer. Check the correct answer to the following question.

> ### *How to Answer Multiple-Choice Questions*
>
> 1. Answer all questions for which you know the correct answer.
> 2. Look for clues to correct answers.
>   - "All of the above"
>   - One of two similar-looking answers
>   - The most inclusive answer
> 3. Look for clues to *incorrect* answers.
>   - An extreme modifier (such as *always*)
>   - An unfamiliar term
>   - A joke or insult
>   - The highest and lowest number in a set

4. Teenage love involves
   - ☐ a. crushes.
   - ☐ b. expensive dates.
   - ☐ c. guilt and shame.
   - ☐ d. all of the above

According to the source upon which this question is based, the correct answer is *a*; however, keep in mind that in college tests "all of the above" is the correct answer much more frequently than it should be.

Also, when you know that two answers are correct and another choice is "all of the above," you must select "all of the above" as the correct answer. For instance,

5. Silver is used to make
   - ☐ a. knives and forks.
   - ☐ b. jewelry.
   - ☐ c. film for photography.
   - ☐ d. all of the above

If you know that silver is used to make knives, forks, and jewelry, you must select "all of the above" as the correct answer even if you do not know that it is also used to make film for photography. If you select *a*, you do not include jewelry; if you select *b*, you do not include knives and forks. You must select *d* to include knives, forks, and jewelry in your answer.

Two Similar-Looking Answers

When two answers are similar looking, the correct answer is often one of the two similar-looking answers. Check the correct answer to the following question.

6. In the brain, language functions are associated mainly with the
   - ☐ a. left hemisphere.
   - ☐ b. right hemisphere.
   - ☐ c. cerebellum.
   - ☐ d. corpus callosum.

You should have eliminated answers *c* and *d* and made your choice between the two similar-looking answers—*a* and *b*. The correct answer is *a*.

Question writers sometimes write multiple-choice questions to eliminate the clue to two similar-looking answers. For instance,

7. The loss of all sensation in your hand would most likely result from damage to
   - ☐ a. afferent spinal nerves.
   - ☐ b. efferent spinal nerves.
   - ☐ c. afferent cranial nerves.
   - ☐ d. efferent cranial nerves.

When questions are written in this way, you cannot use two similar-looking answers as a clue to the correct answer, which in this case is *a*.

Most Inclusive Answer

When one answer to a multiple-choice question is more inclusive than other answers, it is likely to be the correct answer. Check the most inclusive answer to the following question.

8. Output devices on computers produce
   - ☐ a. a permanent copy.
   - ☐ b. a soft copy.
   - ☐ c. both *a* and *b*
   - ☐ d. none of the above

You should have checked *c*, which includes the possibilities stated in answers *a* and *b*; answer *c* is the most inclusive answer, and it is also the correct answer.

It can be a challenge to identify the most inclusive answer. Check the most inclusive answer to the following question.

9. Weight is likely to vary most among a group of
   - ☐ a. men who are football linebackers.
   - ☐ b. women who are ballet dancers.
   - ☐ c. people who are jockeys.
   - ☐ d. people who are college students.

Football linebackers tend to include only heavy people; women ballet dancers and jockeys tend to include only light people. College students, though, include people who are heavy, light, and medium in weight. Answer *d* is the most inclusive, and it is the correct answer.

Extreme Modifiers

In Chapter 24 you learned that extreme modifiers tend to be included in true-false questions that are false; in multiple-choice questions, extreme modifiers tend to appear in distractors. Underline the extreme modifiers in the following question and check the correct answer.

10. Mentally healthy people
    ☐ a. never change their goals.
    ☐ b. are always happy when alone.
    ☐ c. are sometimes anxious or afraid.
    ☐ d. never examine their mistakes.

You should have underlined *always* and *never*, and you should have checked *c*.

Unfamiliar Terms

Unfamiliar terms or phrases are often included in distractors. Underline the unfamiliar terms in the following question and check the correct answer.

11. Mass hysteria results when large numbers of people
    ☐ a. believe something that is not true.
    ☐ b. fear an invasion of iconoclasts.
    ☐ c. have concomitant exigencies.
    ☐ d. share incontrovertible perceptions.

You should have underlined *iconoclasts, concomitant exigencies*, and *incontrovertible perceptions*; and you should have checked *a*.
   The only time it is wise to pick answers with unfamiliar terms is when you are certain that all the other answers are incorrect. For instance,

12. Jeans are always
    ☐ a. dark blue.
    ☐ b. well worn.
    ☐ c. too tight.
    ☐ d. bifurcated.

You know that jeans are not always dark blue, well worn, or too tight; therefore, you are forced to conclude that they are *bifurcated*, even though you probably don't know the meaning of the word. To bifurcate is to divide into two parts or branches; the legs of jeans are in two parts—one for each leg. Skirts, in contrast, are not bifurcated.

Jokes or Insults

Answers that are jokes or insults are usually distractors. Check the answer in the following question that is *not* ridiculous or insulting.

13. A common reason students give for leaving college is that they
    - ☐ a. aren't smart enough to do college work.
    - ☐ b. find that they dislike other college students.
    - ☐ c. are treated badly by their instructors.
    - ☐ d. decide that something else interests them more.

Answers *a*, *b*, and *c* are either ridiculous or insulting; you should have eliminated them as distractors and checked *d*, which is the correct answer.

Extreme Numbers

When answers are a series of numbers that go from high to low, the extreme numbers (the highest and lowest ones) tend to be incorrect. Answer the following question by eliminating the extreme numbers as distractors.

14. According to generally accepted nutritional guidelines, how many servings of fruit and vegetables should we eat each day?
    - ☐ a. two
    - ☐ b. four
    - ☐ c. six
    - ☐ d. eight

You should have eliminated the extreme numbers in answers *a* and *d* and made your choice between *b* and *c*. The correct answer is *b*; we should eat four servings of fruit and vegetables daily.

EXERCISE 25.1 **Multiple-Choice Questions**

Use the clues to correct and incorrect answers summarized on page 349 to select the correct answers to the following questions.

1. Learning how to play the piano while singing occurs in the
   ☐ a. motor domain.
   ☐ b. cognitive domain.
   ☐ c. affective domain.
   ☐ d. motor and cognitive domains.

2. After the Civil War, Reconstruction legislatures in the South were successful in
   ☐ a. making prison reforms.
   ☐ b. integrating schools.
   ☐ c. serving the handicapped.
   ☐ d. achieving all of the above.

3. On June 21, the sun is found directly over the
   ☐ a. Tropic of Cancer.
   ☐ b. Tropic of Capricorn.
   ☐ c. equator.
   ☐ d. North Pole.

4. The normal adult temperature of 98.6°F is equivalent to
   ☐ a. 18°C.
   ☐ b. 27°C.
   ☐ c. 37°C.
   ☐ d. 42°C.

5. Those who believe in the work ethic believe that
   ☐ a. all will do good work.
   ☐ b. work is always rewarded.
   ☐ c. work is good and important.
   ☐ d. only workers should receive money.

6. The biosphere consists of
   ☐ a. air above the earth.
   ☐ b. the earth's surface.
   ☐ c. bodies of water on earth.
   ☐ d. air, earth surface, and water bodies.

7. The median is a measure that is similar to
   ☐ a. the average.
   ☐ b. a histogram.
   ☐ c. the skewness.
   ☐ d. a coefficient.

8. Educators refer to individuals of very low intelligence as
   ☐ a. idiots.
   ☐ b. morons.
   ☐ c. imbeciles.
   ☐ d. totally dependent.

9. Studies of workers' attitudes have found that
   ☐ a. most workers feel they should have better jobs.
   ☐ b. many would rather have better jobs than more pay.
   ☐ c. workers are motivated by conflicting drives.
   ☐ d. all of the above

10. Children begin to understand some of the concepts associated with religious beliefs when they are
   ☐ a. toddlers.
   ☐ b. preschoolers.
   ☐ c. school-aged.
   ☐ d. teenagers.

EXERCISE 25.2   Multiple-Choice Questions

Use the clues to correct and incorrect answers summarized on page 349 to select the correct answers to the following questions.

1. Most Jewish immigrants to the United States came from
   □ a. Eastern Europe.
   □ b. Western Europe.
   □ c. Israel.
   □ d. Africa and Asia.

2. Partners in a marriage are likely to be similar in
   □ a. height and weight.
   □ b. hair and skin color.
   □ c. general health.
   □ d. size, coloring, and health.

3. People work because they
   □ a. need to feel productive.
   □ b. must pay for necessities.
   □ c. want to achieve dignity.
   □ d. all of the above

4. Brazil was colonized by
   □ a. Indians.
   □ b. North Americans.
   □ c. a heterogeneous group of Europeans.
   □ d. a homogeneous group of Europeans.

5. A zero-growth family is one that has
   □ a. no children.
   □ b. one child.
   □ c. two children.
   □ d. three children.

6. Members of one's family of orientation are
   □ a. blood relatives.
   □ b. affinal relatives.
   □ c. tertiary relatives.
   □ d. misogynistic relatives.

7. The difficulty of reading material can be estimated by studying the lengths of
   □ a. words.
   □ b. sentences.
   □ c. both *a* and *b*
   □ d. none of the above

8. Which of the following statements about ability is true?
   □ a. People differ in their abilities.
   □ b. All people are equal in abilities.
   □ c. There is only one basic type of ability.
   □ d. Ability never changes over one's lifetime.

9. More doctors are males than females, probably because
   □ a. women don't want prestigious jobs.
   □ b. of established occupational expectations.
   □ c. males make better doctors.
   □ d. most women crack under pressure.

10. A common physical symptom of depression is
    □ a. constipation.
    □ b. decreased pulse.
    □ c. decreased blood pressure.
    □ d. all of the above

EXERCISE 25.3   Multiple-Choice Questions

Use the clues to correct and incorrect answers summarized on page 349 to select the correct answers to the following questions.

1. About how much time should one spend doing aerobic activity to attain top conditioning?
   - ☐ a. 1 hour 6–7 days a week
   - ☐ b. ½ hour 3–5 days a week
   - ☐ c. ¼ hour 3–5 days a week
   - ☐ d. ½ hour 6–7 days a week

2. Harmony between one's beliefs and behavior is called
   - ☐ a. cognitive consonance.
   - ☐ b. cognitive dissonance.
   - ☐ c. personality agreement.
   - ☐ d. belief-system integration.

3. Our sexual attitudes develop
   - ☐ a. solely from what we learn from our parents.
   - ☐ b. from positive and negative sexual experiences.
   - ☐ c. from satisfying sexual experiences.
   - ☐ d. from unfortunate sexual experiences.

4. The burning of fossil fuel is causing a build-up of carbon dioxide that may eventually
   - ☐ a. affect the global radiation balance.
   - ☐ b. create a warming trend on earth.
   - ☐ c. irreversibly alter world ecosystems.
   - ☐ d. all of the above

5. In the 1840s the great potato famine in Ireland resulted from
   - ☐ a. wet weather.
   - ☐ b. dry weather.
   - ☐ c. population growth.
   - ☐ d. potato disease.

6. Which of the following age groups most commonly experiences frightening dreams?
   - ☐ a. two-year-olds
   - ☐ b. three-year-olds
   - ☐ c. six-year-olds
   - ☐ d. adolescents

7. The abbreviation SEM refers to a type of
   - ☐ a. serological technique.
   - ☐ b. anaerobic bacteria.
   - ☐ c. microscope.
   - ☐ d. avian embryo.

8. In New England prior to 1780, there were
   - ☐ a. no banks.
   - ☐ b. no schools.
   - ☐ c. no hospitals.
   - ☐ d. both *a* and *c*

9. If a five-year-old says, "I flied to New York," this indicates that the child
   - ☐ a. has ignorant parents.
   - ☐ b. has inferior intelligence.
   - ☐ c. knows language rules but not their exceptions.
   - ☐ d. prefers using incorrect grammatical forms.

10. Cancer cells
   - ☐ a. lack contact inhibition.
   - ☐ b. are "immortal."
   - ☐ c. will not readily rejoin cells of the organ from which they originate.
   - ☐ d. all of the above

EXERCISE 25.4   Multiple-Choice Questions

Use the clues to correct and incorrect answers summarized on page 349 to select the correct answers to the following questions.

1. If a woman's worry over her cat's safety prevents her from leaving home more than twice a week, she is
   - ☐ a. obsessive-compulsive.
   - ☐ b. a dipsomaniac.
   - ☐ c. somewhat abnormal.
   - ☐ d. a fruitcake.

2. The first book published in the New World was printed in
   - ☐ a. Peru in 1473.
   - ☐ b. New York in 1486.
   - ☐ c. Mexico in 1539.
   - ☐ d. Massachusetts in 1626.

3. The return to a less mature behavior pattern is called
   - ☐ a. repression.
   - ☐ b. regression.
   - ☐ c. reaction formation.
   - ☐ d. none of the above

4. A nurse's first concern upon discovering a fire is to
   - ☐ a. close doors and windows.
   - ☐ b. put out the fire.
   - ☐ c. safeguard patients.
   - ☐ d. set off the fire alarm.

5. Engaging in aerobic exercise at least three times a week may produce
   - ☐ a. positive body perception.
   - ☐ b. more endorphins in the brain.
   - ☐ c. cardiovascular conditioning.
   - ☐ d. all of the above

6. Mary jogs every day because it makes her feel good about herself. She is motivated by
   - ☐ a. an intrinsic reward.
   - ☐ b. an extrinsic reward.
   - ☐ c. a psychological need.
   - ☐ d. peer-group pressure.

7. Children begin to understand that death is final when they are about
   - ☐ a. 5–6 years old.
   - ☐ b. 8–9 years old.
   - ☐ c. 11–13 years old.
   - ☐ d. 15–16 years old.

8. The central processing unit of a computer
   - ☐ a. controls computer operations.
   - ☐ b. performs arithmetic operations.
   - ☐ c. contains memory for the program and data.
   - ☐ d. all of the above

9. The major problem with selling beverages in throwaway cans is that these containers
   - ☐ a. create costly garbage-disposal problems.
   - ☐ b. are expensive to make and dispose of.
   - ☐ c. use a great deal of expensive metal.
   - ☐ d. require much expensive energy to produce.

10. Most psychologists agree that
    - ☐ a. institutionalized children never succeed in life.
    - ☐ b. fatherless boys always become homosexuals.
    - ☐ c. unloved infants often have personality problems.
    - ☐ d. abused children always abuse their own children.

EXERCISE 25.5 **Multiple-Choice Questions**

Use the clues to correct and incorrect answers summarized on page 349 to select the correct answers to the following questions.

1. The conscious mind
   - □ a. evaluates all that it accepts.
   - □ b. can help us to succeed or fail.
   - □ c. acts only on positive orders.
   - □ d. never changes after age twenty.

2. A hypothesis is
   - □ a. a proposition that can be tested.
   - □ b. a proposition that must be correct.
   - □ c. a statement of fact.
   - □ d. an explanation.

3. Some bacterial cells secrete a viscous envelope called a
   - □ a. pilus.
   - □ b. mesosome.
   - □ c. capsule.
   - □ d. nucleoid.

4. The first mass-circulation newspapers were introduced in the
   - □ a. 1780s.
   - □ b. 1830s.
   - □ c. 1890s.
   - □ d. 1920s.

5. The perceived size of a car
   - □ a. depends only on its distance from the viewer.
   - □ b. is never affected by prior learning.
   - □ c. is the same whether it's near or far away.
   - □ d. is a function of retinal articulation.

6. In the colonial American family, the status of women was
   - □ a. better than that of British women.
   - □ b. of no interest to American men.
   - □ c. lower than that of slaves.
   - □ d. equal to men's status.

7. Which of the following is a domestic animal that shows hybrid vigor and yet is sterile?
   - □ a. snark
   - □ b. unicorn
   - □ c. bandersnatch
   - □ d. mule

8. Between 1870 and 1910, American women gained greater independence, and as a result, more of them
   - □ a. quit their jobs.
   - □ b. divorced their husbands.
   - □ c. became prostitutes.
   - □ d. committed suicide.

9. Unmarried adults are often discriminated against in matters of
   - □ a. housing.
   - □ b. credit.
   - □ c. loans.
   - □ d. all of the above

10. The responsibility for a patient's nursing-care plan belongs to
   - □ a. the head nurse.
   - □ b. the assigned registered nurse.
   - □ c. the assigned student nurse.
   - □ d. everyone assigned to care for the patient.

EXERCISE 25.6 **Negatives in Stems**

When the stems of multiple-choice questions contain the words *not, false,* or *except,* do the opposite of what you ordinarily do—select as correct answers options that contain extreme modifiers or that are jokes or insults.

1. All of the following statements are true *except:*
   □ a. Hitler believed in psychology.
   □ b. Some psychologists believe in astrology.
   □ c. Horoscopes appeal only to the mentally deficient.
   □ d. Horoscopes are published in many newspapers.

2. Which of the following is *not* an effective way to relieve tension?
   □ a. exercising
   □ b. doing something for others
   □ c. going away for a weekend
   □ d. avoiding all situations that might cause tension

3. Famous on-the-scene radio reporters during World War II included all of the following *except*
   □ a. Edward R. Morrow.
   □ b. Lillian Smith.
   □ c. Robert Trout.
   □ d. William L. Shirer.

4. Which of the following statements about punishing children is *false?*
   □ a. It never works.
   □ b. It may inhibit their behavior.
   □ c. It may encourage negative behavior.
   □ d. It may make them immune to punishment.

5. According to Carl Rogers, effective teaching procedures do *not* include using
   □ a. learning contracts when appropriate.
   □ b. only topics that have stood the test of time.
   □ c. a variety of teaching methods.
   □ d. the resources that are readily available.

6. Which of the following would *not* violate the mores of American society?
   □ a. rape
   □ b. murder
   □ c. child molestation
   □ d. burping in public

7. Which of the following types of information does a nurse *not* need to include on a patient's chart?
   □ a. He refused to take medication.
   □ b. He telephoned his wife.
   □ c. His physician visited him.
   □ d. He became dizzy while walking.

8. It is appropriate for a teacher to respond to a student's misbehavior in any of the following ways *except* to
   □ a. praise it.
   □ b. ignore it.
   □ c. ask her questions about it.
   □ d. instruct her how to act.

Matching Questions

Matching questions present two lists of items and require test-takers to associate items in one list with items in the other list. In properly written questions, all items in each list are similar. For example, the following matching question for a music appreciation course requires students to match operas with their composers.

Music Appreciation

_____	1. *Dido and Aeneas*	a. Puccini
_____	2. *Don Giovanni*	b. Mozart
_____	3. *Tosca*	c. Monteverdi
_____	4. *Tristan and Isolde*	d. Purcell
_____	5. *Orfeo*	e. Wagner
_____	6. *Rigoletto*	f. Donizetti
_____	7. *Carmen*	g. Verdi
_____	8. *Lucrezia Borgia*	h. Bizet

It is extremely difficult to guess correct answers to properly written matching questions, such as this one. If you guess at the composers of the operas, you are not likely to guess more than one correct answer.

Answering Matching Questions

When you answer a matching question, scan both lists to understand the types of items you are to match, and then use one list as the starting place for making all the matches. Take care to match only those items that you are absolutely certain are matches because each time you make a mistake, you will be led to make another error. For instance, if you match 3 with *b*

How to Answer Matching Questions

- Examine both lists to understand the types of items you are to match.
- Use one list as the starting place for making all the matches.
- If one list has longer statements, use it as the starting place for making matches.
- Cross out items as you match them.
- Match first only those items that you are certain are matches.
- If possible, use logical clues to match items about which you are uncertain.

---

when you should match *3* with *f*, you will make the mistake of matching *3* with an incorrect letter *and* you will make another mistake when you match *f* with an incorrect number.

Procedures for answering matching questions are summarized in "How to Answer Matching Questions" above.

Lists with Longer Statements

If one list in a matching question has longer statements, use the list of longer statements as the starting place for making matches. For example,

Introduction to Business

_____   1. advertising media   a. telling customers that an advertised special is sold out but offering them a more expensive substitute

_____   2. sales promotion   b. nonpaid information about the company or its products in the mass media

_____   3. bait-and-switch   c. the element of promotional strategy other than personal selling, advertising, and publicity

_____   4. promotional mix   d. radio, TV, newspapers, magazine, and direct mail

_____   5. publicity   e. combination of advertising, personal selling, sales promotion, and publicity

_____   6. frequency   f. average number of times an advertising message reaches a person or household

There are only eleven words in the first column of this matching question, but there are sixty-eight words in the second column. Therefore, if you use the column with the longer statements as the starting place for making matches, you will not have to read through all of the long items each time you want to make a match.

Logical Clues

When matching questions are improperly prepared, you may be able to use logical clues to figure out answers to them, as in the following improperly prepared matching question for a psychology course.

Psychology

_____	1. located in the ear	a. James B. Watson
_____	2. behaviorist	b. ideographic study
_____	3. childhood crisis	c. frequency distribution
_____	4. tally of scores	d. to trust others
_____	5. study of an individual	e. organ of Corti

Since this question is improperly written, you should be able to use logical clues to guess some correct answers to it. For example, you will not match *1* with *a* because you know that *James B. Watson* is not *located in the ear*. Guess the answers.

EXERCISE 26.1   **Starting with Longer Statements**

Use the list with the longer statements as the starting place to make matches. Match first only those items that you are certain are matches and cross out items as you match them.

_____   1. lecture

_____   2. syllabus

_____   3. curriculum

_____   4. mnemonic

_____   5. acronym

_____   6. dean

_____   7. bibliography

_____   8. registrar

_____   9. tutor

_____   10. bursar

_____   11. appendix

_____   12. transcript

a. a word made from the initial letters of other words

b. the part of a book that contains any supplementary materials or information

c. a list of the books, articles, or other sources of information that are referred to by a writer

d. the title of a person at a college who is responsible for money transactions

e. a member of the administration of a college who is in charge of specified aspects of the school's functioning

f. a talk during which an instructor communicates information to students

g. a device used to aid memory

h. the title of a person at a college who is responsible for registering students in courses and for maintaining their academic records on transcripts

i. a summary or outline distributed by an instructor that states the main topics to be discussed in a course

j. the official record of courses taken, grades received, and grade point averages

k. a person who gives individual instruction to students

l. the courses required to earn a particular degree

EXERCISE 26.2 **Using Logical Clues**

Use logical clues to locate the correct answers to the following poorly written matching questions. Match first only those items that you are certain are matches and cross out items as you match them.

_____	1. indentured servant	a. Maine
_____	2. largest city on the eve of the American Revolution	b. made blacks citizens
		c. thirty-eight
_____	3. He established the American factory system.	d. barbed wire
		e. temporary laborer
_____	4. She advocated better care for the insane.	f. Currier and Ives
		g. 1929
_____	5. state where Prohibition was strongest	h. $486
_____	6. number of Southern slaves in 1860	i. Samuel Slater
		j. 4,000,000
_____	7. painters of American life	k. Dorothea Dix
_____	8. the Fourteenth Amendment	l. two-faced
		m. melodrama
_____	9. contribution of black musicians	n. jazz
_____	10. needed for frontier farming	o. Philadelphia
_____	11. describes U.S. policy toward Indians	
_____	12. average yearly income in 1890	
_____	13. percent of population living in cities in 1910	
_____	14. popular nineteenth-century entertainment	
_____	15. year the Great Depression started	

EXERCISE 26.3   **Guessing Answers**

In order to understand how difficult it is to guess the answers to well-written questions, try to match the items in the right column to the names in the left column. If you are unfamiliar with the facts being tested, you should make no more than one correct match by guessing at the answers. Use all but one of the items in the right column, and use an item one time only.

_____	1. Democritus	a. Law of Triads
_____	2. Van Helmont	b. naming of cathode rays
_____	3. Proust	c. conceived of the atom
_____	4. Berzelius	d. discovered sulfanilamide
_____	5. Döbereiner	e. discovered DDT
_____	6. Zeidler	f. Law of Definite Composition
_____	7. Gelmo	g. discovered element 106
_____	8. Urey	h. first atomic pile
_____	9. Goldstein	i. modern symbols for elements
_____	10. Fermi	j. discovered deuterium
		k. foundations of chemical physiology

Fill-in Questions

Fill-in questions are statements with deleted portions that test-takers must supply. For instance,

> Approximately _____ percent of American land is devoted to the raising of crops.

It is usually impossible to guess the correct answers to fill-in questions that appear on college tests. If you do not know how much American land is devoted to raising crops, you are not likely to guess the answer (17 percent).

Strategies for answering fill-in questions are summarized in "How to Answer Fill-in Questions" on page 366.

Decide the Type of Answer

The basic strategy for answering a fill-in question is to decide what type of answer is required. What type is needed for this question?

> After reading _____, President Theodore Roosevelt ordered an investigation of the meat-packing industry.

You should have decided that the answer for this question is the name of a book, magazine, newspaper, or other written material. However, it is probably impossible that you would have guessed the answer is a book entitled *The Jungle*.

When it is unclear what type of answer is required, ask the instructor for clarification. For instance,

> Alexander Hamilton was born in _____.

Since it is unclear what type of answer is needed for this question, you might ask a teacher, "Do you want me to give the place where he was born or the year in which he was born?" Prepare your question carefully. Don't, for example, point to a question and ask a teacher, "What do you mean?" Request clarification by asking questions that help your teacher understand why you are confused. (Alexander Hamilton was born on the island of St. Kitts in the West Indies; the year was 1755.)

365

How to Answer Fill-in Questions

Use these three strategies when you answer fill-in questions.

- Decide what type of answer is required.
- When a question contains two blanks with a space between them, give a two-word answer.
- When a blank is preceded by the word *an*, give an answer that begins with a vowel (*a, e, i, o,* or *u*).

Two Blanks

When a fill-in question contains two blanks with a space between them, a two-word answer is required. For instance,

Always and *never* are examples of _____ _____.

If you studied Chapters 24 and 25, you should know that the correct answer to this question is *extreme modifiers.*

The "An" Clue

The word *an* before a blank is a clue that the answer is a word that begins with a vowel sound, such as those represented by the letters *a, e, i, o,* and *u.* For instance,

Compliments satisfy an _____ need.

Those who have studied the basic human needs know that they are of five basic types: physiological, safety, social, esteem, and self-realization. The word *an* before the blank suggests that the correct answer is the human need that begins with a vowel; the correct answer is *esteem.* However, most instructors eliminate this clue by writing *a(an), a(n),* or *a/an* instead of *an* before blanks.

EXERCISE 27.1   **Fill-in Questions**

Guess the answers to the following questions to understand that it is practically impossible to guess the correct answers to fill-in questions.

1. The sixth letter of the Greek alphabet is _____.

2. Mulkiteo is located in the state of _____.

3. Tirana is the capital of _____.

4. There are _____ inches in a rod.

5. The two parts of a ratchet are a wheel and a(n) _____.

The basic strategy for answering a fill-in question is to decide what type of answer is required and to give that type of answer. Use the words in the following list to write the types of answers required by the following nine fill-in questions: Walt Whitman; morpheme; fifteen; 1962; 4,160; first; cyclone; sadist; Hinduism.

6. The Nile River is approximately _____ miles long.

7. Until as recently as _____, slavery existed somewhere in the world.

8. It was _____ _____ who said, "In the faces of men and women I see God."

9. A(n) _____ killed 300,000 people in Bangladesh on November 13, 1970.

10. A person who derives pleasure from causing others to suffer physical or mental pain is a(n) _____.

11. A(n) _____ is the smallest unit of language that has meaning.

12. One belief of _____ is that life in all forms is an aspect of the divine.

13. If a federal court gives a criminal a life sentence, the earliest possible parole date is after _____ years of the sentence have been served.

14. United States presidents enjoy the highest public support during the _____ year of their terms.

EXERCISE 27.2   **Fill-in Questions**

The following fill-in questions are based on information in Chapters 23–26 of *RSVP*.

1. Test anxiety is uneasiness or _____ students experience because they need to take a test.

2. When you guess the answer to a multiple-choice question with four answers (*a, b, c,* and *d*) you have a _____ chance of guessing the correct answer.

3. When you guess the answer to a true-false question, you have a _____ chance of guessing the correct answer.

4. Cheating in college is a serious offense that could result in disciplinary action or _____.

5. When you are uncertain whether a true-false question is true or false, assume it is _____.

6. A true-false question that contains a(n) _____ _____ such as *always* and *never* tends to be false.

7. True-false questions that state reasons often contain the words *reason, because,* or _____.

8. True-false questions tend to be _____ when they state a reason.

9. The incomplete statement or question that begins a multiple-choice question is called the _____.

10. Jokes and insults tend to be _____ answers in multiple-choice questions.

11. High and low numbers tend to be _____ answers in multiple-choice questions.

12. If one list in a matching question has short statements and the other list has long statements, use the list of _____ statements as the starting place for making matches.

Essay Questions

Essay questions require written responses that are usually a paragraph or more in length.

Students are often instructed *not* to answer all questions on essay tests. For example, the directions for the essay test in Figure 28.1 state that students are to answer only three of the five questions. They will be penalized if they answer more than three questions, because only one of the 50-point answers and two of the 25-point answers will be graded. A good answer to the fifth question on the test is illustrated in Figure 28.2, on page 370.

Students usually write answers to essay questions in **bluebooks,** which are small booklets that contain lined paper. At one time the covers of these booklets were always blue, but today covers of bluebooks may be blue, yellow, pink, or some other color.

Variations of the essay test include take-home and open-book tests. A **take-home test** can be test questions that students actually answer at home or test questions that they study at home but answer in class. The questions on take-home tests are usually more difficult than the questions on tests students see for the first time in class. Also, teachers tend to grade answers to take-home tests very strictly.

An **open-book test** is a test during which students may refer to textbooks, and sometimes to notes, as they answer questions. The term "open-book" is misleading because it suggests that students can copy answers to questions from books; however, open-book tests seldom include questions for which answers can be copied. Whatever benefit students gain by referring to books is directly related to how thoroughly they have studied. Prepare for an open-book test just as you would for any other type of test.

The steps for writing good answers to essay questions are summarized in "How to Answer Essay Questions" on page 371.

Understand Direction Words

The first step in answering an essay question is to interpret correctly the meanings of direction words. **Direction words** are italicized in the following questions.

> *Describe* the five principal types of societies.
> *Explain* the success of Eliza Pinckney.

FIGURE 28.1

An Essay Test

> Sociology Test
>
> Write your answers to the following questions in the booklet that you have been given. Answer any one of the 50-point questions and any two of the 25-point questions. You have 60 minutes to write your answers.
>
> Answer One (50 points)
> 1. Describe the five principal types of societies.
> 2. Compare the functionalist and ecological approaches to understanding cultural variation.
>
> Answer Two (25 points each)
> 3. Discuss the effects of isolation during childhood on human development.
> 4. Contrast Freud's, Cooley's, and Mead's theories of how the self emerges.
> 5. Explain what norms are.

FIGURE 28.2

An Answer to the Fifth Question in Figure 28.1

Norms are guidelines for how people should behave in particular situations; they include folkways, mores, and taboos.

Folkways are norms that pertain to things people do in everyday life. Placing refrigerators in kitchens, watching TV now and then, and eating hot dogs at ball games are some of our folkways. These behaviors are expected but not demanded.

Mores are norms that prohibit such behaviors as theft, murder, and rape. Society severely punishes those who violate mores.

Taboos are norms for behaviors that are unthinkably repulsive. In our society the taboo against eating human flesh is so strong that many states have no law against it. Also, sexual relationships between parents and children are taboos in most societies.

Some norms apply to all members of a society, and others do not. For instance, in the United States nobody may be married to more than one person. However, although we have a norm against killing others, it does not apply to soldiers and police officers in certain situations.

How to Answer Essay Questions

Use these six procedures when you answer essay questions.

1. Give the type of answer the direction words call for.

2. Answer all parts of questions.

3. Write well-organized answers.
   - Plan the major points.
   - Write an introduction that summarizes the answer.
   - Make the major points stand out.

4. Write complete answers.
   - Include all the information that is relevant to the answer.
   - Write as though you are explaining the subject to a person who is uninformed about it (such as a friend or relative) rather than to a teacher.

5. Write answers that are easy for you to proofread and easy for your teachers to read.
   - Write or print neatly.
   - Use an erasable ball point pen, so you can correct errors.
   - Write only on right-hand pages of bluebooks, so you can write changes on left-hand pages.
   - Indent each paragraph.
   - Leave one-inch margins on all four sides of answers.

6. Proofread your answers before you give them to your instructor.

Before you take an essay test, learn the meanings of the following direction words. Pay special attention to the often misinterpreted meanings of *compare*, *criticize*, and *justify* and notice that *describe*, *explain*, and *illustrate* each have two meanings.

Direction Words	Meanings	Sample Essay Questions
Discuss	Write as much as you can.	Discuss test-taking skills.
Describe	Write as much as you can.	Describe early American family life.
	Write about the subject so it can be visualized.	Describe a nutritious diet.
Explain	Write as much as you can.	Explain totalitarianism.
	Discuss reasons.	Explain why the United States entered World War II.
Compare	Discuss similarities and differences.	Compare democracy and communism.

Contrast	Discuss differences.	Contrast Catholicism with Protestantism.
Criticize (or *Evaluate*)	Discuss good and bad points of the subject and conclude whether it is primarily good or bad.	Criticize (or evaluate) the death sentence.
Justify	Discuss good and bad points of the subject and conclude that it is good.	Justify U.S. expenditures on military defense.
Diagram	Draw a picture and label its parts.	Diagram the parts of the human ear.
Illustrate	Draw a picture and label its parts.	Illustrate the parts of the human eye.
	Give a long written example.	Illustrate the use of the SQ3R study formula.
Enumerate	Make a numbered list.	Enumerate good and bad listening habits.
List	Make a numbered list.	List good manners for business employees.
Outline	Make a numbered or well-organized list.	Outline basic test-taking strategies.
Summarize	Briefly state.	Summarize the accomplishments of President Truman.
Define	Give the meaning.	Define *psychopath*.
Relate	Discuss the connection between (or among) topics.	Relate television viewing to reading habits.
Trace	Discuss in a logical or chronological sequence.	Trace the path by which blood flows through the human body.

Answer All Parts of Questions

Failure to answer all the parts of essay questions is a major reason students sometimes get lower grades on essay tests than they should. Compare the following questions.

> Relate cigarette smoking to heart disease.
> Relate cigarette smoking to heart disease and cancer.

The first question has one part, but the second question has two parts. Answers to the second question must explain how cigarette smoking is related to (1) heart disease and (2) cancer. Answers that respond to only one part of the question will not receive full credit.

Sometimes essay questions are not clearly written. When you cannot understand an essay question, ask the teacher who wrote it for clarification. It is appropriate for you to assume that your teachers want you to understand their test questions.

Write Well-Organized Answers

After you have interpreted the direction words and identified all parts of an essay question, write a well-organized answer by planning the major points, by writing a good introduction, and by making major points stand out clearly.

   1. Plan the major points. Sometimes the major points you should include in your answers are directly stated in essay questions. For instance,

> Define the following terms: folkways, mores, and taboos.

The three major points to include in the answer are stated in the question; they are definitions of the three terms listed at the end of the question. However, the question is worded in the following way in the essay test illustrated in Figure 28.1, on page 370.

> Explain what norms are.

To answer this question, students must recall that folkways, mores, and taboos are three types of norms.

   2. Write an introduction that summarizes the answer. A good introduction to an essay question is a clear summary of the answer. If an answer has several parts, the introduction should state the parts in the way illustrated in the first paragraph of the essay answer in Figure 28.2, on page 370.

   When a question requires an answer with one major point, summarize the major point of your answer clearly in the introduction. For example,

Question	**Introduction to Answer**
Explain whether you believe that advertising benefits consumers.	In my opinion, advertising does not benefit consumers.

Other students may have written, "I believe that advertising benefits consumers." Whichever point of view is taken, it should be clearly stated in the introduction.

   3. Make major points stand out. Notice in Figure 28.2 on page 370 that major points stand out because they appear in first sentences of paragraphs and because key terms are underlined for additional emphasis. If major points in your essay stand out clearly, it will be easier for your teachers to grade your answers. If you write answers that are easy to read, teachers may show their appreciation by giving your answers higher grades than they give for answers that are difficult for them to read.

Write Complete Answers

As a general rule, teachers give the highest grades to those answers that include the most relevant information. It is almost always better to include too many facts and details than to include too few. Whenever you are uncertain whether to include a relevant piece of information or example, include it.

© 1992 by Houghton Mifflin Company

FIGURE 28.3

Comparison of a Short and Long Answer to a Question

Use point value as a guide in deciding the length and completeness of answers. Compare these examples of a 10-point and a 50-point answer to the following question.

QUESTION

What are the four speech-making strategies and how do they differ?

10-point response

There are four basic speech-making strategies. Impromptu speeches are presented on the "spur of the moment"; the speaker has no time to organize or rehearse. Extemporaneous speeches are organized in outline form but are not written word for word. Manuscript speeches are written in advance and then read from a written or typed copy. Memorized speeches are written in advance and then learned word for word, to be presented without a written copy. These four strategies allow speakers to suit their presentations to their speaking situations.

50-point response

Situations for speech making vary and speakers, as a result, choose among four different speech-making strategies to present their ideas most effectively.

Impromptu speeches are given on the "spur of the moment"; the speaker has no chance to organize or rehearse. These highly informal speeches are often unfocused (because they are unplanned) and ineffective (because they were not rehearsed), but they are the usual kinds of speeches given at organization meetings and in class discussions.

Extemporaneous speeches are given from prepared outlines, but they are not completely written. Rather, speakers decide what to discuss and what details or examples to use, and then they choose words as they speak. Extemporaneous speeches have the advantage of being organized, but at the same time they are flexible, allowing speakers to modify what they say to suit the needs of their audiences. For this reason, they are often the most effective speeches at informal meetings.

Manuscript speeches are written in complete form and then read, much like a newscast. Because they are prepared in advance, manuscript speeches are well organized and carefully worded. If they are also well rehearsed, manuscript speeches are effective in formal speaking situations because they present an exact, well-worded version of the speaker's ideas.

Memorized speeches are written in complete form and then committed to memory. Because they are carefully prepared, they often present solid content, but few speakers can memorize a lengthy speech and deliver it well. In addition, memorized speeches are not flexible and only work in highly formal circumstances, like awards ceremonies and formal banquets.

Because of the differences among these four speech-making strategies—in organization, presentation, and flexibility—they provide speakers with a number of ways to share ideas with audiences.

You must, of course, use the point value for an answer as a guide in deciding the length and completeness of your answer. Figure 28.3 above contains a 10-point and a 50-point answer to an essay question on a fifty-minute essay test. Compare the one-paragraph 10-point answer to the six-paragraph 50-point answer.

If you tend to write answers to essay questions that are too short, write them thinking that they will be read by a friend or relative rather than by a teacher. The thought that your answers will be read by a person who is uninformed about the subject might help you to write more complete answers and to explain your thoughts more clearly.

An essay test may be printed on sheets of paper with spaces on the paper for writing answers. When a space is not large enough for a complete answer, continue the answer on the back of the page. For instance, if there is not enough space to write a complete answer to a third question, write as much as you can in the space provided and then write *over* in parentheses. On the other side of the page, write *3* and complete the answer.

Write Easy-to-Read Answers

Write neatly so that your answers are easy for you to proofread and easy for your teachers to read and grade.

- Use an erasable ball point pen so you can erase mistakes and correct them.
- Write answers only on right-hand pages of bluebooks so that when you proofread you can write additions and changes on the blank left-hand pages.
- Indent each new paragraph and leave margins that are at least one inch wide at the top, bottom, left, and right of your answers.

It is extremely important that you write or print neatly so that teachers can read your answers quickly and easily; most teachers give lower grades to sloppy papers written in hard-to-read handwriting.

Proofread Your Answers

You cannot do your best writing when you answer essay questions under the pressure of time limitations; therefore, plan for time to proofread answers after you write them.

When you proofread, correct errors in spelling, punctuation, and grammar, and add additional relevant information if you can. Any improvements you make when you proofread will benefit you when your answers are graded.

What to Do if Time Runs Out

It is essential to plan test-taking time carefully when answering essay questions (see page 333). However, no matter how carefully you plan, you will not always have enough time to write complete answers to all questions on an essay test. If you do not write an answer, a teacher will assume that you do not know the answer; and if you write a very short answer, a teacher will assume it is the best answer you can write.

One solution to this problem is to write an outline for the answer you would write if you had sufficient time, show it to the teacher, and request additional time to write the complete answer. Another solution is to simply tell a teacher that you did not have enough time to write an answer. A reasonable teacher will offer a solution to this problem.

EXERCISE 28.1   **Direction Words**

Learn the meanings of the direction words on pages 371–372 and write them on the lines beneath the following questions.

1. **Discuss** three types of social mobility.

   _____

2. **Describe** clothing you enjoy wearing because it is good-looking and comfortable.

   _____

   _____

3. **Explain** why you have chosen the curriculum in which you are enrolled.

   _____

   _____

4. **Compare** your college teachers to your high school teachers.

   _____

5. **Contrast** your college teachers with your high school teachers.

   _____

6. **Criticize** this statement: "All college instructors should correct spelling and grammatical errors in papers they receive from students."

   _____

   _____

   _____

7. **Evaluate** this statement: "The best teachers are the ones who know the most about the subjects they teach."

   _____

   _____

   _____

8. **Justify** guessing at correct answers to true-false and multiple-choice questions.

   _____

   _____

   _____

9. **Diagram** the room in which you are sitting.

   _____

10. **Illustrate** how you have used study suggestions explained in *RSVP*.

    _____

    _____

11. **Enumerate** the guidelines for underlining textbooks.

    _____

12. **Outline** the characteristics of multiple-choice questions that are sometimes hints to incorrect and correct answers.

    _____

13. **Summarize** the basic strategies for answering true-false, multiple-choice, and fill-in questions.

    _____

14. **Define** the following: *appendix, glossary, references.*

    _____

15. **Relate** the use of effective study skills to good grades on college tests.

    _____

    _____

    _____

16. **Trace** the path of the last trip you took.

    _____

EXERCISE 28.2 **Answering All Parts of Questions**

To receive full credit, an answer to an essay question must respond to all parts of the question. Number the parts of the following questions in the way that is illustrated in the first question.

①   ②
1. Compare narration and exposition and give examples of them.

2. Discuss three methods for making ethical decisions, enumerate the problems associated with each method, and evaluate which method is the most difficult to use.

3. Discuss the differences between modern and traditional dating, identify differences you consider to be most important, and hypothesize how dating might be different twenty years from now.

4. How did the following men challenge the accepted religious views during the Age of Enlightenment: Toland, Bayle, Hume, and Voltaire?

5. Is the women's liberation movement a continuation of the women's rights movement, or are they two different movements? Defend your answer.

EXERCISE 28.3   An Essay Question

Write a well-organized and complete answer to the following question and proofread your answer.

Summarize the steps in the study process.

EXERCISE 28.4 An Essay Question

Write a well-organized and complete answer to the following question and proofread your answer.

Summarize the basic strategies for taking any test and the specific strategies for answering true-false, multiple-choice, matching, and fill-in questions.

EXERCISE 28.5 An Essay Question

Write a well-organized and complete answer to the following question and proofread your answer.

Discuss the methods that may be used to write well-organized and complete answers to essay questions.

Appendix: Textbook Chapter for Practice

This appendix contains a textbook chapter entitled "Building High Self-Esteem" from *Effective Human Relations in Organizations*, fourth edition by Barry L. Reece and Rhonda Brandt (Houghton Mifflin Company, 1990). The authors of the chapter believe that high self-esteem is the essential basis of achievement and well-being.

Use the chapter to practice surveying, underlining or highlighting, making notes, and taking tests.

- Exercise 19.1 on pages 269–270 provides practice surveying the chapter.
- Exercise 20.10 on pages 297–298 provides practice marking the chapter.
- Exercise 21.10 on page 316 provides practice making notes from the chapter.
- Exercise 22.4 on page 328 provides practice reciting the information in notes.

If your instructor assigns these exercises, he or she will probably request you to answer test questions about the chapter, such as those in Exercise 23.2 on page 337.

As you study the chapter in this appendix, evaluate whether it contains any suggestions that you want to use to build your self-esteem.

Chapter 4

Building High Self-Esteem

CHAPTER PREVIEW

After studying this chapter, you will be able to

1. Define *self-esteem* and discuss how it is developed.

2. Explain why high self-esteem is essential for effective human relations and success at work.

3. Understand the power of expectations.

4. Understand the impact of workers' self-esteem in an organizational setting.

5. Explain how, when, and why mentors are useful.

6. Identify ways to help build self-esteem.

en years ago, I was at the bottom of the career ladder. I was a single mother raising two small children, going back to school at night while working full time as a receptionist. I really stretched myself — building my self-esteem, and going for goals I hadn't thought possible. My income went from $12,000 a year to more then $100,000 today. I'm living proof of the impact self-esteem has on income." The speaker is Connie Palladin, Ph.D., a career-development consultant in Palo Alto, California, and author of *The Believe in Yourself and Make It Happen Guide*. "I've seen the same process work with some of my clients," she continues. "As their self-esteem increased, they doubled or tripled their income in a few years. The more you look at it, the more you see that the link between self-esteem and success is incredibly strong." [1]

The right mental conditioning is critical for success. If you think negatively, you may set yourself up for failure. To be a winner, you must *expect* to win. People who believe they are worth $100,000 a year and deserve a loving family and a vacation home on the ocean may very well attain these goals, because they push their limits to achieve them. Someone who limits his or her expectations to a one-room apartment and an entry-level job probably won't try for more. The winner's edge, high self-esteem, is the basis for achievement in any organization.

SELF-ESTEEM DEFINED

"Love thy neighbor" is one of the world's best-known human relations principles. Yet most people forget that the phrase ends "as thyself." Those last two words are the foundation for accomplishing the first three. When you maintain your self-esteem, you feel confident and free to express yourself without being overly concerned with others' reactions. You work to fulfill your needs for achievement, strength, recognition, independence, and appreciation — to reach your greatest potential. If you maintain low self-esteem, you are plagued by doubts and anxieties that will limit your ability to achieve success.

Some social scientists believe that self-esteem is closely connected to students' performance in school. Students with low self-esteem tend to do less well than students with high self-esteem.[2] And some believe a person's low self-esteem can cause more serious problems throughout life. The California State Assembly established a twenty-five-member Task Force on Self-Esteem and Personal and Social Responsibility after hearing testimony that people with low self-esteem are more likely to exhibit violent behavior, discriminate against others, and abuse drugs.[3]

Some researchers are finding that generalizations about self-esteem and success can't be made as easily for females as they can for males,[4] while

Chapter 4   Building High Self–Esteem

others are beginning to challenge the correlation between poor self-esteem and delinquency.[5] However, it is clear that low self-esteem can create barriers between friends, family, and business associates, leading to an inevitable breakdown in effective human relations. This is why Alfred Adler, a noted psychologist, has stated, "Everything begins with self-esteem, your concept of yourself."[6]

Self-esteem is the sum of self-confidence and self-respect. If you have high self-esteem, you feel competent and worthy. If you have low self-esteem, you feel incompetent and unworthy. If you have average self-esteem, you fluctuate between these feelings of competence and worthiness. Your measure of self-esteem is always a matter of degree. Your self-esteem reflects what you think and feel about yourself, not what someone else thinks or feels about you, even though you are always reevaluating yourself in light of others' comments about your behavior.

Your self-esteem includes your feelings about your adequacy in the roles you play in life, as a friend, brother or sister, daughter or son, employee or employer, student, researcher, leader, and so on. It includes the personality traits you believe you have, such as honesty, creativity, assertiveness, flexibility, and many more. Often your self-esteem derives from your physical characteristics and your skills and abilities. Are you tall, slender, short, or heavy? Do you like what you see in the mirror? Are you good at writing, fixing appliances, researching topics, playing the piano, or some other skill?

Although high self-esteem is the basis for a healthy personality, it does not mean becoming egotistical, that is, thinking and acting with only your own interests in mind. Genuine self-esteem is not expressed by self-glorification at the expense of others, or by the attempt to diminish others so as to elevate yourself. Arrogance, boastfulness, and the overestimation of your abilities reflect inadequate self-esteem rather than, as it might appear, too much self-esteem. Someone with an egotistical orientation to the world sees everything and everyone in terms of their usefulness to the person's own aims and goals. This attitude undermines good human relations; people become objects to be manipulated or used.

In an insurance office with five agents, a manager, and two secretaries, workers help one another achieve personal and company goals. Everyone gets along well with everyone else — except the number one salesperson. He has such a self-centered view of his work and himself that he expects other people in the office to drop everything and help him first. He leaves a stack of letters on the secretary's desk and tells her, "I need these typed by five." He ignores the fact that she is already hard at work on correspondence for three other agents. He tells the manager how an important client should be handled even though the manager has known the client for over ten years. He may or may not speak to the other agents — they are not as successful, and he has important calls to make, so why waste time? This person's self-esteem has passed beyond healthy self-confidence and has

Part 2   Career Success Begins with Knowing Yourself

become a negative, egotistical personality trait. In terms of human relations, he has become a liability to the company, even though he is successful as a salesperson.

An individual with high self-esteem realizes the value of other people and the role they play in his or her success. Recognizing the difference between a person with high self-esteem and a person with an egotistical personality is important in developing and maintaining good human relations.

How Your Self-Esteem Develops

A Sunday school teacher once asked her class of small children, "Who made you?" Instead of giving the expected reply, an insightful child responded, "I'm not finished yet!" You are not born knowing who and what you are. You acquire your image of yourself over time by realizing your natural abi-

Positive feedback from an authority figure can have a powerful effect on a child's self-esteem.
© Alan Carey / The Image Works

Chapter 4   Building High Self–Esteem

lities and by constantly receiving messages about yourself from the people closest to you and from your environment.

Childhood   Your self-esteem is a reflection of your image of who you are. This image begins to form the minute you have the first conscious realization that you are a living, functioning being. Your family is the earliest source of information about yourself. An ancient Chinese proverb tells us, "A child's life is like a piece of paper on which every passer-by leaves a mark." Parents do not *teach* their children self-esteem. But they do leave negative or positive strokes on their slates:

- Bad boy! Bad girl!
- You're so lazy!
- You'll never learn.
- What's wrong with you?
- Why can't you be more like...
- It's all your fault.

- You're great!
- You can do anything!
- You're a fast learner.
- Next time you'll do better.
- I like you just the way you are.
- I know you did your best.

In most cases, you probably did not stop and analyze these messages; you simply accepted them as true and recorded them in your memory. As a result, your subconscious mind gradually developed a picture of yourself, whether accurate or distorted, that you came to believe as real.

> Everyone was once a child. Our experience today is filtered through the events and feelings of childhood, recorded in detail. We cannot have a feeling today that is "disconnected" from similar feelings recorded in the past, the most intense of which occurred to us in the first five years of life. This does not mean that today's feelings are not real, or that we are to discount them by claiming "they're just an old recording." We are today who we once were.[7]

The type of family discipline you grew up with probably had considerable effect on your self-esteem. Interestingly enough, some psychologists have found that children brought up in a permissive environment tend to develop *lower* self-esteem than those raised in a firmer and more demanding home. Parental discipline is one way of telling children that parents care about them and what they do. When someone cares about you, you tend to think more positively about yourself.

The strength of early parental positive feedback can have far-reaching effects in the course of a person's life. Irene Carpenter, the first woman elected a senior vice president in the ninety-year history of Citizens and Southern National Bank in Atlanta, recalls of her childhood: "My parents raised us to believe we could do anything we chose to do. . . . Many women in management do not start out with that concept of themselves. It has

Part 2   Career Success Begins with Knowing Yourself

enabled me to overcome many of the obstacles I've encountered in the banking industry."[8]

The self-esteem formed in childhood lays the foundation for your attitudes toward work, your future success, your personal abilities, and the roles you play.

Adolescence   Infants love to look at their reflections. They are totally accepting of themselves. As an infant, you looked at pictures of yourself and other children and experienced joy. You probably didn't think, "I wish I looked like that baby," or, "That baby sure is ugly!" The worth of your own image was not dependent on or measured by the images of others. As you got older, however, and entered your teens, you probably started comparing yourself to other people. Typically you became less happy with who you were. You wished you were more like others you perceived as better, and you began to use put-downs as an equalizer. Teenagers often tear down others in order to build themselves up, trying to combat their doubts about themselves and their negative self-image. "Friends" add to the level of self-doubt by using "kidding" statements such as "Hi, Klutz!", "You're such a chicken.", or "You'll probably be late to your own funeral!" These negative images undermined your original strong self-acceptance. Their critical words may have been prompted by their own unmet needs and low self-esteem.

The media play a strong part in how adolescents see themselves. The beautiful people featured on TV and in the movies lead adolescents to use these unrealistic images to measure their own attributes and lifestyles. It is easy to feel deficient or diminished in comparison. Instead of seeing who you really are, you see who you are not and continually reinforce that negative image with your own inner thoughts, often referred to as **self-talk**. The propensity toward self-talk often follows teenagers into adulthood. The issue of self-talk is discussed later in this chapter, where you will discover how you can effectively improve your self-esteem by altering your self-talk.

The ages of twelve to eighteen are among the most crucial in developing and consolidating your feelings about yourself. During these years, you are moving away from the close bond between parent and child and are attempting to establish ideals of independence and achievement.[9] You must also deal with physical changes; relationships with peer groups; an emerging, often confusing identity; and the loss of childhood and assumption of some adult responsibilities. Is it any wonder that your self-esteem seemed to change not only day by day but hour by hour? In fact, many people never move beyond the image they had of themselves while in high school. Outwardly successful, they may still be trying to prove to their old classmates that they can "make it." For this reason, adolescent problems should not be underestimated, for it is in the resolution of these problems and conflicts that the self-esteem of the adult is born.

Chapter 4   Building High Self–Esteem

It is unfortunate that many teenagers look for their self-esteem every-where except within themselves. Strong self-esteem is independent of the opinions of others or of external possessions. It comes mainly from an inter-nal sense of worth. Because many adolescents (and adults) with low self-esteem judge their own value by comparing themselves with others, they have a desperate need for recognition and status. Therefore, they tend to value money and the things money can buy. During a role-playing incident between a teacher instructing a self-esteem unit and a teenage boy, the fol-lowing exchange occurred.

The teacher asked: "What's your favorite car? Describe it."

"A Mustang with black interior," the student replied.

"Now imagine you just washed that car and drove it to school. I come along in a crane, swing a wrecking ball, and the whole thing shatters. Wham, and the door falls off. Wham, and the body is spread out like scrambled eggs. You are not insured. How would you feel inside?"

The student looked stricken.

"If that car is the *only* image you project," the teacher explains, "I have just destroyed you. I have taken away everything you represent. If you do not work from the inside out, somebody will come along at some point in your life — believe me — and take everything away."*

Adulthood   When you reach adulthood, your brain has a time-enforced picture of who you are, molded by people and events from all your past experiences. You have been bombarded over the years with positive and negative messages from your family, friends, strangers and the media. You may compare yourself to others, as was so common in adolescence, or you may focus on your own inner sense of self-worth.

As an adult, you are expanding the roles you play, taking on the role of wife or husband and even parent. Work experiences and your relationships with your coworkers and supervisors can have a major impact on your feel-ings about yourself. Doing a job well and being respected as a competent worker enhances your self-esteem. On the other hand, a difficult work situa-tion that provides few opportunities to experience success can diminish your self-respect and inhibit your ability to learn and develop your skills. Thus, spouses, coworkers, friends, and professional colleagues are among those who will continue to influence your self-esteem throughout your life. In some cases, they may reinforce an already negative concept of yourself, whereas in others they may reaffirm the positive images you have built. Per-haps in your adult world you will be able to correct an outmoded, adoles-cent picture of your abilities and potential.

———

*Reprinted from *The Detroit Free Press*, December 5, 1985, by permission.

Part 2   Career Success Begins with Knowing Yourself

Dr. Denis Waitley, psychologist and well-known author and public speaker, discusses his changing self-esteem.

> I've had my own struggles with a poor self-image. Even though my parents told me I was special, my peer group in grammar school and junior high told me different. They offered me such labels as "buzzard beak," "beaver teeth," "Waitley Come Lately." ...During my plebe year at Annapolis the superlatives were, "Mr. Waitley, you couldn't lead a one-cadet parade," "You're so dense you couldn't lead a silent prayer!" or, "If your eyes were any closer together, we'd call you Cyclops." As I began to wear the labels others pinned on me, I began to play my own games....In response to a birthday gift I would say, "You shouldn't have gone to all this trouble for *me*." In response to a compliment, "Don't mention it. It was nothing." In response to a compliment on a great golf shot, "Yeah, bet I won't do that again!" After a seesaw career as a young adult, I finally learned to stop associating myself with external labels, negative self-talk, and humiliating self-presentation. In my early thirties, I began to talk affirmatively about my accomplishments and goals. I began to say "thank you" when other people would bestow any value upon me. I began to accept myself as a changing, growing, and worthwhile human being, imperfect but capable of becoming a Double Winner. And I began to feel good about myself.[10]

As an adult, you will be constantly adjusting the level of your self-esteem to the real world around you. It is important to be aware of how other people have influenced and will continue to influence your beliefs about yourself. You will need to learn how to protect your self-esteem against those who try to diminish or limit your potential and how to listen to those who will encourage and challenge you. Such knowledge can help you distinguish between what is helpful and what is destructive, what is true and what is false, and help you expand the range of what you believe you can be and do in the future.

Characteristics of People with High Self-Esteem

When several leaders were asked about the qualities exhibited by people with high self-esteem, they pointed out the following characteristics:

1. *They are future oriented and not overly concerned with past mistakes or failures.* They learn from their errors and are not immobilized by them. Every experience has something to teach — if you are willing to learn. A mistake can show you what doesn't work, what not to do. One consultant, asked whether he had obtained any results in trying to solve a difficult problem, replied, "Results? Why man, I've had lots of results. I know a hundred things that won't work!" The same principle applies to

Chapter 4   Building High Self–Esteem

TOTAL PERSON INSIGHT

❝ But if we never make mistakes, if we never look foolish, if we never take a risk, we'll never grow and we'll never experience the exhilaration that exists on the other side of those fears. We become self-limiting. ❞

Larry Wilson

---

your own progress. Falling down does not mean failure. Staying down does.

When Peter Ueberroth was only in his mid-twenties, he formed an air-shuttle company to provide service between Los Angeles and the Spokane, Washington, World's Fair. Within a year, because of a drop in the demand for charter service, his company failed and he was $100,000 in debt. Nevertheless, Ueberroth did not give up. He established another transportation company the following year. This new company provided central reservation services for the smaller hotels, airlines, and passenger ships that did not have their own representatives. Though he started with only $5,000 and one employee, this time Ueberroth's business grew. He took over several failing travel agencies and formed First Travel Corporation, now one of the largest travel companies in America. One success led to another. He agreed to head the 1984 Los Angeles Olympic games and helped turn a $300,000 debt into a $215 million surplus.[11]

2. *They are able to cope with life's problems and disappointments.* Successful people have come to realize that problems need not depress them or make them anxious. It is their attitude toward problems that makes all the difference. In his autobiography, Lee Iacocca recalls many disappointments. At the top of his list was the experience of being fired as president of Ford Motor Company after the firm had recorded two years of record profits. After being fired by Henry Ford he moved to Chrysler Corporation and brought the ailing company back from the brink of failure. Years later, he recalled the loss of his job at Ford: "A lot has happened since July 13, 1978. The scars left by Henry Ford, especially on my family, will be lasting, because the wounds were deep. But the events of recent years have had a healing effect. So you move on."[12]

3. *They are able to feel all dimensions of emotion without letting those emotions affect their behavior in a negative way.* This characteristic is one of the major reasons people with high self-esteem are able to establish and maintain effective human relations with the people around them. They realize emotions cannot be handled either by repressing them or by giv-

Part 2   Career Success Begins with Knowing Yourself

ing them free rein and lashing out at other people. You may feel better after such an explosion, but the people around you will not. Although you may not be able to stop feeling what you feel, you can control your thoughts and actions while under the influence of a particularly strong emotion. Robert Conklin, author of *How to Get People to Do Things*, suggests keeping the following statement in mind: "I can't help the way I feel right now, but I *can* help the way I think and act."[13] Remembering this principle can help you bring an emotionally charged situation under control.

4. *They are able to help others and accept help.* People with high self-esteem are not threatened by helping others to succeed, nor are they afraid to admit weaknesses. If you are not good at dealing with figures, you can bring in an accountant who will manage the records. If you see someone whose abilities are not being used to their fullest, you can suggest ways in which the person might develop his or her talents. An old adage in business goes, "First-rate people hire first-rate people. Second-rate people hire third-rate people." Individuals with secure self-esteem realize that in helping others succeed they benefit themselves as well.

5. *They are skilled at accepting other people as unique, talented individuals.* People with high self-esteem learn to accept others for who they are and what they can do. A relationship built on mutual respect for one another's differences and strengths can help both parties grow and change. It is not a relationship that limits or confines either person. Acceptance of others is a good indication that you accept yourself.

6. *They exhibit a variety of self-confident behaviors.* They accept compliments or gifts by saying "Thank you," without self-critical excuses, and without feeling obligated to return the favor. They can laugh at their situation, without self-ridicule. They let others be right or wrong, without attempting to correct or ridicule them. They feel free to express opinions, even if they differ from those of their peers or parents. They enjoy being by themselves without feeling lonely or isolated. They are able to talk about themselves to others without excessive bragging.

THINKING/LEARNING STARTERS

1. Can you recall two or three people from your childhood or adolescence who had a positive effect on your self-esteem? What did these people say or do? Were there any who had a negative effect on you? What did they say or do?
2. Identify at least two people who you feel exhibit the characteristics of people with high self-esteem. Explain what behaviors helped you identify them.

Chapter 4   Building High Self–Esteem

SELF-ESTEEM AND SUCCESS AT WORK

Your self-esteem is a powerful factor influencing your choice of career and how well you progress in that career. According to Richard Grote, president of Performance Systems Corp. in Dallas, "People take you at the value you put on yourself. If you believe in your own power, other people will believe you and treat you with the respect you've provided for yourself."[14]

In an organizational setting, workers with high self-esteem are inclined to form nourishing rather than destructive relationships. They tend to do more than what is strictly required on the job, and they are receptive to new experiences, to meeting new people, to accepting responsibility, and to making decisions. People who accept themselves can usually accept others, tolerate differences, share their thoughts and feelings, and respond to the needs of others. They do not perceive others as threats. Such people contribute to the well-being and productivity of a group and can explore the opportunities offered by an organization.

Moreover, research studies repeatedly show this connection: individuals with lower self-esteem are more likely to feel hostile, show a lack of respect for others, and attempt to retaliate against others to save face in a difficult situation.[15] Author and psychologist Dr. Milton Layden believes that a hostile response to others is a natural outcome of feelings of low self-esteem and inferiority. It occurs because the emotional system, like other systems of the body, is controlled by a "balancing mechanism." When a person feels a lack of respect toward himself or herself, or feelings of inferiority, the mechanism is knocked off balance and the person starts to feel hostile and anxious. These feelings then get translated into hostile actions.[16]

If a person is in a position of power, and has low self-esteem, it is improbable that subordinates or coworkers will be treated fairly. Workers with low self-esteem can also cause problems on several levels. They can affect the efficiency and productivity of a group because they tend to exercise less initiative, hesitate to accept responsibility or make decisions on their own, and may ask fewer question and take longer to learn procedures. They often have trouble relating well to others. Self-rejecting people generally have a pessimistic view of human nature and may always be on the lookout for an insult or "attack" from someone else, an attitude that can cause interpersonal conflicts. Also, their lack of self-confidence can be misinterpreted by coworkers as unfriendliness. They may require more supervision because they are afraid of making a mistake or appearing ignorant if they ask questions. Even when offered a chance to receive training or career development courses, they may feel they are being singled out as workers who need more instruction than other employees.

Part 2   Career Success Begins with Knowing Yourself

"HEY! C'MON, MAN! I'm 'arrogant, rude and smug' because I got LOW SELF–ESTEEM." Reprinted by permission of NEA, Inc.

Your Self-Esteem Influences Your Behavior

When you accept what others say about you during your early years, these comments are "programmed" into your subconscious mind. You form a mental picture of yourself, which influences your behavior. Your subconscious mind does not evaluate what is put into it; it merely acts on the information it receives — good or bad.

Most people do not realize that the subconscious mind represents a powerful creative capacity within their control. By controlling what goes into your subconscious mind, you can influence your self-esteem. This awareness can be used for positive or negative ends. For example, if you see yourself as a failure, you will use your creative capacity to find some way to fail. William Glasser, author of *Reality Therapy* and other books on human behavior, calls this the **failure syndrome**. No matter how hard you work for success, if your subconscious mind is saturated with thoughts and fears of failure, it will make your success impossible. On the other hand, if your subconscious has been intentionally or unintentionally programmed with positive thoughts to help you succeed, you will be able to overcome many

Chapter 4   Building High Self–Esteem

barriers, even those considered handicaps, such as age or a disadvantaged background.

The late Colonel Harland Sanders of Kentucky Fried Chicken Corp. (now KFC Corporation) began his franchise business at an age when most people start collecting Social Security. He had been a moderately successful businessman but had little to show for it beyond the belief that people would buy his fried chicken prepared according to his secret recipe. All the conventional wisdom of the business community was against him. They told him he was too old; people wanted hamburgers, not chicken; his recipe was too spicy; the franchise market was already flooded with fast-food items; and he could never make it on his own.

But Colonel Sanders did not see himself settling down in a retirement home and sitting on the sidelines for his remaining years. He was so confident of his own judgment that he took the risk and started his own business. Within a few short years, his name was as familiar to consumers as the McDonald's golden arches. Eventually, the colonel sold his franchise business for several million dollars.[17]

Maltz Discovers the Power of Self-Esteem

Although physical appearance, talents and abilities, background, and education all play a part in our success, *what we believe about ourselves* is the controlling factor that can override or undermine all the rest. This principle was vividly demonstrated by the work of the noted plastic surgeon Dr. Maxwell Maltz in his book, *Psycho-Cybernetics*. Throughout his twenty-five years of practice, Maltz operated on soldiers wounded in war, accident victims, and children with birth defects. Many of these individuals saw only their defects and could not believe they would ever be successful in life. In many cases, after he removed a scar or corrected some type of physical deformity, dramatic and sudden changes in personality resulted. Improving the person's physical image seemed to create an entirely new individual.

Yet, curiously, not all patients responded this way. Dr. Maltz discovered that, for some, corrective surgery did little to change their low self-esteem. The deformity continued to exist in the patient's mind. Further, some people came to see him who did not need plastic surgery at all. Their "deformity" was in their mental pictures of themselves.

Maltz soon realized that if people could not reprogram their subconscious minds and change what they believed about themselves, plastic surgery would not help them. Once they understood how to use the creative power of their subconscious minds, their physical appearance became less important to them. The real change happened within; they began to believe in themselves.[18]

THE POWER OF EXPECTATIONS

Your thoughts about yourself are often expressed in terms of expectations — how far you believe you can go and what you feel you can do. Many behavioral psychologists agree that people's expectations about themselves have a significant impact on their performance and how much risk they are willing to take. If you set out to learn a new skill and expect to master it, chances are you will succeed. If you secretly believe you will fail, that expectation is also likely to come true. Once you have acquired an idea about your abilities and your character, you will tend to live up — or down — to your expectations.

Your Own Expectations

People tend to behave in a way that supports their own ideas of how successful or incompetent they are. This somewhat mysterious power of expectations is often referred to as **self-fulfilling prophecy**. Your career successes and failures are directly related to the expectations you hold about your future.

In looking over applications for an M.B.A. program, an admissions director noticed that some students had answered questions about their future plans with phrases such as "I *am...*" or "I *can...*" Other students had written "I *hope* to..." or "I *might...*". The words used by the first group represented a statement of belief that they could achieve specific goals. Not surprisingly, their academic records and outside accomplishments showed that these students had set and reached high performance levels. The second group of students had lower expectations and less confidence in their ability to accomplish their goals.

The effect of self-fulfilling prophecies can be dramatic in terms of an employee's career aspirations and personal development. More than one manager has witnessed the phenomenon of capable, talented employees refusing promotions or being afraid to move out of the positions they have occupied for a time. On the other hand, managers have also seen average employees become motivated to succeed. These workers achieve far more than their personnel records or the opinions of their coworkers suggested they could accomplish.

Holding positive expectations about oneself can lead to positive results. Natalie wanted to become a field representative for a computer hardware company, but lacked self-confidence and the ability to mix easily with other people. She finally decided that she could learn to become more outgoing and self-assured, just as she had learned about the company's products. She enrolled in sales courses, practiced overcoming her shyness and reserve,

Chapter 4   Building High Self–Esteem

watched and imitated other people who had the skills she wanted to culti-vate, and acted as if she were confident even when inwardly nervous. At some point along the way, she began to *enjoy* talking with clients. She didn't have to worry about what to say or how to introduce herself.

Not long afterward, a field representative position in the company be-came available, and Natalie applied. When she was offered the position a week later, one of the interviewers commented on her "self-confidence and ability to relate well with others." She was launched on her new career.

The Expectations of Others

Self-fulfilling prophecies reflect a connection between your own expecta-tions for yourself and your resulting behavior. But people can also be great-ly influenced by the expectations of others. The **Pygmalion effect** sometimes causes people to become what others expect them to become.

This term was first used by Dr. Robert Rosenthal, a professor at Har-vard University, and is based on a Greek legend about Pygmalion, the king of Cyprus. In the legend, the king longs for an ideal wife. Since no mortal woman meets his expectations, he fashions a statue of his ideal woman out of ivory and eventually falls in love with his creation. His desire to make the statue his wife is so intense that his belief brings it to life.

Zig Ziglar, author and motivational speaker, tells his own Pygmalion story in his book, *See You at the Top*. Early in his career, Zig attended a sales training session conducted by P. C. Merrill. When the training session was over, Mr. Merrill took Zig aside and quietly told him, "You know, Zig, I've been watching you for two and a half years, and I have never seen such a waste. You have a lot of ability. You could be a great salesman and maybe even one of the best in the nation. There is no doubt in my mind if you really went to work and started believing in yourself, you could go all the way to the top."[19]

Zig described himself as an "average" person as far as intelligence or ability was concerned. He did not suddenly acquire a new set of skills that day, nor did his I.Q. jump fifty points. Zig admired and respected Merrill. When the man told him, "You can be a great salesman," Zig believed him and started seeing himself as a top salesperson. He began to think, act, and perform like one. Before the year was over, Zig ranked number two in a company of over seven thousand sales personnel. By the next year, he was one of the highest-paid managers in the country and later became the youngest division supervisor in the nation. P. C. Merrill's image of Zig helped him see himself as someone special who had something to offer oth-ers. Merrill was Ziglar's Pygmalion.

Organizations are beginning to realize the impact of management ex-pectations on employee performance. Many companies are redesigning

Part 2   Career Success Begins with Knowing Yourself

their training programs to provide a supportive or enabling environment that fosters and encourages positive expectations in employees.

In one company, data processing trainees were regularly told that it would take them three weeks to master the program and that they would be able to program about two hundred cards per hour. Not surprisingly, employees met those expectations precisely. They learned the program in three weeks and could process only two hundred cards per hour. Then a new personnel director was hired, who scrapped the old training sessions, hired new trainees, and set up a program oriented toward increasing management expectations of employees. New recruits were told only that they could master the program quickly and were not given any limits on the number of cards per hour they could process. The new recruits learned the program in less than a week and by the end of the training session were programming five hundred cards per hour. Management realized the value of setting open expectations rather than limiting productivity by past performance.

Mentors

Mentors are people who have been where you want to go in your career and who are willing to act as your guide and friend. They take you under their wing and show you how to get to the next step in your career. They act as sponsors, teachers, devil's advocates, and coaches.

As sponsors, mentors will create opportunities for you to prove yourself. In an organization, this might mean they will ask you to help them on a project, analyze a problem, or make a presentation to higher levels of management. As teachers, mentors will present you with hypothetical situations and ask you, "What would you do?" An important part of the teaching responsibility is to explain both the written and unwritten rules of the organization. As devil's advocates, mentors challenge and confront you to give you practice in asserting your ideas and influencing others. Mentors can act as coaches, supporting your dreams, helping you find out what's important to you and what skills you have.

There are certain criteria you might want to consider as you select your mentor or mentors. Susan Nycum, senior partner in the international law firm of Baker & McKenzie, declares she has changed her mentors as often as she has changed bosses. The criteria by which she has chosen each mentor has depended upon his or her influence and perspective on her specific job. "I believe that the Lancelot who can ride through the world doing good, banishing evil, and coming out ahead exists only in Camelot. One simply must have the mentor or advisor to get through the underbrush of politics and rivalries and lack of information that block the road to advancement in most organizations."[20] In a book co-authored with Nancy Collins and Susan Gilbert, Nycum suggests certain criteria for selecting a mentor, some of which are paraphrased on the next page.

Chapter 4   Building High Self–Esteem

People who develop mentoring relationships are often happier with their careers, earn larger salaries, and follow a systematic career path.
Frank Siteman/The Picture Cube

1. Mentors must never be your boss, or someone in your chain of command. A mentor's career should not be affected by the advice he or she gives you or the work you do.

2. Mentors must be authorities in their field.

3. Mentors must be higher up on the professional ladder than you are.

4. Mentors must be influential.

5. Mentors must have a genuine interest in your personal growth and development so that they can recognize opportunities that will meet your potential.

6. Mentors must be willing to commit time and emotion to the mentoring relationship.

7. Mentors are not designed to be permanent, but usually last several years.[21]

Although mentors are not mandatory for success, they certainly help. Research indicates that business executives with a mentoring relationship earn larger salaries, engage in more formal education, and are more likely to follow a systematic career path. They are also happier with their careers and derive more satisfaction from their work.[22]

Part 2   Career Success Begins with Knowing Yourself

When 160 women listed in *Who's Who of American Women* were asked about their mentors' contributions to their careers, they responded with statements like the following:

> Thought of me as a person first, a woman second.
> Helped my orientation and assisted me in "learning the ropes."
> Gave motivation and guidance.
> Shared their philosophies with me.
> Instilled determination and desire to excel.
> Developed my long-term strategy.
> Gave me access to powerful people.
> Helped me to take risks.
> Groomed me to be the boss.[23]

Mentoring is an important part of the Management Readiness Program (MRP), a six-month career development program established at Merrill Lynch & Co., Inc. One important goal of this program is to build bridges between high-level managers and employees. It helps participants learn about the firm's culture and career opportunities. Mentors at Merrill Lynch are department or higher-level managers who volunteer to serve as counselors or advisors to four individuals during a six-month period. They agree to meet with these persons once a month in either group or individual meetings.[24]

There will always be days when you feel nothing you do is right. Your mentor can help repair damaged self-esteem and encourage you to go on. With the power of another person's positive expectations reinforcing your own native abilities, it's hard to fail.

THINKING/LEARNING STARTERS

1. Do you believe you can alter your self-esteem once you have reached adult-hood? If so, what actions can you take to raise your current level of self-esteem?
2. Do you agree with the statement "People tend to take you at the value you place on yourself; if you believe in your own potential abilities, so will others"? Explain your answer.

HOW TO BUILD YOUR SELF-ESTEEM

Now that you are aware of the power self-esteem has over your life, you can take the next step — examining the image you have of yourself and identifying what might need to be changed. You wouldn't think of trying to fix a machine until you attempted to understand something about how the ma-

Chapter 4   Building High Self–Esteem

chine was supposed to work. On the other hand, you don't need to understand the machine completely before you try to make improvements. The same applies to your self-esteem. Even though you may not be totally aware of your current level of esteem, you can begin making plans for improving it.

It isn't easy to meet yourself face to face. But bringing your present self-image out into the open is the first step in understanding who you are, what you can do, and where you are going.

Each day can mean another step toward higher self-esteem. The person you will be tomorrow has yet to be created. Most people continue to shape that future person in the image of the past, repeating the old limitations and negative patterns without realizing what they are doing. The development of a new level of self-esteem will not happen overnight, but it *can* happen. Such a change is the result of a slow evolution that begins with the desire to overcome low self-esteem.

Accept the Past, Change the Future

The first step toward higher self-esteem is to accept yourself as you are now. The past cannot be changed, but the future is determined by how you think and act. Various practices and theories have been developed to help people build high self-esteem. None of these approaches offers a quick, easy route for changing your picture of yourself. You developed your self-esteem over many years; it will take time to change it. But the results can be well worth the effort. Some of the basic principles common to all approaches are summarized here.

Identify and Accept Your Limitations   Part of creating a high level of self-esteem is learning to tolerate limitations in yourself and becoming more realistic about who you are and what you can and cannot do. Demanding perfection of yourself can make you less tolerant of others' faults as well as of your own. It can also place undue importance on failures and mistakes, robbing them of their potential to serve as learning experiences and to provide perspective.

Some women in business, such as Marcie Schorr Hirsch, director of career planning at Brandeis University, have decided they no longer want to live up to the "superwoman" image, juggling home, family, and career. They realize their time and energy are limited, and they are adjusting their schedules to accommodate those realities. She states: "I'm concerned about the quality of my existence. I'm willing to work hard; but I don't want to work so hard at everything that nothing gets done well, and I end up feeling like a failure."[25] Many men, also, are rejecting the super-achiever image.

If you often exhibit a behavior of which you are not proud, and want to change, hate the behavior but do not condemn yourself. Hating yourself tends to make the behavior worse. If you condemn yourself for being weak,

Part 2   Career Success Begins with Knowing Yourself

for example, how can you muster the strength to change? However, if you become an "observer," and view the activity as separate from yourself, you leave your self-esteem intact while you work on changing the behavior. Acting as an observer and detaching yourself from negative thoughts and actions can help you break the habit of rating yourself according to some scale of perfection and can enable you to substitute more positive and helpful thoughts.

Visualize the Results You Want   The power to visualize is in a very real sense the power to create. We often visualize ourselves succeeding or failing in some enterprise without knowing that such mental pictures can actually affect our behavior. It is the *intentional* successful visualization that can slowly lead your self-esteem and your life in the direction you want it to go. Shakti Gawain, author of *Creative Visualization*, states that when we create something, we always create it first in the form of a thought:

> Imagination is the ability to create an idea or mental picture in your mind. In creative visualization you use your imagination to create a clear image of something you wish to manifest. Then you continue to focus on the idea or picture regularly, giving it positive energy until it becomes objective reality...in other words, until you actually achieve what you have been visualizing.[26]

Diane Von Furstenberg, noted fashion designer, has used mental imagery to produce positive changes in her life. She started her business in 1970 with the dining room table as her office and a small amount of money obtained by pawning her jewelry. Six years later her business was grossing over $60 million, and she was on the cover of *Newsweek* — a superstar at twenty-nine. Reflecting on her career, she says: "I believe nothing happens unless you can imagine it. I have to have images of where I want to go next." [27]

Former Olympic diving star Greg Louganis mentally rehearsed before each dive. He visualized the perfect performance in his imagination and then often executed the dive as perfectly as he imagined it. Salespeople often close the sale in advance. Most hosts plan the party in advance. When it comes time for the actual performance, the mentally rehearsed events have become habits.

Your concept of yourself is no exception. Visualize the behaviors you want to exhibit. When you consciously decide to improve your self-esteem, you are harnessing the mind's creative force to work for you. You are constructing an image of your ideal self and imagining all the qualities and skills you would like to have. Although it sounds like an exercise in fantasy, it is an accepted fact that mental practice has improved the performances of salespeople, executives, and others in the business community.[28]

Chapter 4   Building High Self–Esteem

Turn Your Goals into Positive Self-Talk   A person without goals is like a football team without a game plan. Can you imagine the Dallas Cowboys running onto the field, hoping that someone else will tell them what to do out there? By visualizing who you want to be, you have already begun your life's game plan. The secret to goal setting is very simple: establish clearly defined goals, write them down, and then dwell on them with words, mental pictures, and your emotions. Break down long-term goals into several attainable short-term goals. Don't set them out of sight, but rather just out of reach to pull you in the direction you want to go. Author Richard Grote recommends that at the beginning you set moderate goals for yourself. "Set reasonable objectives for each hour, each day, each week. Keeping long-term sights in mind is important, but don't put unnecessary obstacles in your way by setting objectives too high. People who don't reach those high goals many times feel like failures."[29] The feeling of success you will gain from achieving short-term goals will spur you on to set and attain even higher ones.

To help internalize these goals, it is helpful to create self-talk statements that describe the end result that will occur when you accomplish the goal. You talk to yourself every minute of the day. Through this self-talk, you are constantly in the process of conditioning yourself — negatively or positively, depending on the tone of your thoughts. Many people internalize negative self-talk, which produces negative behaviors. When you want to take control of your self-esteem, focus self-talk on your positive thoughts. Learn how to write **affirmations** for each of your goals. Affirmations are self-talk statements declaring your goals and the qualities you want to develop. When creating your personal and professional affirmations, be sure to follow these guidelines:

1. Begin each affirmation with a first-person pronoun, such as *I*, or *my*.

2. Use a present-tense verb, such as *am, have, feel, create, approve, do,* or *choose*.

3. Describe the end results you want to achieve. Be sure to phrase the statement *toward* where you want to go, not away from what you don't want. Say, "I am a slim, trim 120 pounds," as opposed to "I am losing 30 pounds." Table 4.1 offers several general affirmations that might help you improve your self-esteem.

Write affirmations for different facets of your personal and professional life. Put them on three-by-five-inch index cards and attach them to your bathroom mirror, refrigerator, car dashboard, desk blotter, and so on. Another technique for internalizing these thoughts rapidly is to record your affirmations on a blank cassette tape while quiet, one-beat-per-second music (largo) is playing in the background.[30] Play the tape repeatedly, especially when you are in a relaxed state, such as just before you fall asleep at

Part 2   Career Success Begins with Knowing Yourself

TABLE 4.1 Positive Self-Talk Affirmations

I look forward to new experiences confidently.

I do my own thinking and make my own decisions.

I am an employee who is able to be a strong team member.

I can sincerely recognize the accomplishments of others.

I am filled with a feeling of quiet calmness.

I am in control of my eating habits.

I am able to listen with full concentration to what is being said by the other person.

night. Your brain will accept the information without judgment. When these statements become part of your "memory bank," over time your behavior will follow accordingly. Your brain is like a computer. It will put out exactly what you put in. If you put positive self-talk in, positive behavior will result.

Make Decisions   Psychologists have found that children who were encouraged to make their own decisions early in their lives have higher self-esteem than those who were kept dependent on their parents for a longer period of time. Making decisions helps you develop confidence in your own judgment and enables you to explore options.

At age thirty, Mary Boone became one of the most successful art dealers in the United States. Her galleries are showplaces. But she can recall a time when her self-confidence was conspicuously lacking. "In a family of three girls," she states, "I was the oldest and homeliest." Her mother helped develop her artistic abilities, but Boone found she had more talent for organizing other students' shows than for her own painting.

After a few years as an assistant art dealer in New York, she made the decision to open a gallery of her own. "I had great ambivalence about making art a business. But I realized that [art] dealing had become important to me. Not knowing what you're going to do is like not knowing who you are," Boone says. "When I opened the gallery, I'd found my place in life."

The painters whose work she exhibits agree. As one commented, "In a business like this, clients are as much buying the vision of the dealer as they're buying the work. They look into her eyes and they think...'she really believes what she's saying.'"[31]

Take every opportunity you can to make decisions both in setting your goals and in devising ways to achieve them. Along with making decisions, be willing to accept the consequences of your actions, positive or negative. Organizations with supportive management personnel encourage decision making by employees at all levels in order to develop more employee initiative and self-management skills.

Chapter 4   Building High Self–Esteem

Updating job skills through adult education classes can help maintain high self-esteem.
© Frank D. Smith/Jeroboam, Inc.

Develop Expertise in Some Area   Developing "expert power" not only builds your self-esteem but increases the value of your contribution to the organization. Identify and cultivate a skill or talent you have, whether it is a knack for interviewing people, a facility with math, or good verbal skills. Alice Young, a resident partner in the law firm of Graham & James in New York, developed an expertise in her youth that she didn't know would be a major asset in her career. "I speak Japanese, Chinese, French, and English," she says. "I have a knowledge of Asian cultures that I developed before trade with the East opened up." She has been able to capitalize on her expertise to help American and Asian companies do business with one another and to smooth over many cultural differences that would otherwise make negotiations difficult or impossible. She advises others to "use what you know to benefit yourself and your company."[32]

Developing expertise may involve continuing your studies after completing your formal education. Some institutions offer professional courses to enable people to advance in their careers. For example, the Institute of Financial Education conducts courses for persons employed by financial institutions.

Your Organization Can Help

While each of us is ultimately responsible for the level of his or her self-esteem, we have the option of supporting or damaging the self-confidence and self-respect of everyone we work with, just as they have that option in their interactions with us. Organizations are beginning to include self-esteem modules in their employee and management training programs. R. J. Reynolds, Deere & Company, IBM, Shell Oil, and Calgon, to name just a few, realize the impact low self-esteem has on a worker's ability to learn and grow. These programs help employees at all levels understand how they can influence their own self-esteem as well as that of their coworkers. Participants are given the opportunity to look at and remove some of the self-limiting behaviors that create barriers to fully using their abilities. They are also encouraged to consider new areas of work and responsibility as well as to acquire new skills. William J. Rothwell, a special services officer in the Illinois Office of the General Auditor, has found that one of the main reasons people seek training is the desire to increase their self-esteem. He sees this as an opportunity for management to encourage workers to build their self-esteem. "We can emphasize to participants the strengths of training as a means of unlocking creativity and hidden potential."[33]

Research clearly shows that high-tech employees of the future will need more than training and good salaries to maintain their high self-esteem.[34] Today, many organizations are adopting long-range plans for investing in their people as well as their physical plants. They realize that employees with high self-esteem are more creative, more energetic, and more committed to both the work and the organization. While boosts to self-esteem may come from technical achievements, they must also come from other sources, such as increased opportunities for decision making and more personalized management-employee relationships.

Effective organizations are demonstrating to employees that their opinions and views matter and that their ideas are being implemented in significant ways. They are making sure that each person has a sense of belonging through warm, empathic relationships and open two-way communication that expresses feelings as well as facts. Organizations need to help employees feel they are accomplishing their own goals while helping the organization reach its goals as well. These steps will enable organizations to meet the self-esteem needs of their employees.

SUMMARY

Self-esteem is what you think and feel about yourself. It is the sum of your self-confidence and self-respect. If you have high self-esteem, you feel competent and worthy. If you have low self-esteem, you feel incompetent, unworthy, and insecure. Self-esteem includes your feeling of adequacy about the roles you play, your personality traits, physical appearance, skills, and abilities. High self-esteem is the foundation for a successful life and good human relations. Organizations are beginning to recognize the impact of employees' self-esteem on their ability to learn and to contribute to the organization's productivity.

Chapter 4   Building High Self–Esteem

People start acquiring and building their self-esteem from the day they are born. Parents, friends, associates, the media, and professional colleagues all influence the development of a person's self-esteem. Most of this process takes place in the subconscious mind; people do not objectively evaluate or censor the formative influences they take in. As a result, their self-esteem may represent an accurate reflection of their true abilities or a negative and distorted one.

High self-esteem is essential for success in an organization. Peoples' self-esteem is often expressed in terms of expectations — how much or how little they believe they can do. These expectations can become self-fulfilling prophecies. The power of other people's expectations is also very strong. They can result in a Pygmalion effect in which an individual lives up to the image another has of him or her. Mentors can strengthen a person's self-esteem by expressing belief in that individual's abilities and talents. They can act as sponsors, teachers, devil's advocates, and coaches. Managers in organizations can act as mentors to employees and provide a supportive or enabling environment for strengthening workers' self-esteem.

Building high self-esteem is important both personally and professionally. People who have high self-esteem tend to be future oriented; cope with problems creatively; handle their emotions; give and receive help; accept others as unique, talented individuals; exhibit self-confident behaviors.

Although there are many approaches to improving low self-esteem, such as writing positive self-talk affirmations, certain underlying principles are common to all. These principles include identifying and accepting personal limitations, visualizing positive results, setting goals, making decisions, and developing an expertise in one area. While everyone is ultimately responsible for the level of his or her self-esteem, each of us has the option of supporting or damaging the self-confidence and self-respect of anyone we work with. Several organizations are offering their employees training sessions on how to improve their own and coworkers' self-esteem.

KEY TERMS

self-esteem   Pygmalion effect
self-talk   mentor
failure syndrome   affirmations
self-fulfilling prophecy

REVIEW QUESTIONS

1. What is self-esteem? Why is the development of high self-esteem important in a person's life?

2. What influences help shape a person's self-esteem?

3. How do the expectations of yourself and others affect your self-esteem? Give examples from your own life.

Part 2 Career Success Begins with Knowing Yourself

4. What are some of the characteristics that people with high self-esteem exhibit?

5. Why are organizations concerned about employees' self-esteem? In what ways are they helping workers build high self-esteem?

6. List the basic guidelines for building high self-esteem. Which two do you feel are the most important? Why?

7. What role does the subconscious mind play in developing and changing a person's self-esteem?

8. How can visualization help change a person's behavior and self-esteem?

9. List the three elements necessary for the construction of positive self-talk statements. Give three examples of such statements.

10. Review Larry Wilson's Total Person Insight on page 391. Describe a mistake you have made and how it proved to be a growth experience for you.

CASE 4.1

Slowing the Revolving Door

Kenn Ricci, president of a Cleveland air-charter operation called Corporate Wings, figured the high pilot turnover in his company was unavoidable. Deregulation of the airline industry in 1978 had opened possibilities for new and expanded routes by established carriers and for market entry by fledgling carriers. But to keep all those airplanes flying, the airlines needed more pilots, and most could pay them twice what Corporate Wings could. Like other air-charter organizations and the regional and commuter air companies, Ricci had built his business employing pilots who didn't mind relatively low pay and unpredictable schedules because they needed flight experience. That they would leave when they racked up enough flying time, he thought, was a foregone conclusion.

In fact, salary and schedules aren't the only considerations affecting pilots. Many corporate pilots weigh the higher salaries offered by airlines against the greater anonymity of working for a large company and decided to stay with the small-scale air charter. Others are attracted to small companies by the prospect of flying a wide variety of corporate-owned aircraft, some with well equipped, often advanced avionics. For flexible professionals who find satisfaction in performing both the flying and nonflying details of flight service — from greeting traveling executives to loading luggage — corporate air-charter employment can be rewarding.

Chapter 4   Building High Self–Esteem

Corporate Wings did well in the years from 1981 to 1985, but toward the end of 1986 Ricci began to realize he had underestimated the value of the one-to-one relationship between his pilots and his clients. The mounting rate of turnover meant new faces in the cockpit, and this so concerned two of the company's biggest clients they decided to go elsewhere for service. In five months Corporate Wings lost one-third of its business, and Ricci took a hard look at his employee policies. "We were programmed for turnover," he said.[1] To keep his clients, Ricci now needed to entice his pilots to stick with Corporate Wings.

Sources: Bruce G. Posner, "To Have and to Hold," *INC.*, October 1988, pp. 130–131; Eric Weiner, "Corporate Pilots; Are Airline Jobs All that They Are Cracked up to Be?" *Flying*, April 1986, pp. 59–62; Eric Weiner, "Boom Skies: As They Expand Their Markets, Airlines Are Snatching up Eager Pilots in Record Numbers," *Flying*, October 1986, pp. 69–71.

Questions

1. What did the interplay of expectations between pilots and management have to do with Ricci's problems? How could this situation have been avoided?
2. Beyond increasing salaries and modifying flying schedules, what could Ricci do to help retain his staff? What would be the benefits to the organization and the clients?
3. Could these improvements be carried over to the office and maintenance personnel as well? How?

CASE 4.2

Unmanagement at W. L. Gore & Associates

When Bill Gore founded his company, he "set out to recreate the sense of excited commitment, personal fulfillment, and self-direction" for his employees that he had in his own life. He organized a new system of management in which there were no titles, no orders, and no bosses. Everyone was expected to work effectively with everyone else. Associates, as all Gore employees are called, chose to work in an area of the company that they felt best matched their interests, skills, and abilities. They were urged to develop their potential to the fullest.

Gore found that the system worked well until the number of associates reached about two hundred. At that point, human relations and worker productivity began to suffer, and the group became less cooperative. Instead of

---

[1] Bruce G. Posner, "To Have and to Hold," *INC.*, October 1988, p. 130.

Part 2   Career Success Begins with Knowing Yourself

adding layers of management to the company to take care of the problem, Gore opened another plant. As the number of associates dropped to one hundred and fifty, morale lifted and the workers felt part of the team again. Each time the number of associates exceeded two hundred, Gore opened another plant. He has opened a total of twenty-seven plants, with plans for more if the need arises.

How is the system working? Sales have neared $125 million, and the company is profitable. Customers admit they have "seen at Gore remarkable examples of people coming out of nowhere and excelling." For the employees, the atmosphere is hard to describe; it's "a feeling, a state of mind."[1] And if that means a sense of excitement and personal growth, that, as much as anything, is what Bill Gore set out to create.

Source: Lucien Rhodes, "The Un-Manager," *INC.*, August 1982, p. 38.

Questions

1. List some of the ways that employees at Gore are encouraged to develop and expand their self-esteem.
2. Bill Gore found that when the company grew too large, it had a negative effect on workers. Besides making employees feel more anonymous, why would size tend to affect workers negatively? What impact might it have on their self-esteem?
3. What would you say are Bill Gore's expectations about the people who come to work for him?

SUGGESTED READINGS

Branden, Nathaniel. *How To Raise Your Self-Esteem*. New York: Bantam Paperback Edition, 1988.

Dyer, Wayne W. *Your Erroneous Zones*. New York: Funk & Wagnalls, 1976.

Gray, James, Jr. *The Winning Image*. New York: AMACOM, 1982.

Maltz, Maxwell. *Psycho-Cybernetics*. New York: Pocket Books, 1972.

Waitley, Denis. *The Seeds of Greatness*. Old Tappan, N.J.: Fleming H. Revell Company, 1983.

NOTES

1. Robert McGarvey, "The Confidence Factor," *Executive Female*, July/August 1988, p. 28.
2. William Watson Purkey, *Self-Concept and School Achievement* (Englewood Cliffs, N.J.: Prentice-Hall, 1970), pp. 14–17.

---

[1] Lucien Rhodes, "The Un-Manager," *INC.*, August 1982, p. 38.

Chapter 4   Building High Self–Esteem

3. "Task Force Feelgood," *Time*, February 23, 1987, p. 33.
4. Purkey, *Self-Concept and School Achievement*, pp. 14–17.
5. Judy Folkenberg, "Delinquency and Self-Dislike," *Psychology Today*, May 1985, p. 16.
6. A. H. Maslow, "A Theory of Human Motivation," in *Psychological Foundations of Organizational Behavior*, ed. Barry M. Staw (Santa Monica, Cal.: Goodyear Publishing, 1977), pp. 7–8.
7. Amy Bjork Harris and Thomas A. Harris, *Staying OK* (New York: Harper & Row, 1985), p. 24.
8. Sue Baugh, "Cool Path to the Top," *NABW Journal*, January/February 1982, pp. 28–30.
9. Margaret Henning and Ann Jardim, *The Managerial Woman* (New York: Anchor Books, 1977), pp. 106–107.
10. Denis Waitley, *The Double Win* (Old Tappan, N.J.: Fleming H. Revell Company, 1985), pp. 76–77.
11. *Current Biography Yearbook*, 1985, pp. 421–425.
12. Lee Iacocca with William Novak, *Iacocca* (New York: Bantam Books, 1984), p. 137.
13. Robert Conklin, *How to Get People to Do Things* (Chicago: Contemporary Books, 1979), p. 69.
14. "How to Gain Power and Support in the Organization," *Training/HRD*, January 1982, p. 13.
15. Judith Briles, *Woman to Woman: From Sabotage to Support* (Far Hills, N.J.: New Horizon Press, 1987), p. 77.
16. Milton Layden, "Whipping Your Worst Enemy on the Job: Hostility," *Nation's Business*, October 1978, pp. 87–90.
17. Zig Ziglar, *See You at the Top* (Gretna, La.: Pelican Publishing, 1975), p. 99.
18. Maxwell Maltz, *Psycho-Cybernetics* (New York: Pocket Books, 1972), pp. 6–7.
19. Ziglar, *See You at the Top*, p. 23.
20. Nancy W. Collins, Susan K. Gilbert, and Susan Nycum, *Women Leading: Making Tough Choices on the Fast Track* (Lexington, Mass.: The Stephen Greene Press, 1988), p. 43.
21. Ibid., p. 41.
22. Breda Murphy Bova and Rebecca R. Phillips, "Mentoring as a Learning Experience for Adults," *Journal of Teacher Education*, May/June 1984, p. 17.
23. Collins, Gilbert, and Nycum, *Women Leading*, p. 46.
24. Caela Farren, Janet Dreyfus Gray, and Beverly Kaye, "Mentoring: A Boon to Career Development," *Personnel*, November/December 1984, p. 22.
25. Anita Shreve, "Careers and the Lure of Motherhood," *New York Times Magazine*, November 21, 1982, pp. 38–43, 46–52, 56.
26. Shakti Gawain, *Creative Visualization* (San Rafael, Cal.: Whatever Publishing, 1978), p. 14.
27. Bob Colacello, "Diane Von Furstenberg: I Don't Believe in Fairy Tales," *Parade Magazine*, August 30, 1987, p. 5.
28. Albert Ellis and Robert A. Harper, *A New Guide to Rational Living* (North Hollywood, Cal.: Wilshire Book Company, 1975), pp. 210–215.
29. Richard Grote, "Make Sure Training Builds Self-Esteem and Peer Acceptance," *Training/HRD*, December 1981, p. 13.

Part 2   Career Success Begins with Knowing Yourself

30. Sheila Ostrander and Lynn Schroeder, *Superlearning* (New York: Dell Publishing, 1979), pp. 87–109.
31. Maggie Pale, "Mary Boone: A Confident Vision," *Savvy*, July 1982, pp. 62–67.
32. Cheri Burns, "The Extra Edge," *Savvy*, December 1982, p. 42.
33. Grote, p. 13.
34. Pete Bradshaw and Sandra Shullman, "Managing High-Tech Employees Through Self-Esteem," *Infosystems*, March 1983, pp. 111–112.

Master Vocabulary List

This section contains information about the meanings and pronunciations of the words that are underscored in blue in Chapters 9, 10, 11, 12, 15, and 20 of *RSVP*. Place checks in the boxes in front of the words in the Master Vocabulary List that you want to learn, and use the suggestions in Chapter 5 to learn their meanings.

Information in Entries

The following entry for the word *pit* illustrates the five types of information that are provided for words listed in this section.

> **pit** (pit) *v.*   To set in competition; to set against, match [to *pit* the two best teams in a championship play-off]

1. The *spelling* is printed in boldface: **pit.**

2. The *pronunciation* is enclosed in parentheses: (pit).

3. The *part of speech* is printed in italics: *v.*

4. The *definition* begins with a capital letter: To set in competition; to set against, match.

5. An *example* of the way the word is used is enclosed in brackets following the definition: [to *pit* the two best teams in a championship play-off]

The meaning of each word in the Master Vocabulary List corresponds to the ways the word is used in this book. For instance, the word *pit* has many meanings including "the hard stone in a fruit [a cherry *pit*]" and "an area where animals are kept [a bear *pit*]." However, the entry above indicates that in this book *pit* is used as a verb that means "to set in competition."

Parts of Speech

The following abbreviations are used for the traditional parts of speech:

noun (*n.*)
noun plural (*n.pl.*)
verb (*v.*)
adjective (*adj.*)
adverb (*adv.*)
preposition (*prep.*)

The words in the Master Vocabulary List do not include a conjunction (*conj.*) or an interjection (*interj.*).

Pronunciation Spellings

Interpret pronunciation spellings using the pronunciation key at the bottom of this page, on the bottom of other pages in this section, and on the inside back cover of the book. For instance, by using the key you can determine that *chaos* (kā′os′) is pronounced using the following sounds:

k
ā as in **pay**
o as in **pot**
s

Vowels. Vowel sounds present the major problem in interpreting pronunciation spellings because the five vowels, *a, e, i, o,* and *u,* are used to represent sounds.

pat (pat)	**pet** (pet)	**pit** (pit)	**pot** (pot)	**cut** (cut)
pay (pā)	**be** (bē)	**pie** (pī)	**toe** (tō)	**cute** (kyo͞ot)
care (câr)		**pier** (pîr)	**paw** (pô)	**firm** (fûrm)
arm (ärm)			**took** (to͝ok)	
			boot (bo͞ot)	

In addition, pronunciation spellings include the two-vowel combinations found in the term *boy scout* (boi skout) and the de-emphasized sound in words such as *ago, agent, sanity, comply, and focus,* which is represented by a symbol called the schwa: *a*go (ə′gō). The schwa, which looks like the letter *e* printed upside down (ə), has the vowel sound heard in *of* when the phrase "bag *of* candy" is said quickly (bag əv kan′dē).

Consonants. Consonant letters are used to represent consonant sounds in pronunciation spellings. For example:

half (haf)	phone (fōn)
ghost (gōst)	wrap (rap)
gem (jem)	his (hiz)
knit (nit)	rhyme (rīm)
debt (det)	sign (sīn)

The letters *c, q,* and *x* are not used in pronunciation spellings. The letter *c* is usually pronounced *k* as in *can* (kan) or *s* as in *cent* (sent); the letter *q* is usually pronounced *kw,* as in *quit* (kwit); and the letter *x* is usually pronounced *ks,* as in *tax* (taks).

Accent Marks. Pronunciation spellings usually include accent marks to indicate the relative force with which syllables are spoken. Compare the placement of the primary accent marks (′) in the pronunciations for the verb and noun forms of the word *extract:*

extract (ek-strakt′) *v.* To pull out [to *extract* a tooth]
extract (ek′-strakt) *n.* A passage selected from a book [to read a short *extract* from a long book]

The second syllable of *extract* is stressed when the word is used as a verb [*ex-tract'* a tooth], whereas the first part of the word is stressed when the word is used as a noun [to read a short *ex'-tract* from a long book].

The secondary accent mark (') is used to indicate stress that is weaker than primary stress but stronger than the stress of unaccented syllables. Primary and secondary accent marks in the following words indicate which syllables receive primary and secondary stress.

rec' og nize'
in' dis pen' sa ble

Say *recognize* and *indispensable* aloud, giving primary and secondary stress to the syllables with the primary and secondary accent marks.

☐ **aberrant** (ab-er'ənt) *adj.* Not normal or typical; abnormal, atypical [the *aberrant* behavior of a murderer]

☐ **abrasion** (ə-brā'zhən) *n.* A scraped, rubbed, or worn-away place on skin [an *abrasion* caused by falling off a bicycle]

☐ **absorption** (ab-sôrp'shən) *n.* The state of being very interested in or completely occupied by someone or something [total *absorption* in one's work]

☐ **abstract** (ab-strakt') *adj.* Existing as an idea in the mind rather than in physical form [the *abstract* ideas of beauty, love, perfection, and freedom]

☐ **acute** (ə-kyōōt') *adj.* Severe, powerful, critical [an *acute* headache]

☐ **adhere** (ad-hîr') *v.* To follow closely; to keep to, stand by [to *adhere* to the rules of a game]

☐ **adherent** (ad-hîr'ənt) *n.* A supporter or follower [an *adherent* of Christianity]

☐ **affective** (ə-fek'tiv) *adj.* Having to do with feelings; emotional [a psychologist studying *affective* behavior]

☐ **affiliate** (ə-fil'ē-āt') *v.* To associate, connect, ally [to *affiliate* oneself with worthwhile organizations]

☐ **affluence** (af'lōō-əns) *n.* Great wealth or riches [the *affluence* of movie stars]

☐ **allocate** (al'ō-kāt') *v.* To set aside for a specific purpose; to designate, earmark, assign [to *allocate* money for rent and groceries]

☐ **alternative** (ôl-tûr'nə-tiv) *n.* A choice among or between things [the *alternative* of attending college or going to work]

☐ **altruism** (al'trōō-iz'əm) *n.* Unselfish concern for others; unselfishness, humanitarianism, philanthropy [the *altruism* of those who spend their lives feeding the starving]

☐ **ambiguous** (am-big'yōō-əs) *adj.* Having two or more possible meanings; unclear, vague [*ambiguous* directions on a test]

☐ **ambivalent** (am-biv'ə-lənt) *adj.* Having conflicting feelings toward something, such as sometimes loving and sometimes hating somebody or something [to be *ambivalent* about one's job]

☐ **analogy** (ə-nal'ə-jē) *n.* The showing of a similarity between things that are otherwise not alike; comparison [to draw an *analogy* between a computer and the human brain]

☐ **anticipatory** (an-tis'ə-pə-tôr'ē) *adj.* Looking forward to; expecting, anticipating [*anticipatory* nervousness before giving a speech]

☐ **antipathy** (an-tip'ə-thē) *n.* A deep-seated dislike; distaste [an *antipathy* for people who eat with food falling out of their mouths]

☐ **appalling** (ə-pô'ling) *adj.* Dismaying, shocking, horrifying, sickening, revolting [the *appalling* sight of soldiers dying on a battlefield]

☐ **aquifer** (ak'wə-fər) *n.* An underground layer of rock and sand that contains water

☐ **arbitrary** (är'bə-trer'ē) *adj.* Done without the use of fixed rules; random, inconsistent [an *arbitrary* decision]

☐ **archaeologist** (är'kē-ol'ə-jist) *n.* A person who studies the life and culture of ancient people by examining the remains of objects they used [an *archaeologist* who studies the civilization of Native Americans]

☐ **ascetic** (ə-set'ik) *adj.* Living in self-denial for religious reasons [to lead an *ascetic* life in a desert]

☐ **assertive** (ə-sûr'tiv) *adj.* Positive, self-assured, confident, forceful, decisive [an *assertive* officer in military service]—**assertively**, *adv.*

☐ **asset** (as'et') *n.* Something valuable or desirable to have [the *asset* of a good sense of humor]

ə ago/a pat/ā pay/â câre/ä arm/e pet/ē be/i pit/ī pie/î pier/o pot/ō toe/ô paw/ōō took/ōō boot/ oi boy/ou scout/u cut/yōō cute/û firm **Also see the inside back cover.**

☐ **attribute** (ə-trib'yо̄ot) *v.* To regard as belonging to someone or something [to *attribute* success to hard work]

☐ **autonomy** (ô-ton'ə-mē) *n.* Independence or self-government; the state of functioning independently [unmarried people who value their *autonomy*]

☐ **barter** (bär'tər) *v.* To trade using goods or services rather than money [to *barter* lawn care for a bicycle]

☐ **behavioral science** (bi-hāv'yər-əl sī'əns) *n.* The study of human and social behavior, including psychology, sociology, and anthropology [the *behavioral science* department at a college]

☐ **bias** (bī'əs) *n.* Prejudice, leaning, inclination, or partiality [a *bias* for young, good-looking people]

☐ **bizarre** (bi-zär') *adj.* Very odd; strange, weird, outlandish [to wear a *bizarre* costume to a Halloween party]

☐ **brash** (brash) *adj.* Hasty, reckless, careless, incautious [the *brash* decision to purchase a used car without having it inspected by a competent mechanic]—**brashly,** *adv.*

☐ **breach** (brēch) *n.* Failure to observe correct procedures; violation, infraction, noncompliance [to make a *breach* in a contract by failing to observe its terms]

☐ **brew** (brо̄о) *v.* To make from malt or hops by boiling, steeping, or fermenting [to *brew* beer]; to begin to form [trouble *brewing*]

☐ **bubonic plague** (bо̄о-bon'ik plāg) *n.* A deadly disease transmitted by fleas from rats

☐ **burgeon** (bûr'jən) *v.* To grow rapidly; to expand, enlarge, mushroom, increase [swimmers *burgeon* at the seashore in summer]

☐ **buttocks** (but'əks) *n.pl.* The rounded parts at the back of the hips; rump, seat, rear, bottom [to inject medicine in the *buttocks*]

☐ **canonization** (kan'ə-niz-ā'shən) *n.* The formal act of a church in declaring a person a saint [the *canonization* of St. Mary]—**canonize,** *v.*

☐ **caption** (kap'shən) *n.* A heading or title [a *caption* stating the content of a photograph]

☐ **cardinal** (kärd'n-əl) *adj.* Of main importance; foremost, basic, primary, key, principal [a *cardinal* rule of etiquette]

☐ **channel** (chan'əl) *v.* To direct along a desired path; to route, direct, guide, lead [to *channel* one's energy toward studying]

☐ **chaos** (kā'os') *n.* Extreme confusion, disorder, turmoil, disorganization [*chaos* in a city created by fires following an earthquake]

☐ **coercive** (kō-ûr'siv) *adj.* Forcing, pressuring, compelling, making, intimidating, bullying [being *coercive* when disciplining children]

☐ **coin** (koin) *v.* To make up, devise, or invent a new word [to *coin* a name for a new product]

☐ **compassion** (kəm-pash'ən) *n.* Sorrow for the suffering of another; sympathy, pity, mercy, kindheartedness [*compassion* for the sick and starving]

☐ **compassionate** (kəm-pash'ən-it) *adj.* Showing sorrow for the suffering of another; sympathetic, pitying, merciful, kindhearted [*compassionate* feeding of the hungry and clothing of the naked]

☐ **compatible** (kəm-pat'ə-bəl) *adj.* Capable of getting along well together; like-minded, congenial [a *compatible* husband and wife]

☐ **competence** (kom'pə-təns) *n.* Capability, skill, ability [to demonstrate *competence* in the game of tennis]

☐ **competent** (kom'pə-tənt) *adj.* Well-qualified, capable, skillful, able [a *competent* typist]

☐ **compliance** (kəm-plī'əns) *n.* The tendency to give in to others [a child's *compliance* with his parents' wishes]

☐ **compulsive** (kəm-pul'siv) *adj.* Being driven by some inner force to perform some act repeatedly; uncontrollable, compelled, driven [a *compulsive* shopper who has closets filled with unworn clothing]

☐ **concise** (kən-sīs') *adj.* Brief and to the point; short and clear; succinct [a *concise* summary of a long book]

☐ **concrete** (kon-krēt') *adj.* Specific, particular, factual, definite [*concrete* evidence that the murder was committed with a butcher knife]

☐ **confidant** (kon'fə-dant') *n.* A trusted friend with whom one shares intimate secrets [to be a spouse, lover, and *confidant*]

☐ **conjure** (kon'jər) *v.* To call to mind or cause to appear from nowhere [to *conjure* up a meal from leftovers found in the refrigerator]

☐ **connotation** (kon'ə-tā'shən) *n.* An idea or notion associated with or suggested by a word [The *connotations* of "mother" include love, care, and tenderness.]

☐ **connotative** (kon'ə-tā'tiv) *adj.* Being an idea or notion associated with or suggested by a word [using a word in its *connotative* sense]—**connotatively,** *adv.*

☐ **consolidation** (kən-sol'ə-dā'shən) *n.* The act of combining things into a single whole; unification, integration, amalgamation [the *consolidation* of three small businesses into one large business]

☐ **constraint** (kən-strānt') *n.* The act of restricting by force [a *constraint* against businesses that misrepresent products they sell]

☐ **constructive** (kən-strukʹtiv) *adj.* Leading to improvements or advancements; helpful, useful [*constructive* suggestions for vocabulary development]—**constructively,** *adv.*

☐ **consumerism** (kən-sooʹmə-rizʹəm) *n.* The consumption of goods and services; also, practices and policies designed to protect consumers

☐ **context** (konʹtekst) *n.* The entire background or environment of a particular event; framework, surroundings [the inappropriateness of hysterical laughter in the *context* of a funeral]

☐ **contraceptive** (konʹtrə-sepʹtiv) *n.* A device or medication used to prevent pregnancy [an oral *contraceptive*]

☐ **convention** (kən-venʹshən) *n.* A customary practice; custom, usual practice [the *convention* of serving cake at birthday parties]

☐ **criterion** (krī-tîrʹē-ən) *n.* A standard by which something is judged; measure, yardstick, model [a *criterion* for judging students' written work]—**criteria,** *n.pl.*

☐ **crucial** (krooʹshəl) *adj.* Of great importance; critical, decisive, essential, urgent [the *crucial* decision to wage a war]

☐ **decapitate** (di-kapʹə-tāt´) *v.* To cut off the head of [to *decapitate* using a guillotine]

☐ **defense mechanism** (di-fensʹ mekʹə-nizʹəm) *n.* Any thought process used by individuals to protect themselves from experiencing feelings such as guilt, shame, and anxiety [rationalization as a *defense mechanism* against feeling shame for mistreating a friend]

☐ **deintensify** (dēʹin-tenʹsə-fī´) *v.* To make less intense; to decrease, weaken [to *deintensify* one's feelings of rage]

☐ **delusional** (di-looʹzhən-əl) *adj.* Holding a belief that is contrary to fact or reality [a *delusional* episode during which one believes himself to be God]

☐ **delve** (delv) *v.* To dig deeply for information; to search, examine, explore, look for [to *delve* into the secrets of somebody's past life]

☐ **demigod** (demʹē-god´) *n.* A godlike person

☐ **denotation** (dēʹnō-tāʹshən) *n.* The direct meaning or reference of a word [The *denotation* of "bird" is a "feathered animal with wings."]

☐ **denotative** (dēʹnō-tāʹtiv) *adj.* Being the direct meaning or reference of a word [using words in their *denotative* senses]—**denotatively,** *adv.*

☐ **depict** (di-piktʹ) *v.* To picture in words or represent in art [a story or sculpture that *depicts* Abraham Lincoln]

☐ **derive** (di-rīvʹ) *v.* To get from a source [to *derive* maple syrup from a tree]

☐ **deter** (di-tûrʹ) *v.* To discourage, hinder, prevent [Cold, wet, and windy weather may *deter* outside activities.]

☐ **deteriorate** (di-tîrʹē-ə-rāt´) *v.* To worsen; to decline, decay, fall apart [to watch a person's health *deteriorate*]

☐ **deterioration** (di-tîrʹē-ə-rāʹshən) *n.* The condition of becoming worse [the *deterioration* of a vacated house]

☐ **determinant** (di-tûrʹmə-nənt) *n.* A thing that determines [country of birth as a *determinant* of citizenship]

☐ **deviate** (dēʹvē-āt´) *v.* To turn aside from an approved behavior; to stray, wander [to *deviate* from the truth—lie]

☐ **devise** (di-vīzʹ) *v.* To create, design, invent, contrive, formulate [to *devise* a program for losing excess weight]

☐ **devotee** (devʹə-tēʹ) *n.* One who is strongly devoted to something; fan [a *devotee* of the arts]

☐ **dialect** (dīʹə-lekt´) *n.* A form of spoken language that is peculiar to a specific region or group of people [a *dialect* spoken on a remote island in the Atlantic Ocean]

☐ **dilemma** (di-lemʹə) *n.* A situation in which one must select between unpleasant choices [the *dilemma* of whether to remain in a burning building or jump from a high window]

☐ **directive** (di-rekʹtiv) *n.* An official instruction or order [a *directive* stating company policy with regard to drug use during working hours]

☐ **disclosure** (dis-klōʹzhər) *n.* The act of revealing or disclosing; revelation, communication, making known [the *disclosure* of one's affection for another]

☐ **discrepancy** (dis-krepʹən-sē) *n.* Lack of correspondence; difference, disagreement [a *discrepancy* among eyewitness reports of a crime]

☐ **discrimination** (dis-krimʹə-nāʹshən) *n.* An act of showing prejudice against a person or group, especially members of a minority group [laws prohibiting *discrimination* in the workplace]

☐ **disreputable** (dis-repʹyə-tə-bəl) *adj.* Having a bad reputation; shady, dishonorable, notorious, infamous [a *disreputable* businessperson known to cheat customers]

☐ **distill** (dis-tilʹ) *v.* To produce a refined substance by heating a mixture and then cooling and condensing the resulting vapor [to *distill* alcoholic beverages]; to purify, refine, or concentrate [to *distill* one's thoughts about the meaning of life]

ə ago/a pat/ā pay/â câre/ä arm/e pet/ē be/i pit/ī pie/î pier/o pot/ō toe/ô paw/oo took/oo boot/ oi boy/ou scout/u cut/yoo cute/û firm **Also see the inside back cover.**

□ **distinctive** (dis-tingk′tiv) *adj.* Having characteristics that are different from those of others; unique, different, special, extraordinary [a *distinctive* way of speaking]

□ **diversify** (di-vûr′sə-fī) *v.* To give variety to; to vary [to *diversify* the kinds of foods one eats]

□ **documentary** (dok′yə-men′tə-rē) *n.* A television show or motion picture that presents newsworthy, factual, or educational information [a *documentary* broadcast on a public television station]

□ **dogmatic** (dôg-mat′ik) *adj.* Asserting opinions that are not supported by evidence; opinionated, dictatorial, domineering [having *dogmatic* opinions about how to solve the problems of the world]

□ **dogmatism** (dog′mə-tiz′əm) *n.* The assertion of opinions that are not supported by evidence [to detest the *dogmatism* of a dictator]

□ **drudgery** (druj′ə-rē) *n.* Difficult, menial, tiresome, or distasteful work; toil [the *drudgery* of washing diapers]

□ **dullard** (dul′ərd) *n.* A stupid person; dunce, dumbbell, nitwit [a harebrained solution offered by a *dullard*]

□ **ecclesiastical** (i-klē′zē-as′ti-kəl) *adj.* Pertaining to the church; churchly [an *ecclesiastical* decision made during a meeting of clergy]

□ **ego** (ē′gō) *n.* The part of the personality that is conscious, most in touch with external reality, and that controls behavior [to have an *ego* that accepts all challenges]

□ **eject** (i-jekt′) *v.* To drive out, force out, throw out [to *eject* troublemakers from a party]

□ **elastic** (i-las′tik) *adj.* Changes to suit the circumstances; adaptable, flexible, accommodating [*elastic* regulations that apply differently to management than to workers]

□ **electroencephalogram** (i-lek′trō-en-sef′ə-lə-gram) *n.* A record made by a machine that shows variations in the electrical force in the brain

□ **elliptical** (i-lip′ti-kəl) *adj.* Oval in shape [*elliptical* rather than perfectly circular]— **elliptically,** *adv.*

□ **emanate** (em′ə-nāt′) *v.* To come forth; to flow, issue, come from [heat *emanating* from a fireplace]

□ **embodiment** (em-bod′i-mənt) *n.* The definite visible form of an idea or concept; representation, personification [motherhood as the *embodiment* of loving and caring]

□ **embroil** (em-broil′) *v.* To draw into conflict or trouble; to tangle, trap, implicate [to be *embroiled* in a court battle]

□ **empathy** (em′pə-thē) *n.* The ability to share in another person's thoughts or feelings [a mother's *empathy* for her child's difficulties]

□ **emulation** (em′yə-lā′shən) *n.* The desire to equal or surpass; imitation, rivalry [a boy's *emulation* of his father]

□ **enhance** (en-hans′) *v.* To improve or make more attractive; to heighten, intensify, elevate [to wear clothing that *enhances* one's appearance]

□ **entail** (en-tāl′) *v.* To require, necessitate, involve [a business that *entails* stocking shelves]

□ **entity** (en′tə-tē) *n.* A thing that has a separate existence and that is real in itself; thing, object, body, individual [Each of us is an *entity* unto ourselves.]

□ **envision** (en-vizh′ən) *v.* To picture in the mind; to imagine, visualize [to *envision* a world free of want]

□ **equity** (ek′wə-tē) *n.* Fairness, justice, even-handedness [to expect *equity* in a court of law]

□ **ere** (âr) *prep.* Archaic. Before ["Sent to the devil somewhat *ere* his time"—BYRON]

□ **erotic** (i-rot′ik) *adj.* Arousing sexual feelings or desires; stimulating [to disapprove of *erotic* literature and drawings]

□ **ethical** (eth′i-kəl) *adj.* Taking the moral action; moral, decent, honorable, proper, just, fair [*ethical* treatment of the homeless]

□ **ethics** (eth′iks) *n.pl.* A code of morals and standards of conduct [the *ethics* of the medical profession]

□ **ethnic** (eth′nik) *adj.* Pertaining to membership in a group that shares characteristics such as cultural heritage, customs, language, and history [Japanese taking pride in their *ethnic* heritage]

□ **ethnicity** (eth-nis′i-tē) *n.* Membership in a group that shares characteristics such as cultural heritage, customs, language, and history [New York City residents of Italian *ethnicity*]

□ **euphemism** (yoo′fə-miz′əm) *n.* An acceptable or inoffensive word or phrase used to describe something distasteful, unpleasant, or intimate; inoffensive expression; delicate term ["passed away" as a *euphemism* for "died"]

□ **euphoric** (yoo-fôr′ik) *adj.* Having high spirits or a feeling of great well-being [to be *euphoric* over a raise in one's weekly pay]

□ **evolve** (i-volv′) *v.* To develop through gradual stages; to unfold, ripen, mature [a great tree that *evolved* from a tiny seed]

□ **exclusive** (eks-kloo′siv) *adj.* Not shared or divided; unshared, undivided [the *exclusive* right of single people to spend the money they earn]

□ **excreta** (ek-skrē′tə) *n.* Body waste such as urine and sweat

☐ **expenditure** (ek-spen′də-chər) *n.* An amount of something such as money, time, or effort spent or used up; outlay, output [an *expenditure* of energy to shovel snow]

☐ **explicit** (ek-splis′it) *adj.* Clearly stated; definite, precise [*explicit* directions that a child can understand]—**explicitly,** *adv.*

☐ **exploitation** (eks′ploi-tā′ shən) *n.* The act of making unethical use of someone or something for profit or advantage [the *exploitation* of the poor by the rich]

☐ **extol** (ek-stōl′) *v.* To praise highly; to commend, compliment, acclaim, applaud, laud [to *extol* a firefighter for saving a child's life]

☐ **extract** (ek-strakt′) *v.* To draw something out as if by pulling; to remove [to *extract* all the joy from living]

☐ **facet** (fas′it) *n.* A side or aspect of something [the many *facets* of one's personality]

☐ **facilitate** (fə-sil′ə-tāt′) *v.* To make easy or less difficult; to ease, help [a well-written textbook that *facilitates* learning]

☐ **factor** (fak′tər) *n.* A circumstance or condition that brings about a result; reason, influence [a *factor* to consider when selecting a mate]

☐ **feces** (fē′sēz) *n.* Waste matter from the bowels

☐ **ferment** (fûr′ment′) *v.* To cause the breakdown of organic compounds [Grain must *ferment* to produce alcohol.]

☐ **fibrocystic** (fī-brō-sis′tik) *adj.* Having or being like a fibrous cyst

☐ **flamboyant** (flam-boi′ənt) *adj.* Showy, flashy, extravagant, sensational, theatrical [a *flamboyant* coat made of red velvet and ostrich feathers]

☐ **free-floating** (frē flōt′ing) *adj.* Experienced from time to time for no apparent reason [*free-floating* worry over the well-being of one's children]

☐ **frenzy** (fren′zē) *n.* An outburst of feelings, excitement, or emotion; fury, craze [the *frenzy* of people fleeing from a burning building]

☐ **frustration** (frus-trā′shən) *n.* Prevention from attaining satisfaction or achieving a goal; hindrance, interference, obstruction [the *frustration* of not having one's love returned]

☐ **gaol** (jāl) *n.* The British spelling of the word *jail* [prisoners in a London *gaol*]

☐ **gastrointestinal** (gas′trō-in-tes′tə-nəl) *adj.* Pertaining to the stomach and intestines

☐ **generic** (jə-ner′ik) *adj.* Having the name of a product but not a trademark; common, nonexclusive, unspecified [*generic* aspirin as opposed to Bayer aspirin]

☐ **genitourinary** (jen′ə-tō-yŏŏr′ə-ner′ē) *adj.* Pertaining to the genital and urinary organs

☐ **grist for the mill** (grist fôr thə mil) *n.* Anything that can be used profitably or turned to one's advantage [A letter of recommendation becomes *grist for the mill* when one is seeking employment.]

☐ **habitual** (hə-bich′ŏŏ-əl) *adj.* Done by habit; customary, usual, accustomed, moral, typical [*habitual* lateness to class]—**habitually,** *adv.*

☐ **harbor** (här′bər) *v.* To shelter, house, conceal, or hide [to *harbor* criminals who have escaped from prison]

☐ **heresy** (her′ə-sē) *n.* A religious belief that opposes a belief taught by a church [the *heresy* of believing that there is no God]

☐ **heretic** (her′ə-tik) *n.* A church member who has religious beliefs that differ from beliefs taught by the church [a *heretic* who believes that there is no life after death]

☐ **human resources** (hyŏŏ′mən rē′sôrs-əz) *n.* A personnel department of a company that maintains records and manages the hiring and training of employees [to work in a *human resources* office]

☐ **idiosyncratic** (id′ē-ō-sin-krat′ik) *adj.* Peculiar, unusual, distinctive [an *idiosyncratic* way of thinking]

☐ **imperialist** (im-pîr′ē-əl-ist) *adj.* Seeking to control world markets and other countries and to establish colonies [the *imperialist* activities of Spain in Central and South America]

☐ **implicit** (im-plis′it) *adj.* Suggested but not directly stated; hinted, implied [a child's joy *implicit* in her cheerful smile]

☐ **imposing** (im-pō′zing) *adj.* Making a strong impression because of qualities such as size, dignity, or power; impressive, awe-inspiring [the *imposing* presence of George Washington]

☐ **impoverished** (im-pov′ər-isht) *adj.* Without material resources or means; poor [left *impoverished* when a fire destroyed their home and all they owned]

☐ **imprecision** (im′pri-sizh′ən) *n.* The condition of not being exact, definite, or precise; vagueness [*imprecision* in the manufacture of a valve that led to the failure of a spacecraft]

ə ago/a pat/ā **pay**/a câre/ä arm/e pet/ē be/i pit/ī pie/î pier/o pot/ō toe/ô paw/ŏŏ took/ōō boot/ oi boy/ou scout/u cut/yŏŏ cute/û firm **Also see the inside back cover.**

☐ **impulsive** (im-pul′siv) *adj.* Acting suddenly and without much forethought; unpredictable, spur-of-the-moment, offhand, unplanned, spontaneous [the *impulsive* decision to marry after they had known each other for only two days]

☐ **inactivate** (in-ak′tə-vāt′) *v.* To make inactive [to *inactivate* a hand grenade so it will not explode]

☐ **incapacitation** (in-kə-pas′ə-tā′shən) *n.* The condition of being unable to engage in normal activity [*incapacitation* due to illness]

☐ **incentive** (in-sen′tiv) *n.* Something that stimulates one to take action; encouragement, motivation [a test as an *incentive* to study]

☐ **incompetent** (in-kom′pə-tənt) *adj.* Lacking the ability or knowledge necessary for a task; unskillful, incapable, unqualified [an open-and-shut case that was lost by an *incompetent* lawyer]

☐ **incur** (in-kûr′) *v.* To acquire, become liable for, bring on [to *incur* unexpected expenses due to an automobile accident]

☐ **indicative** (in-dik′ə-tiv) *adj.* Giving an indication; indicating, showing, suggesting [laughter *indicative* of amusement and enjoyment]

☐ **indifference** (in-dif′ər-əns) *n.* Lack of concern, interest, or feeling [to have *indifference* for the suffering of others]

☐ **indifferent** (in-dif′ər-ənt) *adj.* Having no particular interest or concern; unconcerned [rebellious teenagers who are *indifferent* to what their parents tell them]

☐ **indistinguishable** (in′dis-ting′gwi-shə-bəl) *adj.* Cannot be distinguished as being different; identical, carbon copy [twins who are *indistinguishable* from each other]

☐ **indoctrination** (in-dok′trə-nā′shən) *n.* Instruction in values and beliefs; teaching, initiation, training, education [the *indoctrination* of sailors into navy life]

☐ **induce** (in-do͞os′) *v.* To bring about or cause; to persuade, influence [to *induce* vomiting]

☐ **inept** (in-ept′) *adj.* Clumsy, inefficient, awkward, incompetent, unqualified, ineffective [an *inept* electrician who electrocuted himself]

☐ **inevitable** (in-ev′ə-tə-bəl) *adj.* Certain to happen; unavoidable, inescapable, unpreventable [the *inevitable* daily setting of the sun]

☐ **inference** (in′fər-əns) *n.* A conclusion arrived at by using reasoning, knowledge, and accumulated experience [Seeing dark clouds leads to an *inference* that it may rain soon.]

☐ **inhibit** (in-hib′it) *v.* To hold back from doing or feeling something; to prevent, stop, restrict [to be *inhibited* from telling people exactly what you think of them]

☐ **initial** (i-nish′əl) *adj.* Occurring at the beginning; first, introductory [the *initial* letter of a word]—**initially,** *adv.*

☐ **injunction** (in′jungk′shən) *n.* A command or order [an *injunction* not to kill, steal, or cheat]

☐ **innovation** (in′ə-vā′shən) *n.* A new method, custom, device, or way of doing something [the air bag as an *innovation* for safety in case of an automobile accident]

☐ **intact** (in-takt′) *adj.* With no part missing; complete, whole, entire [a fire that damaged the kitchen but left the rest of the house *intact*]

☐ **integral** (in′tə-grəl) *adj.* That which is necessary to make something complete; essential, necessary, indispensable [each brother and sister an *integral* part of the family]

☐ **interaction** (in′tər-akt′shən) *n.* Action on each other [the *interaction* that takes place during heart-to-heart conversation]

☐ **internalize** (in-tûr′nə-līz′) *v.* To make something part of one's way of thinking [to *internalize* your parents' values]

☐ **interrogation** (in-ter′ə-gā′shən) *n.* The asking of questions in a formal examination; questioning, examination, investigation [the *interrogation* of witnesses during a trial]

☐ **intervention** (in′tər-ven′shən) *n.* The act of doing something to change a situation; interference, mediation [the *intervention* of a teacher in a fight among children on the playground]

☐ **intricate** (in′tri-kit) *adj.* Having many parts with complicated relationships among them; complicated, complex, involved [an *intricate* pattern on an Oriental rug]

☐ **invest** (in-vest′) *v.* To spend time, money, or effort in hope of future gain; to devote, give [to *invest* time and effort in building good friendships]

☐ **irreversible** (ir′i-vûr′sə-bəl) *adj.* Cannot be reversed or turned back [an *irreversible* decision]

☐ **jeopardy** (jep′ər-dē) *n.* Great danger; hazard, peril [in *jeopardy* while driving on icy roads through a blinding snowstorm]

☐ **legacy** (leg′ə-sē) *n.* Something handed down from the past; gift, bequest [Greece's *legacy* of democracy]

☐ **levy** (lev′ē) *v.* To impose and collect a tax or other charge; to demand [to *levy* a toll on a bridge]

☐ **lewd** (lo͞od) *adj.* Showing lust or desire in an offensive manner; indecent, vulgar [the *lewd* behavior of customers in a strip joint]

☐ **liability** (lī′ə-bil′ə-tē) *n.* An obligation for

which one must make good in case of loss or damage; debt, responsibility [the *liability* of debts charged to one's credit card]

☐ **liken** (lī′kən) *v.* To describe as being alike; to compare [to *liken* life to the game of baseball]

☐ **literal** (lit′ər-əl) *adj.* Being an exact representation of the original; precise, word-for-word [a *literal* English translation of a German novel]

☐ **low-ball** (lō′bôl) *v.* To state a lower price or estimate than one intends to honor; to underestimate, understate [to give a *low-ball* estimate of $100 for auto repairs while intending to charge $150 when repairs are completed]

☐ **maim** (mām) *v.* To deprive of the use of a body part; to cripple, disable [to be *maimed* in an automobile accident]

☐ **mainstream** (mān′strēm) *n.* The prevailing current trend of thought or influence [a movie that is popular because it is in the *mainstream* of public taste]

☐ **mandate** (man′dāt′) *n.* An order or command [The new *mandate* does not allow smoking on domestic airplane flights.]

☐ **martyr** (mär′tər) *n.* A person who chooses to suffer or die rather than deny belief [to seek sainthood for a *martyr* of a church]

☐ **martyrdom** (mär′tər-dəm) *n.* The condition or act of choosing to suffer or die rather than deny beliefs [the *martyrdom* of a civil rights leader]

☐ **medium** (mē′dē-əm) *n.* A substance in which bodies exist or move; environment, surroundings, atmosphere [the watery *medium* in which fish live]

☐ **menial** (mē′nē-əl) *adj.* Fit for servants; lowly, degrading [the *menial* task of cleaning toilets]

☐ **microbe** (mī′krōb′) *n.* A microscopic bacterium that causes disease; germ [to be infected by a *microbe*]

☐ **monetary** (mon′ə-ter′ē) *adj.* Having to do with money [the *monetary* policies of the United States]

☐ **motivate** (mō′tə-vāt′) *v.* To provide a reason to be moved to action; to stimulate, activate, arouse [to *motivate* a student to learn]

☐ **negativism** (neg′ə-tiv-iz′əm) *n.* Behavior characterized by ignoring or resisting suggestions or instructions from others [the *negativism* of a two-year-old who refuses to follow parental instructions]

☐ **newsworthiness** (nyōōs′wur′thē-nis) *n.* The quality of being timely, important, or interesting [the *newsworthiness* of an announcement made by the president]

☐ **niche** (nich) *n.* A place or position that is particularly suited to a person or thing; slot, position [In fatherhood he found his *niche* in life.]

☐ **nip in the bud** (nip′ in thə bud) *v.* To stop something before it gets started [an attempt to borrow money *nipped in the bud* by a firm and final no]

☐ **norm** (nôrm) *n.* A standard for behavior that is considered to be appropriate; yardstick, criterion [*norms* that govern the courteous treatment of others]

☐ **normative** (nôrm′ə-tiv) *adj.* Having to do with norms or standards [the *normative* behavior of attending school while young]

☐ **nuance** (nōō-äns′) *n.* A slight shade of difference; delicate distinction [the *nuance* that separates bad from worse]

☐ **nuclear family** (nōō′klē-ər fam′ə-lē) *n.* Parents and children living in one household

☐ **nurture** (nûr′chər) *v.* To promote the development of; to nourish, rear, educate [to *nurture* one's children]

☐ **nutrient** (nōō′trē-ənt) *n.* A nourishing substance in food [the *nutrients* in a bowl of chicken and vegetable soup]

☐ **obese** (ō-bēs′) *adj.* Extremely fat; overweight, heavy [too *obese* to engage in sports]

☐ **oblige** (ə-blīj′) *v.* To require, obligate, demand, compel, force [to be *obliged* to pay taxes]

☐ **obscure** (ob-skyoor′) *adj.* Not well-known or famous; unknown [an *obscure* author of the seventeenth century]

☐ **offset** (ôf′set′) *v.* To balance, compensate for, make up for [an A in math that *offsets* a D in history]

☐ **oppress** (ə-pres′) *v.* To keep down by the unjust use of power; to abuse, persecute [to *oppress* the poor]

☐ **optimal** (op′tə-məl) *adj.* Most favorable or desirable; best [to get *optimal* mileage from each gallon of gasoline]

☐ **optimize** (op′tə-mīz′) *v.* To make the most of or to make the best possible use of; to maximize [many windows in a house to *optimize* the sunlight that enters it]

☐ **orientation** (ôr′ē-en-tā′shən) *n.* The act of adjusting to an environment, situation, or idea; familiarization [*orientation* to the ways things are done in college]

☐ **orifice** (ôr′ə-fis) *n.* An opening, hole, or cavity

ə ago/a pat/ā pay/a câre/ä arm/e pet/ē be/i pit/ī pie/î pier/o pot/ō toe/ô paw/ōō took/ōō boot/ oi boy/ou scout/u cut/yōō cute/û firm **Also see the inside back cover.**

[the mouth, nostrils, and other *orifices* of the body]

☐ **ostensible** (o-sten′sə-bəl) *adj.* Apparent, seeming, assumed [the *ostensible* reason for arriving late for an appointment]

☐ **overdraft** (ō′vər-draft′) *n.* A withdrawal from a bank that is greater than the amount on deposit in the bank [a check that bounced because of an *overdraft*]

☐ **overintensify** (ō′vər-in-ten′sə-fī′) *v.* To make too intense; to increase or strengthen too much [to *overintensify* one's feelings]

☐ **overplay** (o′vər-plā′) *v.* To overdo or overemphasize [to *overplay* the danger of walking on the streets of New York City]

☐ **parallel** (par′ə-lel′) *adj.* Corresponding, similar, comparable, equivalent [the *parallel* goals of physical, spiritual, and intellectual improvement]

☐ **passive** (pas′iv) *adj.* Being influenced by others but not influencing them; inactive, submissive, unassertive [to be *passive* rather than to fight back when abused]

☐ **patronage** (pā′trə-nij) *n.* Support, encouragement, sponsorship [*patronage* of the arts]

☐ **perceive** (pər-sēv′) *v.* To acquire knowledge by using the senses of sight, hearing, touch, taste, or smell; to sense, observe, detect [by counting, to *perceive* how much money is in your wallet]

☐ **perception** (pər-sep′shən) *n.* Knowledge gotten by using the senses of sight, hearing, touch, taste, or smell; awareness, comprehension, recognition [the *perception* from the sound of a siren that a fire engine, ambulance, or police car is near]

☐ **perspective** (pər-spek′tiv) *n.* A point of view used in understanding or evaluating something; viewpoint, overview [to see yourself from the *perspective* that others see you]

☐ **pertinence** (pûr′tə-nəns) *n.* Appropriateness, relevance, relatedness, suitability [the *pertinence* of thanking gift givers]

☐ **phenomenon** (fi-nom′ə-non′) *n.* A happening, occurrence, or event [the *phenomenon* of a snowstorm in winter]—**phenomena,** *n.pl.*

☐ **phoneme** (fō′nēm′) *n.* A sound that is heard when a word is spoken (the *phoneme* k that begins the word *cat*]

☐ **pious** (pī′əs) *adj.* Showing religious devotion; devout, religious, spiritual [a *pious* and trusted member of the community]

☐ **pit** (pit) *v.* To set in competition; to set against, match [to *pit* the two best teams in a championship play-off]

☐ **placenta** (plə-sen′tə) *n.* An organ in most mammals within which a fetus is partially encased in the uterus

☐ **placidity** (plə-sid′ə-tē) *n.* The condition of being calm, quiet, tranquil; peacefulness [to enjoy the *placidity* of the mountains of Vermont]

☐ **plum** (plum) *n.* Something desirable to have —especially a good position at work [a *plum* that pays well and that requires little effort]

☐ **plurality** (ploo-ral′ə-tē) *n.* The difference between the number of votes cast for the leading candidate and the candidate with the next highest number of votes; majority [the *plurality* of votes for the office of president]

☐ **portico** (pôr′ti-kō′) *n.* A porch or walkway covered by a roof that is supported by columns [the *portico* at the entrance to the White House]

☐ **predominant** (pri-dom′ə-nənt) *adj.* Most frequent, noticeable, dominant, important, major [financial necessity as a *predominant* reason to hold a job]—**predominantly,** *adv.*

☐ **prestigious** (pre-stij′əs) *adj.* Having influence or the power to impress; respected, reputable [a *prestigious* address on Rodeo Drive in Beverly Hills]

☐ **prevail** (pri-vāl′) *v.* To be widespread; to exist widely [policies that *prevail* at your college]

☐ **procreation** (prō′krē-ā′shən) *n.* The act of producing children [the *procreation* of the human race]

☐ **profound** (prə-found′) *adj.* Thoughtful, deep, wise, intense [the *profound* writings of a great philosopher]

☐ **pronounced** (prə-nounst′) *adj.* Unmistakable, distinct, clear, unquestionable, noticeable, conspicuous, apparent [to have a *pronounced* limp when walking]

☐ **prospective** (prə-spek′tiv) *adj.* Expected, likely, future [an engaged couple who are *prospective* marriage partners]

☐ **provinces** (prov′ins-əz) *n.pl.* The parts of a country that are distant from major cities and cultural life [to live on a farm in the *provinces*]

☐ **provocative** (prə-vok′ə-tiv) *adj.* Arousing an action or feeling; stimulating, fascinating, intriguing [a *provocative* discussion about child abuse]

☐ **public domain** (pub′lik dō-mān′) *n.* The state of being open to use by anybody because of freedom from copyright or patent [plays by Shakespeare in the *public domain*]

☐ **punctual** (pungk′choo-əl) *adj.* Taking action at an appointed time; prompt, on time, not late [to be *punctual* for appointments]

☐ **ratify** (rat′ə-fī′) *v.* To approve, confirm, or support [to be *ratified* by a majority]

☐ **rationale** (rash′ə-nal′) *n.* The reasons for something; reasoning, explanation [a *rationale* for raising taxes]

☐ **recipient** (ri-sip′ē-ənt) *n.* A person who receives something; receiver [to be the *recipient* of an A in an English course]

☐ **reciprocal** (ri-sip′rə-kəl) *adj.* Done in return; mutual, shared, exchanged [to enjoy *reciprocal* friendship]

☐ **reciprocity** (res′ə-pros′ə-tē) *n.* The doing of things in return; mutual action or exchange; mutuality, sharing; give-and-take [the *reciprocity* of Christmas gift exchange]

☐ **regiment** (rej′ə-mənt′) *v.* To organize under strict discipline and control; to regulate [to *regiment* soldiers, sailors, and marines]

☐ **regression** (ri-gresh′ən) *n.* The return to an earlier, more infantile behavior [the *regression* to thumb sucking of children who have not sucked their thumbs in years]

☐ **rehabilitation** (rē′hə-bil′ə-tā′shən) *n.* Restoration to sound condition [the *rehabilitation* of a house that had been damaged by flood water]

☐ **résumé** (rez′oo-mā′) *n.* A written summary of a job applicant's employment, education, and other qualifications [to give a *résumé* to a prospective employer]

☐ **retailer** (rē′tāl-ər) *n.* A company that sells goods in small quantities to customers [the *retailers* who have stores at a local mall]

☐ **retribution** (ret′rə-byoo′shən) *n.* Punishment for evil; revenge, retaliation [to seek *retribution* for having been injured]

☐ **revelation** (rev′ə-lā′shən) *n.* Something disclosed or revealed; disclosure, prophecy [the *revelation* to Moses of the Ten Commandments]

☐ **revere** (ri-vîr′) *v.* To regard with respect, love, affection, or honor [to *revere* one's grandparents]

☐ **rig** (rig) *n.* An arrangement of masts and sails on a sailing vessel

☐ **salient** (sā′lē-ənt) *adj.* Prominent, noticeable, obvious, conspicuous [noting *salient* flaws in a proposal to free all prison inmates]

☐ **sanction** (sangk′shən) *n.* A punishment for failure to conform to society's expectations [the *sanction* of prison or death for murderers]

☐ **scourge** (skûrj) *n.* That which causes suffering or inflicts punishment; curse, terror, affliction [the *scourges* of earthquake, flood, fire, and famine]

☐ **segmentation** (seg′men-tā′shən) *n.* A dividing into segments, or parts [the *segmentation* of those in favor, those opposed, and those who don't care one way or the other]

☐ **self-esteem** (self′ə-stēm′) *n.* Pride in oneself; confidence, self-respect [to have healthy *self-esteem*]

☐ **seniority** (sēn-yôr′ə-tē) *n.* A status achieved by length of service in a position; longevity, tenure [the *seniority* of workers who have been on a job longest]

☐ **shoestring** (shoo′string′) *n.* A small amount of money [to take a vacation on a *shoestring*]

☐ **sibling** (sib′ling) *n.* A brother or sister (a female *sibling*—a sister)

☐ **simultaneous** (sī′məl-tā′nē-əs) *adj.* Happening at the same time; accompanying, concurrent [the *simultaneous* shouting and stomping of football fans]—**simultaneously,** *adv.*

☐ **sophisticated** (sə-fis′ti-kā′tid) *adj.* Complex, refined, or highly developed [*sophisticated* computer technology]

☐ **spatial** (spā′shəl) *adj.* Happening or existing in space [an asset for architects to have an excellent *spatial* sense]

☐ **spectrum** (spek′trəm) *n.* A continuous range of something [the *spectrum* of public opinion about whether murderers should be put to death]

☐ **spontaneous** (spon-tā′nē-əs) *adj.* Done naturally without forethought [a child's *spontaneous* demonstration of love]—**spontaneously,** *adv.*

☐ **staggering** (stag′ər-ing) *adj.* Shocking, astonishing, or overwhelming [the *staggering* price of $700,000 for a three-bedroom house]

☐ **static** (stat′ik) *adj.* Not moving; inactive, stationary, motionless, unchanging [to be *static* in a job that offers no advancement or pay raise]

☐ **stereotype** (ster′ē-ə-tīp′) *n.* A fixed notion about a person or group of people [the *stereotype* that all weight lifters are stupid]

☐ **stipulate** (stip′yə-lāt′) *v.* To specify as a condition; to insist upon [a syllabus that *stipulates* the requirements for a course]

☐ **stocks** (stoks) *n.pl.* A device for punishment that is no longer in use consisting of a heavy wooden frame with holes for holding ankles or wrists

☐ **subculture** (sub′kul′chər) *n.* A group of people in a society who are similar in such characteristics as age, social status, interests, and goals [a teenage *subculture*]

☐ **subject** (sub-jekt′) *v.* To cause to experience

ə ago/a pat/ā pay/a câre/ä arm/e pet/ē be/i pit/ī pie/î pier/o pot/ō toe/ô paw/oo took/oo boot/ oi boy/ou scout/u cut/yoo cute/û firm **Also see the inside back cover.**

an action or treatment; to expose, put through [to *subject* students to writing papers and taking tests]

☐ **subsequent** (sub'sə-kwənt) *adj.* Next, following [to have smoked cigarettes in 1989 but not in *subsequent* years]—**subsequently,** *adv.*

☐ **subtle** (sut'l) *adj.* Not very obvious; not easily detected [a *subtle* hint of lemon in a cheesecake]

☐ **succinct** (sek'singkt') *adj.* Expressed in few words; to the point, brief, short, concise [a *succinct* answer to a complicated question]—**succinctly,** *adv.*

☐ **superimpose** (soo'pər-im-pōz') *v.* To put something on top of something else [to *superimpose* a cotton beard on a picture of Santa Claus]

☐ **surname** (sûr'nām') *n.* Family name or last name [the *surnames* Larsen, Lopez, and Levy]

☐ **susceptible** (sə-sep'tə-bəl) *adj.* Easily affected by; sensitive to, vulnerable [to be *susceptible* to acquiring a severe sunburn]

☐ **taboo** (tə-boo') *adj.* Forbidden by tradition; prohibited, banned, unthinkable, unmentionable [the *taboo* of eating human flesh]

☐ **technology** (tek-nol'ə-jē) *n.* The application of science to the solution of practical problems [the use of computer *technology* in planning highways]

☐ **terminal** (tûr'mə-nəl) *adj.* Ending in death; fatal, deathly [a *terminal* heart attack]—**terminally,** *adv.*

☐ **terminate** (tûr'mə-nāt') *v.* To bring to an end; to stop, finish, conclude [to *terminate* an unhappy marriage in divorce]

☐ **theoretical** (thē'ə-ret'i-kəl) *adj.* Based on theory; unproven, hypothetical [a *theoretical* framework for understanding the workings of the human brain]

☐ **thrive** (thrīv) *v.* To grow, prosper, and flourish [A plant needs water and sunlight to *thrive.*]

☐ **timeliness** (tīm'lē-nis) *n.* The condition of happening at the right time [the *timeliness* of a Christmas card that arrives on December 22]

☐ **timely** (tīm'lē) *adj.* Happening at the right time; well-timed, opportune [a *timely* birth occurring nine months after the beginning of a pregnancy]

☐ **tirade** (tī'rād) *n.* A long, angry speech, harangue, lengthy lecture, reprimand [a coach's *tirade* about errors players made during a game]

☐ **tortuous** (tôr'choo-əs) *adj.* Full of twists, curves, and turns; winding, twisting, meandering, hard to follow [a *tortuous* road up a steep mountain]

☐ **trauma** (trou'mə) *n.* A painful emotional experience that has a lasting effect [the *trauma* of seeing one's child killed]

☐ **traumatic** (trou-mat'ik) *adj.* Causing psychological damage that has a lasting effect [the *traumatic* experience of battlefield combat]

☐ **ultimate** (ul'tə-mit) *adj.* Final, last, conclusive [the *ultimate* victory of the North in the Civil War]

☐ **undercut** (un'dər-kut') *v.* To sell at a lower price than others [to *undercut* the price offered by competitors]

☐ **unseemly** (un'sēm'lē) *adj.* Not decent or proper; improper, unbecoming, undignified [the *unseemly* conduct of a child molester]

☐ **vacillate** (vas'ə-lāt') *v.* To show indecision; to waver, fluctuate, change [to *vacillate* about whether to remain single or to marry]

☐ **valid** (val'id) *adj.* Able to withstand criticism; genuine, sound, well-founded, logical [a *valid* argument]—**validly,** *adv.*

☐ **validity** (və-lid'ə-tē) *n.* The quality of being able to withstand criticism; genuineness, soundness, reasonableness [the *validity* of an argument]

☐ **vector** (vek'tər) *n.* An insect or other animal that carries a germ

☐ **vehicle** (vē'i-kəl) *n.* A means whereby something is moved from one place to another [a dirty napkin as the *vehicle* by which germs are carried to the mouth]

☐ **vicious cycle** (vish'əs sī'kəl) *n.* A situation in which the solution to one problem creates a new problem and brings back the first problem [the *vicious cycle* of a person frustrated because he is overweight who deals with the frustration by overeating]

☐ **victimize** (vik'tə-mīz') *v.* To make a victim; to cause to suffer [to be *victimized* by a bully]

☐ **virtually** (vûr'choo-ə-lē) *adv.* For all practical purposes [a price of $99.99 is *virtually* a price of $100]

☐ **virulent** (vîr'yə-lənt) *adj.* Extremely poisonous; deadly, lethal, toxic [a *virulent* fever that killed many children]

☐ **vomitus** (vom'ə-təs) *n.* Matter that has been vomited

☐ **wampum** (wom'pum) *n.* Small white and black beads made of shells and used by native Americans as money; money [to exchange goods for *wampum*]

☐ **wane** (wān) *v.* To fade, weaken, decline, diminish, decrease [The singer's popularity *waned*.]

☐ **wangle** (wang′gəl) *v.* To get by using persuasion, influence, or manipulation [to *wangle* an invitation to a party]

☐ **wary** (wâr′ē) *adj.* On one's guard, careful of, cautious, suspicious [to be *wary* of strangers]

☐ **wholesaler** (hōl′sāl′ər) *n.* A person or company who sells goods in large quantities to stores

☐ **willful** (wil′fəl) *adj.* Intentional, deliberate, planned [the *willful* destruction of property]

☐ **zealous** (zel′əs) *adj.* Extremely devoted to a purpose or cause; enthusiastic, eager, passionate [to be *zealous* in pursuing a college degree]—**zealously,** *adv.*

ə ago/a pat/ā pay/a câre/ä arm/e pet/ē be/i pit/ī pie/î pier/o pot/ō toe/ô paw/o͞o took/o͞o boot/ oi boy/ou scout/u cut/yo͞o cute/û firm **Also see the inside back cover.**

Glossary

Words in italics within these definitions are also defined in this glossary.

Acronym. A word made from the initial letters of other words. *Scuba* is an acronym made from the first letters of the following words: *s*(elf)-*c*(ontained) *u*(nderwater) *b*(reathing) *a*(pparatus).

Advisers. Instructors assigned to help students select college courses; advisers' offices are usually located in the offices of the departments in which they teach.

Affix. A *prefix* or *suffix*.

Appeal to ignorance. An attempt to secure agreement with a conclusion by requesting those who oppose the conclusion to disprove it.

Appeal to pity. An attempt to secure agreement with a conclusion by asking for sympathy rather than by presenting evidence that supports the conclusion.

Appendix. A part of a book that contains supplementary materials or information; it is usually located in the back of a book, immediately following the last chapter.

Associate degree. A *degree* that is usually offered by two-year colleges, often the A.A. (Associate of Arts), A.S. (Associate of Science), or A.A.S. (Associate of Applied Science).

Attack on the person fallacy. An illogical argument in which a person's conclusion is ignored and he or she is discredited instead.

Author index. An *index* that lists the names of authors referred to in a book.

Authoritative. Said of information that is written by people who are experts on the subjects about which they write.

Bachelor's degree. A *degree* offered by four-year colleges and universities, usually the B.A. (Bachelor of Arts) or the B.S. (Bachelor of Science).

Bandwagon. The solicitation of support for a product or viewpoint by creating the impression that everyone, or practically everyone, uses the product or holds the opinion.

Bar graph. A drawing in which parallel bars are used to show differences in amounts. A bar graph can be used to show differences in the amounts of tar in various brands of cigarettes.

Bibliography. A list of books, articles, and other sources of information that are referred to by a writer.

Black-or-white fallacy. See *either-or fallacy*.

Bluebook. A booklet, not necessarily blue, that contains lined paper on which to write answers to *essay questions*.

Bulletin. A booklet published by a college or university that includes information about *curriculums*, courses, and other important facts; a *catalogue*.

Bursar. The title of a person at a college who is responsible for money transactions; a treasurer.

Card stacking. Presenting information that supports a specific opinion while deliberately not presenting information that opposes the opinion.

Cartoon. A drawing depicting a humorous situation, often accompanied by a caption.

Cashier. Same as *bursar*.

Catalogue. Same as *bulletin*.

Chancellor. Sometimes the same as *president*, and sometimes the title for a special assistant to a president.

Circle graph. A drawing in the shape of a circle that is used to show the sizes of the parts that make up a whole. A circle graph can be used to show what parts of a family's income are used for rent, food, clothing, and other expenses.

Classification chart. A format for recording notes about information that explains how two or more people, places, or things are alike or different in two or more ways.

Combining form. A Greek or Latin word part that is joined with other such forms, words, or *affixes* to form a word. For example, "-logy" is a combining form that indicates "science" or "study of" in "biology," "theology," and many other words.

Context. A sentence, paragraph, or longer unit of writing that surrounds a word and determines its meaning.

Copyright page. The page following the *title page* of a book that states the year the book was copyrighted or published.

Counselors. People who provide students with guidance in achieving their educational and occupational goals and in resolving their personal problems; counselors' offices are usually located in a counseling center.

Credit. A unit for completion of any study that applies toward a college *degree.*

Critical reading. Reading done for the purpose of judging the merits or faults of written material.

Curriculum. The courses required to earn a particular *degree.*

Dean. A member of the administration of a college who is in charge of specified aspects of the school's activities, such as a dean of students, dean of faculty, dean of instruction, or dean of a *school* or *division* within a college or university.

Definition. A statement of the meaning of a word; the definition of "happy" is "having a feeling of great pleasure."

Degree. A rank given to students who have successfully completed specified courses of study, usually the *associate degree, bachelor's degree, master's degree,* or *doctoral degree.*

Department. In colleges, the organizational unit that offers courses in a specific subject or a specific group of subjects. For instance, a foreign language department may offer courses in Spanish, French, German, and other languages.

Details. See *major details* and *minor details.*

Diagram. A drawing that explains something by outlining its parts and by showing the relationships among its parts. For example, a diagram may show the relationships among the parts of the human eye.

Direction word. A word in an *essay question* that informs test-takers about the type of answer they are to give. The direction word "diagram" usually indicates that students are to draw a picture and label its parts.

Distractor. An answer for a *multiple-choice question* that is not the correct answer.

Division. In some colleges, departments are organized under larger groups called divisions. For example, the social sciences division of a college may include a psychology department, sociology department, anthropology department, and other departments.

Doctoral degree. The highest *degree* offered by colleges and universities. Many college teachers earn a Ph.D. (Doctor of Philosophy) or an Ed.D. (Doctor of Education).

Either-or fallacy. An illogical argument in which we are asked to believe that there are only two extreme possibilities when there are in fact additional alternatives.

Essay questions. Test items that require students to give written answers that are usually one paragraph or more in length.

Etymology. Information about the origin and development of a word.

Examples. Something selected to show the general characteristics of whatever is named by a term; examples of beverages include milk, orange juice, and coffee. Also, in dictionary entries, examples are phrases or sentences that illustrate the ways words are used.

Exercise. In a textbook, a *problem* or series of problems.

Exposition. Writing that gives explanations and information.

Extreme modifiers. Words such as "always" and "never" that tend to be in false statements. For instance, "*All* children love candy" contains an extreme modifier, and it is false.

Fact. A statement that can be proved to be true or false: "There are twelve inches in a foot." Contrast with *opinion.*

Fill-in questions. Statements that have deleted portions that test-takers must supply: "There are _____ letters in the English alphabet."

Glittering generalities. Words and phrases used to arouse a favorable response when describing a product, policy, or person.

Glossary. A list of words and their definitions; usually located in the back of a book, just in front of the *index.*

GPA values. Values given to *letter grades* so that *grade point averages* may be computed. The following values are used at many colleges: A—4.00; B—3.00; C—2.00; D—1.00; and F—0.00.

Grade point average (GPA). A number that usually ranges from 0.00 to 4.00 and that indicates a student's average course grade.

Hasty generalization. A conclusion drawn from too small a sample or from a sample that is not typical.

Heading. In a textbook, a word or words at the beginning of a division within a chapter.

Highlight. To mark important words or sentences in a book using a pen that contains watercolor ink. This is done so that important statements will stand out clearly and not be overlooked while *studying*.

Hour. A unit, usually less or more than sixty minutes, that designates time students spend in classrooms, laboratories, or conferences.

Idiom. A phrase that has a meaning that is not clear from the common meanings of the words in the phrase; it is an accepted phrase that cannot be interpreted literally.

Imply. To hint, suggest, or otherwise indicate indirectly.

Incomplete grade (INC). A grade given at many colleges when students are doing passing work but have not completed all course requirements. Usually an INC grade is changed to F or some other grade if incomplete work is not completed within a specified time.

Index. An alphabetically arranged listing of subjects and the page numbers on which they are discussed in a book; it is usually located at the very end of a book.

Infer. To use known facts, information, or evidence to arrive at a conclusion.

Insert. Material set off in a textbook; it may be enclosed within lines or printed on a shaded background of light blue, yellow, gray, or some other color.

Intersession. A short session of study offered between two *terms*, such as a four-week session offered in January between a fall term and a spring term.

Introduction. The part of a book that gives the author's explanations of why the book was written. It often includes a summary of the purposes, philosophy, or contents of a book and is usually located right after the *table of contents*. This information may also be located in a *preface*.

Learning goals. A list of statements or questions at the beginning of a textbook chapter that summarizes information in the chapter.

Letter grade. A grade such as A−, B+, or C that designates the quality of work students do. Letter grades have the following meanings at many colleges: A—excellent; B—good; C—satisfactory; D—passing; and F—failing.

Line graph. A drawing in which lines are used to show increasing or decreasing amounts. A line graph can be used to show increases or decreases in the numbers of students enrolled at a college over a period of time.

List. A presentation of a series of items of any kind.

Main idea. A statement about the specific way in which a *topic*, or subject, is discussed.

Major details. Explanations, examples, or other supporting information about a *main idea*.

Manipulation. The use of shrewd means to persuade readers to hold certain opinions or to take specific actions.

Map. A diagram or other drawing that shows the relation between a topic and major details or among a *topic*, *major details*, and *minor details*.

Marginal note. A definition of a term or other information printed in the margin of a textbook.

Master's degree. A degree that ranks higher than a *bachelor's degree* but lower than a *doctoral degree*, usually the M.A. (Master of Arts) or M.S. (Master of Science).

Matching questions. Test items that present two lists and require test-takers to associate words or statements in one list with words or statements in the other list.

Method. The procedure or process used to do something.

Minor details. Explanations, examples, or other supporting information about a *major detail*.

Mnemonic device. A device used to aid memory. "Use *i* before *e* except after *c*" is a mnemonic rhyme for remembering a spelling principle.

Mnemonic sentence. A sentence in which the first letters of words in the sentence are the same as the first letters of words to be recalled.

Multiple-choice questions. Test items written in a format that requires test-takers to select a correct answer from among four or five possible answers that are listed.

Name calling. The association of an unfavorable label with something to create an unfavorable impression of it.

Name index. An *index* of the authors and other people referred to in a book.

Notes. See *bibliography*. Also, handwritten summaries of information stated in classes or printed in course textbooks.

Number grade. A grade such as 91, 85, or 68 that designates the quality of work students do. Many colleges agree on the following correspondences between number grades and letter grades: A 90–100; B 80–89; C 70–79; D 60–69; F 0–59.

Ombudsman. A special assistant to a *president*.

Open-book test. A test during which students may refer to books, and sometimes to notes, as they answer questions.

Opinion. A statement that cannot be proved to be true or false and about which equally knowledgeable and informed people may argue or debate: "No American citizen should have to pay for health care." Contrast with *fact*.

Orientation. A period of time or a series of events planned to help students adjust satisfactorily to college or university life.

Outline. A summary of information that lists important points in a well-organized manner. In the traditional outline format, details are labeled with Roman numerals, capital letters, and Arabic numerals.

Plain folks. The association of an idea or product with "ordinary" people or the things that "ordinary" people do.

Preface. See *introduction*.

Prefix. A letter or group of letters that is added to the beginning of a word. The "mis-" in "misspell" is a prefix.

Prerequisite. A requirement that must be completed before a student may take a course. For example, the prerequisite for an intermediate algebra course might be a course in elementary algebra.

President. At a college or university, the chief administrative officer, who has ultimate responsibility for all aspects of the functioning of the school.

Primary source. A firsthand source of information. A movie starring Marilyn Monroe is a primary source of information about her appearance on screen. Contrast with *secondary source*.

Process chart. A drawing in which information is enclosed within geometric figures that are arranged to show how someone or something progresses through the steps of a process.

Problem. In a textbook, a question to answer, a proposition to solve, or other activity to do.

Qualifier An adjective that modifies a noun or an adverb that modifies a verb. In the phrase "young women talking quietly," the adjective "young" is a qualifier of the noun "women," and the adverb "quietly" is a qualifier of the verb "talking."

Quarter system. A system that divides a school year into three parts, usually a fall, winter, and spring *term* of about ten weeks each.

Reading. The process used to understand information that is presented in writing. Contrast with *studying*.

Reciting. The act of repeating information silently or aloud to learn it and be able to recall it.

References. See *bibliography*.

Registrar. The title of a person at a college who is responsible for registering students in courses and

for maintaining their academic records or *transcripts*.

Registration. A period of time during which students register for the courses they will take.

Reviewing. The repeated *reciting* of information to learn it or the practicing of *skills* to acquire them.

Review questions. Questions at the end of a textbook chapter that students may answer to determine whether they have understood or learned information in the chapter.

School. A division within a college or university, such as a school of medicine.

Secondary source. A statement made about a *primary source*. A movie review describing Marilyn Monroe's appearance on screen is a secondary source about her appearance.

Semester system. A system that divides a school year into two parts, usually a fall and spring *term* of fifteen to sixteen weeks each.

Sequence. The order in which things follow each other in time, space, rank, or some other dimension.

Skill. An ability acquired as a result of training and practice. Reading and writing are skills.

Slanted. Written to convince readers of a particular opinion.

Stem. The part of a *multiple-choice question* that comes before the first answer. The first answer is usually preceded by the letter "a."

Studying. The process used to remember and recall information. Contrast with *reading*.

Subject index. An *index* of the subjects discussed in a book.

Subject label. A term printed in italic type in a dictionary entry to indicate the field of knowledge to which a definition applies.

Suffix. A letter or a group of letters that is added to the end of a base word. The "-ee" in "employee" is a suffix.

Summary. A section at the end of a textbook chapter that provides a brief overview of the information in the chapter.

Summer session. A period in the summer during which students may take courses for academic *credit* but that is usually not considered a *semester*, *quarter*, or *trimester* for the purposes of a school's business.

Survey of a book. The examination of the major features of a book, such as the table of contents, introduction, appendix, and glossary.

Survey of a chapter. The quick examination of introductory paragraphs, headings, pictures, tables, and other features of a chapter to learn what major topics it discusses.

Syllabus.   A summary or *outline* distributed by an instructor that states the main topics to be discussed in a course.

Synonym.   A word that has the same or nearly the same meaning as another word. "Big" and "large" are synonyms.

Table.   A systematic listing of statistical information that is presented in orderly columns and rows to facilitate comparisons among data.

Table of contents.   A list that shows the page numbers on which chapter headings and subheadings of a book appear; it is usually located in the front of a book, right after the *title page*.

Take-home test.   A test for which students are given questions to answer at home or to study at home before they answer them in class.

Term.   A period of study in a college that usually ends with the administration of final examinations. A term may be a *semester, quarter, trimester,* or *summer session.*

Terminology.   Words or phrases that are used with specific meanings when a subject is discussed. The important terminology used in a textbook is usually defined in a *glossary.*

Test anxiety.   Uneasiness or apprehension students experience because they must take a test.

Testimonial.   A statement made by a famous or respected person favoring or opposing something.

Textbook.   A book that summarizes information about the subject matter of a college course. This book is a textbook.

Title.   The name of a book, chapter, play, poem, essay, or other written material.

Title page.   The page of a book that gives information about the title, author, and publisher; it is usually the first or second printed page of a book.

Topic.   Something dealt with in writing or conversation—the person, place, or thing that is the subject of a discussion.

Transcript.   The official record of courses taken, grades received, and *grade point averages.* Transcripts are maintained by a *registrar.*

Transfer.   A technique in which a product or idea is associated with something that is known to be viewed favorably.

Trimester system.   See *quarter system.*

True-false questions.   Test items that are statements that test-takers must decide are either true or false.

Tutor.   A person who gives individual instruction to students.

Underline.   To draw lines under important words or sentences in a book so they stand out clearly and will not be overlooked while *studying.*

Vice chancellor.   Sometimes the same as *dean.*

Vice president.   Sometimes the same as *dean.*

Visual material.   Pictures, graphs, charts, diagrams, and other nonprose components of a book.

Visualization.   An image that can be pictured in the mind and used to recall information. If you picture in your mind the room in which you sleep, you can use the image to recall information about the room.

Withdrawal grade (W).   A grade given at many colleges so that students may drop courses when they have good reasons for doing so. Usually W grades do not lower *grade point averages* when they are requested within specified time limits or when students are doing passing work at the time of withdrawal.

CREDITS *(continued from copyright page)*

Page 104: "Pygmalion Effect" adapted from Barry L. Reece and Rhonda Brandt: *Effective Human Relations in Organizations,* 2nd ed. Copyright © 1984 by Houghton Mifflin Company. Used by permission.

Page 105: "The Old Testament" from Marvin Perry, et al., WESTERN CIVILIZATION, 3rd ed., pages 32–33. Copyright © 1989 by Houghton Mifflin Company. Used by permission.

Page 106: "The Double Bind" from Morris K. Holland, USING PSYCHOLOGY, 3rd ed., pages 93–94. Copyright © 1985 by Little, Brown, and Company. Used by permission.

Page 108: "Displaying Feelings" from COMMUNICATE! 4/E by Rudolph F. Verderber © 1984 by Wadsworth, Inc. Reprinted by permission of the publisher.

Page 109: "Roman Baths" from John P. McKay et al., A HISTORY OF WORLD SOCIETIES, 2nd ed., page 181. Copyright © 1988 by Houghton Mifflin Company. Used by permission.

Page 110: "Consumer Income" from Robert J. Hughes: *Business.* Copyright © 1985 by Houghton Mifflin Company. Adapted by permission.

Pages 111 and 113: "Flextime" and "Minority Groups" from David J. Rachman and Michael H. Mescon, *Business Today,* 6th ed. and 4th ed., page 233 and page 20. Copyright © 1990 and 1985 by McGraw-Hill Publishing Company. Used by permission.

Page 114: "Stereotypes" from COMMUNICATE! 4/E by Rudolph F. Verderber © 1984 by Wadsworth, Inc. Reprinted by permission of the publisher.

Page 115: "Retail Stores" from Mary Beth Norton: *A People and a Nation,* 2nd ed. Copyright © 1986 by Houghton Mifflin Company. Adapted by permission.

Page 116: "Memory Systems" from PSYCHOLOGY, 3/e by Andrew B. Crider, et al., pages 247–248. Copyright © 1989 by Andrew B. Crider, George R. Goethals, Robert D. Kavanaugh, and Paul R. Solomon. Reprinted by permission of HarperCollins Publishers.

Page 118: "Brands and Trademarks" from David J. Rachman et al., BUSINESS TODAY, 6th ed., page 323. Copyright © 1990 by McGraw-Hill Publishing Company. Used by permission.

Page 120: "The Supreme Court" from Kenneth Janda et al., THE CHALLENGE OF DEMOCRACY, Brief Edition, page 321. Copyright © 1990 by Houghton Mifflin Company. Used by permission.

Page 122: "Stages of Dying" from DEATH: THE FINAL STAGE OF GROWTH. Copyright © 1975 by Elisabeth Kubler-Ross, pages 508–509. Reprinted by permission of Simon & Schuster, Inc.

Page 124: "Pricing Strategies" from David J. Rachman et al., BUSINESS TODAY, 6th ed., page 340. Copyright © 1990 by McGraw-Hill Publishing Company. Used by permission.

Page 126: "Compliance." Reprinted by permission from ESSENTIALS OF PSYCHOLOGY 4th ed., by Dennis Coon copyright © 1988 by West Publishing Company. All rights reserved.

Page 128: "Roletaking" from Ian Robertson, *SOCIOLOGY: A Brief Introduction,* pages 76–77. Copyright © 1989 by

Worth Publishers. Used by permission.

Page 130: "The Third World" from John P. McKay et al., A HISTORY OF WORLD SOCIETIES, 2nd ed., pages 1226 through 1228. Copyright © 1988 by Houghton Mifflin Company. Used by permission.

Page 132: "Defense Mechanisms" from Morris K. Holland, USING PSYCHOLOGY, 3rd ed., pages 158 and 159. Copyright © 1985 by Little, Brown and Company. Used by permission.

Page 134: "The Maid of Orleans" from John P. McKay et al., A HISTORY OF WORLD SOCIETIES, 2nd ed., pages 437 and 438. Copyright © 1988 by Houghton Mifflin Company. Used by permission.

Pages 136–137: "Listening" adapted from Barry L. Reece and Rhonda Brandt: *Effective Human Relations in Organizations,* 2nd ed., pages 57 and 59. Copyright © 1984 by Houghton Mifflin Company. Used by permission.

Pages 139–140: "Career Planning" from Robert J. Hughes: *Business.* Copyright © 1985 by Houghton Mifflin Company. Adapted by permission.

Pages 142–143: "Conflict." Reprinted by permission from INTRODUCTION TO PSYCHOLOGY, 4th ed., by Dennis Coon copyright © 1988 by West Publishing Company. All rights reserved.

Pages 145–146: "Stages of Relationships" from COMMUNICATE! 4/E by Rudolph F. Verderber © 1984 by Wadsworth, Inc. Reprinted by permission of the publisher.

Page 151: "George Sand" from John P. McKay et al., A HISTORY OF WORLD SOCIETIES, 2nd ed., page 851. Copyright © 1988 by Houghton Mifflin Company. Used by permission.

Page 151: "Supply and demand" from David J. Rachman and Michael H. Mescon, BUSINESS TODAY, 4th ed., page 9. Copyright © 1985 by McGraw-Hill Publishing Company. Used by permission.

Page 151: "Ethnicity" from Ian Robertson: SOCIETY: A BRIEF INTRODUCTION, 1989. Worth Publishers, New York.

Page 152: "Female attractiveness" from Ian Robertson: SOCIOLOGY, 2nd ed., pages 207–208. Copyright © 1981 by Worth Publishers, Inc. Used by permission.

Page 153: "School" from Ian Robertson: SOCIOLOGY, 2nd ed., page 118. Copyright © 1981 by Worth Publishers, Inc. Used by permission.

Page 153: "Advancement of science" from Marvin Perry et al., WESTERN CIVILIZATION, 3rd ed., page 531. Copyright © 1989 by Houghton Mifflin Company. Used by permission.

Page 154: "What Is News?" from Melvin L. Defleur: *Understanding Mass Communication*, 2nd ed. Copyright © 1985 by Houghton Mifflin Company. Adapted by permission.

Page 154: "Advantage of children" from Marvin L. Levy et al., ESSENTIALS OF LIFE AND HEALTH, 4th ed., page 221. Copyright © 1984 by McGraw-Hill Publishing Company. Used by permission.

Page 154: "Prisoners" from Marvin Perry et al., WESTERN CIVILIZATION, 3rd ed., page 397. Copyright © 1989 by Houghton Mifflin Company. Used by permission.

Page 157: "Grammar" from Robert S. Feldman, UNDERSTANDING PSYCHOLOGY,

pages 204 and 205. Copyright © 1987 by McGraw-Hill Publishing Company. Used by permission.

Page 158: "Normal Childhood Problems." Reprinted by permission from ESSENTIALS OF PSYCHOLOGY, 4th ed., page 413, by Dennis Coon copyright © 1988 by West Publishing Company. All rights reserved.

Pages 158–159: "Professions" from Ian Robertson: SOCIOLOGY, 2nd ed., pages 458–459. Copyright © 1981 by Worth Publishers, Inc. Used by permission.

Page 159: "Emotional Health" from Marvin R. Levy et al., ESSENTIALS OF LIFE AND HEALTH, 5th ed., page 20. Copyright © 1988 by McGraw-Hill Publishing Company. Used by permission.

Page 161: "Dreams" from PSYCHOLOGY, 3/e by Andrew B. Crider, et al. Copyright © 1989 by Andrew B. Crider, George R. Goethals, Robert D. Kavanaugh, and Paul R. Solomon. Reprinted by permission of HarperCollins Publishers.

Page 163: "Corrections" from Ian Robertson, *SOCIOLOGY: A Brief Introduction*, page 129. Copyright © 1989 by Worth Publishers. Used by permission.

Page 164: "India's Legacy" from John P. McKay et al., A HISTORY OF WORLD SOCIETIES, 2nd ed., page xxii. Copyright © 1988 by Houghton Mifflin Company. Used by permission.

Page 165: "Value of Water" from Marvin R. Levy et al., ESSENTIALS OF LIFE AND HEALTH, 4th ed., pages 322 and 323. Copyright © 1984 by McGraw-Hill Publishing Company. Used by permission.

Page 165: "Fresh water" from Ian Robertson, SOCIOL-

OGY, 3rd ed., page 619. Copyright © 1987 by Worth Publishers. Used by permission.

Page 166: "Characteristics of money" from David J. Rachman et al, BUSINESS TODAY, 6th ed., page 456–457. Copyright © 1990 by McGraw-Hill Publishing Company. Used by permission.

Page 166: "Chinese Money" from John P. McKay et al., A HISTORY OF WORLD SOCIETIES, 2nd ed., page 303. Copyright © 1988 by Houghton Mifflin Company. Used by permission.

Page 167: "Death is peaceful," from Marvin R. Levy et al., ESSENTIALS OF LIFE AND HEALTH, 4th ed., page 443. Copyright © 1984 by McGraw-Hill Publishing Company. Used by permission.

Page 167: "Theories of afterlife" from Paul M. Insel and Walton T. Roth, CORE CONCEPTS IN HEALTH, 5th ed., page 536. Copyright © 1988 by Mayfield Publishing Company. Used by permission.

Page 168: "Effects of divorce" from Marvin R. Levy et al., ESSENTIALS OF LIFE AND HEALTH, 4th ed., page 228. Copyright © 1984 by McGraw-Hill Publishing Company. Used by permission.

Page 168: "Children get hurt" from Marvin R. Levy et al., ESSENTIALS OF LIFE AND HEALTH, 5th ed., page 451. Copyright © 1988 by McGraw-Hill Publishing Company. Used by permission.

Page 170: "Romantic and Mature Love" adapted from pp. 333–336 in UNDERSTANDING HUMAN SEXUALITY by Joann S. Delora Sandlin et al., copyright © 1980 by Harper & Row, Publishers, Inc. Reprinted by permission of Harper & Row Publishers, Inc.

Page 174: "Daydream plots." Reprinted by permission from

INTRODUCTION TO PSY-
CHOLOGY, 2nd ed. by Dennis
Coon copyright © 1983 by
West Publishing Company. All
rights reserved.

Page 175: "The Presi-
dency" from John H. Aldrich:
American Government. Copyright © 1986 by Houghton
Mifflin Company. Adapted by
permission.

Pages 177–178: "Ego-
Defense Mechanisms" from
PSYCHOLOGY, 3/e by An-
drew B. Crider et al. Copyright
© 1989 by Andrew B. Crider,
George R. Goethals, Robert D.
Kavanaugh, and Paul R. Solomon. Reprinted by permission
of HarperCollins Publishers.

Page 180: "Idioms" from
Robert Perrin, THE BEACON
HANDBOOK, 2nd ed., page
262. Copyright © 1990 by
Houghton Mifflin Company.
Used by permission.

Pages 180–181: "Affirma-
tions" from Barry L. Reece and
Rhonda Brandt: *Effective Hu-
man Relations in Organiza-
tions,* 4th ed., page 109.
Copyright © 1990 by
Houghton Mifflin Company.
Used by permission.

Page 181: "Metamemory"
from PSYCHOLOGY, 3rd ed.
by Andrew B. Crider et al.,
copyright © 1989. Reprinted
by permission of Scott, Foresman and Company.

Pages 182–183: "Courtship"
from Marvin R. Levy et al.,
ESSENTIALS OF LIFE AND
HEALTH, 5th ed., pages 197–
198. Copyright © 1988 by
McGraw-Hill Publishing Company. Used by permission.

Page 184: "Dreams" from
Morris K. Holland, USING
PSYCHOLOGY, 3rd ed., pages
73–74. Copyright © 1985 by
Little, Brown, and Company.
Used by permission.

Page 185: "Romantic Love"
from Ian Robertson, *SOCIOL-
OGY: A Brief Introduction,*

pages 254–255. Copyright
© 1989 by Worth Publishers.
Used by permission.

Page 186: "Black Death"
from John P. McKay et al., A
HISTORY OF WORLD SOCIE-
TIES, 2nd ed., pages 429–430.
Copyright © 1988 by
Houghton Mifflin Company.
Used by permission.

Page 187: "Conversations"
from COMMUNICATE! Sixth
Edition by Rudolph F. Verderber © 1990 by Wadsworth,
Inc. Reprinted by permission
of the publisher.

Page 188: "Caffeine" from
Marvin R. Levy et al., ESSEN-
TIALS OF LIFE AND
HEALTH, 5th ed., pages 108–
109. Copyright © 1988 by
McGraw-Hill Publishing Com-
pany. Used by permission.

Page 189: "Inequality" from
Ian Robertson, *SOCIOLOGY:
A Brief Introduction,* page 201.
Copyright © 1989 by Worth
Publishers. Used by
permission.

Page 190: "News" from John
H. Aldrich: *American Government,* page 309. Copyright
© 1986 by Houghton Mifflin
Company. Adapted by
permission.

Page 191: "Looking-Glass
Self" from Ian Robertson, *SO-
CIOLOGY: A Brief Introduction,* page 75. Copyright © 1989
by Worth Publishers. Used by
permission.

Page 192: "Intimate Rela-
tionships" from Paul M. Insel
and Walton T. Roth, CORE
CONCEPTS IN HEALTH, 5th
ed., pages 116–118. Copyright
© 1988 by Mayfield Publishing
Company. Used by permission.

Page 193: "Demography"
from Ian Robertson, *SOCIOL-
OGY: A Brief Introduction,*
page 350. Copyright © 1989 by
Worth Publishers. Used by
permission.

Page 194: "Sports" from Ian
Robertson, SOCIOLOGY, 3rd

ed., page 96. Copyright © 1987
by Worth Publishers. Used by
permission.

Page 203: "Chart: Employ-
ment Process" from Robert
Kreitner et al., BUSINESS, 2nd
ed., page 225. Copyright © 1990
by Houghton Mifflin Com-
pany. Used by permission.

Page 210: "Classification
Chart" from Barry L. Reece
and Rhonda Brandt: *Effective
Human Relations in Organizations,* 4th ed., page 358. Copyright © 1990 by Houghton
Mifflin Company. Used by
permission.

Page 211: "Check Clearing"
from O. C. Ferrell and Geof-
frey Hirt, BUSINESS, page 540.
Copyright © 1989 by
Houghton Mifflin Company.
Used by permission.

Page 212: "Computer Dia-
gram" from David R. Sullivan:
Using Computers Today,
p. 18. Copyright © 1986 by
Houghton Mifflin Company.
Used by permission.

Page 221: "Establishing
Credit" from E. Thomas Garman, PERSONAL FINANCE,
2/e., page 151. Copyright
© 1988 by Houghton Mifflin
Company. Used by permission.

Pages 221–222: "Keys to
Credit" from David J. Rachman and Michael H. Mescon,
BUSINESS TODAY, 4th ed.,
pages 424–425. Copyright
© 1985 by McGraw-Hill Publishing Company.

Pages 229–328: Chapters 16
through 22 are based on material in *College Study Skills,*
4th ed., Copyright © 1990 by
James F. Shepherd. Used by
permission of Houghton
Mifflin Company.

Page 240: "Cornell System"
from Walter Pauk, HOW TO
STUDY IN COLLEGE, 3rd ed.,
page 134. Copyright © 1984 by
Houghton Mifflin Company.
Adapted by permission.

Page 244: "Simplified Handwriting" from Walter Pauk, HOW TO STUDY IN COLLEGE, 4th ed., page 137 and 139. Copyright © 1984 by Houghton Mifflin Company. Used by permission.

Page 244: "The Breakthrough" from Walter Pauk, HOW TO STUDY IN COLLEGE, 3rd ed., page 123. Copyright © 1984 by Houghton Mifflin Company. Used by permission.

Page 254: "Title Page" from William M. Pride et al., BUSINESS, 2nd ed., page iii. Copyright © 1988 by Houghton Mifflin Company. Used by permission.

Page 255: "Copyright Page" from William M. Pride et al., BUSINESS, 2nd ed., page iv. Copyright © 1988 by Houghton Mifflin Company. Used by permission.

Page 256: "Table of Contents" from William M. Pride et al., BUSINESS, 2nd ed., page vii. Copyright © 1988 by Houghton Mifflin Company. Used by permission.

Page 257: "Preface" from William M. Pride et al., BUSINESS, 2nd ed., page xxv. Copyright © 1988 by Houghton Mifflin Company. Used by permission.

Page 258: "Appendix" from William M. Pride et al., BUSINESS, 2nd ed., page A1. Copyright © 1988 by Houghton Mifflin Company. Used by permission.

Page 259: "Glossary" from William M. Pride et al., BUSINESS, 2nd ed., pages G1–2. Copyright © 1988 by Houghton Mifflin Company. Used by permission.

Page 260: "References" from William M. Pride et al., BUSINESS, 2nd ed., page N1. Copyright © 1988 by Houghton Mifflin Company. Used by permission.

Page 261: "Name Index" from William M. Pride et al., BUSINESS, 2nd ed., page I1. Copyright © 1988 by Houghton Mifflin Company. Used by permission.

Page 262: "Subject Index" from William M. Pride et al., BUSINESS, 2nd ed., page I5. Copyright © 1988 by Houghton Mifflin Company. Used by permission.

Page 268: "Marginal Notes in a Textbook" from William M. Pride et al., BUSINESS, 2nd ed., page 213. Copyright © 1988 by Houghton Mifflin Company. Used by permission.

Page 275: "Brain Death" from Marvin R. Levy et al., ESSENTIALS OF LIFE AND HEALTH, 4th ed., page 438. Copyright © 1984 by McGraw-Hill Publishing Company. Used by permission.

Page 275: "Colloquialisms" from Joseph F. Trimmer and James M. McCrimmon, WRITING WITH A PURPOSE, 9th ed., page 214. Copyright © 1988 by Houghton Mifflin Company. Used by permission.

Page 276: "The Family" from Ian Robertson, SOCIOLOGY, 3rd ed., page 128. Copyright © 1987 by Worth Publishers. Used by permission.

Page 277: "Reasons for Using Credit" from E. Thomas Garman: *Personal Finance.* Copyright © 1985 by Houghton Mifflin Company. Adapted by permission.

Page 278: "SQ3R" from Bruce E. Shertzer: *Career Planning*, 3rd ed. Copyright © 1985 by Houghton Mifflin Company. Adapted by permission.

Pages 279–280: "Conversationalists" from COMMUNICATE! Sixth Edition by Rudolph F. Verderber © 1990 by Wadsworth, Inc. Reprinted by permission of the publisher.

Pages 281–282: "Altruism" from Gary L. Belkin and Ruth

H. Skydell: *Foundations of Psychology*, pages 469–470. Copyright © 1979 by Houghton Mifflin Company. Used by permission.

Pages 283–284: "Coping with Adversity" from COMMUNICATE! Sixth Edition by Rudolph F. Verderber © 1990 by Wadsworth, Inc. Reprinted by permission of the publisher.

Pages 285–287: "Spoken Language" from PSYCHOLOGY, 3/e by Andrew B. Crider, et al. Copyright © 1989 by Andrew B. Crider, George R. Goethals, Robert D. Kavanaugh, and Paul R. Solomon. Reprinted by permission of HarperCollins Publishers.

Page 288: "Personal Space" reprinted by permission from ESSENTIALS OF PSYCHOLOGY, 4E by Dennis Coon copyright © 1988 by West Publishing Company. All rights reserved.

Pages 289–291: "Advertising Media" from William M. Pride et al., BUSINESS, 2nd ed., pages 418–421. Copyright © 1988 by Houghton Mifflin Company. Used by permission.

Pages 292–293: "Television" from Melvin L. DeFleur and E. E. Dennis: *Understanding Mass Communication*, 3rd ed., pages 75–78. Copyright © 1988 by Houghton Mifflin Company. Used by permission.

Pages 294–296: "Infection Chain" from J. R. Ellis and E. A. Nowlis, NURSING, 3rd ed., pages 385–387. Copyright © 1985 by Houghton Mifflin Company. Used by permission.

Page 301: "Computers and people" from Robert H. Blissmer and Roland H. Alden, WORKING WITH COMPUTERS, pages 71–74. Copyright © 1989 by Houghton Mifflin Company. Used by permission.

Pages 329–381: Chapters 23 through 28 are based on material in *College Study Skills,*

Index

Abbreviations, for class notes, 244–245
Absences, from classes, 7–9
Absolute modifiers, *see* Extreme modifiers
Academic difficulty, finding help for, 14
Acronyms, as mnemonic aids, 321–322
Admissions offices, 34
Advisers, 14
Affixes, 64–65
    see also Prefixes; Suffixes
Anticipating test questions, 230–233
Anxiety, *see* Test anxiety
Appeal to ignorance, 217
Appeal to pity, 217
Appendixes, of books, 253
Assignments
    having ready on time, 11–12
    scheduling time to do, 17–24
Associate degrees, 34
Attack on the person, 217
Attendance, importance of, 7–9
Audiocassette recorders, as aid to learning, 230–231
Author indexes, 253
Authoritativeness, 214–215

Bachelor's degrees, 34
Bandwagon, 218
Bar graphs, 199
Bibliographies, in books, 253
Blackboard, *see* Chalkboard
Bluebooks, 369
Boxed inserts, 267
Bulletins, for schools, 31
Bursar, 34

Calendars, for schools, 31–32
Card stacking, 219
Cartoons, 195
Cashier, *see* Bursar
Catalogues, for schools, 31
Chalkboard, ways used in lectures, 241

Chancellors, 33
Charts
    Classification, 202
    Process, 203
Circle graphs, 198
Class notes
    abbreviations in, 244–245
    completeness of, 242
    Cornell System for, 238
    details in, 240–241
    example of, 239
    as guide for studying, 230, 243
    how to organize, 237–238
    importance of chalkboard for, 241
    improving listening for, 235–237
    increasing speed of taking, 243–245
    major thoughts in, 239–240
    preparation for taking, 235–236
    reviewing after class, 242
    selecting notebooks for, 235–237
    study hints for, 241–242
    studying before tests, 243
Combining forms, 84
Comparison charts, *see* Charts
Computers, 12
Concentration, improvement of, 27–30
Connotation, 112
Context
    definition of, 73
    finding word meanings implied by, 74–75
    finding word meanings stated in, 73–74
Copyright pages, 251
Cornell System for class notes, 238
Counseling services, 32
Courses
    attendance for, 7–8
    checklist for requirements for, 8
    credits for, 34

finding help for difficulty in, 14
keeping up with work for, 11
knowing requirements for, 7
lateness to classes for, 9
notebooks for, 9–11
suggestions for selecting, 5–6
syllabuses for, 7
see also Chalkboard; Class notes; Grades; Prerequisites; Scheduling; Study
Credits, for courses, 34
Critical reading, 213–219
Curriculums, 4–5

Deans, 32
Definitions
    in dictionaries, 62
    in textbooks, 179–180
Degrees, 34
Denotation, 112
Departments, of schools, 32
Details, 156, 170
    see also Major details; minor details
Diagrams, 204–205
Dictionaries
    affixes in, 64–65
    definitions in, 62
    desk, 61–62
    etymologies in, 63
    examples in, 62
    idioms in, 64, 180
    multiple meanings in, 63
    paperback, 61–62
    recommended, 62
    subject labels in, 63–64
    synonyms in, 62, 64
Direction words, in essay questions, 369–372
Divisions, of schools, 32

Either-or fallacy, 216
Essay questions
    answering all parts of, 372
    direction words in, 369–372
    example of answer to, 370
    examples of, 333, 370

Assignments

Course Name	Monday Date:	Tuesday Date:	Wednesday Date:	Thursday Date:	Friday Date:

Assignments

Course Name	Monday Date:	Tuesday Date:	Wednesday Date:	Thursday Date:	Friday Date:

Assignments

Course Name	Monday Date:	Tuesday Date:	Wednesday Date:	Thursday Date:	Friday Date:

Assignments

Course Name	Monday *Date:*	Tuesday *Date:*	Wednesday *Date:*	Thursday *Date:*	Friday *Date:*

Study Schedule

	MON	TUE	WED	THU	FRI	SAT	SUN
7—8							
8—9							
9—10							
10—11							
11—12							
12—1							
1—2							
2—3							
3—4							
4—5							
5—6							
6—7							
7—8							
8—9							
9—10							
10—11							
11—12							

Study Schedule

	MON	TUE	WED	THU	FRI	SAT	SUN
7—8							
8—9							
9—10							
10—11							
11—12							
12—1							
1—2							
2—3							
3—4							
4—5							
5—6							
6—7							
7—8							
8—9							
9—10							
10—11							
11—12							